CW00923945

RB

THE ILLUSTRATIONS

Various unprovenanced woodcuts or engravings, by anonymous artists, have been used or adapted to illustrate this book. A few of the new drawings are from sources outside of Fobbing, being included solely to convey an impression and complement the text. For example, monumental brass copies of a priest and nun on pages 62 and 115 are from Littlebury and St. Albans, while the eelspear (p. 37) may be from either the Corringham or Fobbing marshes. An early Saxon gilt button brooch from Mucking decorates page 51.

No visual evidence of Fobbing's post-windmill has been discovered and the jacket illustration is therefore imaginative, as are various wartime drawings of aircraft and incidents. John Garbutt's and the author's identified scenes and the labelled artefacts illustrated are, however, all based upon direct historical data from within Fobbing parish.

Opposite: *East Vineyard and cottages in Wharf Lane.*

FOBBING: LIFE AND LANDSCAPE

ESSAYS ON AN ESSEX PARISH

BY

RANDAL BINGLEY

(FORMERLY CURATOR, THURROCK MUSEUMS SERVICE)

WITH THIRTY SPECIALLY
DRAWN VIGNETTES

BY

JOHN GARBUTT

AND REPRODUCTIONS OF THE WORKS OF

DONALD MAXWELL
&
FRED ROE.

ADDITIONAL ARTWORK BY THE AUTHOR

A production by Pheon Heritage
in association with Thurrock Council Museum.

Lejins Publishing
Stanford le Hope
Essex

Printed and bound in Great Britain
by Redwood Books, Trowbridge, Wiltshire
ISBN O 9528789 1 7

for

SUSAN ANN FLANDERS,

fond and equal friend.

Also their love, and their hatred, and
their envy, is now perished; neither have
they any more a portion for ever in any
thing that is done under the sun.

Ecclesiastes 9.6

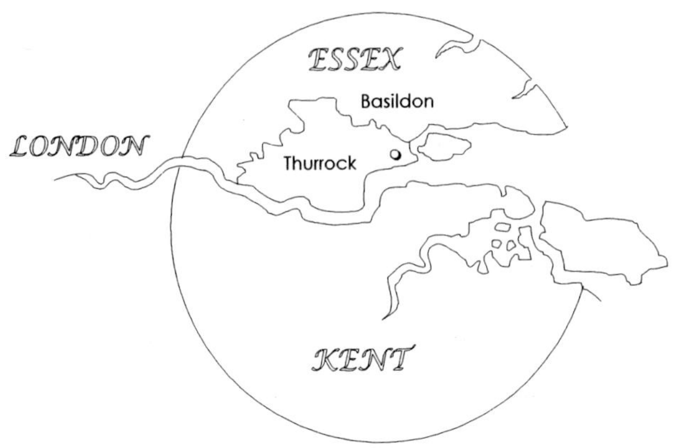
ESSEX
Basildon
LONDON
Thurrock
KENT

CONTENTS

1.	Warp and Weft	1
2.	"Peg O' Lantern": The Marshlands	20
3.	Anphilogoff's Prophesy: Manor and Settlement	50
4.	Treasoning Men	77
5.	"Yoke Fellows in Arms ..."	89
6.	The Vale of Intolerance	111
7.	Van This, Van That and "Goodman Paul"	130
8.	King George Uber Alles	149
9.	Middlin' Sort of Folk	166
10.	Pastures New	191
11.	Growing Pains	207
12.	Look for the Silver Lining	232

Manorway at Iron Latch farm

"FROM THE BEACON TOWER OF ST. MICHAEL'S, FOBBING, HALF THE WORLD CAN BE SEEN."

FORESAY

No one has yet attempted to write with any range or depth about Fobbing – a place which ought long ago to have had its own book. The dozen essays which follow aren't primarily for the academic: I have left too many thoughts only part worked-through for that, am aware of numerous village themes still unpursued. Nevertheless I have, as a basic necessity, combed the published literature of earlier writers, from our antiquarians such as Salmon and Palin, to modern newspaper communicators – notably the late and prolific F. Z. Claro – distilling out what has seemed accurate from a amidst the dubious and rash; often re-assessing and interpreting in the light of my own widely garnered evidence. In clearing this ground of its myth and misconception, I conceive a useful purpose to have been served.

My aim is to reach the *explorer* that lies in most of us – those who might become alert to the ways in which fields and roads and the furniture of landscape interlace wholly with the actions of past men and women. The occasionally introduced tune of national happening is, of necessity, overly simplistic, but is put there to suggest at whiles what makes our country figures dance.

A *good* historian is not any kind of an egg-head who is invariably right about his subject – just a careful creature who can provide impeccable sources for why he has it, so often, so dreadfully wrong. If therefore, the footnotes seem a trifle burdensome upon the page, they possess for me a certain defensive charm, as well as providing, I hope, some tangent avenues for those who wish enquiry beyond my immediate theme. Throughout, I have allowed a little of what Tennessee Williams fancied once to call man's *"personal lyricism"* to show through, because I do not see why local history mightn't be a creative, an expressive journey, as well as a journey after truth.

What I intend this to be, when all's said, is a *portrait* – a personally acquired view of one parish, its mood, landscape and a succession of its people, mainly over fifteen or twenty human generations; from around the fifteenth century up to 1940. This limited time zone provides a convenient (but else unjustifiable) device. By it, I need re-hash almost nothing about Fobbing's dynamic role in political events during its violent summer of 1381, while still being able to impose what seems a wise curfew when reaching those first misty corners of modern recollection. This way, Fobbing and I may stay friends. Besides, to some yet alive, 1940 must have looked like being an end of things.

That September, the village could perceive from its elmy height the dreadful inferno that was Thameshaven. Day and night, its marshland oil-holders had been burning from the *Luftwaffe's* after-lunch onslaught of Thursday 5th and from the swift attack a day following: a rising spume of dark smoke visible for miles out across the North Sea. *"This month"*, wrote Fobbing's defiant parson from behind white-taped windows in his stout brick rectory, *"has witnessed the beginning of the Blitzkrieg ... our Hurricanes and Spitfires, the clever heads that designed them, the devoted ground workers who condition them, and above all, the gallant young pilots ... have won the admiration of the whole world."*

Some of the reasons why a twentieth century *fuhrer's* air fleet should target our South Essex spirit depots were, of course, already forming in embryo far back at the close of the medieval period. Unconsciously, events were preparing a path. These chapters are someways about those connecting threads of community and consequence which, to my mind at least, make any vanished human environment a fascinating thing to try again to see ...

Fobbing Wharf

1. WARP AND WEFT

A month earlier, 6th August 1940, Dick Coffey, married Home Guard volunteer and father of a young family, had become Fobbing's first fatal casualty in the war. But not *of* it. A "blind bend" near the foot of Lion Hill had proved his undoing: cycling speedily down past the pub's many-paned facade to confront the sudden metal of a black taxi-cab.[1]

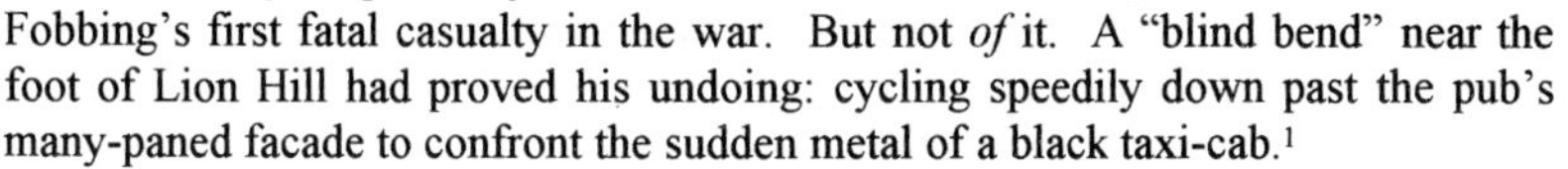

A long chapter of accidents is included in the hill's story, not often so tragic, but frequently alarming. For years Elijah Bearman of Stanford le Hope would remember taking his closed, single horse brougham from the *Railway* tavern to the funeral of Annie Ewen at Fobbing churchyard; a warm August day in 1900 and his vehicle full of important family mourners. Bearman and his passengers were on their way down what was considered "perhaps the steepest declivity in this part of the county", when the handsomely plumed animal became restive at the tremendous weight thrusting upon him and began to kick, shattering carriage glass "to atoms" and finally careering loose from its shafts. Both of Bearman's legs went under the front wheels in the wreck, but he survived.[2]

Those who used wheels of any kind were beginning to pay the price, perhaps, of human acquisitiveness, for by now Lion Hill had become too confined: fenced in upon its lower, southward, side. Since time immemorial there had existed at this spot a wide sanctuary of wasteland fronting one small copyhold cottage at the glebe edge and extending toward some rushy pasture of the parish boundary brook. Yet already by mid 1770, the widow Elizabeth Smith, occupier there, had been summoned before her manor court, having "enclosed with a Hedge and ditch a piece of the Kings Common Highway ... lying by the Road Side leading from Fobbing to Corringham."[3] An order for her fencing to be got rid of straightway followed, and doubtless it *was*, on that occasion anyway, for this extensive fringe of grazing herbage would still appear upon the parish tithe map of 1839. But in time, as the manor courts – which had for so many centuries seen to these things – became dismantled and memories faded, the old spacious arrangement was nibbled away again.

---

1 G.T.G. 6th August, 1940: News column, Rev. E. A. Gardner, O.G.R.D., September, 1940.

2 G.T.G. 18th August, 1900.

3 Manor of Fobbing and Stanford le Hope, Court Books, 1653-1910 E.R.O. D/DCx.

It had been long an important thoroughfare; no mere lane up to some unvisited backwater. Progress would alter the case, but in medieval context Fobbing's main settlement lay right upon an old "coastal" land route between London – 28 miles distant – and estuarine townships of Thames like Grays and Leigh, the latter a thriving small harbour of the lower reaches well into the seventeenth century and one from which important missions of commerce and war had sailed forth. This highway's upkeep had been a subject of constant concern to a wide circle of business folk and yeomen, as the will of John Drywood of Dunton (an affluent Fobbing landowner) was to show in the 1570s, directing a legacy toward the repairing of just one section between "Bowers cross and Vange Church."[4]

Aside from that important eastward projection into the Rochford hundred parishes, the High Road, or "towne street" as local parlance had preferred it during the 1640s, could be taken directly onward to the north, climbing the edge of high-perched Hawkesbury manor and between deeply clustered banks of bluebell and oak, to Billericay's market; or beyond into the county-town of Chelmsford. It was along this route that much parish business ran, moreso as a local government bureaucracy increased throughout the Georgian age. The early June of 1744 had seen Fobbing's churchwardens providing – at the great cost of six shillings – a "frock and Weskote" (a hard-wearing smock) for a poor lad called Durnston. Some master was being sought, to whom he might be bound apprentice and, by the 26th, an additional bill was to be paid for a "journey to Billericky to bind Francis Durstnon" – a routine parish transaction successfully tied up by a few saddle-horse hours along leafy summer lanes.

More problematical were those determined opportunists of the highway, characters like the husbandman William Styles of Fobbing who (aptly, a week before Christmas) in 1604 had stolen up at Runwell a couple of turkeys valued at three shillings;[5] or the labourer, William Garnish, perpetrator in 1831 of another December felony in "Oxberry Bush" farmhouse (Hawkesbury) which was then standing tenantless – forcing the ancient brewhouse door and parlour windows to steal a feather bed and coverings. Ten days later, Garnish was to be apprehended after a night at the *Shepherd and Dog* in Crays Hill, a few miles upcountry. He would hang the year following at the county gaol.[6]

A few passerines trudging these ancient ways are glimpsed in the parish registers and churchwardens' accounts, or in the files of the Justices of the Peace: an abusive Suffolk cattle drover in 1752, or with the spring of 1759, when conflict

---

4 *Elizabethan Life: Essex Gentry's Wills*, F. G. Emmison, 1978.

5 E.R.O. *Assize Files* 1599-1622.

6 *The Brooks Scrapbook*, entry Housebreaking 1832, PAN. Vol. 27, 1985.

with the Gallic foe had again arisen, the appearance of "two Soldiers" who had either paused for beer or been billeted "at the Lyon", their bill being settled from Fobbing's rates. During the April of 1783 a shilling had been risked by one parish official to hasten upon their way "a man wife and four Children pasing threw the Street to Sea Church" (Southchurch) evidently for fear they might linger, to become a budgetary burden upon Fobbing's householders. Thousands continued onward: some remained, like the stranger Richard Smith, found in the early Maytime of 1679 "dead in ye highway".

Doubtless in earlier years and through the medieval centuries when pilgrimages to the sundry shrines of East Anglia, Canterbury, or of continental Europe were at their zenith, each of these trafficways had recorded its share of wayfaring characters whose destinations lay with the boat-ferries operating from a half dozen shores upriver from East Tilbury. At that spot lay the lowest crossing of London's river, its ferry tolls devolving to the wardens of the great stone bridge over Medway at Rochester: an important stage on the route for Becket's place of martyrdom. At nearby West Tilbury, right beside the tiny chapel of St. Mary Magdalen, could be found oarsmen ready to row the half-mile of water to Gravesend's thriving market town, a modest plod only from the pilgrims' old Roman artery into Canterbury. Gravesend's status had long been more than locally prestigious for it was the nation's official maritime gateway; customs entry-port for the city of London. When in 1380, during a high period of French raiding around southern England, audacious galleys of war had swept in sight of Hadleigh castle's pristine stone towers and by Holehaven mouth, to destroy Gravesend's wooden houses, it had been a venture of particular significance, for in propaganda terms the foreigner might claim to have set torch to a suburb of England's capital.[7]

Through these times, and long after, any journeyer seeking swift transport toward London from eastward, might avoid dirty and dangerous highways to some extent, taking that same Tilbury crossing, to connect with a "long" ferry by public "tiltboat" from Gravesend's manor wharf to Billingsgate stairs. Its service would endure beyond the Georgian age, ceasing only with the adoption of paddle steamer vessels, in 1830. But even through such relatively civilised periods, there were setbacks and difficulties, including several long-term disasters at times of storm, and Arthur Young had bemoaned in the late 1760s intolerable delays while awaiting boatmen upon the Essex side. The July of 1811 had seen an example of how a public might fare at this same fortside landing stage: in a moment of annoyance, John Miles, perhaps a common boatman employed

[7] *History of the Town of Gravesend*, R. P. Cruden, 1843.

Thames tiltboat, 18th century

at the *Worlds End*, had hurled the rector of Fobbing's pet dog into the insalubrious billows of Thames. A lengthy period of correspondence between minister and the Board of Ordnance (the ferry owners) would ensue before Miles obtained the parson's forgiveness – a gesture for which probably he cared anyway not a fig.[8]

So far as inland transportation of goods was involved, the Thames and its tidal creeks had been utilised to the fullest extent possible, even into remote times, as the positioning of Domesday's Saxo-Norman farmsteads so plainly evidences. Navigable channels – many of which are today disguised beneath reclamation schemes – served such highground manor halls as West Tilbury, Mucking and Corringham, and other medieval steadings around the Garlands area of Stanford le Hope, each with its timber revetted hythe for the lading of outgoing produce or essential imports required for craft-trades and farmwork within the district. For these communities were by no means so self-sufficient as we might conceive. Moreover, the manor quays were not limited only to the requirements of their own direct community; they were movement points for commodities going to other townships, often well inside the Essex hinterland, importing wealden timber perhaps, iron for smithies, mill-stones, and so on.

Fobbing's own territory was either bounded or intersected by some of Barstable hundred's most significant creeks. Its westernmost, called Shellhaven as early as the Tudor period, must at some distant time have meandered inland right to Fobbing's hillslopes. To eastward lay the greater inlet, long known as Hole haven (*le Hole havene,* 1263) draining out from sand-capped heights above Canvey by means of a half dozen serpentine tideways such as the now diminished Pitsea Hall fleet, Benfleet and Vange creeks, and the tortuous Fobbing Creek itself – which met the greater water at *Fobbing Horse* island. Further Thamesward down Holehaven's course, lay the oozy expanses of two other *"horses"*, the Upper and Lower. Mariners know various mud banks or silt bars by this name, and the entry to Liverpool even plots a "Horse Channel". Holehaven's mouth had traditionally served as a minor harbour for seagoing vessels, both merchantmen and ships of war. Beyond, the wide "Sea Reach" of Thames began. Here, against the Fobbing shore during the spring of 1732, the artist William Hogarth and a few jaunting London friends had moored, miserable and sick and without as much as fire for their clay tobacco pipes, till one had climbed aboard Captain Robinson's royal gun-sloop to return joyously in time with a comforting match.[9]

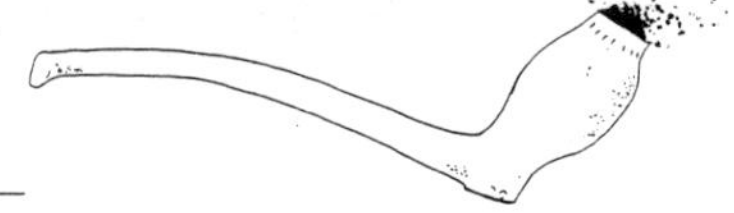

8 *Behold the Painful Plough: Country Life in West Tilbury, Essex 1700-1850,* R. Bingley (unpublished) 1985.

9 *An Account of ... five days' peregrination ... (to Sheppey)*, E. Forrest, 1732, reprinted 1872.

Making their way into all of these inlets, poling with long oars up tortuous narrows, had come the smallish brown-canvassed "hoys" of the post-medieval age and the mightier sprit-sail barges of later creation. Occasionally, Fobbing's registers or wills identify the men whose livelihood centred upon these robust, flat-bottomed craft; the Elizabethan sailor John Cryps who in May, 1597 would bequeath to his son Eleazar "a quarter of myne hoy ... (and) to Jone my wife the other quarter", or Robert Smith "an ancient Hoyman of ffobbing parish" whose last breath had come, during 1643, "in Goodman Landish his house who buried him honestly and in an handsome fashion".[10] The charitable Landish, we discover, was another coastal mariner of the place, whose spouse Ellen was to perish also before the same year's end.[11]

Subsequent chapters will glimpse the town wharf, its activity and personal associations. But this was not Fobbing's only quay. Each of the marshland farmsteads had its own – Borley house at Holehaven edge, Oil Mill and Shellhaven, while far inland, within hailing distance of the *Ship* inn, lay Great Ilford's homestall, advertised in the late 1770s as a hythe "very conveniently situate for shipping and landing Goods, to and from Fobbing Creek".[12] A detailed map of 1800 shows the wharf's position, fronting a porched three-bay corn barn with its open cattle yard nearby.[13]

There was no land-borne means of commercial transport to compare; the meanest hoy under sail could convey cargoes far in excess of a whole convoy of snail-paced road-waggons and far into the seventeenth century it would be rare on rural byways to meet any vehicle more impressive than a two-wheeled farm tumbrel. By the dawn of the Georgian age, Essex yeoman farmers were obtaining true harvesting *waggons* – four wheelers of sturdy gracefulness, their form evolving slowly by the ingenuity of unsung village inventors: carpenters and wheelwrights who tussled with the mysteries of lightness-versus-strength and the intriguing technology of wheel-lock. For the turning of these majestic red-spoked vehicles in tight country lanes was no small problem. Unlike the nimble field cart, they required a wide arc by which to change direction and it was this factor which established those wasteful triangles of grass at old road junctions which travellers still find today. With the nineteenth century, Essex waggon builders were incising

[10] Wording of wills in these essays may vary from versions given in the E.R.O. Wills series by F. G. Emmison, as the latter are generally in modernised form.

[11] *Fobbing Parish Register* 1539-1652 burials. Original at St. Michael's.

[12] *The Particulars of a ... Freehold Estate ... (by Order of the Trustees of Jasper Kingsman, Esq.) 1789.*

[13] *Great Ilford Marsh Farm, the Estate of Sir Mark Wood, Bart.* 1800 E.R.O. D/DCx.

the bodywork with scooped "locking-holes" into which the great wheels could bite on the turn, giving much greater manoeuvrability and establishing a regional waggon-type all their own, which would be recognised even into the motorised age.

They were used for all kinds of work and social purposes; not only the shifting of sheaves to spacious autumn barns, but sack hauling to the mill, shifting sheep hurdles onto marshland pasture grounds, ballast carrying and cottage removals. The Michaelmastide roadways would always provide a *"sight"*, the farmers' Prussian-blue harvest waggons fetching across country their newly hired labourers, children, chattels, dogs and caged up fowls to fresh villages. At life's end, these beautiful farm implements carried the coffined yeoman, his bailiff, or even sometimes an agricultural servant, to the churchyard gate, a custom which was to prevail widely even into the 1930s.

"Bad roads", an eighteenth century humorist had jibed, "are the wheelwright's best friend", and indeed most of the district's lanes must have been rough travelling for any horse-drawn vehicle in our period, despite a constant will – through the Justices of the Peace and local surveyors of the highways – to pressurise for each season's necessary repairs. Doubtless tradesmen of the spokeshave and cart-jack like the wheelwright Jacob Samuel who had wed Mary Bigg at Fobbing in the July of 1658, could pluck the best from all circumstances – with a busy village arterial passing alongside his big-doored work sheds and a constant business to be had from nearly twenty farmsteads in this one parish alone. The manor field sides towered with elm for wheel-naves and waggon-boxes; above Hawkesbury and into Langdon parish grew tough spoke-and-felly timber; two or three hundred years old pedunculate oak. Almost certainly, Samuel's woodworking premises occupied a High Road corner site long in use thereafter and which, by early 1825 (upon the death of William Rust, carpenter) was to be offered for sale, "a good House, with convenient workshops, saw-pit and shed, with a large yard", suitable for either wheelwright or carpenter, or any person "that can carry on both trades, as they are both much wanted."[14]

Not so, however, would be the future cry of Walter Payne, Fobbing's undertaker and wheelwright, who was to take up business there during 1893 and whose eventual bankruptcy provided a morsel of fireside gossip for villagers in the armistice winter of 1919. *"No trade"* and a heavy mortgage had been his plea.[15] Motor cars could be spotted every day of the week now, cautiously risking Lion

---

[14] *The Farm Waggon in Thurrock*, part II, R. Bingley, PAN.Vol. 17, 1973-4.

[15] G.T.G. 15th March, 1919.

Hill, but in continuous putter through the level parish crossways adjoining the *Five Bells,* just a mile or so beyond Mr. Payne's own street entrance. That was the present order of things since the war: speed, and the ongoing quest for weekend amusement.

A seeking for the delights of the seaside had really begun, for the wealthy, far back in the Georgian nineties, spawning mildly fashionable watering-places within a few hours post-chaise gallop from London along the Thames, even round to Ramsgate. Prittlewell village would quickly see its "South-end" mushroom with brick-and-stucco villas and lanky boarding houses. By the late 1850s the London, Tilbury and Southend Railway Company's line was to sunder Fobbing's central upland in a hideous way – mutilating most pastures alongside the pleasant Brook House and Hovels farms and purloining a few outlying acres of the Rev. William Thomson's glebe that were called *"Church Hills".* Unlike nearby Stanford le Hope, there would be no case for a handy railway station to compensate.

Southend, in fact, had changed the old medieval pattern of communications, leaving Fobbing village out upon a mere by-road that served for nothing by the nineteenth century except as a domestic link between a few neighbouring villages; for as early as 1793 had arrived the Hadleigh Trust turnpike scheme, improving the whole east-west highway into a grand coach-route that linked Southend with the fort and ferryplace at Tilbury, and to London beyond. In Fobbing parish, the Hadleigh toll-road would upgrade an old section of lane that had been mapped by Ogilby in the 1670s, leading by Hovels, under the scenic shoulder of Martinhole wood and through Corringham's damp backlands towards the *King's Head* at Stanford.[16]

Thus, in a nutshell, was born the parish's own half-mile of holiday-makers' speedway, which with the 1920s would become the asphalted A.13, steam trains puffing beside it only a few dozen yards away along the old Victorian line. But already by the celebration of Edward's crowning in 1902, Messrs. Deeley & Kesterton were auctioning building plots along the leisure-highway's edge and village traders could see how the magnet of this road-to-Southend-pier was pulling things that way, playing into the hands of Vange enterprise. Soon appeared the

[16] *An Act for Repairing ... the Roads from Hadley Turnpike Gate to Stifford Bridge.* 30th April, 1793.

loyally-titled *Coronation Villas*, and *King's Terrace*,[17] but the Edwardian years were not to see this development succeed to great extent. Its long anticipated shops would arise only with the post-Kaiser's war motor boom, in 1929.

Meanwhile, during 1926 an ex-army hut of sombre red had opened for church services as a far flung mission of Fobbing (St. Michael's) aside Bells Hill lane; the enthusiastic parson Gardner's attempt to draw in worshippers from the Vange border and from various cottages along the ways to Dry Street and Fobbing Farm. Through the greater part of that quarter century, when these two "ends" of Fobbing vied with each other, the village centre itself would remain strangely static, developing few further building plots of its own, yet not *dying* because of its third "end" – the part off which it largely ate and drank, but which (for civil purposes) had been thought of after 1889 as a piece of Corringham marsh. If the innocent lure of bucket and spade tickled Fobbing's torso, its *boots* were surely deep amidst the "muck and bullets" of a sorrier world. For the once pastoral Borley farm's river barges were shipping explosives now out of Holehaven, from Kynoch's vast marshland munitions plant, where hundreds of workers found employ.[18] So much had changed.

LANE, SHOT AND CROFT

South Essex lay within an area of "ancient landscape", similar in aspect to counties southward of the Thames: a countryside which had been arranged and ordered by farming into hedge-hemmed areas long before the coming of the "Enclosure Acts" which reached their peak of influence in the 18th century. Its smallish, rectangular field systems are now known to be the result of exceedingly old factors and here, the "rectilinear" pattern of the hedged upland – with its criss-cross of more or less symmetrically running lanes – indicates that pioneer communities in the later Iron Age or early Roman period were its creators.[19]

---

[17] Coronation Villas: TQ78.7089.8654. King's Terrace: TQ78.7086.8620.

[18] *Kynochtown: A Great Explosive Factory on the Essex Marshes,* A. Clifton Kelway, E.R. Vol. 16, 1907.

[19] *Settlement in the later Iron Age and Roman Period,* Drury and Rodwell, C.B.A. Research Report No. 34, ed. D. Buckley, 1980.

Incredibly enough, a near two thousand years old landscape can still be traced. It still directs everyday logistics to a great extent: the means by which we are made to drive from place to place; the minor boundaries of village gardens, the siting of modern residential enclaves.

Within a far wider area of this symmetrical countryside, recognised by archaeologists as a key example of the type, Fobbing provides a very important though fast vanishing fragment. Distinct from the clay marshes (which show the influence of curling water-boundaries) the high ground was methodically and mathematically apportioned over undefined periods of years into blocks that are interlinked by regular lanes, or lesser farm access ways. Though much has been erased, even a current ordnance survey map provides a moderate indication of the former structure. High Road, a north-south thoroughfare, is matched by parallel lanes to the westward[20] which represent former cartways ("West Street" in 1679) and by Public Footpath 23. Opposed to these are the significant east-west tracks of Whitehall Lane, Marsh Lane, Great House Chase and others. Nearly two miles from the village hub, but still within the church's former tithable territory, a tag-end of Dry Street crosses Fobbing eastward from Langdon Hills in an equally planned way, edged by the remains of a chequer-board of neat "crofts", or hedged enclosures, that have now been largely overbuilt by Basildon's New Town. Each of these lanes – and there are and were various others – signifies a fragment of a communications framework known to the last prehistoric farmers. They are our oldest man-made landscape structures and they are still in everyday use.

Were it possible to view the whole parish fieldscape as it appeared before massive change ensued, the warp and weft of numerous crossing lines, of hedgerows, enclosure banks and their counterpart ditches, would impress us at once. Each averaging only about eight acres, well over a hundred upland fields could be envisaged along the village ridge; sweeping pleasantly to Hawkesbury's summit and beyond, down the valley to old Basildon parish edge: oblongs whose perimeters had been overwhelmingly dictated by those straight lanes and homestead tracks of a distant time. By good fortune, not only *can* they be perceived in near-completeness thanks to such surveys as the early Victorian Tithe Apportionment map, but occasionally other documents enhance our sight of how the system of field waggonways became gradually eroded, falling by stages to a mere remnant of an original plan.

Fobbing's manor court had heard in June 1766 of two instances where farmers had encroached upon a highway near Whitehall farm, one having snatched a piece of the lane to be "converted into a Garden", while during 1742, a prosperous copyholder, Benjamin Jocelyn, had tried to stop it up with a ditch and

20 *"West Street"* Rental of Fobbing Hall manor, 1679 D/DCx M12-21.

Pedunculate Oak

new hedge "leading from the Want field ... to Thistley Field now in the Occupation of John Houlding", so hindering his neighbour's agricultural work. This much-used track – referred to during 1679 as "Barr Lane" – climbed northward as yet another parallel to the High Road from the present Wheelers Lane and crossing Marsh Lane in its course to Whitehall. Jocelyn's attempt on this occasion was to be thwarted, for almost forty years on, in 1781, the attractive estate map of Thomas Drew's Vineyard farm could depict the whole "Ancient Lane leading to Bakers Croft" as quite intact. But our illustration of man's continual pressure to gain farming acres at the expense of such highways is plain enough. By 1839 a narrow finger of woodland had grown across the lane south of Whitehall. Today, its whole mile course is lost to plough and pasture.

With regard to the rich pattern and variety of the hedgerows themselves, a similar massive reduction has taken place. Compared even to sixty years ago, Fobbing's present picture is one of a sadly threadbare countryside. This is not merely a scenic loss: the ways in which hedgeline plants can help the field-historian in dating his landscape are now well appreciated. Multiple-species hedges are today seldom found in our parish except in areas northward of the village and increasingly towards Basildon, though *there* housing estates have vanquished a great part of the evidence forever. Those shrubby field and lane boundaries such as remain near Fobbing's main settlement, are further diminished (so far as dating evidence goes) due to elm-suckering.

Elm was, of course, always present to a considerable extent, but its method of natural propagation through extending suckers underground, tends to slowly eradicate other shrub kinds. Marsh Lane, Wheelers Lane and Mill Lane are all ready examples of very old highways whose edges have been overtaken by masses of elm; though the latter trackway is somewhat more species-rich in its northerly progress towards Inglefield Road.[21] In the vicinity of Great House farm, for example, an excellent impression of the "ancient" character of this old vehicle-way can be gained. Some earlier names (for this part of it at least) were Blind Lane (1781) or Chase Lane (1810)[22] and its ten feet wide unmetalled surface is accompanied by quite broad ditches and sizeable banks, which support a moderate range of hedge-trees; standard oaks, attractive field-maple and hawthorn, and the sloe-bearing blackthorn. A certain amount of spindle – a useful indicator for early hedgerows – is also present along its course, together with wild briar (or dogrose).

[21] Strictly, north of Waterworks Lane. F.P. 23 is part of the ancient "West Street".

[22] *A True Terrier of all the ... Glebe Lands ... belonging to the Rectory of Fobbing ...* Jerome Alley, 28th June, 1810.

Spindle

The much shorter Whitehall Lane also offers a fairly mixed sample, especially upon its southward hedgeline where there is elm, hawthorn and blackthorn, field-maple and crab apple, honeysuckle and dogrose. A shrub list of this kind could indicate a hedge of at least medieval date, though this is no more than we might anticipate for an approach into a farmstead which we believe to have been present in the early 14th century. Its name had possibly derived from the family of John le White, alive in 1332, while during 1367 a Nicholas White had also held lands somewhere in Fobbing.[23]

Upon the slope above Whitehall, *Bakers Croft* has suffered from de-hedging except along the line of its northern ditch and bank. Sadly, a predominance of elm there suggests that its clones are succeeding in wiping out a once richer hedgerow of particular historical importance. For here stood the copyhold enclosure of Fobbing's rebel captain, Thomas Baker.[24] With six species – oak, hawthorn, blackthorn, field maple, ash and elm – it retains however an adequate shrub range to imply as many centuries of living existence and, quite remarkably, we are able to corroborate from a late 14th century source that it was already "enclosed with hedges and ditches" at this period. Some sallow-willow is now also adding itself within its deep field ditch. Slightly more varied is the hedge of *Upper Abbots* lying north-eastward of the former windmill site, on a brown clayey loam with stones. Estimates of its age might vary according to whether the field historian accepts such plants as elder or briar-rose in his counting. These aside, Upper Abbots shows a seven species total, adding dogwood to the list obtained from Bakers Croft.[25]

Few of the hedgerows anywhere near Fobbing's village centre could be said to reveal indications of old forest landscapes. Except in dubious patches which may only represent garden-dumping, bluebell never occurs within hedgerows upon the upland ridge of the main settlement. A little wild honeysuckle and an odd crab apple tree *may* be chance survivals from this kind of landscape however. The implication is strong nevertheless that southward of Hawkesbury's foot, pioneering and cultivation happened much earlier than elsewhere in Fobbing so that nearly all woodland vestiges have been erased, not only along highway edges, but across the whole network of enclosures also, with the deliberate setting of boundary thickets comprised of a mix of shrubs. This was an operation which possibly began seven centuries ago; though invariably using as its baseline the much older symmetry of already-present cartways.

23 *The Placenames of Essex,* P. H. Reaney, 1935.

24 *Remember the Poll Tax,* R. Bingley, E.C. Vol. 39, 414, June, 1991.

25 *Hedgerow Dating,* R. Bingley, PAN.Vol. 29, 1988.

Field Hawthorn

Those ways, at least the greater traffic-carrying ones, have of course been widened considerably – and not because of motorised vehicle's needs alone. During 1778 Bells Hill, and possibly the westward half mile of the Southend Road, had been improved under a military project to push a "trident" of marching routes out from Tilbury Fort, through Stifford, Horndon and Basildon, into higher Essex.[26] Such schemes would naturally involve removal and replanting along at least one roadside hedgeline all the way. The present seventeen-feet width of the Bells Hill route appears to derive from the Royal Engineers' undertaking, broadening its original trafficway to Billericay by perhaps a couple of yards throughout.[27] Plainly here, they hacked into banks of ancient woodland prolific with bluebell, honeysuckle, crab apple trees and oaks, a terrain distinctly more uncultivated than that which we have previously viewed.[28]

Yet not a quarter mile beyond, Dry Street's course was of an entirely different character. Again, its bordering shrub-species told variety – plentiful dogwood, field maple, ashes and oak – but these did not press the lane's edge. For even back into the medieval, it seems, wide verges of grass and herb must have existed at either side, so that the whole climbing course between its junction with the Billericay highway and Blackmans farm below Langdon Hill, served as a grazing common for livestock. Dry Street farmstead and other cottage homes further west – perhaps in origin of a squatter sort – seem to have snatched in past centuries their bits of this generous roadside green, but enough is still visible for us to understand the whole linear scheme of pasturage.

Bounds oaks, Martinhole edge

All across this greater high-land of the parish, rising to Hawkesbury's 230 feet, the wayside and field hedges bear a more marked influence of that woodland which preceded them. Not all by any means have blatant signs such as bluebell flowers or honeysuckle bines, but the incidence of shrubs like

---

[26] *Military Land Communications around East Tilbury*, R. Bingley, PAN. Vol. 30, 1989.

[27] R.E. GRA/10/1.

[28] *Bells Hill*: There is a strong inference on the Tithe Map (1839) in the linear progression of hedgelines from Crooked Brook to Dry Street, that both the north end of High Road and Bells Hill are "adjusted" lines and that previously the highway travelled somewhat to the west, directly *over* Hawkesbury top.

crab apple, dogwood, native privet, wild rose and a good mix of trees from ash to field maple is greater by far. In a number of these cases, it seems reasonable to see the kind of hedgerow which was not *planted*, but survived as a managed barrier of shrubs and timber between newly pioneered fields as each was claimed out of the woodland. In the sense of their *use* as agricultural boundaries, they are possibly creations of a very similar period to those closer in on Fobbing village; merely indicating that the large coppices and swine-woods of Domesday were now coming under pressure by arable or flock-grazing husbandmen.

From the brow of Bells Hill, the long straight course of High Road can easily be seen leading back toward Fobbing village. A raking sunlight across the sloping field surfaces of autumn will also reveal with field glasses, distant ripples that are the remains of ridge and furrow fields – each roughly an acre piece – which predate and underlie the larger rectangular croft enclosures beyond Whitehall's farmland. These were the common strips, many in number, of "open-fields" that were for the main part unhedged and which within our surrounding district were usually called "shots". Only the slightest fieldname evidence has lingered relating to these early strips, because so many would acquire new identities as they became swallowed into the croft-scape. "Double Shots" was spoken of by farm workers even into the present century and at Hawkesbury manor during 1649 one enclosed sixteen acre field had kept its long obsolete title of "Strayt Shotte". Generally groups of these ribbon acres were cultivated "in common" by manorial tenants in exchange, to varying degrees, for services to their lord: in 1329 for example on Hawkesbury's monastic estate, the customary tenant John Sueyn would be bound to reap for the lady Abbess 11 acres of corn at harvest-time as boon work for his holding. Sueyn's fields for all we know may not have been of "shot" strips, for it appears to be around this time that Fobbing's highground landscape was in its phase of revision, compacting the old ridge-and-furrow acre lands into groups of four or six, perhaps ten acres, and hedging them independently round so that a new era of mixed farming would proceed.

Because a settled place of community had already emerged, with cottages and farmhouses straggling Fobbing's central highway, the new chequerwork of croft-fields was in one aspect as inconvenient as the old; the apportionment of enclosures still involved cart journeys and plough-hauling to squares of land that were sometimes inconveniently far from each homestead. Doubtless through the early years, agreements for exchange and rationalisation were to be made, further drawing together groups of fields for the convenience of one or another of the manor copyholders. But overall, even by the Victorian period, Fobbing's map of land occupation showed an arrangement of wantonly scattered properties. Sprivens Hall (Prosbus) at the church-side was a case in point, with much of its grounds remotely placed out beyond Whitehall and Brookhouse lands, while Curtis' boasted never more than two fields that touched each other. More compactly arranged were the farms like Dry Street, Fobbing Farm and Hawkesbury Bush, again implying direct organisation as medieval woodland clearance went ahead.

The 1300s generally seem to have been those years in which our "croft" landscape was developing. A document of 1424 would refer to the *"Bakerescroft"* we have already viewed, but giving it aside an alias *"Pokattescroft"* which must on other evidence refer to a copyholder of before 1381; while another parcel of three acres near St. Michael's churchyard, called *"Burgeyescroft"* whose name continued far into the Georgian century, plainly existed in 1381 as part of the countess of Hereford's estate.[29] It was then being farmed by William Gildeborne, Thomas Baker's close ally in the Fobbing uprising and must have derived from the family of John Burgeys, who during 1367 had obtained royal licence for the shipping of 60 weys of cheese and as many barrels of ale out of Fobbing, to Flanders.[30] Following the rebellion, its executed leader's small parcel of ground, held at 2 shillings yearly rental from the Abbott of Waltham Holy Cross and called *"Bakerescroft"*, had been taken over by this Burgeys' presumed son, "John Burgeys the younger of Fobbyngg (who) has ever since occupied it (1389) and taken the issues." Well into future generations, court rolls would hint at the many other "croft" fieldnames that had perhaps originated in those medieval years – such as Crouchmans Croft (a John Crouchman had paid the Lay Subsidy of 1317); Motts Croft, Hall Croft and Rogers Croft. Recorded by successive court Steward's hands, they retained their original clarity, though in rustic parlance matters might easily drift. Down the pebbly slope of Marsh Lane could be found in Victorian times a *"Calves Crotes"* field, typifying the later Essex corruption of the croft name.

Earliest among the inquisitions (documented enquiries) traced relating to Thomas Baker's small possession, is that taken at Billericay before the king's escheator for Essex upon 27th October 1389, above eight years after he had been "drawn and hanged for divers felonies and treasons at Chelmsford on Thursday after St. Peter and St. Paul" (4th July, 1381). In it, *"Bakerescroft"* had been identified as "6 acres of land worth 6s. yearly", yet several subsequent medieval references such as that of the Fine Rolls of 1424, define this same confiscated arable parcel as of only 4 acres extent.[31] By the period of the tithe apportionment, in 1839, it had become known merely as "Whitehall Six Acres" and so had lost its unique historical identity of name.

---

[29] Joan de Bohun, lady of the manor in the year of insurrection.

[30] A wey, 224 lbs., thus a cargo of 13,440 lbs. of cheese.

[31] P.R.O. *Calendar of Inquisitions Miscellaneous,* Vol. V (1387-1393) H.M.S.O., 1962.

Conceding that Thomas Baker's parcel of ground had been of the lesser (4 acre) size, how could such an apparent increase happen by the 1830s without intake from neighbouring fields? Allowing for some variation in survey, or in the current definition of a statute acre – or the frequent fact that any proprietor might claim to be allowing his tenant a little more ground than was the reality – considerable enlargement *was* possible simply through the reduction of hedges. Farming tenants had traditionally calculated differently to their landlords; using the practical concept of the area *available* for direct seasonal use. Their term was "as the plough and scythe goes."

So generously hedged had many ancient crofts been, that often as much as one tenth of the total acreage of a steading could be denied the ploughshare. An equal part again might be blighted by the effects of shade from towering elms, or maiden oak and ash. As the 18th and 19th centuries bowed to the import of nasty softwoods and to the use of brick around its farmyards, native sources of timber would become devalued. Arable production increased to the hilt at their expense and thousands of enclosure hedgerows would be grubbed away to leave mere slender fences of laid quickthorn. It was not difficult, where profit beckoned, to turn by axe and spade something above four acres into somewhere close upon six. The 1389 Inquisition besides would establish that *Bakerescroft* had been adjoined by the traitor's "messuage and curtilage" (his dwelling place with its surrounding workbuildings) separately owned by Joan, countess of Hereford and held in jointure by both Baker and his wife Avice, "who is still alive". This lost houseplot, too, had presumably in subsequent centuries been absorbed into the overall acreage of the arable field.

THE HILL OF THE HAWKS

Despite all the transforming influences that were working upon the sound and written form of fieldnames (a constantly shifting village population for example, varying accents, an unstandardised spelling among even the most literate) the identity of many locational names has remained surprisingly constant in our parish. Original meanings can frequently be understood even after seven or eight hundred years of modification. The *burh*, or hill of the hawks, was first recorded as *Hauechesburga* during the mid 13th century, but had acquired its modern form within the parish registers by the 1640s ("Hawkesbury"). There were still however various erratic attempts by educated villagers to write it far later than this

("Ashbury", 1870, "Oxberry", 1877) the latter giving us a momentary image of how the Essex voice would have pronounced it in almost any period.[32] Imprecise diction seems also to have played tricks with the couple of fields of Great House farm, called in 1839 Upper and Lower *"Abbots"*, lying towards the marshes eastward of the High Road. When, during the January of 1886 the old and deluded Charles Ballard had been found dead in a water-filled ditch here, a coroner at Fobbing's *White Lion* had heard the local name of *"Rabbits"*, an easily made transformation when the "R" of "Lower" or "Upper" was tagged onto the next vowel.[33]

"Abbots" must have derived from a personal name. In 1839 the tithe apportionment map had listed other such fields to which names of old or recent occupiers had become – for chance reasons – affixed for a while before succumbing to some new fashion. There was Abrey Field (the farming Abreys were established at Pitsea Hall in 1841) and Sand Hills just off Wheelers Lane, clarified upon Thomas Marsh's map in 1781 as *"Sandalls or Sandhills"* and evidently once connected with that Sandal family which had been lords of Basildon's Barstable Hall manor.[34] A fine of 1525 was to name William Sandall the younger as lessee of a messuage and thirty acres in Fobbing and Corringham; perhaps the Vineyard farm to which these present parcels of land still belonged. *"Byrons Acre Piece"* was another which kept its personal name and we shall meet later the Edmund Byron who had worked this dipping ribbon of ground that touched the western parish boundary stream. It seems to have been one of the very few medieval "shot" acre pieces to have escaped absorption, right into Victorian times.[35]

Bounds oak, Martinhole edge

By the period of the tithe apportionment map in 1839, many attractive and informative landscape names had already slipped from usage. Indeed, their vanishing and retitling had been a constant feature of the agricultural story. Facing the pretty red Brickhouse along High Road had been a close called *"Sheep Stealers"* referred to in Fobbing's manor rental of 1713 and still so known during 1781 – recalling surely some

32 *Fobbing, Overseers' Rates* 1870-1878, microfilm E.C.L. Grays CR18645.

33 G.T.G. 23rd January, 1886.

34 *A Plan of an Estate ... belonging to Thos. Drew* (Vineyard farm) *Surveyed by Thos. Marsh, 1781,* E.R.O. D/DCx P1.

35 Tithe Apportionment (map) 1839 E.R.O. D/CT 141.

undocumented village felony of a distant past. A barn had stood upon it; by 1839 it had become a mundane "Barn Four Acres". The will of Henry Doe, who had died in the April of 1579, enables us to hear an earlier pronunciation of the farmstead called *"Hovels"* lying beside the Crooked Brook's pastures and which was then known as *"Hofild"* meaning cleared land in a hollow – an apt picture of its valley-bottom situation. His father, Richard Dowe, in the early 1540s had clarified it even further, leaving at his decease "all my corne growyng in ffange and holefeld", while the notoriously inaccurate Ordnance Survey of 1805 was to implant "Howell Farm", a rendering possibly picked up by its military surveyors from some labourer met upon their way. "Hobbles" was the Fobbing census enumerator's spelling in 1851, evidently a locally acceptable substitute for "hovel" since during 1887 a Fobbing unfortunate called Aaron Bacon had been fined by magistrates for living in a "hobble" that had an earth floor and sacks for a roof.[36]

Close to Hovel's brick farmhouse in 1839 had been marked "Marten Hole Field", which abutted the similarly called coppice at Corringham's edge. Reaney's authoritative study of Essex placenames pins down an early reference to this area as *Mantels Hole* (1493) though reasonably its connection had been with the weasel-like pine marten, now locally extinct but whose alternative name occurs on occasions within Fobbing's churchwardens' accounts. The bounty to a villager called Groves for handing in a dead "Marten Catt" had been 8d. in 1769, and three others would be destroyed during springtime a decade later. Hawkesbury farm, whose grounds ranged downslope to meet this boundary of Hovels, had possessed a field here named "Meaden Hole" in 1649. More northward yet over the upland lay Fobbing farm, which had assumed its title only in late Georgian years perhaps, being earlier spoken of as *"Lesons"* (1507)[37] *"Leesings"* (1661) and *"Leasons"* (1679) an extensive 400 acre holding which ranged into Langdon Hills and East Lee parishes.[38] Its derivation is still obscure, but may refer in part to *"leases"* (leas); for a grassland character pertained over much of its fieldscape towards Lee Chapel and indeed can still today be enjoyed around Basildon's Dry Street area.[39]

More plain in their meaning are those land names which came about because of some nearby feature of note; a house, highway, or cattle shed perhaps. A "Mylnehill" is found in 1539; and the will of John Fowler had referred during 1567 to a two acre "Mill Hill field", while *Bullock Lodge, Big Barn field* and *Bell field* are all present in 1839, the latter quite

[36] G.T.G. 25 July and 30 June, 1887.

[37] Incorrectly given in Inquisitions P.M., 2nd series Vol. III as *Lesous.* (1507).

[38] *Essex Recusant*, Vol. 7, Will of William Whitbread, gent 1661, farm purchased of John Petrie (Petre); *Fobbing Manor Rental,* 1679.

[39] *The Freehold Estate known as Fobbing Farm:* Sale Catalogue, Surridge & Son auctioneers, 1876.

close to the *Five Bells* alehouse. *Well field, Old Bar* (denoting a gateway perhaps to Blind Lane) were mentioned too, with others whose name objects were seemingly transient things like a *Pear Tree* or even a *Straw Stack.* The "Want Field" already referred to in our progress, had gathered its title because of two adjacent cross tracks (Marsh Lane and the lost Barr Lane) and evolved from "Went" and the old English *Wendam*, meaning to turn, or go. Chaucer had spoken in his fourteenth century *Book of the Duchesse* of "a floury grene *wente* ful thicke of gras", in other words a green country lane.

Of even more remarkable antiquity was the quaint tag of *"Diddles"*, a parcel of Fobbing farm's pasture mapped near Dry Street in 1839, but given alternatively as *"Didlands"* during 1876. We may trace this beautiful grassland hummock back to 1244 when it has been spoken of as *"Dedefeld"*, an indication of having been held by title deed from the crown in Saxon times, or soon after. As *Dedefeld*, it had been enfeoffed to the rector of West Lee from Peter de Newport, Archdeacon of London, to hold upon a ninepenny rent with the proviso that it should never be sublet to either any Jew or other persons of certain religions.[40]

Few field names anywhere in south Essex have Scandinavian origins, though *"Waits"* may be one of these, its title remaining in use by Fobbing's farm workers into our own lifetimes. This field is identified in 1839 as lying aside the *White Lion* and during 1679 had been listed on the manor rental as both *Weights* and *Waites*. Eilert Eckwall points out that *Waithe* refers in old Scandinavian to a fording place and certainly the topography of Lion Hill's highway and the boundary stream which crosses it, fits entirely that interpretation. Presumably this had been the location of the "West Pond at the Towns End" to which the above rental had alluded during 1679 and which – at least in flood times – all traffic must have forded upon journeys to and fro' Corringham parish.

Though respectably antique, of no such impressive pedigree is the *"Vineyard"* – the one agricultural fieldname that is mentioned daily and which is soon known to even the latest village-comer.[41] P. H. Reaney gives its earliest reference as among the Minister's accounts of 1539 ("le vynyarde") and consistently Fobbing's lawyer-stewards would record it through the Stuart and Georgian years under that general guise, "le Vyneyard" or "Tenement and eight acres of land be the same more or less called the Vineyard" (1746). We shall glimpse later its connection with the vine-culture which featured modestly along these warm south facing terraces of Thames, but its subsequent use was to be for arable production

RB.

40 P.R.O. Calendar of Ancient Deeds, 1243-4. H.M.S.O.

41 Vineyard farmyard, vestiges at TQ78.7174.8385.

Medieval key, Vineyard

and meadow grassland. An East and West *Vineyard* had been marked upon Thomas Marsh's 1781 map and the present thickets of elm and cherry-plum of our time still demark their dividing line to some extent, as does its distinct field ditch within. Latterly, Ernest Gardner, Fobbing's rector from 1925 to 1949, would purchase the Vineyard, placing it in diocesan trust as a playground for village youngsters and for the benefit, social and moral, of "the neighbouring population".[42] Upon occasions, some might doubt its moral aspect realised, but its value as a precious natural space none can deny.

With the distressing constitutional politics of a royal abdication put aside, Orsett Deanery's magazine was whispering early in 1937 of plans to set the Vineyard fields at Fobbing aglow with a glorious bonfire for the coronation of the empire's new monarch, George VI. But none of those who congregated happily amidst creaming hawthorn buds to enjoy their merry blaze on the following 12th May, were privy to a truly sensational press secret; that upon only the previous day a *Junkers 52* airliner had passed over this Thameside horizon, bound from Nazi Germany into Croydon airport. On board, eager to observe the south country's pattern of ancient landscape unfold below him – highway, village, town, factory, oil depot – was one *Reichmarschall* Hermann Goering, soon to be given supreme command of Hitler's invincible air force. He had arrived in civilian clothes, a legitimate German citizen, hoping to see the forthcoming street pageantry of an admired "Teutonic people", but had been humiliated and turned away on the tarmac by British officials.[43]

Lufthansa's passenger services into England and its roll of aircrew personnel, had markedly increased of late. Coolly, secretly, the *Fuhrer's* young eagles were building up their navigational training on routes to and from London: ready for the big show. They could promise this valley a somewhat grander conflagration, when their time was ripe.

Vineyard cottage

[42] Will. Rev. E. A. Gardner, 22 June, 1948 devising "the Vineyards" to the St. Albans and Chelmsford Church Trust.

[43] *Croydon Airport. The Great Days 1928-1939,* D. Cluett, J. Nash and B. Learmonth, 1980. For flight-path and Thames-approach procedure, see *Wings over the Lower River,* A. G. Linney, P.L.A. no. 129, July, 1936.

D. Maxwell

2. "PEG O'LANTERN": THE MARSHLANDS

Like so many places abutting Thames, Fobbing had been devised as a strip of territory that was long – in this instance nearly six miles – and a mile and a half or so wide at most. If a certain symmetry was visible in its fairly straight upland boundaries, the creek-riddled nature of its low marshes made for contorted edges to the parish outline, while from westward a waisted band of Corringham's grounds thrust in to breach its shoreward pastures. It cut Fobbing clean in two, a fact somehow overlooked by P. H. Reaney when mapping his Essex parishes for the English Place-Name Society, a work nevertheless without which no one can develop an understanding of how this region's landscape became tamed and settled.[1]

Other, quite distant inland parishes such as Dunton and Little Warley possessed for many generations detached pockets of grazing upon the eastward side of Shellhaven Creek and, as a result, various agricultural holdings overlapped one parochial sector or another. Upon Oil Mill farm, the house and barnyard and some 200 acres of ground were Fobbing's, though about another 30 acres draped themselves over the Corringham border by Manorway Fleet. Shellhaven farm, its greater neighbour, would be calculated in the year 1753 as some 378 acres. Though an entirely compact block which occupied the peninsular above Shellhaven Point, only its northerly 80 acres lay inside Fobbing's jurisdiction, the rest spreading into three other parishes.[2] Small wonder that, when in April 1881 the census enumerator called at a boarded dwelling on Fobbing's High Road to collect details of John Baker – a shepherd of the marsh then in his mid sixties – the old fellow could not declare with certainty in what parish he had been born. Either "Wharley or Dunton" was his reply, though a decade earlier Baker had considered himself a native of Fobbing. Between the lines, he was pinpointing his birthplace to a worker's cottage on Shellhaven farm, amidst that jumble of boundaries which few folk entirely understood.

---

1 *The Place Names of Essex,* P. H. Reaney, Cambridge, 1935. Others have followed suit, erroneously implying that the ecclesiastical parish had no Thames-fronting marshland at all.

2 *An Accurate Plan of Shell Haven Farm ... Surveyed and Plan'd by W. Fairchild,* 1753.

Local writers have constantly misplaced the marsh farms into wrong parishes, and indeed they *are* difficult to pigeonhole, not least because of another tendency (like farmsteads everywhere) to alter their names fairly frequently over periods of time. Simply, there were six main marshland holdings whose grounds lay either wholly or partly within Fobbing: Nazewick (264 acres) which extended eastward of the settlement ridge; then, southward towards the Thames were Little Ilford (93 acres) Great Ilford (114 acres) Borley farm (197 acres within Fobbing) whose sea walls edged Holehaven's water, and the two we have already touched upon called Oil Mill and Shellhaven farms. Aside from these, there was also a smaller remnant of marsh acreage which remained attached to the better upland farms (Fobbing Hall and Whitehall) tagged onto the foot of the easterly ridge slopes as meadow feed-ground. Well above one thousand acres in total of Fobbing's agricultural land was therefore to be found upon these rich brown clays that weathered quickly after tillage to a lightish grey and which were called by countrymen "*the levels*". This was near to a half of the parish farming grounds, but represented in natural fertility by far the more prosperous portion.

Beyond the two Ilford farms and within the several old navigable loopings off Shellhaven creek that were called Oilmill Fleet and Manorway Fleet, stood further marshland farmsteads; *Reedham* ("Buttons Farm" upon Chapman & Andre's survey of the mid 1770s) and the drearily named Oozedam, an extensive property of well above 300 acres.[3] Both were Corringham holdings, yet were located by crow's flight closer to Fobbing's village nucleus than to their own, so that it was not unusual to find their occupants included in St. Michael's registers at whiles; as during September 1598 when a daughter of "John Kent of Ooes" was buried; or the marriage far later in October 1753 of Joseph Coot and Mary Skinner, single persons, "both of Ouzey house – part of the ffarm belonging whereto is in this parish".

Such a name as "Ouzey" *sounds* right, suggesting soft, even treacherous grounds of the kind which we might associate with a boggy vicinity, because to the modern mind "marsh" usually accords with something akin to "swamp". But agriculturally the word has long meant almost the reverse, implying a fully drained area of the levels suitable for a great range of arable and grass crops. While still in its natural unimproved and oozy state, it was normally called a saltern or salt-marsh, the habitat of a great variety of brine-tolerant herbs and providing good, nutritious browsing for sheep and horned cattle. A will of John Wyberd dated 1560 would identify exactly this kind of tide-washed ground in some part of Fobbing "bought of Mr. Robert Turrell called ... Castell being salt marsh", while less than twenty years later a fine, or agreement over land between Robert Benne

---

[3] Oozedam TQ78.7383.8328. Reaney refers to this holding and its name under Corringham; *waes*, 'mud'.

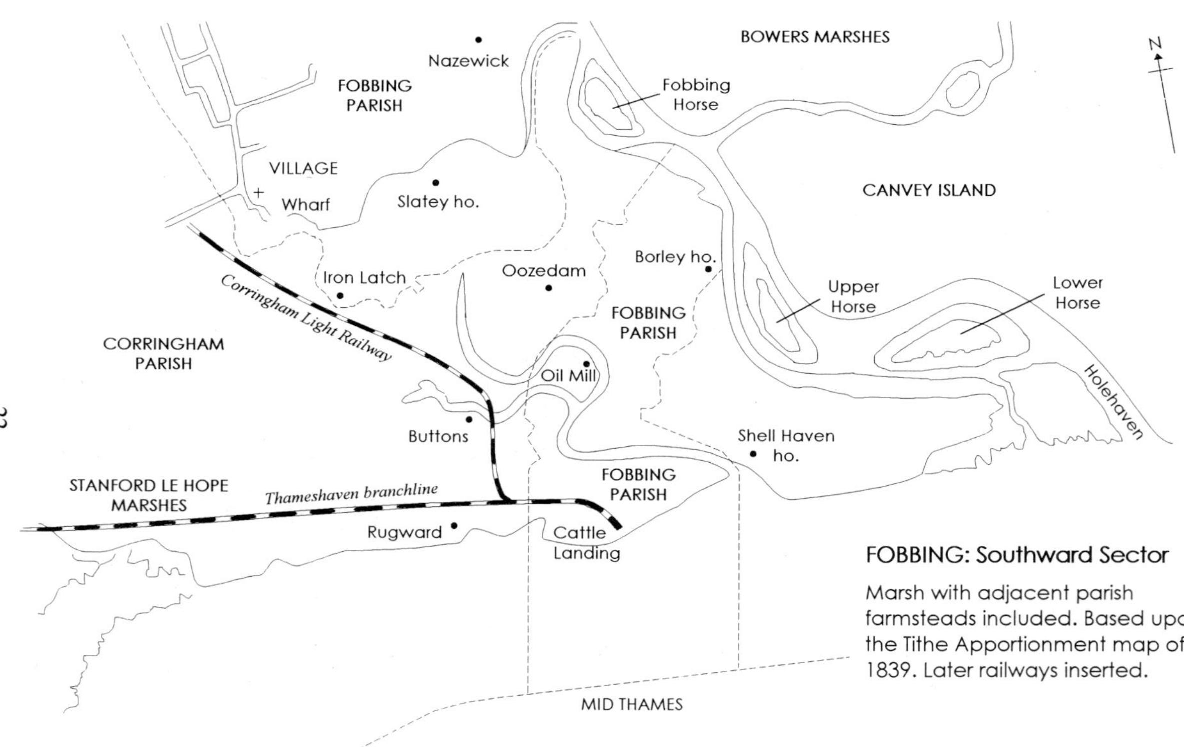

FOBBING: Southward Sector

Marsh with adjacent parish farmsteads included. Based upon the Tithe Apportionment map of 1839. Later railways inserted.

and the widow Alice Oglander, was to list a hundred acres of "salt marsh in Fobbing" and another equal area of "fresh meadow". Winning this "fresh" or "sweet" marsh from the swampy wild-flower salterns was to be the endeavour of sundry parish generations, and hence "marshland" came more and more to imply a land surface rescued from the flood that could be ploughed and harvested in much the way of the upland fields.

But paradoxically, what we call "marshland" was not in a medieval terminology *land* at all – as the feet of fines so often indicate to us.[4] Prior to the Tudor period, "land" really pertained only to grounds that were higher than the river flood plain. A single fine, dated to Easter 1446, will suffice to clarify this: it arranges the transfer between William Wetenhale (a London grocer and alderman) his business colleagues, and John and Emma Bernard, of "1 messuage 80 acres of land and 40 acres of marsh in the towns of Fobbyng and Fange ...". Wherever the sea tides might break in and overflow, even occasionally, the title of "land" seems not to have applied.

Whether as a group, or individually during this embryo period of reclaiming the wetlands, the fields attached to any holding normally took to themselves the name of "marsh" (or one of its variant spellings) – during 1218 *"Wadmerse"* had been mentioned at Fobbing, presumably long to remain in its wild, salt-mire condition, for it was so described in 1560. Its identity a decade on, in 1570 when its lease would be willed by Thomas Kent (of Oosedam?) to John Hayes, was in the form of *"Wade Wick"*, illustrating an often-found change of suffix which refers to a *"wic"* or dairy pasture for milch sheep. Nazewick (Nasshemershe, 1487) is alternatively noticed both before and after that date with this "wic" element (Nasshewykmersshe, 1419 or Naswick, 1741) and even into our own century as Narswick (1914) a broad medieval sound would linger.[5] In all likelihood, its origin had been with *naes*, a word akin to nose, or promontory, for Nazewick (now an Essex Wildlife Trust reserve) is of distinctly beak-like form to the south east, where it is embraced on three sides by Vange and Fobbing creeks.[6]

Reviewing for a moment our *Wadmerse* of the early thirteenth century, we appear to have its derivation amongst what P. H. Reaney groups as the "werde" fieldnames, all found "in low-lying marshland" along the lower Thames and some of which have modified into spellings like *"worth"* or *"word"*.[7] Fobbing's two holdings called Great and Little Ilford demonstrate well the kind of bizarre

---

4 Feet of Fines for Essex, Vol. I-VI (1182-1603); contains abstracts of agreements of land-transfer, with indexing of locality.

5 P.R.O. Calendar of Close Rolls, 18th October, 1419, H.M.S.O.

6 Nazewick, farmstead mound and cattlepond at TQ78.7235.8486.

7 *The Place Names of Essex*, P. H. Reaney, 1935.

Sea aster

language changes which may arise to perplex the amateur in this most perilous area of study, for during the mid Tudor period they were just the westerly and the easterly *word* or marsh farmstead; hence *Westelword* (1521) and *Estylward* (1539). This is very much the form still found as late as 1679, when Fobbing's manor rental had shown John Peter (Petre) of Thorndon renting "East Tilward Marsh", yet within the short period up to 1736 a radical alteration to a single name of "Ilford" for both farms (Great and Little) had taken place. The common south-eastern practice of interchanging spoken Ws with Vs and Vs with Fs (*Vobbyng*, 1392; *Fange*, 1203) depicts this drift perfectly.

Some marshes were also termed "hopes", simply meaning an enclosure within fenny ground and even as late as 1904 those reedy streamside meadows near Lion Hill foot attaching to Fobbing Vineyard were being referred to by that title.[8] Stanford *"le Hope"* is the most familiar local survival from this class of fieldnames, though in this case more fanciful origins are generally put forward.[9] At Fobbing in May 1657 the Court Rolls had documented a certain "marsh called Mill hope", presumably close to the Oil Mill farmstead and seemingly identical to the "Northop Marsh" where dwelled in the spring of 1635 one Thomas Gouldwin, father of a newly baptised child called Sarah. A sale catalogue of 1789 sheds further light upon: "Three Marshes, called Northope, with the contiguous Saltings and Fleet", as containing altogether about forty six acres and being clearly a portion of the Oil Mill farm. It seems on the evidence to have lain within the wide curve of Oil Mill fleet abutting the farmhouse and can be traced back as yet another medieval holding of the hanged rebel William Gildeborne. Both "a marsh called Northope" and the "Wadewyk" that we have noted, would be listed at an inquisition post mortem in Horndon upon Saturday, the eve of the nativity of the Virgin Mary, 1382, following Gildborne's execution.[10]

Even if landscape names themselves do not fascinate us, they surely inform that in *some* way these marshes provided an integral resource of the manor and parish more than half a millennium ago, while Domesday Book can tug that continuity back for us onto the edge of the Saxon age. But names themselves do not assist very much in determining *when* the first attempts to "inn" or reclaim "fresh marsh" out of the saltern quagmire took place. There are inferences however. From the saltmarsh that was called "le Castell" at Fobbing and which is named so in an inquisition of 1507, a guess might be made that it stood either within, or close to, some early protective sea-wall, because the word *castellard* corresponds to the strengthening or repair of earthen banks. Upon Canvey *"Castlewick"* appears to have similar derivation. When Justinian Champneys and

---

8 Fobbing P.C.C. minutes, 1904.

9 *Place names, Stanford le Hope,* R. Bingley, PAN. 30, 1989.

10 P.R.O. Calendar of Inquisition Post Mortem. *William Guldeburn of Fobbyng, 5 Richard II.*

his wife Elena quitclaimed to William Hammond in the early Elizabethan years a certain Fobbing farmstead, more than a half of its several hundred acres upon the levels was noted to have been already embanked and improved. At a similar period (1565-6) a description of other Fobbing manor grounds (albeit including various detached holdings such as Bowaters farm at East Tilbury) would reveal an even more impressive reclamation; only a hundred acres of wild saltern now remaining compared to 300 of "fresh" marshgrounds.

Obviously so great an endeavour as wholesale reclamation was a long term enterprise. But *how* long? Plentiful queries arise. Was it an outward pioneering process extending by easy stages from the settlement shelf; or were those muddy islands of sea aster and scurvy-grass seized in some cases far out, due to fortunate tidal circumstances and ripening terrain? And to what extent had men in, say, 1300 A.D., inherited vestiges of walled and managed marshland from the Roman occupiers of a thousand years before? For just as the upland pattern of landscape had been created by late Iron Age and Roman needs, so the marshes, too, had known exploitation and change. At present little is known about these people's use of the Thames Valley wetlands: they may have been responsible for the laying of those areas of marsh trackways which later farmers would term "manor ways": certainly to an intense degree the later-prehistoric people were to industrialise the whole lower river with salt-producing factories that were of major regional importance. Some, like the recently discovered Marsh Lane brine-evaporation site, and another near Great Ilford (Slated House farm) are far inland and plainly utilised creeklines that are still traceable today. A degree of protective embankment building may well have accompanied this kind of industrial activity nearly 2000 years ago.

Whatever might have existed, there had been in the interval a significant lowering of land levels throughout southern England. Sinking still continues at a rate of about one inch every three or four generations – as the present Woolwich barrier far upstream reminds us. Through the early medieval phase, a number of calamitous floods had been chronicled; disasters which were to instigate a sequence of royal decrees – mainly concerned with the County of Kent and its Thames coastline – furnishing orders for the better prevention of future ruin "in respect of the raging of the sea."[11] Within Essex, a "law of the marsh" would as early as 1210 A.D. embody the concept that each landholder must contribute to the upkeep of such defensive walls as then existed. Roger de Cramavil, clearly a kinsman of the manor lord of Fobbing, had been one of those magnates accused of negligence upon his Thameside embankments at Rainham in the same year. Indirect though such a reference may look, it establishes that the movement

[11] *The History of Imbanking and Draining of Divers Fens and Marshes,* W. Dugdale, 1772.

towards controlled agricultural land-use behind flood-walls was already underway by the dawn of the thirteenth century right along London's river and would reasonably be already a feature at the de Camvill manor at Fobbing.

Marshfoot meadows

THE SIX ISLANDS

Nature itself provided a gauge by which the decision to intake saltern pasture was made. For, even though regionally the land's surface was slowly subsiding, still there were localised zones – often quite small acreages – that were being raised by a constant deposition of silts and other tidal material. As this occurred, the resultant muds took on their initial mix of brine-tolerant plants, usually fleshy leafed species such as the beautiful golden samphire, or various kinds of scurvy-grass, a herbage which would diversify, acquiring new species as the area built up and became more deprived of salt. At a final stage, excellent fodder stuffs like the sea-lime grass proliferated.

Exceptional tides might well still overflow such zones, but in the main an intersecting network of small streamlets, called "*guts*" provided swift drainage of brinewaters away from these higher clumps. Such raised saltmarshes were deemed "ripe"; ready, with some trouble and outlay, to be inclosed and made secure from the sea.[12] But the ordinary marsh clays themselves were not suitable alone for heaping into a barrier against the river and though no ancient seawalls have yet been archaeologically sectioned to determine their make-up, a good deal of their base material must be of chalk rubble and mined flint, presumably laid against a resilient palisade of interwoven coppice-wood. In creating the river defences throughout all of this district, a mining industry centred upon Grays surely featured considerably. A very reasonable correlation exists between the period of medieval marshland reclamation and the accepted dates which we have for the numerous "denehole" mine-shafts that exist over western Thurrock. Many

---

12 *The Great Tide,* Hilda Grieve, E.R.O. 1959. (Outlines this development of saltern to reclaimed marsh, pp. 3-4).

thousands of tons of mineral had been extracted from these during the years before 1500. Subsequently open-cast quarrying would provide similar materials into modern times.

By separating in colour on a good scale map the marsh grounds of each farm estate that we have talked about, it becomes fairly easy to comprehend how Fobbing finally captured within walls (from the maze of winding creeks and lesser saltstreams) its six considerable islands.[13] In doing so, its human force had stopped up various small tidal rivulets, diverting others along fresh courses; perhaps in the earliest phases draining and reclaiming only moderately sized acres sufficient to gain a couple of "fresh marsh" fields. To these, other enclosures might be added at intervals. Over years, a jigsaw of managed *islets* would be turned into the final island block. No kind of agricultural fieldscape is more truly akin to the wavy-edged jigsaw idea than a medieval marsh, salvaged, as were these at Fobbing, from amidst numberless serpentine channels.

Slight though it may be, our evidence has at least suggested that *some* areas of the parish marshlands were being pioneered and improved in this way well before the mid-Elizabethan period and there is some further information to support this in retrospective data found upon an estate map of Great Ilford surveyed during 1800.[14] At that time, a substantial "hall house" with typical medieval or Tudor crosswings had occupied its homestall area, indicating that a reclamation of this island estate must have been completed at least three centuries or so earlier. For a building of this status would surely not be sited amidst unprotected salterns.

Quite to what degree Dutch embanking included the Fobbing manor levels we do not know, but extensive activity is implied during the first quarter of the seventeenth century; a crucial period during which Fobbing Hall's lands would be sold off from crown possession. These disposals seem to have coincided closely with the appearance of a Dutchman (by descent) called Giles Vanderputt,[15] a merchant of St. Andrew Undershaft parish in London,[16] to whom during late February 1624 Sir Henry Appleton of South Benfleet had sold his marsh of Northope in Fobbing. In this same month, Appleton, a descendant of the Tyrell family of Heron Hall, was to engage with the celebrated wetland engineer Joas Croppenburgh in an agreement for draining more than three and a half thousand acres upon Canvey Island. Moreover, other Fobbing connections appear to be present, for among the half dozen Canvey owners who had signed over to

[13] Canvey also had been described as of some half-dozen islands: *The History of Rochford Hundred*, P. Benton, 1888, p. 79.

[14] *Great Ilford Marsh ... estate of Sir Mark Wood, Bart.*, E.R.O. D/DCx (map).

[15] I.G.I., 1992 (Church of Jesus Christ of Latter Day Saints) Vandeputt (various counties) and *Canvey Island: The History of a Marshland Community*, B. Cracknell, 1959.

[16] *The Complete Baronetage*, G. E. Cokayne (ed.) 1983; *General Armory*, Burkes, 1884.

Croppenburgh third portions of their land in fee simple, were John, William and Mary Blakmore. This surname appears in an earlier decade at St. Michael's, where in 1607 "fayth", daughter of William Blakmore had been brought for baptism, while a will of Joane Blakemore would be proved during mid 1634. Apparently a spinster her "tenement in Fobbing" which her father William Blakemore had purchased, would go to South Benfleet people called Pinson. So late as 1690, Corringham's register was to record the burial of Joanna, wife of Thomas Blackmore "from ffobing".

More than fifty years later than the above agreements, in 1675, an area of reclaimed saltern some way westward of Fobbing, near Old Garlands at Corringham, was to be mapped, identifying the *"Curry Marsh"* there as having been "lately Inned by the Dutch men".[17] From this survey, we may guess that the Garlands wall-system as depicted was continuous, back across the Fobbing river frontage as far as Shellhaven at least. In contemporary parlance "lately" might suggest only an event within human memory and indeed there *is* confirmation that Vanderputt's scheme of the mid 1620s had included works at Fobbing, Corringham and in the tiny detached fragment of Mucking called Rugward marsh, which abutted Corringham's terrain. For with April 1627, an Essex sessions had heard this Dutch merchant's petition concerning a payment of composition imposed upon these improved grounds, "pretending himself to be much oppressed by the (parish) officers and neighbours" of all three places where saltmarshes had been "by him drained and recovered." It must most logically have been during this great reclamation that the "Parting Gut" creek, once leading towards Whitehall farmyard alongside Nazewick's pastures, had been dammed up, forming in time an extensive reedbed area which still features there.[18] Until that improvement had been effected, the sea's occasional surges must have reached at whiles so far in as to spoil sweet meadows high up the Crooked Brook, towards Vange *Bells*.

There were still internal areas of the marshes that remained unimproved long afterward however, and not until 1796 was the landlord of Little Ilford (the Rev. James Filewood of Sible Hedingham) to enclose his property "from the Sea by a strong Embankment ... on the South side of Fobbing Creek";[19] an area of some 60 acres which was then being popularly called *"Lady's Island";* an attractive landscape name that seems to have come about through its association in the mid-century with Lydia Catherine Duvall, lady of the manor of Fobbing Hall. A stockman's cottage stood upon its westward flank, an area which by the 1730s

---

[17] *Sundrie parcells of marsh land* ... 1675 E.R.O. D/DU 112/2 (Map).

[18] "Parting Gut" creek divides the parishes of Fobbing and Vange throughout its course. Chapman & Andre Plate XXIII, 1777 and *Old Time Marsh Farms,* F. Z. Claro in *Corringham* ed. I. G. Sparkes, 1965.

[19] *Memo,* Fobbing Parish Register, Baptisms, 1783-1812.

had become known as *"Iron Latch"* – a name which would tarry long after the dwelling had been ploughed away.[20] At Oil Mill, a sale advertisement as late as 1829 would indicate other saltern pieces that were not yet enclosed, though ripe for taking. About forty six acres were available for reclamation "at simple expense" – a pleasant little example of estate agent's guile.

To steal new lands from the flood was one thing; to keep them secure was another. Reclamation meant that within a period of years the freshly inned grounds lost their salinity, but as this process went on, so they dried through, and slowly shrank and settled. Over a period of generations there would be a tendency for their settled surfaces to lie well below the horizon of the muddy saltern forelands just beyond the protective walls. Thus, should chance storm conditions bring the tides upon them, inundation would be far greater than of old. Such elementary soil knowledge was understood far back, at the very commencement of pioneering the levels and, as more enclosed land had come into productive use, so the responsibilities of a whole riverine community in safeguarding one another's interests would be enforced. Sporadic disaster-based commissions from the thirteenth century onward would gradually give way to a more ordered and preventative approach, culminating in 1531 with the Statute of Sewers, under which a national arrangement of local courts would be set up to deal with all aspects of maintenance and repair within areas where coastal flooding was likely to have effect. This system was to endure for the following three centuries or so, though much of that while it excluded Canvey, because the island was to remain within a special jurisdiction of the Dutch community.

To assist in its management, bodies of examining jurors were to be appointed and a marsh bailiff employed for each level; the latter to enforce, or undertake in the event of proven neglect, all necessary repairs of sea defences, sluices or ditches. Nearly all of these officials were themselves agricultural men, normally tenant farmers, both practically knowledgeable and directly concerned with the economy of the marsh. Throughout the broad district which most involves us, courts would be regularly convened for the "Rainham levels" (as far downstream on the Essex shore as Mucking) and the "Fobbing levels", which embraced parts of Mucking, Stanford le Hope, Corringham, Fobbing, as well as the several detached fragments of Laindon, Dunton and Little Warley. General funding for the continuance of the multifarious aspects of operation, such as that for example, incurred by the elected Marsh Bailiff in investigating offences, was raised from among all tenants who farmed coastal grounds and was called a "level lot". To this end, the Commissioners of Sewers appointed from time to time their "collector and expenditor" for each particular level; in 1740 would appear in that

---

[20] Iron Latch: possibly from the "new" cottage there which possessed iron rather than the normal wooden doorlatches. TQ78.7238.8325.

guise the Fobbing born Zachariah Button, while another parishioner, John Clifford of Prosbus Hall, filled the marsh bailiff's post. Good, commodious public houses normally served as meeting places for the Commissioners' courts and during this period the *Bell* at Horndon on the Hill generally proved a sensible (and central) spot for any business pertaining to the Fobbing level, though, with later Georgian years, sittings would gravitate toward Brentwood's *White Hart.*

Though their records (court minutes and order books) survive only from 1729, they open one of the most revealing sources of local agrarian history, identifying a continuous sequence of land ownership and tenant occupiers, listing the appointment of officials and providing massive topographical detail, as well as affording a close insight into the technical workings of marsh-country farming. At the Vineyard foot watercourse during 1770, Thomas Drew, esquire (landlord) and tenant Hearman Prescott would be ordered to "mend the piling and fill it up with Chalk near Fobbing barrs" (adjacent to the *Ship* inn) before the ensuing Michaelmas, upon pain of three pounds fine, while in 1781 at the glebeland, we find that rector John Ryley and the carpenter Leonard Rust must "raise their dam at the parting stile to prevent the fresh Water (flowing down the parish boundary brook) running into the Salt and the Salt mixing with the fresh ..." (at Fobbing Wharf).[21] The horny-handed tradesman Rust himself would serve with other Fobbing menfolk as juror a decade later, after severe floods had damaged the level at large in 1791, being ordered to "go their View and walk the Walls within the limits of their Charge ...". Breastworks, or outer faces, of sea walls became often subject to shrinkage or slippage, bringing to their respective proprietors mandates from the court for attention and the mid 18th century had seen the governors of "the Great Hospital" (at Norwich) owners of Borley farm, being called (with their Fobbing tenant, John Digby) to "mend the Breasting of their wale in several places where it is decayed ...". During May, 1754 Thomas Crow and his landlord were similarly required to "Breast and Turf Fifteen Rods of their wall leading from Oozey house to the South Corner of Shell-Haven by Xmas ...", an entry which indicates the importance of protecting the new works with herbage – not so much against water's action as that of sun and frost, which could soon work havoc upon clay surfaces.

Traversing the levels, could be seen numerous "driftways" or droving roads between fields, while the sea-walls themselves (generally surfaced with gravel fetched from the uplands) were also of sufficient width to act as lanes for light farm traffic. Through the 1750s the Court of Sewers would direct the enhancement of these: John Bostock and Thomas Crow, for example, were to work on "the Cartway at the Head of Oil Mill Creek" and (at the farm of Zachariah Button) another vehicle-track from Oil Mill's sluice to a certain gate at

---

21 Court of Sewers, Fobbing Levels: Order Books, 1770, 1781.

"Oozey House Barrs" was to be raised "two foot Higher and (made) Sixteen feet Wide" over a distance of ten rods, upon pain of a fine of ten shillings the rod.

These are but random glimpses of the kind of seasonal arrangements that would continue through the centuries, usually only of a mundane and precautionary nature. From time to time however, tidal disasters were to bring a flurry of court activity in their wake. Though no record survives of local relevance, we know that the January of 1552 had witnessed a widespread deluge along this eastern coast, and upon the shorelines of Holland and Flanders too. Sheppey and Foulness had been mentioned upon this occasion as "quite drowned". Again in 1570 Fobbing must have seen its lowlands under the cold lap of tide right to the hill's edge, for Holinshed had told how *"From a towne call Rainham unto ... Maulden all alongst by the waterside were the marshes all over flowen, wherein a great number of cattell drowned".* Well might the versifying farmer Tusser[22] remind his Tudor confederates to guard their pastured herds –

As well at the full of the moon as the change
Sea rages in winter be sodainly strange.

But not until February's "outrageous tide" in 1736 do we discover a first-hand report of our parish at time of flood-crisis; an event occasioned in the words of the Essex historian Nathaniel Salmon, "by a strong north-west wind at the time of the full moon".[23] Round the North Sea and within its estuaries the waves' violence had overwhelmed many sea walls and William Blake, curate of Fobbing (in that year one of the Commissioners for his district) was to tell of a "highest Tide that was ever known which ... laid the whole Level several Feet under Water ...". If there was to be any solace from that Monday's calamity, it had been because the flood had swept inward with an hour or two of daylight remaining, by which to handle the escape of humans and grazing livestock. Nevertheless some thousands of sheep were still to be lost along the Essex marshes. Hilda Grieve observes that a number of farmsteads in the marsh country had been originally built upon slight mounds, allowing some refuge in the circumstances of total

22 *Five Hundred Points of Good Husbandry,* T. Tusser (1580 text, reprinted Oxford, 1984).

23 *The History and Antiquities of the County of Essex,* N. Salmon, 1740.

flood, and plainly during the 1953 inundation Oozdam's homestead and curtilage remained an impressive island sanctuary,[24] while a recent examination of Great Ilford's ruined stockyard suggests that this, too, may well have provided dry-standing during past calamities.[25]

Nevertheless, the watery surge of 1736 had damaged over sixty rods' length of Jasper Kingsman's (Great Ilford) wall, bringing swift demands for its coping. Other works along this inward area of Fobbing creek had included coping the damaged wall at various points bounding the Duke and Duchess of Chandos' marsh (Lady's Island) and along Drew's Vineyard fleet (the point to which ordinary tides normally flowed). At Borley farm twenty five rods of the Holehaven wall had been weakened, but overall across the parish lowlands no actual structural collapse had been reported. The waves had overtopped, but not finally breached, their defensive curtain wall.

With the turn of the weather, and by effectual operation of watercourses and outlets, dispersal of the floods might be a fairly rapid process, though its economic sequel was always both grim and protracted. Thousands of acres had again become polluted with salt, the most immediate result of which was a destruction of its earthworm population. At the water's recession they lay in countless numbers like a grey-pink film over sodden cornland and pasture alike. Several years must pass before worm aeration of the soil returned to a level conducive to profitable husbandry. Cattle ponds stood contaminated and brackish, chronically affecting milk yields and rendering calves feeble and useless. If, as Defoe observes, the marsh landlords of Essex "let good penny-worths" to farm tenants, their consideration must, to a marked extent, have been for the financial risks shouldered by these men. Whereas during 1743 the Fobbing "level lot" had been set at threepence the acre, the following severe overflowing of defences (in 1791) had seen it rise by four hundred per cent, and one could never know when outright ruin might befall due to some colossal breach (like that which had occurred up at Dagenham in the time of queen Anne). On the other hand, there were no more productive soils to be found in all Essex than these and tenants could reasonable predict that high tides would overwhelm their agricultural endeavours only once in each generation; thrice a century even by the most pessimistic estimation. Those were reasonable odds.

---

24 *The Great Tide,* H. Grieve, E.R.O. 1959.

25 Great Ilford. Building footings of brick survive TQ78.7297.8398. A farmstead mound of impressive proportions, still possessing its circular cattle-pond, is visible on the marsh eastward of Whitehall: it may be the lost site of *'Fowlers'* copyhold. Recognised first by the author during 1996, it is raised some 10 feet higher than the present levels and extends to c.100 yards diameter. Ceramic litter indicating domestic use since at least the 14th century is present, giving the earliest archaeological evidence to date of a peasant holding on the marshes of this district. *Considerations Upon Possible Terp-Mounds ...* R. Bingley, PAN. 37, 1997.

Oil Mill farmhouse

"MIGHTY STRONG MEAT ..."

A pastoral character still typifies Fobbing's remnants of landscape at the oil refineries' fringes, though obviously quite different to that of the rough *saltmarsh* feeding grounds of earlier times. Essex writers aplenty have repeated antique descriptions of the ewe-sheep dairying which prevailed along this part of Thames, but it may be worthwhile to outline the picture anew as we proceed, and to place it in context with our own slight parish evidence of the practice. By the mid 1360s cheeses were being shipped from some loading place within Fobbing manor, while long after, in 1579, we discover an inhabitant called William Pitman bequeathing at his death "half a lead of cheese" (a lead: 56 lb.) to one John Fenill, and to two other associates each twenty pounds of cheese. From their father, Richard Love (Lowe?) would come to two Fobbing women, Alice and Mary in 1557 not only his best cows and ten sheep, but "All my woll: All my butter: All my cheese."[26] In other wills of this period ewes or lambs are frequently found as bequests, again hinting at the important "white meat" or dairy husbandry of the marshlands which had flourished throughout the medieval age.

To Thomas de Camvill, lord of Fobbing, belongs what appears to be an earliest reference along all Thameside to the connection between ewes and cheese production, for during 1201 Thomas had claimed a marsh called *Richerness* on Canvey, declaring that as far back as the reign of Henry II, his grandfather had taken the profits of "cheese, wool and rushes" there. The Camvill's successors were to be of the mighty de Bohun line, in whose possession nearly all the Fobbing claylands and salterns remained as portion of "a powerful complex of estates" in Essex comprising some fifty-one manors that had been acquired by the time of the death of William de Bohun, earl of Hereford, in January 1373. Work by J. R. Smith[27] reveals the extent to which these de Bohun territories had been inter-related, many containing saltmarsh "sheepwalks". One of the greater had been Foulness Island where, in 1424, no less than fourteen hundred milking sheep would be accounted upon the "wicks" – one pasture among them being "Nazewick", like our own at Fobbing.

---

26 *Wills at Chelmsford,* F. G. Emmison, Vol. I (1400-1619) indexes the above. Individual E.R.O. references will be omitted throughout therefore.

27 *Foulness,* J. R. Smith, E.R.O. publication No. 55, 1970.

Canvey Island's constantly overflown salt-pastures, said Camden in the later Elizabethan period, sustained about four thousand sheep "whose flesh is ... most sweet and delicate", where "young lads taking the womens function (go) with stooles fastened to their buttocks to milke in those dairy sheddes of theirs that they call wickes." Doubtless, the identical scene persisted through Fobbing, and down the entire coastal marshes also. A little after, during 1594, John Norden was to tell of the Essex style of cheeses, "wondered at for their massiveness", adding that they were shipped for sale "not only into parts of England, but into foreign nations" besides. If not highly prized for flavour, these local marshland products provided a solid domestic standby for the poorer classes. They were widely seen amongst the common roadside alehouses of Tudor times – like that of Surrey's fictional "comely dame" Elenour Rumming of Leatherhead, whose scandalous premises and coarse table-fare the laureate John Skelton described:

A cantle of Essex cheese
Was well a foote thicke
Full of magots quicke
It was huge and great
And mighty strong meat
For the Devill to eat ...

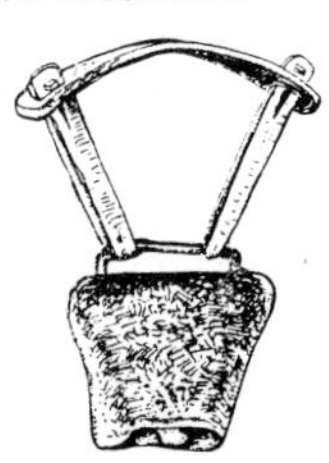

The medieval and Tudor sheepwalks, of course, furnished as well their share of springtime wool, soft fells to the skinner's trade and ample butchers' mutton, while to a lesser extent there were other "great cattle" browsing these saline pastures alongside. But it was the ensuing period, the 1600s, which saw the shift away from sheeps' cheese production to a fatstock grazing and milch cow interest, as newly claimed "fresh" marshes came into condition. A voracious London market spread its influence far down Thames and the whole corridor of the estuary was a live larder for foddering horned stock that had been herded along the highways, often from far away – the midlands and north, or from Wales. In the early 18th century, Defoe tells of Lincolnshire and Leicestershire wether sheep fetched down for disposal at Smithfield market during early autumn, then placed out into these Essex feeding grounds till Christmas: "and tho' they are not made at all fatter here ... yet the farmer, or butcher finds very good advantage in it, by the difference of the price ... between Michaelmas, when 'tis cheapest, and Candlemass, when 'tis dearest ...".[28] Not least of this meat's attractions, thought David Hughson in later Georgian years, was the yellowish cast in its fat, supposedly brought about by marsh-country browsing yet "taken by persons who are ignorant" to result from turnip-feeding and hence to be of superior quality.[29]

---

[28] *A Tour through the Whole Island of Great Britain,* D. Defoe, 1724 (Everyman Edition, 1966).

[29] *London and its Neighbourhood,* Vol. IV D. Hughson, 1809.

Perhaps Hughson had been overly cynical: for the turnip husbandry that had begun to interest a growing number of farming experimenters by mid Stuart times was already long practised here, the cattle wintering on roots in upland stockyards and depasturing with each spring over the green low grounds. With the young Victoria's reign, the bigger flockmasters of Orsett were observed to hold farms along a number of river-front parishes. "At Corringham, Mucking and Fobbing," says agricultural historian Ted Collins, "the great flocks, together with their shepherds, would migrate each May from the lambing pens and hurdle folds ... to the lower levels where they were shorn each June by travelling gangs of shearers." Marsh holdings such as Oozedam, Shellhaven and Slatey House (the name adopted by Great Ilford since its square yellow brick and grey-roofed farmhouse arose around the 1840s) were all brought into the extensive landed estate centred upon Orsett Hall during this broad period – following a first acquisition as far back as the 1750s of Fobbing Hall and its few marsh meadows.[30] Small wonder that well respected Orsett tenantry like the Sacketts could snatch up attractive leases here, and it is significant that, from the mid century, Fobbing's trade directory pages advertise very few farmers who were resident, *those* clinging to the wholly upland quarter: Fobbing farm, Dry Street, Hawkesbury, Hovels.

In contrast, occupying Great Ilford[31] at the 1851 census we find John Hornsby, a 34 year old shepherd and his family: at Nazewick homestall (called *Fowler's*, after John Fowler, who worked part of this marsh in 1746) dwelled the flock-tender William Rye. Ralph Bearham, another ordinary shepherd, was comfortably set up at Whitehall farmhouse overlooking his grazing grounds through more than twenty years up to 1871. To Shellhaven's neat brick-fronted Georgian residence came later that decade Simon Gilder, a shepherd born at Finchingfield around 1850 accompanied by his Stanford spouse. With the 90s they had shifted into the smart and rebuilt Slatey House, where not least amongst modern conveniences was a deep freshwater well of the highest quality – a luxury generally absent from domestic life upon the levels. Superior housing was evidently one of the compensations a reliable stockman might expect in return for his specialised talents and unenviable working hours.[32]

Pastoral farming naturally dominated the whole lower Thames marshes, though temptations of ploughing for cereals, beans and latterly potatoes were at times strong. Attempts to create arable from some of Fobbing Hall's marshes under Richard Baker in 1823, observes Collins, were quickly deemed unsuccessful, the soils "expensive to cultivate and in many parts low and wet", though at a similar period Shellhaven farm's reputation for White Wheat was

---

30 *A History of the Orsett Estate 1743-1914,* E. J. T. Collins, 1978.

31 Great Ilford, Slatey House: shown as "Newhouse" on the re-engraved 1843 1" O.S.

32 Census Returns 1851-1871.

standing high in London at the Mark Lane cornmarket. There is a reasonable weight of evidence also to suggest that the Dutch embanking of the mid 1620s had led directly to cultivation around Shellhaven creek for oil bearing crops such as linseeds or the gaudy yellow-flowered rape, already well known in the Netherlands and across France, and soon to be particularly encouraged (by Act of 1649) as "of singular use to make soap and oils within this nation". Such oils were used not only for lighting and foodstuffs but in the treatment of cloth and the manufacture of paints for instance and long before, in 1579 (upon the Norfolk coast) Sir Thomas Gresham had been purchasing rape-seed for an oil-milling enterprise. At some point during the late 1630s there had appeared in Fobbing's church rate-list a "Millhouse in the marsh", a premises placed within the highest category of payments and so evidently the centre of some major farming enterprise. At the same period, during October 1638, Corringham's register was to record the burial of a certain native of Picardy, Claude Martin "borne in Boloigne dying at ye Oylemill in ffobbing ..." whom we may reasonably believe to have been either involved in the continental shipment of grist or oils, or some mill operative whose familiarity with the French trade had gained him employment here.[33]

Its position at the blocked head of Shellhaven creek makes clear that this was a tide-mill – operating by means of penning *inflowing* waters, which were then released at a regulated rate to power its wheel-system – and it is regrettable that there is now no surface evidence of its features. Photographic records show only a long brick farmhouse, acceptably of early 17th century date, with a boarded bay and a lean-to at one end, while a sale advertisement of 1789 had mentioned only its stable, yard and garden, with no suggestion of either a barn, wharfage or water-mill as being present.[34] A dozen years previously, the excellently observant Chapman & Andre map had suggested that no mill-sluices survived even by that time and it seems the sea wall had been remade along its frontage. "Island Mill" was what the surveying team accepted[35] as Oil Mill's title; an easily conceived error, though strangely most other records would keep its name perfectly remembered into an age when – by peculiar chance – the site was to be swallowed by a greatly developed lube oil and petroleum industry.

As control of the reclaimed areas advanced, a new calling of countrymen specialising in wetland management had emerged, acquiring knowledge somewhat from the Dutch workmen and settlers and applying its expertise in various ways to the advantage or exploitation of the levels. By Elizabethan times, even, these

---

33 Oil Mill TQ78.7405.8273.

34 *The Particulars of a ... Freehold Estate ... (by order of the Trustees of Jasper Kingsman Esq. ...) at the Rainbow Coffee House in Cornhill*, 19th and 20th October, 1789.

35 Plate XXIII, surveyed 1774/5, published 1777.

Eel spear

"marshmen" were a distinct parish species, effective in controlling and keeping scoured the many watercourses, in the laying of "wholves", or run-throughs beneath field entrances; in the maintenance of heavy timber sluice gates and so on. When needed, they might lend a hand at rope-on-shoulder work, "*hovelling*" barges wharfward up the shallow creek miles. They could hand-auger water pipes out of elm trunks, decoy waterfowl for the master's table, spear eels with barbed iron glaves and attend to the tasselled harvest of ditchside reed in season, carting it ready for summer's thatching work to upland barnyards. George Munnes of Fobbing would leave numerous bequests upon his death in January 1583, including ten shillings to Richard Mocke, "one of my marshmen" – a character whom we can briefly see as twice-married in the parish, during 1574 and again in September 1579. Mocke the marsh-specialist had himself witnessed the will of farmer William Bell in that period and was to die a dozen years later, having seen the little English ships go downstream beyond Leigh to join Drake's Armada battle in the summer of 1588. Henry Shelton was another described as of the marshman breed when buried at St. Michael's during the plague time of 1666.

To some degree amongst the Essex coastal parishes, salt making had continued through the medieval age. References to a "salte cote" (cottage) occur as late as 1784 in Fobbing's manor rolls, though plainly it was by then already somewhile demolished and possibly its name had been long obsolete as far as any direct connection with the industry was concerned.[36] Almost two centuries earlier, during December, 1607, Hugh Bridg(e) of Fobbing had made a will that spoke of a local "Maker of Saltt c coll" (charcoal) and outlined certain financial arrangements "to save the salte house from any thirdes" – a customary third portion of real estate which would otherwise pass for her lifetime to Susan, his widow. She was to enjoy his freehold tenement "standing in the towne" and would have two loads of firewood supplied through each winter during such whiles as she remained unremarried. Their son, Thomas Bridge, must besides "let his mother have salte brought home to her dwellinge house"; in all a goodly provision for this bereaved lady. Whether the nearby tidal fleets were being used to supply brine evaporation pits by this Bridge family – as had long been practised at Woodham Ferrers and other creekside places – we cannot yet tell, but it seems highly probable. Hugh Bridge's provision of hearth-fuel is also of interest, since great quantities of coppice wood were required for heating within saltcote areas, where the murky

[36] A ploughed out foundation of 17th century red brick near the foot of Marsh Lane, adjacent to a once tidal creekline, TQ78.7226.8465 may be the "Salte Cote" location because it lies atop an earlier salt production mound of the Iron Age phase.

crystalline blocks obtained from steaming brine-pans were subsequently refined to whiteness by a second evaporating process in clean water. Dr. Emmison,[37] explains that salt-making was a seasonal occupation, undertaken during winter, adding that other sources of "bay" salt were entering Essex from the Rochelle district of France long before the Cheshire rock-salt mines began to export from the 1670s onward. To some extent, then, Bridge's supply *could* have been impure stock from foreign sources, fetched into Fobbing wharf for refining and distribution.

It seems likely that a village-side quay[38] was already in operation before the early 16th century: a commission of the 1560s for control of east coast piracy had named all Essex trading hythes, including Pitsea Wharf, Vange and other nearby places of lading at Mucking and Fobbing though the place probably possessed little in the way of shipping itself. Compared to Leigh's 21 boats (Harwich and Colchester were in the same league) an attempt to raise maritime revenues from the ports during 1619 had shown Fobbing to declare only one vessel, almost certainly a "hoy".[39] Some hint of the variety of commerce throughout its history has been made; but there was chalk, too, arriving in vast quantities for marshland wall-building and repair, ballast, and flints, as well as the whole outgoing produce of local farms, from corn and hay, to butter and cartwheel cheeses for a swelling metropolis. During 1688, the Fobbing blacksmith Richard Upton and a Grays associate called Godfrey would prosecute Sarah Skilder of Laindon and John Jones, labourer of Fobbing, for carrying away "one hundred of ostery faggetts" from the wharf – bundles of *"hostry"* or hornbeam wood, which undoubtedly represented fuel for Upton's High Road forge-house. Jones had purloined the faggots that cheerless January, while Sarah Skilder – one of Fobbing's Dutch community and probably not long absconded to her present abode beyond Dry Street – would be named receiver, "knowing them to be stolen".

Although the parish possessed some workable ceramic clays, red housebricks were coming into the wharf very shortly before 1700 for cottage building, not inconceivably from Daniel Foe's kilns upstream at Chadwell, near to Tilbury fort.[40] Two centuries on, Rushbrook Bros.' brickfield which extended over the marsh-edge within a few minutes walk of the wharfside, would dominate

---

[37] F. G. Emmison, *Elizabethan Life: Home, Work and Land*, Vol. 3. E.R.O. 1976.

[38] Fobbing Wharf TQ78.7200.8379.

[39] V.C.H. *Maritime History*, M. Oppenheim, Vol. 2, 1907. Fobbing was long embraced within the Port of Maldon, which extended round into Thames as far as its meeting with the Port of London – at Gravesend's 'Round Tree', or upon the Essex shore, at Pincocks Creek, later called 'Bill Meroy' (in West Tilbury).

[40] Usually referred to as Defoe, a name adopted c.1703. *Daniel Defoe: His Trail Uncovered,* R. Bingley, PAN. Vol. 27, 1985.

the barge business with their shipments of yellow stocks. Newcastle collier brigs since the Tudor age at least had been constantly fuelling London, though as a domestic commodity fossil coal was possibly not much used across the countryside until the 18th century. Still, by 1802, "carting the Coals from Fobbing" had been penned among the Bowers Gifford churchwardens' accounts, indicating an established dump at the creek-head, which by 1839 would be under the ownership of Abraham Daniels, proprietor of *The Ship* tavern and let to William Bogue, bargemaster and coalmerchant.

A dozen years previously, on 15th February 1827, the bankruptcy of Wilson Simons junior of Fobbing had brought to disposal by auction "THE ENTIRE INTEREST of the INSOLVENT, for the term of 9 years ... in that excellent WHARF, situated next to the Ship Inn ..." including a pair of Simon's sprit-sail barges. His superior vessel the *"Ceres"* of Maldon captained by Mark Martin "with all her sails, rigging, stores and utensils" was currently available to view at Goodchild's barge-building premises at Mill Wall, Poplar, while the *"Nicholas"* of Maldon ("George Howard, master") in like completeness, with "A LONG BOAT and Pair of Oars" now lay berthed for examination on Fobbing quayside. Sale catalogues had been made available along Thames, from Aldgate to Gravesend.[41]

At that time a newcomer to Fobbing parish, William Bogue may have been purchaser of these vessels. During 1834, he was to marry the bankrupt Simon's niece, Elizabeth Rust of the *White Lion*, whose attentions were being sought also by a villager called Labor – a saga of thwarted desires which would lead to a few rounds of fisticuffs upon "Captain" Bogue's wedding night.[42] Labor had apparently attended the couple's marriage festivities, a jocose newspaper account of which survives to tell of jealous brawling that had led to Labor being held down over the pub fireplace for a roasting by some of the guests and of having his nose "turned into a musical instrument". Presumably the latter assault had been by Bogue himself, who would admit to the bench in due course "that when passing under quick sail his yardarm touched the (*nasal*) promontory". He would be fined a shilling with costs.

[41] C.C. 9th February, 1827.

[42] *The Brooks Scrapbook;* undated, unsourced cutting, 1834, PAN. Vol. 27, 1985.

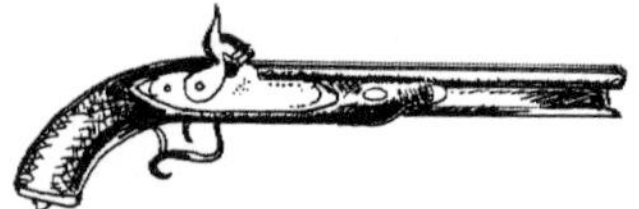

"A MAN UNKNOWN ..."

It was a remote and treacherous terrain, out here where the bittern's booming call sounded amidst brown reeds, and the lank heron stabbed at cold waters of reflected sky. The first spring droughts baked its ditch hollows and driftways iron hard, leaving them ruckered with deeply driven hoof prints. Tawny adders drowsed upon the laid summer grass at the 'feedings' edges and vengeful orange clegg-flies sipped in the heat, clustering like amber highlights upon each day's heapings of new dung. From the autumn clays curled strange phosphorescent vapours that Essex countrymen called *"Peg-o'-Lantern"* and which, met after dark, aroused unwished considerations of spirit-folk, or of *"owd Nick"* himself. Those who dwelled in these dank levels were a people deprived often of company: there were too many hours in this melancholy place for morbid fancies to flourish. It was common thing for the river's dead to roll with the lap of tide onto grey saltern edges and, since the parish boundary reached into mid-Thames, the unidentified bundles must be hooked to the sea wall and carted away for disposal at Fobbing's expense. "A Man unknown. Found drowned upon the shore", or simply "on the river bank Adult" typify such casual burial entries (from 1822 and 1857). The year following, an 85 years old male corpse was washed in upon the mud, to be subsequently interred at the village. Later, from afar, came evidence of identity and his remains would be exhumed for reburial in Hertfordshire. But most were never named.

Beyond the scum-washed sea lavender lay at anchor hopeless prison hulks, whose felon inmates awaited transport to distant penal settlements: the American plantations, in later times to South Australia. At Holehaven mouth, another old wooden vessel, formerly the gunship H.M.S. *Elk*, maintained her coastguard watch through the mid 19th century against smuggling into this shoreline of multifarious hiding places and creeks.[43] A further preventive-service post operated within Fobbing parish upstream at Thameshaven, employing a small 170-ton watch vessel around the mid 1850s, though plainly certain officers (called Hawes and Crocker) were on-station with wives before this period, since their babies had been baptised at St. Michael's through late 1849. Reliable records of the locality's "free-traders" fall entirely short of the persistent village myths concerning running contraband goods: upon Fobbing's hilltop every mundane beer-cellar is pointed to as proof of illicit imports and its proliferation of imagined "secret tunnels" seems to endanger the very progress of heavy traffic over its streets.

Eastern coast smuggling was never really so widespread as in the counties facing France and an outright defiance of revenue officers, which had distinguished the 18th century trade, would be markedly subdued during the 19th,

---

43 *Coastguard Stations of Thurrock*, S. A. Chase, PAN. 16, 1972-3.

by which period a characteristic runners' method was the "sinking" of liquor-tubs offshore. These could later be grappled for and quickly fetched "over the wall" (sea-wall) at leisure. A recent work which sensibly studies this romantic subject, speaks of the convenient inlet for receiving contraband "where Holehaven Creek cuts deep into Fobbing Marshes",[44] adding that, "The innkeepers of Fobbing ... were always well supplied with tax-free liquor", though sadly its author introduces not a single archival reference. Nevertheless, F. Z. Claro was able to scrape up minor newspaper evidence from the "Haven-marshes", where, he states, a Customs Riding Officer called George Poynter had arrested whilst on patrol during 1819, two men "with goods which had been landed". A prosecution followed, both for smuggling and assault upon officer Poynter, and the horse and cart used in this offence was to be confiscated.

Early in 1843, sixty-five tubs (half-ancher casks) had been seized by customs men a mile upriver of Thameshaven. At a similar period, says Benham, the Newcastle brig *Coquet* brought up at the head of Sea Reach in the darkness and calm, but her anchor 'rode' and she drove close inshore "just above the place where the large sign is placed for the collier dock at Shellhaven". Complications and a half-gale had led to the steam brig *Lion* helping her off the shore, when round her anchor fluke a new 3½" rope was found "attached to a string of green-painted tubs", which, when cut free, sank to the bottom. Only one floated up later on the flood tide.[45]

Four families of coastguard personnel had been present at Thameshaven at the census of March, 1851, including that of Mark Brand, whose nephew would arrive some years afterward to settle nearby, giving rise to the generations of wheelwrights, builders and undertakers so well known around the Stanford district. Mark Brand typified the mobile coastguardsman; born at Burnham-on-Crouch during the late Napoleonic wars and marrying there in 1833 Elizabeth Strongman, a Penzance girl with whom he travelled in the service from Southend to Aldeburgh in Suffolk and thence to stations along the Lincolnshire coast before returning to Essex. With 1869 the Thameshaven coastguard station ceased, though a customs presence remained throughout the century, often staffed by westerners such as Examining Officer William Hawke, a Cornishman, or the Irish Frank Gauram, both present in 1891.[46] Unfamiliar accents had long been heard around this dank outpost of Fobbing; mariners of all races, characters from the Dutch and Thames fishing fleets, were constantly ashore, and the cattle-droving trade introduced its element of tartan-plaided strangers from beyond the English border. The few farmhouses and cottages around Oil Mill, Borley, or Thameshaven, never

---

44 *Rogue's River,* F. Martin, 1983.

45 F. Z. Claro, G.T.G. 11th May, 1973 and *The Smugglers' Century*, H. Benham, E.R.O. 1986.

46 P.R.O. Census Returns, Home Office, 1851, 1891.

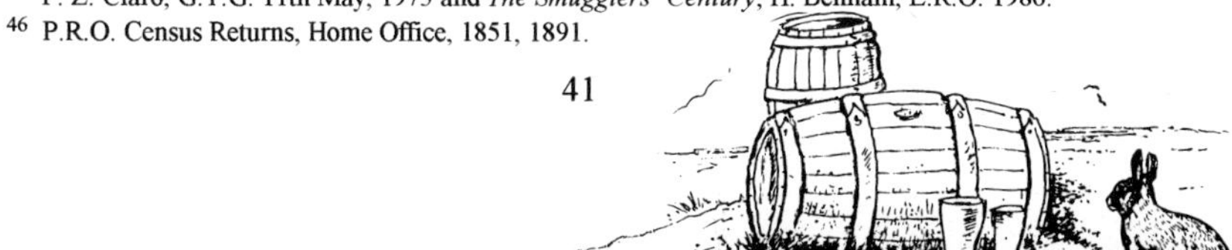

quite knew what incidents tide or season might bring, though none could have conceived the notoriety which would fall upon this parish nook with the arrival, at Michaelmas 1829, of the proud and personable ex-Army officer, Capt. William Moir.

Shellhaven farm's four hundred or so acres lay across several parishes, Fobbing, Corringham, Dunton and Little Warley, all marshgrounds and salterns abutting the creek's eastern side.[47] Its double-pile farmhouse lay just over the Fobbing bounds, in a detached portion of Little Warley parish and it was within that area of fields that Capt. Moir's fatal action was to unfold. Born around 1794, this gentleman appears to have been gazetted Lieutenant with the 1st Hampshire Regt. during December 1813, being placed later for some while upon half-pay before obtaining a commission, also as lieutenant, with the 14th (West Yorkshire) Regt. of Foot. During 1829 he left military service, never – by the Army's evidence – having attained during that time the captain's rank.[48] A few other personal details will suffice to portray Moir: he was married and a father of young children, his physique struck all as impressive and he bore "handsomely masculine features", while his height would be described by the *Chelmsford Chronicle* at the time of Moir's conviction for homicide, as "upwards of six feet". By repute, he was a descendant of king Robert the Bruce of Scotland.[49]

Captain Moir and his family had been occupiers of Shellhaven through the winter of early 1829 and were plainly as yet unfamiliar with customs that had pertained among men of the visiting Barking fishing smacks and others, to come and go unchallenged over parts of his estate. Nearby, a cottage on the sea wall inhabited by a Mrs. Baker had evidently been known as a place of call, possibly for general provisions and a little social intercourse, by some of the fleet; for netting might involve often a period of some days before completion of the catch and departure to the London market. On 12th March, 1830 William Malcolm, a fisherman of Hammersmith, and his mate, a lad called Dukes, departed from Wandsworth downstream for Holehaven, where they worked together for four days, bringing their boat into Fobbing's Borley farm wharf area on Wednesday, the 17th and thence walking the south-westward field mile or so, toward Thameshaven creek. They had nets and a pole, and it was apparently Malcolm's intent to cull a few fish before going onward to the Baker cottage. The time was

---

47 Shell Haven farmhouse TQ78.7488.8209.

48 N.A.M. *Army Lists.*

49 C.C. *Trial of Captain Moir*, 30th July, 1830.

about mid-day when, in William Duke's testimony "*Mr. Moir came up to us, and desired my master to take the net up directly, which he did; some angry words passed between them, in the course of which Mr. Moir said to Malcolm, "If you were anything of a man, I would give you a damned good thrashing". Malcolm replied, "If you can", and immediately pulled off his jacket; Malcolm called Moir a bloody Scotch bugger.*"[50]

Moir's position seems up to this point to have been defensible, since he allegedly believed that the waters of Shellhaven creek, to mid-channel, formed part of his estate, and plainly Malcolm's response had been overly aggressive. William Raven, a labourer, who may have managed Captain Moir's practical farming affairs, would later attest that Malcolm had treated his master's attempts to laugh off the challenge with further language: "You're a great paunch-gutted bugger, or else you would have *fit* me". Finally, Captain Moir was to demand of the fisherman whether or not he had crossed the marsh in coming here to the creek edge – in his view a trespass. Malcolm admitted he had done so, to be informed that he must return to Borley house the longest way, along the sea wall, turning round by Holehaven point. "I don't mind the walk", Malcolm had replied, "I've been walking now the best part of the day", and then while Moir departed for his farmhouse the fisherman moved off towards the Mrs. Baker's cottage. There, Malcolm and Duke tarried some while, having exchanged fish for a half peck of potatoes and doubtless relating of the quarrel which would soon lead to the former's death.[51]

Working in Shellhaven farmyard, the labourer William Raven was to be called shortly after by his employer, and ordered to prepare Moir's horse. Evidently, Malcolm and his assistant were defying his earlier warning, "walking across the marsh in sight of the house", only about sixty yards from where Raven would watch the ensuing drama. He observed his master ride off towards them, by William Duke's account "in great haste". Malcolm "had the potatoes on his left arm" (in a basket) and a fourteen foot pole on his right, when the captain galloped in close, upbraiding him upon the matter of their trespass. Malcolm is said to have replied "I will go", before the horseman moved his mount ahead, then turned and confronted him with a pistol. He fired once, the ball striking Malcolm's inner right arm above its elbow. A second shot may have occurred, passing through the flesh of the same arm. "Damn your eyes, I will go and send the doctor for you", cried Moir, seeing his victim fallen and in pain, and urged his mount for the farmstead again before summoning his servant (Raven) to assist by fetching Stanford surgeon James Barrow Dodd to the scene.

---

[50] Censored words have been restored in this text from blanks in the newspaper report: *Chelmsford Chronicle*, 26th March, 1830.

[51] Ibid.

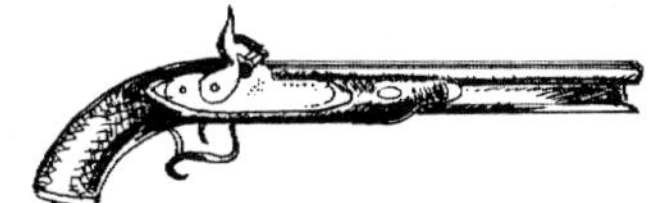

Malcolm meanwhile had been carried bleeding back to the Baker cottage, where by about half past three o'clock, Dodd examined and attended him. There was no bone fracture and bleeding had ceased, proving that the main artery had not been severed. Dodd ordered a couple of glasses of brandy to his patient, "in order to see if the haemorrhage would return, but it did not ..." and as evening approached, the fisherman would be conveyed on a cart that Moir had loaned, along Fobbing's manorway and up to the *Cock and Magpie* inn at Stanford. Dodd's next business was to have a few words with Moir, who had met him somewhat jestfully at the farm gate, to arrange payment for his medical care and to see if he could gain an impression of the assailant's state – drunk or sober. The Captain showed no signs of having partaken, but said of his action, *"by God, Sir, I will do the same tonight, tomorrow, or at any time when I am trespassed on."*

Such at least, was the surgeon's evidence at the inquest upon William Malcolm's death, which followed over a week later, early in the morning of Thursday, March 25th (of lock-jaw proceeding from a pistol wound). Dr. Dodd's situation, after all, was by now at least unenviable, since there might be talk of professional neglect, especially since the injury itself had been initially fairly slight and Malcolm a young and perfectly healthy specimen. Indeed, by early April some London newspapers were carrying the accusation of "unskillful treatment" by the Stanford surgeon, perhaps in the hope of opening opportunities for the defence of Capt. Moir, who by that time had voluntarily placed himself in custody.

"Wilful murder" was the inquest's finding. On 30th July, Moir would be taken from Chelmsford gaol to his trial, where "with a voice and demeanour, unaccompanied by the least outward appearance of agitation, whatever might have been his inward feelings", he declared himself "not guilty". With the close of the prosecution's evidence, no defence would be offered, though a number of character witnesses spoke on Moir's behalf, including his late regimental colonel, who emphasised the officer's reputation for "humility and kindness." Within a quarter hour the jury would return, proclaiming the soldier's guilt. Moir heard the judge's awful pronouncement; Death, to be followed by dissection at the hands of the surgeons.[52] Before leaving the bar, his tall frame bowed respectfully to the court. On Monday, August 2nd, 1830 he went to the public scaffold erected near Chelmsford's stone bridge, attended by the Rev. Hutchinson, prison chaplain and died in the sight of a numerous concourse of villagers from Fobbing and its neighbouring district.[53] The captain's case had become a *cause celebre*, which would retain its small niche in the annals of crime – because it was rare for one of his social background to meet execution for the death of a social inferior. More

---

[52] C.C. *Trial of Captain Moir*, 30th July, 1830.

[53] *Chelmsford Prison*, J. G. Torry, 1980.

significant perhaps had been the sympathetic feeling that the medical circumstances of Malcolm's decease argued for a more lenient sentence. One of Moir's last acts had been to arrange some kind of financial provision for the victim's widow, while his own wife was to have, by happy chance, at least one burden lifted from her. Though, as decreed, Captain Moir's corpse *was* handed to the surgeons "to satisfy the letter of the law", it would be returned straightway, unmutilated, to be buried by relatives upon the northern family estate. Mrs. Moir is said to have afterward adopted a new identity for herself and their children, and was henceforth known by the reversed surname of Riom.[54]

Within a decade (1836) moves were afoot for a large-scale dock development for the landing of slaughter-cattle westward of Shellhaven creek, upon the marsh grounds of Oil Mill farm.[55] From here, a proposed cattletruck rail-line had been originally conceived to run through the Orsett area towards Romford – a significant livestock market at that period.[56] But not until July 1855, as the London, Tilbury and Southend holiday-makers' steamline made its messy progress through Fobbing's uplands, would a branch striking out from the Mucking sector bring, at last, the rail to "Thameshaven". Nevertheless, as early as 1844 Fobbing's rating assessors would note new "cottages erected by the Thameshaven Railway Company" in the Oil Mill vicinity, which at the census of 1851 housed plasterers, a painter and other maintenance workmen-in-waiting.

As the excavation and building of shipping berths continued, so from the mid 1850s was introduced a facility for the increasingly popular river-jaunts between London and seaside towns like Margate and Ramsgate in Kent. "Aquatic" adventurers could step direct from their passenger train onto Thameshaven's deep-water pier, for embarkation upon the high-stacked and

---

[54] T.E. 13th May, 1978. "Bystander" Series (R. Bingley).

[55] *Visions of Thameshaven*, W. Levett in *Corringham* (ed.) I. G. Sparkes, 1965.

[56] *An Act for the Incorporation of the Thames Haven Dock and Railway Company,* 1836.

gaudily carved paddle steamers that were the delight of many a weekending cockney clerk. Rail connections with the steamer pier were, a little later, to be especially arranged from Chalk Farm, London[57] and, though the mid Victorian directories pointed out that pleasure-boat rail services would operate throughout the summer only, there were those who saw out of season opportunities in the *private* hire of trains to this wild metropolitan fringe for entirely different purposes.

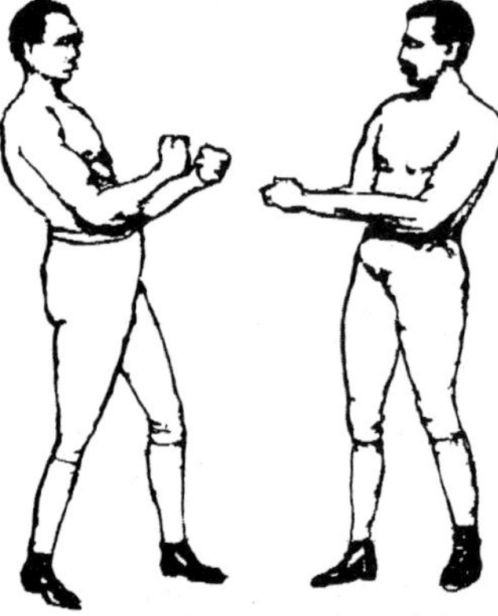

Mace versus King, 1862

There had been for years a tradition of bare-fist prize fighting on the Thameside marshes.[58] Though pronounced illegal by the mid 19th century, knuckle-contests still continued in defiance of the police – with historic and bloody battles like that of Sayers and the eminent Welsh champion, Aaron Jones, being fought (over 35 rounds) at Canvey Island during 1857.[59] In November, 1862, England's last heavyweight competition under prize-ring rules would be thrashed out near Oil Mill's sea wall: between the fiddle-playing Jem Mace, popularly called "the Swaffham gypsy" and his towering opponent Tom King. Hundreds of spectators had travelled to this "secret" rendezvous from Fenchurch Street on early morning trains, paying an admission fare of two sovereigns, and it was said that the city constabulary were unable to inform their Essex colleagues of the event's precise location. Certainly there had been no police interference; the contest went its full twenty-one rounds before the swarthy Mace was struck to the turf by a wild swing on the temple from his near-exhausted foe and the sponge thrown in.[60] Within a few months (1863) George Newbold was to publish Otto Brewer's fine commemorative lithograph of the Mace-King match, in which over 250 photographically-based portraits of the silk-hatted gentry and followers of the fancy are recognisable. This was one of the early ventures of the plate-camera into the sporting realm.

[57] *The Corringham Light Railway,* I. Gotheridge, Branch Line News. December, 1957.

[58] *Essex Blood and Thunder,* G. Caunt, privately printed, 1967.

[59] F. Z. Claro, G.T.G. 15th December, 1972 and *Knuckle Fights in Essex* in *Corringham* (ed.) I. G. Sparkes, 1965.

[60] *English Sporting Prints,* J. Laver, 1970.

Faces in the crowd

Faces in the crowd

It would be difficult to conceive the courage required to halt the progress of this kind of fight, but Fobbing in due time was to witness a police officer who possessed it – Detective Constable Earnshaw of Scotland Yard. As late as 1885, on the 14th September, a prize-fight had been set up in the same vicinity – close to Thameshaven's *Pig and Whistle* alehouse – between pugilists now largely forgotten called William Mellas and "professor" William Natty (alias Dodd) and advertised among London's ring-going fraternity by the usual "word of mouth" process. Doubtless, Earnshaw had been tipped-off in this way as to time and place, duly departing from town amongst the excited throng and presumably backed by a robust force of similar plain-clothes men.[61] A later Quarter Sessions would hear of Detective Earnshaw's "fearless" intervention in the ring, the account of his direct arrest of the bruiser Mellas bringing applause from the bench. Though no reward was possible for this officer, a hope had been expressed that superiors at the Yard might be informed of his bravery and so perhaps acknowledge it "in some other direction". Had the plucky Mr. Earnshaw thwarted one promotion, to find himself introduced to another?

The original concept of "Thameshaven" – a fabricated name devised by business minds so as to identify its location for prospective shareholders far away – had been for the rapid supply of the city with both fresh fish from the estuary's fleets as well as with live pigs, sheep and horned cattle imported from Europe; though it was to be in the latter field that the dock gained its brief reputation. The advantage of rail-truckage to the metropolis lay in its relative speed, for the tidal limitations of Thames were such that exasperating delays were met by the captains of sailing vessels along its serpentine upper reaches leading to the Pool. Under such slow-moving conditions, the cattle-barque's ventilation louvres tended to become inoperative, so that, as one horrified observer remarked, it was "difficult to conceive the amount of heat and effluvium ... in the middle and lower decks" by the time an animal cargo could be unshipped. Dockers, working half naked, were reported unable to withstand the temperatures and stench encountered when first entering below to drive the wretched beasts ashore.[62] At Thameshaven, from whence some livestock, in the early days especially, had been herded by country roads overland to various slaughterhouses, local shoeing smiths were able to find new trade in applying grip-nails to animals' hooves before off loading down the steep gangways. So tells the local writer F. Z. Claro, from other oral sources, adding recollections about the importation here of black continental horses

[61] G.T.G. 24th October, 1885 and R. J. Eastabrook notebooks, T.MUS. 3464.

[62] *The Story of Thameshaven*, B. Cracknell, Port of London Monthly, Vol. 30, 1955.

detailed particularly for London undertakers' work, besides casks of apples, and cheeses "sometimes weighing ½ ton each", – all conversational gleanings which probably refer to the later Victorian years.[63]

But through the 'fifties and onward, activity remained unimpressive and it was really by commercial luck alone that the dock began to handle the kind of trade it had initially hoped for. An outbreak of cattle-plague which affected over 27,000 animals during 1865, would be adjudged by a Royal Commission of Inquiry in October that year to have originated with certain continental consignments and its subsequent recommendations were to include a stringent prohibition of droving imported beasts on the hoof across-country. Throughout the United Kingdom, only twenty six entry points for livestock would be authorised, Thameshaven, with its excellent rail connections, now becoming one of a very few licensed landings within the London river area. New stock sheds for the accommodation of 5,000 sheep and 3,000 horned cattle would soon appear as a result, and during the half dozen years following 1867 the dock was to import and distribute something like a third of all live imports into Britain. But again the scales of fortune tipped, this time with a further epidemic of "foot and mouth" during 1875, resulting in regulations for the immediate slaughtering of European livestock on arrival at British quays. Thameshaven at once lost its advantage for want of the necessary abattoir arrangements and the resultant shipment of consignments up to Deptford, where the cattle could be more readily butchered.

This was to be a significant year; for Fobbing's marshland "cow-town", in so many aspects like a clap-board copy of the American west, was to attract to itself more of the New World's influence than it supposed. Less than a couple of decades previously, the first Pennsylvanian well had given forth its historic gush of oil and by the dawn of the 1860s petroleum was being shipped under sail to Britain in wooden casks – largely at this period for use in linoleum processing and the treatment of domestic coal gasses. Another ten years and several near-disastrous explosions along the river, were to see the Thames Conservancy introducing byelaws that forbade seagoing vessels fetching any inflammable cargoes within the London reaches higher than Thameshaven.[64] With a suitable jetty and convertible cattle sheds already *in situ*, the Petroleum Storage Company was able to begin trading in 1876, while by the late 1890s some fifteen great circular tanks – operated now by its successors, the Thameshaven Oil Wharves, Ltd. – would dominate the riverside's wide expanses of marsh and reed-hemmed

---

[63] *The Historic Essex Havens,* F. Z. Claro, PAN. 9, 1965.

[64] *A Century of Petroleum (in) Corringham* (ed.) I. G. Sparkes, 1965.

creeks.[65] Hundreds were to follow, those of the pre-Great War built for stability upon rafts of bundled coppicewood cut from medieval shaws at Northlands farm, high above the parish boundary. Like life itself, the landscape produced its little drolleries of circumstance as it struggled to modernise and change.[66]

But if hugely transformed by densely clustered metal roundels, roadways, engine houses, offices, the immemorial pattern of an agricultural past could still be traced with strange clarity from on high; in damp crescentic hollows that marked lost rivulets, in the humping angled-bastions of old Dutch embankments, vanished cottage foundations, traces of old cart tracks and the worn pathways of cattle. By the late 1930s, steadily growing files of timed and dated aerial photographs in Berlin could probably have told just at what hour Sam Jordan's herd began its bovine plod back through the fieldways for milking at Shellhaven homestall. With a decent German lens, one could calculate the very number of tiles upon the foldyard roofs, pinpoint some shovelled soil preparations for his family's dugout Anderson shelter alongside.

With so many industrial operatives about the place, and the army ensconced all around, it was to be an ironic turn of fate which plucked this one man out for death as the Battle of Britain moved towards its climax. The modest brass memorial plaque at St. Michael's to personnel of the armed forces who did not survive World War II, thus includes Samuel Jordan, a civilian, among its few names: the last truly pastoralist inhabitant of Fobbing marsh – caught out in the open while getting his startled cows to safety amidst the high explosive onslaught of *"Black Friday"*, September 6th, 1940.

Shellhaven farmhouse

[65] *The Romance of Thames Haven; reprint* from *The Petroleum Times*, G.T.G. 2nd October, 1926. Jetty superintendent in the late 1880s was R. J. Eastabrook, whose notebooks in T.MUS. list vessels offloading at Thameshaven: for example the steam tankship *'Odessa'* 5th October, 1888 with 5,500 barrels of petroleum from Russia; the barque *'Conductor'* 3rd December, 1889 containing 6,545 barrels of naphtha and petroleum and 200 cases of gasolene, from Philadelphia.

[66] *Langdon Hills Country Park,* C. J. Glover, E.C.C. 1983-4.

3. ANPHILOGOFF'S PROPHESY: MANOR AND SETTLEMENT

Britain's most arid climate is to be found in south Essex: but Fobbing's rising ground was abundantly watered in past times, its springs and streams available to every upland farmstead. The agricultural bane here was less drought, than drainage. Nearly half of its 3000 acres[1] lay upon the "strong" lands – a rich, adhesive Thames alluvium; the higher landscapes of variable brown or yellowish London clays pocketed with some brickearths and capped in places by thinly pebbled gravels and sands. A few buffish septarian rocks littered many of its field surfaces.

Hawkesbury's doming top was its greatest summit (at 230 feet) overlooking an adjacent countryside of steepish hummocks with one mile-long ridge that set its eastward flank to the marsh and upon whose nose the medieval village had grown up. At most, these heights were 50 or 100 feet above sea-level and, though not impressive even in home-counties terms, there was nothing loftier beyond them in a direct line (the pundits told) as far as *Russia*. Its prevailing air currents were south westerly and so generally benign. But few of its hill scarps caught the best of the sun and through the cold, short days, even with eyes shut, the proximity of the North Sea was believable.

From across that channel had come the people who gave the spot its spoken identity – the two syllables which, after 15 centuries, continue recognisably on the tongue, just as they figure visibly on road signs and post-office packets. Its sound was arguably something like "*FOBBING" (Phobinge*, 1086) and it is sad that we cannot know with precision just what the expression meant to its originators. Prior to the Domesday reference, there survives no record of how it was written, or uttered, and hence modern placename specialists cannot be entirely sure whether (like the nearby *Mucking*) it derives from "the followers of" a Saxon migrant land-taker called *Fobba*, or denotes instead a creekside location occupied by this leader. Whether the final element had been of an *Ing* or *Ingas* sound, makes all the difference. Wherever that first Saxon highground settlement had

1 Officially computed in 1839 as 3,015 acres; of which 1,513 were meadow or pasture, including saltings.

been established, it must surely have owed its existence to some kind of tidal access from the Thames however, strongly implying that *"Fobba's land by the creek"* was its initial identity sometime in the late 5th or 6th century A.D.

We have glimpsed in the previous chapter P. H. Reaney's placename work upon areas within Fobbing's wetlands and elsewhere, which contain "werde" and "worth" elements and which – although their precise interpretation was unknown – were all "in low-lying marshland" and could therefore be understood as "a marsh"; though the Dutch "weerd" – an island – had also been implied. He did not have the benefit, however, of newer archaeological data from Mucking, where, by the 1970s, early Saxon (5th-6th century A.D.) pottery parallels and loomweights were indicating connections upon the German coast at Feddersen Wierde and at the Dutch Ezinge *terp* mound-settlement.

The *terp* was a type of man-constructed raised island, positioned out among the tidal wastes of the north European coasts and is variously known, in the plural, by other names, such as *Wurthen* and *Wierden*. Those European communities who occupied such tide-lapped mounds were plainly the same people who, during the post-Roman generations, made their migratory voyages of colonisation here and it must be considered that our local "werde" marsh names are strong candidates for having derived from a European terp-mound culture, thus specifically signifying "a raised island farmstead". Certainly in the medieval years one distinct mound settlement, containing a peasant dwelling and of unknown antiquity was to be seen. It lay out amidst marshes eastward of Whitehall, but is unlikely to have been a unique feature. Nazewick house (now vanished) is another marsh farmstead which seems to be upon a raised platform, with its cattle pond alongside.[2]

Many questions will overshadow our thoughts upon the development of *Fobba's* territory and the growth of Fobbing's present village site. We cannot in any degree be certain that the Saxon "village" – for want of a clearer term – underlies our present centre and no previous historical writing has even put forward, let alone explored, such a doubt. Plainly, Fobbing is a hill community today and has been for some while, but its "old" core hugs a fairly low southern brow of the long north-south ridge, using land at a height of only 50 or 60 feet above sea level. Far higher and better strategic ground lies behind it, reaching 100

Saxon brooch, Mucking

2 *Considerations Upon Possible Terp-Mounds in the Mucking, Corringham and Fobbing Wetlands.* R. Bingley, PAN. 37, 1997.

3 Roman-British occupational evidence has emerged from this brow, 1994 at TQ78.7141.8520.

feet around the medieval windmill position and bordering the head of Marsh Lane. Perhaps significantly, it is within that more elevated zone that other indications of ancient occupation exist.[3]

One of these is Great House, a now erased farmstead abandoned within the present century, whose cart lane has held on to the title of "Great House Chase". Such a house-name (in a prior context) implied more than ordinary status and may suggest a manor hall had existed nearby, set upon the southwestern slope of the 100 foot contour and embracing picturesque valley prospects towards Langdon Hill.[4] An arrangement of surrounding field enclosures shows clearly that in earlier times, an old lane (now Public Footpath 23) had joined directly to its home farmyard precincts, providing a communication of equal convenience to that of the current High Road, both northward into Basildon or Vange, or Corringhamwards. Before modern farm reorganisation, Great House had been an estate of a little less than 150 acres; a typically-sized upland holding, matching within just a few acres the manor-house farm of Fobbing Hall (and prior to the 17th century in identical ownership).

Secondly, at the High Road's fringe – a few hundred yards eastward of the vanished Great House and at one time, within its farming jurisdiction – is a parcel of ploughed grounds long known by the name of *"Great Moat field"*. A depression can quite easily be detected in low sunlight, pinpointing the erased moat's general position. In 1839 the tithe map surveyor had been able to discern in detail 3 sides of its rectangular plan, a ditch that was doubtless fed during the 14th century or thereabouts (when such moat-features were fashionable) by a spring which yet persists within a nearby north hedgeline. Kentish ragstone fragments, imported Scandinavian schist stone and a range of coloured domestic pottery surfacing at this site point to continuous occupation through the medieval years, possibly into the Tudor age.[5] A domestic moat enclosing a building of local key importance therefore occupied this hill crest overlooking the Thames estuary and it is regrettable that current metal-detector activity is devaluing its potential as a site of historical meaning.

The agricultural surroundings of Great Moat field are important, too, for this area acts as the pivot to what were seemingly four large "common" fields of classic medieval kind. Originally comprising working strips of about an acre each,

---

4 Great House Farm TQ78.7135.8475. It may be simply the demesne farmstead *of* the "Great House", which is the adjacent moated manor house (below).

5 Moated site TQ78.7155.8478. "Domestic" i.e. not defensive except to deter livestock-predators. *A Moated site at Fobbing*, R. Bingley, PAN. 35, 1995.

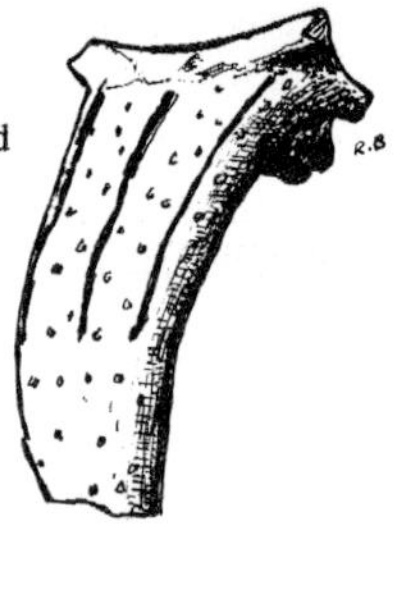

R.B

Medieval jughandle, Wharf Road

they were later (perhaps through the 14th century) to be consolidated by half dozens or so, into those squarish hedged "crofts" already described in our first chapter. A remarkably hotchpotch assortment of copyhold farm grounds of like nature could be seen right across this central band of Fobbing – from the Vineyard in the south and northward to the railway's course – until even our own century. Of what we may call the "village" farms of Fobbing, therefore, their individual "common" fields centred predominantly around the hub of the 100 foot knoll at Great House and Great Moat field, strongly implying that this may have been a settlement nucleus prior to the emergence of the "later" village. Of all those farms, Fobbing Hall's 150 acres stands as the only exception, for its lands had at some period been shuffled into a single block which circled around the southern and easterly village skirts to take in most of the excellent and close-at-hand marsh meadows. Its unorthodox compactness smacks of an attempt to set up a new home farm site close to its manorial wharf at a period later than the usage of the medieval common fields – possibly a further proof of the shift of habitation to the lower hill slope and marsh edge where our present "Fobbing" is situated.

As we have seen, the water supply essential to habitation *was* present even upon such a ridge summit. But was there also a wharf facility available within reasonable distance of the Great House area at some early period? Before considering that question, let us look for a moment at the present Wharf Road which, viewed from the air, plainly staggers away in a series of curves from the long and fairly undevious main street. It is steep; not by any means *convenient* for the movement of animal-drawn transport or even for the loaded land-sledges of past times. It is the only route we may visualise for the getting of cargoes up from Fobbing Wharf to the High Road level. But it was not *there*, it seems, during the full medieval period and may have only been created in the later 15th century when the present Fobbing Hall farmhouse appeared. It reveals the usual signs of having been deliberately engineered, its middle slopes shovelled away and tipped downhill, so giving an enhanced traffic climb by means of an earthen ramp off the marsh, while upon either side the land-plots seem to align their boundaries very neatly, suggesting that strips of ground formerly ran *right across it*. To the field observer, this is an ordinary clue to a roadway being *newer* than its surrounding pattern of settlement.

From the settlement-ridge top, Marsh Lane (*Mershlane,* 1521) drops down steadily over terrace ledges towards manorial meadow levels where – though sea-walls have come to protect this claggy terrain from the tides – the purple reeded hollows of a former *fleet* (suitable for small craft) are straightway detectable among the ploughed surfaces. Obviously, it once made its winding way into proximity with Marsh Lane's foot, where nowadays a sunken counter wall

Medieval jughandle, Lion Hill

FOBBING: Village Settlement

Based upon the Tithe Apportionment map of 1839. Fobbing's essentially medieval street and houseplot layout is seen here: it embraces the top of a low mile-long ridge and continues downslope to the marshfoot creek-head and wharf.

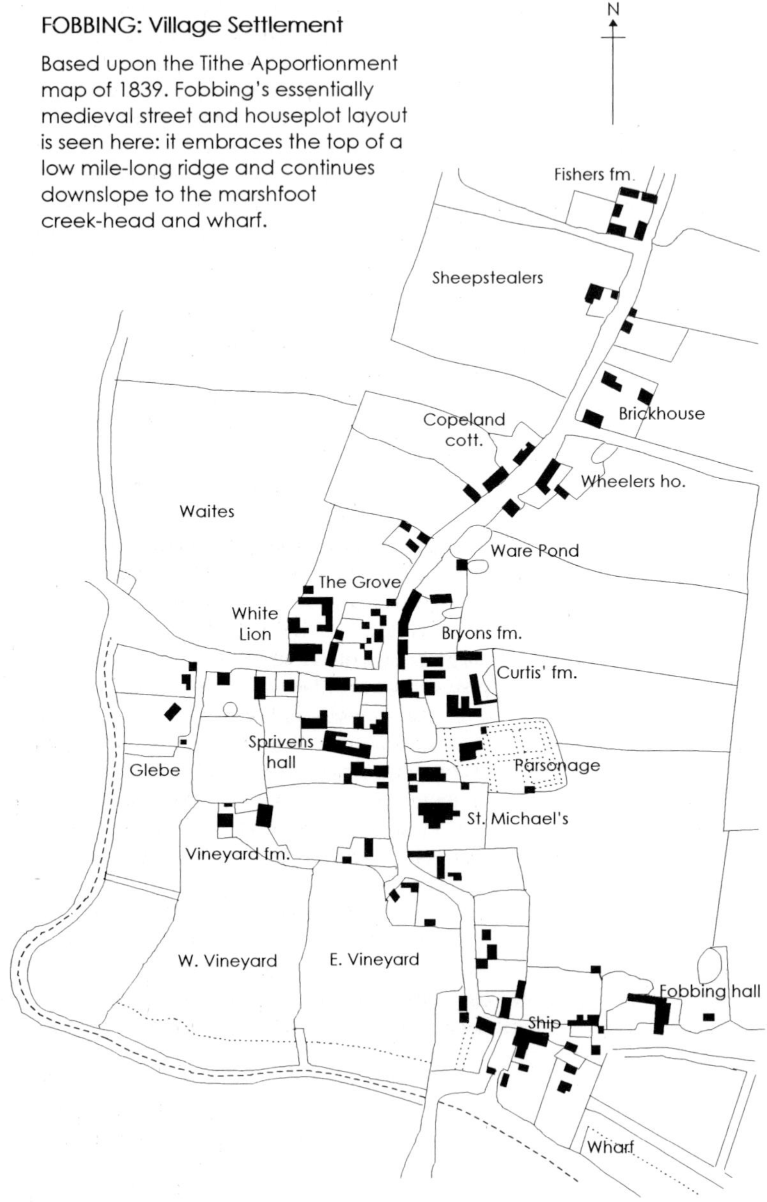

Lattice and pellet shards, Fobbing Marsh

contains it.[6] That the creek was fully tidal in early Roman times is evidenced by its utilisation for saltmaking, a debris of coarse ceramic brine-pans littering the agricultural surfaces around its banks, while some medieval continuity is indicated by the discovery of a water-abraded red jug with cream lattice-and-pellet decoration, dredged from its bed in recent years.[7] Navigation connecting *either* with what we now call Fobbing creek, or a former extension of Shellhaven creek was surely entirely feasible from the terminus of Marsh Lane, though at present evidence for any wharf structure there is absent.

As all field historians would affirm, the most modern ordnance survey map will be found to contain a certain amount of "fossil" evidence upon the origins of the landscape it portrays. Even better, from our point of view, is the late 19th century coverage of Fobbing's terrain, printed before so much of the scene became obscured by petro-chemical installations, for from this we can grasp something of the ancient nature of these reclaimed tracts. *Nature* is not without particular significance here, for one can view very plainly how numerous must have been the creekways and *guts*, great and little, winding in coiled mazes; blocked, turned by man in fresh directions, embanked over so as to hold back abnormal flood. As our previous chapter has hinted, the making of these agricultural marshlands had been a mighty enterprise.

It comes nevertheless as a surprise discovery, when the map gains sense, to see that Fobbing creek's approach towards the village has all the appearance of a humanly created channel for something like the innermost mile of its course. Its "natural" line had apparently once meandered much further south, perhaps to meet in a complete union with Shellhaven's creek, another narrower arm snaking down to entwine about Great and Little Ilford before turning again by Iron Latch (Lady's Island) towards Fobbing's scarp. *That* is the serpentine configuration which was to remain in "ghost" form as the legal parish boundary line across the marshes for hundreds of years afterwards. And that, in turn, is good evidence of how this undrained landscape appeared, back in the twelfth century or even long before, when either a parish or a Saxon manor preceding it, had first been marked out. If Fobbing wharf *was* sited immediately below St. Michael's church at such an early period as the twelfth century, its boats cannot have used the channel which became called Fobbing Creek, for that is a navigation superimposed on the landscape possibly as late as the Dutch scheme of the 1620s. It was with the

---

6 As late as the 1770s Fobbing's first relatively detailed complete landscape mapping had implied an importance to this watercourse (Chapman & Andre, Plate XXIII).

7 Pottery 14th century, probably Mill Green kiln, Ingatestone. Author's possession.

creation of this new cut, that the Marsh Lane creek became separated from its southward entry into the (now called) Manorway fleet and Shellhaven's mouth.

What other happenings though, might have caused Fobbing's main community to focus around it present village location?[8] Perhaps the widespread "new planning" concept of the thirteenth century, which had given rise to numerous radical re-makings of both towns like Hull, or Winchelsea and even small settlements (that had been of Saxon origin) such as West Tilbury not far upriver.[9] These planning innovations were often associated with the granting to manor lords of market charters that promised special trading franchises in suitable locations. Under Thomas de Camvill, Fobbing would be allowed a weekly-held market by the crown in 1227, together with the right of a yearly fair upon the vigil and feast of St. Martin, the 11th November.

De Camvill's market had been chartered to be held each Wednesday, though when confirmed to its later lord, Humphry de Bohun, almost a century afterward, a Thursday would be named.[10] By now (1318) *two* annual fairs were in operation, in the Whitsun week as well as "at Martinmas and the two days following" and so it would appear that Fobbing's commerce was steadily increasing in these years prior to the Black Death.[11] We do not know for certain the market's location, for the lord's stalls might be set anywhere within his manor. Normally, a wide green or street supplied its venue however, and one need only glance at the typical "broadway" alongside St. Michael's to imagine a practicable sort of area, with its house frontages respecting the common public space.[12] If the present facade-alignment of the older houses is inherited directly from some earlier streetplan, a distinct widening toward the southern end of High Road must have existed, sufficient even to suggest a longish triangular medieval village green.

And then, as every local is deeply aware, another possible impetus for movement and replanning might lie in the aftermath of the Essex rebellion of 1381. We know only in the merest detail of the Fobbing men who, with their dependent kinsfolk suffered in varying degrees the retribution which was especial to traitors. Some had been executed; more, like Robert Knyght – incidentally identified as owner of "a boat with rigging" – were to have their possessions and

---

8 *A Saxon Grubenhaus at West Tilbury*, R. Bingley, PAN. 16, 1972-73.

9 Extensive lynchet earthworks at Fobbing have not been discussed in this chapter. They enclose the settlement landplots on S. and W. and are impressive, though of unknown date; banks especially well defined west of *White Lion*, aback south side of High Road near St. Michael's church and aside parish boundary (S.W. brook) where alignments have been ploughed away.

10 P.R.O. *Calendar of Charter Rolls*, 1226-1257, H.M.S.O.

11 P.R.O. *Calendar of Charter Rolls*, 1300-1326, H.M.S.O.

12 Nearly all the present houseplot perimeters here are probably encroachments onto the medieval market-space.

homes confiscated. John Wolk was one of these, deprived of his cottage holding worth 6d. a year. Such family heads were only the outstanding participants, selected for particular punishment and whose circumstances have found record because of their being of some substance within the lordship. But the parishioners' involvement during the great revolt was far deeper than has generally been supposed, for of all the 145 accused within the shire of being "ringleaders" of insurrection, no less than 27 had been Fobbing people. *So many* adult males from a population of about 12 times that size (estimated at c.338 in 1377) would imply that men from at least half the resident families were deeply implicated in crimes against the king.[13] Was no example made of this viper's nest by those armed horsemen under the de Bohun son-in-law Thomas of Woodstock, earl of Buckingham, who rode into Essex during the ensuing weeks of summer, to massacre its rebels only a half dozen miles away in sight of Hawkesbury top, amongst woodland near Billericay? Some homes at Fobbing may well have been ransacked and destroyed (a normal process of war against peasant terrorists, even into our own time) giving stimulus to movement and eventual resettlement within the general area.

Such influences, dramatic though they may have been, leave no documentary trace. Nor does the scant archaeological picture assist. So far, it has to be stated that the few chance finds and excavations for domestic pottery which point to dwelling sites of this broad period, have come from house plots at the *southern* parish end, in Wharf Road and aside Lion Hill. But this is mainly because gardens are most likely to unearth material that attracts notice. Fobbing's outward fields have not yet been surveyed with this question in mind. On the other hand, no soils around our present village centre have yet produced potsherd finds of the *initial* medieval phase, neither Saxon, Norman, nor even certainly into the thirteenth century, an interesting reflection upon our previous debate.

One building only is known to survive from the fourteenth century, close upon the period of Fobbing's uprising; Copeland cottage, which can be dated to the final quarter of the 1300s and which, as its handsome crown-posts and moulded tie-beams reveal, had then been a residence of extraordinary quality. Its fortuitous dating indicates that somewhere in the crucial period *around* 1381, new housing was being erected upon (in this case) a previously

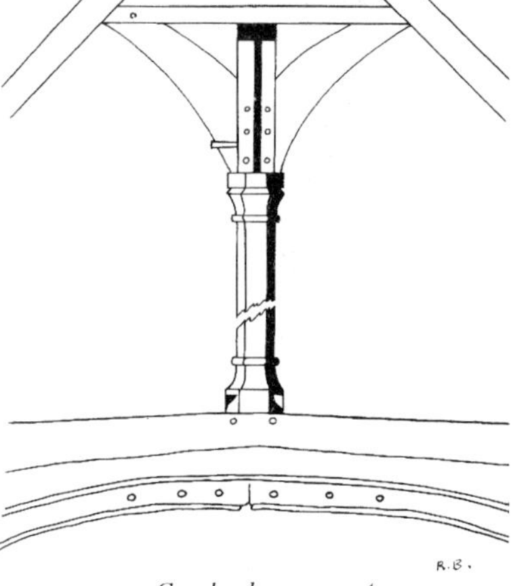

Copeland, crown post

[13] *Essex and the Great Revolt of 1381*, W. H. Liddell and R. G. Wood (eds.) E.R.O. No. 84, 1982.

uninhabited site well south of the 100 foot contour, at the streetside.[14] This is demonstrated by the excavation of its floor layers, which showed a gravelly ploughsoil, or topsoil, directly beneath its groundcill framework. Copeland cottage had therefore been assembled either upon the edge of the cultivated land or perhaps upon a broad verge of grazing waste fringing the highway.

So far as any overall pattern of settlement is concerned, Fobbing by the later medieval period, was a place typical of south Essex and the southern counties in general; with its main zone of community life hinged closely upon manor house, its church and presumably a market green, while beyond at distances of a mile and more were its compact or dispersed clusters of habitation, comprising farm homestalls and their few dependent cottages. The latter groups had invariably come about through manorial gift, or permission to an applicant to clear woodland or waste for the making of a home. Outlying steadings such as Hovels, or Brookhouse[15] appear to have sprung up in this way. Occasionally, too, the most modest of dwellings might mushroom overnight upon broad patches at roadsides where liberty had been obtained from the manorial authority. Even as late as mid 1808, John Wilson, victualler at the Vange *Bells* had been granted the right "to erect a cottage and enclose part of the waste ... on the west side of the Road nearly opposite the public house (in Fobbing) ... and fronting the road leading to Southend ..." at a half guinea rental per annum".

Radiating for a little distance out from the village hub were other farmsteadings, the "street farms", discerned in a number of examples which still in some way survive despite radical changes and re-building. As we find them today, they date from between the 15th and 18th centuries; the flimsily framed *Fishers*, a minor yeoman's house of c.1470, situated rather towards the ridge peak; *Wheelers* of possibly similar date; the 18th century *Byrons*,[16] which is now Fobbing's general store and the late 17th century *Curtis'*[17] alongside it, whose fabric appears to contain far earlier remnants. This remains the one working "street farmyard" of our own time. The *White Lion* was formerly another, operating as did so many alehouses in the dual role, but certainly what we would nowadays define as agricultural activity was by no means exclusive to these. For many roadside dwellings, possessing no property other than their immediate yards, were set cheek-by-jowl with wooden cowhouses and other livestock pens, and even into the 1820s bargemaster William Simons had kept good piggeries within his village garden space.

---

14 *Site discussion: plan and section drawings,* Brenda Watkins, E.C.C. Planning Dept., 1989.

15 Hovels TQ78.7031.8610, Brookhouse TQ78.7081.8614.

16 *Byrons* farmhouse TQ78.7170.8399.

17 *Curtis'* farmhouse TQ78.7176.8397.

That territory which was to become Fobbing, had been settled and partly tamed into a scene of upland farms long before any concept of parish, or parish church was known. The Christianising of this district had effectively begun during the mid 7th century by bishop Cedd, from a newly founded minster at Tilbury, and thereafter, possibly for a further 400 years while the *ministeria* of the East Saxons served the wild, rural populace, it would have been unusual to see any kind of church upon these hilltops of Thameside because religious communion was not dispensed in that way. At Corringham, there is certain structural evidence to certify a late Saxon church, though possibly existing only from the mid 11th century, while Fobbing's visible remnants of a Norman nave also come from about the Conquest period.[18] Architectural fabric is, of course, no proof of a primary date; sub-ground evidence of earlier use is always possible, though only competent archaeological survey might detect it with authority.[19]

Pagan temples were, at a very early period, ordered to be cleansed and made fit for Christian worship and certainly St. Michael – if this were the saint to whom Fobbing was first dedicated – is closely associated with the Roman cult of Mercury and various other heathen deities. Those Germanic migrants who had established their presence here by the 6th century were a pagan people, remaining so through perhaps four or five generations and disposing of their dead in some place of reverence that was not a Christian ground, but which may in time have been adopted by the incoming Church. And in this may lie an answer to the question of why the present St. Michael's site had been established for Christian worship, even though its community was still mainly focused rather distant from it, upon Fobbing's higher ridge.

The old manorial arrangement of landscape which somewhile predated in Fobbing the idea of *parish* organisation, can be glimpsed far back at the close of the Saxon period and though we have no need to examine Domesday Book in depth, *some* of what it tells with regard to our manor grounds continues as relevant into the later years, when Church and parish had become a significant influence. There was extensive woodland, which must have covered most of the northward countryside beyond the Crooked Brook, topping Hawkesbury and reaching beyond the line of Dry Street – sufficient for the autumn foraging of 700 swine. Considerable expanses of saltmarsh pasture to eastward and south of the main settlement were in use: enough to graze 700 sheep through the benign months. Perhaps between 500 and 600 acres of Fobbing's high grounds also, were ox-cultivated for sundry arable crops so that out of the 2,600 or so acres (which we believe the whole manor to have comprised) a third perhaps, was under a mixed

---

[18] *East Saxon Heritage*, S. Pewsey and A. Brooks, 1993. The R.C.H.M. suggests pre-Conquest work.

[19] *The Archaeology of the English Church,* W. Rodwell, 1981. Fobbing St. Michael's TQ78.7180.8390.

farming, either as feed-grounds, or in plough. Its woodland, we may be sure, was no treed wilderness, but wholly under management; as the wood-pasture already seen and for the rotational coppicing and felling of hazel for sheepfolds or thatch-spars, of building oak and elm, ash (used in many kinds of farming implements) hornbeam for forge-heat, clean dairy maplewood, and lime. And there were doubtless many additional acres of laneside waste and marshland, to be exploited for reed and fire-turf, that the Domesday record ignores simply because those grounds were not yet pioneered into mainstream agricultural use.[20]

Faint though these images be, we can detect with a fieldsman's understanding that the manor of the 11th century Count Eustace was very much the same unit of high clays and salterns which, after a hundred years or more, had become fixed as the *parish* of Fobbing and that when one traces today – as with patience we can – those streams and hedgebanks, creeksides and shores which define its old parish boundaries, we are following at most stages our Saxo-Norman *manor* outlines as well.[21] At some undeduced date besides, a second manor called Hawkesbury would be carved out from within the parent estate and gifted to the abbey of Barking. But this made no difference to the physical outline of the ancient plan. Of this sub-manor's beginning we know almost nothing. At Domesday, in 1086, the nunnery of Barking's possessions included none at Fobbing, but with 1258 *Hauecisburi* would be referred to in a grant from John de la lee (of West Lee) as being already in the abbess' ownership.[22] Almost certainly it had been part of those wooded pig-pastures which were to be *assarted* with axe and with browsing livestock by chosen pioneer tenants of the abbey, so as to create the pasture farms which prevailed there into very recent years.

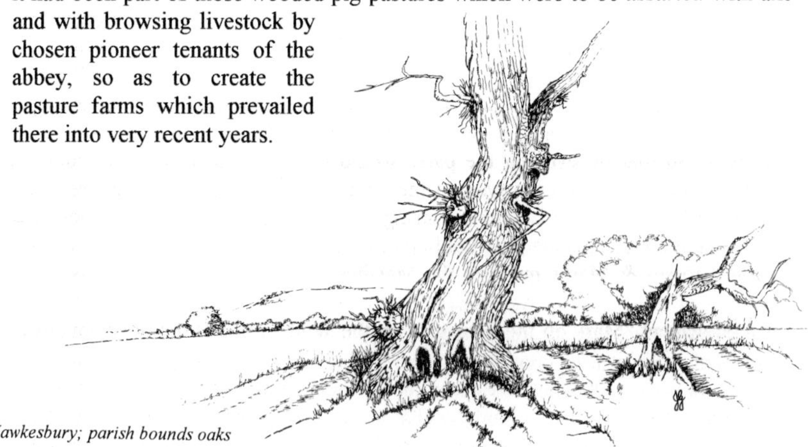

Towards Hawkesbury; parish bounds oaks

[20] *Domesday Book: Essex,* A. Rumble (ed.) Phillimore, 1983.

[21] Holdings of the manor of Fobbing outside this main block are referred to elsewhere. In the present meaning, these detached properties, such as at Billericay, are discounted. See also Chapter 9 (Tithes).

[22] Hawkesbury manor house TQ78.7037.8675.

THROUGH BUSHES AND THROUGH BRIARS

"Wide was his parish and houses far asunder" sang Chaucer of the diligent priest, *"light upon his feet"*, going staff in hand to visit the sick and troubled among his flock. Once we begin to envisage both *"manor"* and *"parish"* as they formerly operated, the medieval poet's blithe description of his holy clerk becomes something of a reality. The priest's livelihood, and indeed his avoidance of much unnecessary dispute, depended upon knowing the locality intimately; his parish boundaries were a girdle that embraced the properties and fields out of which he extracted his tithe, by coin or by crop. Though perhaps a written "terrier" – a description of his own church glebe grounds – was usually in his keeping, there were in earlier times no maps to assist the priests' knowledge of where exactly the secular farmlands and wastes met those of a neighbouring incumbent's jurisdiction. So, time out of mind, it had been the custom to conduct, towards the end of spring, a walking survey, or "perambulation" around the parish perimeter accompanied by both knowledgeable old folk and the young, so that one generation could pass its information on to the next. The event was both of a ritual and of a practical nature; prayers were given *en route*, and pollard "bounds trees" freshly scored or mutilated, while on certain occasions the lads might be ceremoniously beaten so that they should remember a particular location as significant along their way.

As a Rogationtide ceremony, similar journeys continued to be taken long after the time of competent mapping and as late as 1838 Fobbing's churchwardens would be found coughing up 5 shillings for refreshments "at Vang bels" after a gathering had walked "the Bounds of the Parish". By tradition, their course upon that day should have been with the sun, from east, in clockwise progress round to the west, so that by evening the party would have circled back to its convivial starting point. Yet not always was the circuit so arranged, nor the entire travail accomplished at a single session. During 1763, it appears that only the lowlands had been of concern, someone troubling to note in the parish registers his "account of the Crosses & Marks made in the Marshes of Fobbing when the Parishioners went the bounds ... on Holy Thursday." A dozen or so important indications such as a permanent "Mark on the Spur gate on the Wall (seawall) the most southward part of the Oil Mill" would be recorded, another "On the Post at the head of the Salt Fleet".[23] Conversely, 1794 had sent its communal ramblers (from a *westward* startpoint) over the higher landscape, first inspecting their "cross on the waste, close to Gibson's Ditch" at the bottom of Fobbing Hill, thence climbing the lower slopes of *Weights* enclosure, where a certain marked elm tree grew in "Colmans

[23] Memorandum in Fobbing Parish Register (bapts.) 1736-1783.

Field".[24] A tenant called Gibson had occupied Tan House farm, just across the parish edge, during 1789 and the stream ditch which now transiently bore his name had separated Fobbing manor from Corringham since the Saxon age.

An impressive portion of these upland parish (and manor) bounds still survive. The very footsteps of medieval priest or Georgian parson and their chattering parishioners, can be *exactly* traced over the tawny London clays, up beyond "Colemans" cool ditchside (where hazel and dogwood loomed lush and full) to what was once perhaps a sturdy line of pollard oaks (a single tree remains) topping the brow westward of Mill Lane. Several springs arose about here, where views were open to the pleasant Langdon heights, trickling down to form the eastern Hassenbrook rivulet, another looping north as a small feeder to the Crooked Brook. But the brow had another, greatly attractive feature; a steeply cut lynchet bank and deep boundary ditch of some 15 feet width which bordered one cornfield edge. At this dramatic point, Fobbing's soil sat 9 feet *higher* than the Corringham ground next to it; a deliberately engineered earthwork division, which no perambulating party can ever have overlooked.

A priest

Thereon, the way led along hedges of field maple and thorn, towards Hovels farm and into coppice fringes where jays screeched and a brisk stream edging Martinhole wood tumbled to meet the journeyers on its way toward Thames. Here was a natural divider which the centuries would barely change, but soon the bounds-line switched away by a small meadow edge and up over the claygate beds, so that a further row of pollard oaks had been created to define its exact course. Beyond, an ancient trafficway (passing One Tree Hill) was followed between hedgerows dense with honeysuckle and bluebell, into the grassy-verged Dry Street – a lane so labelled, surely, in rustic sarcasm unless its origin lies in the Essex dialect word "dreen" (drowning); for even in modern times its metalling is frequently awash from nearby field-springs. Nevertheless, Hawkesbury's court rolls give us *Drystrete* or *Dreystrete* as early as the 1450s.[25]

Streams and mire continued to feature as parson and parishioners journeyed their way onward over tilting pastures toward Lee Chapel, walking aside a handsome boundary of gnarled oaks that can still be discovered, and which bears evidence of many old pollardings at about 6 or 7 feet above ground. Ahead, lay alder swamps, unworthy of reclamation, around the waters of another brook which curled away northeastwards, reaching the farthest lands of Fobbing. We know of no name for this stream, which forms nowadays the back-limit to gardens of

---

[24] Memorandum in Fobbing Parish Register (bapts.) 1783-1811.

[25] Manor of Hawkesbury, Court Rolls E.R.O. D/DSg.

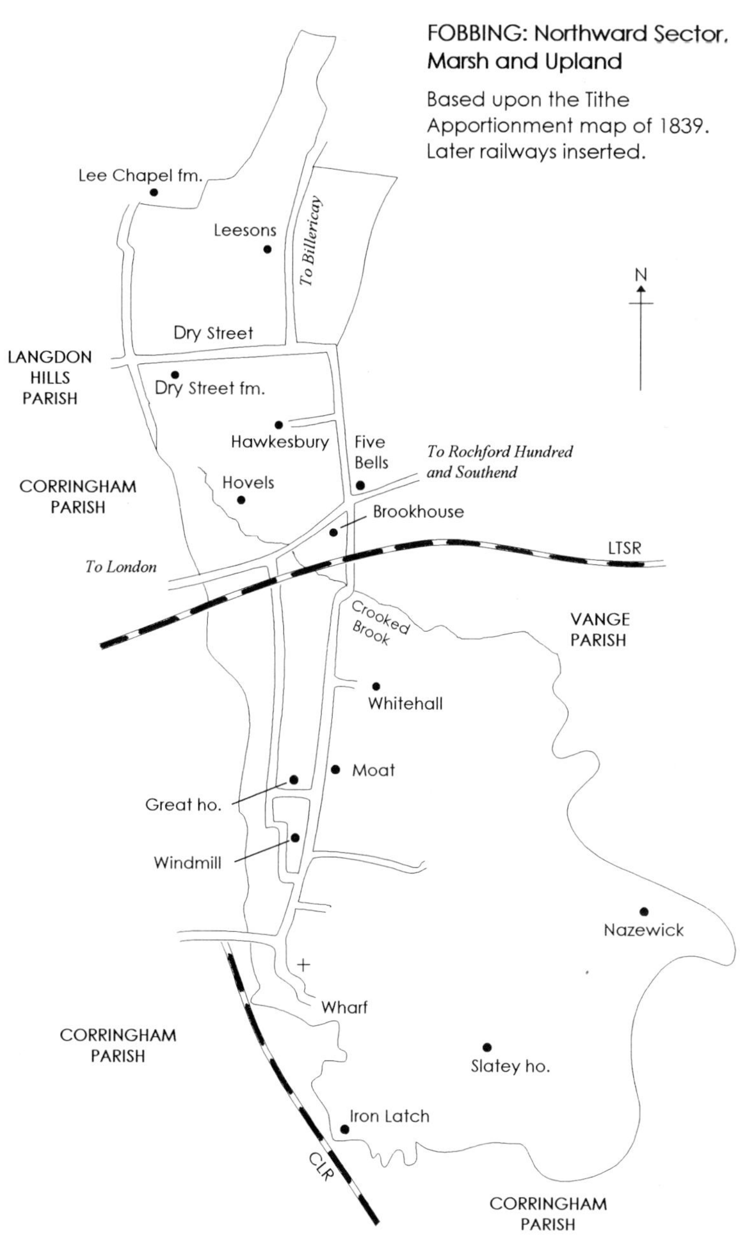

FOBBING: Northward Sector, Marsh and Upland
Based upon the Tithe Apportionment map of 1839. Later railways inserted.
Lee Chapel fm.
Leesons
To Billericay
N
Dry Street
LANGDON HILLS PARISH
Dry Street fm.
Hawkesbury
Five Bells
To Rochford Hundred and Southend
CORRINGHAM PARISH
Hovels
Brookhouse
LTSR
To London
Crooked Brook
VANGE PARISH
Whitehall
Moat
Great ho.
Windmill
Nazewick
Wharf
CORRINGHAM PARISH
Slatey ho.
Iron Latch
CLR
CORRINGHAM PARISH

"Spoorhams", the first of Basildon New Town's enclaves which we find obscuring our medieval landscape hereon. Fobbing's ecclesiastical territory however, continued inland over those modern roads which are today called *Laindon Link*, *Knightleys* and part of *Upper Mayne*, then returned on a rectangular course back southward to *Cherrydown* before darting east to the foot of the housing area called *Waldegrave*. Waldegrave's curving incline follows our medieval boundary precisely to Clayhill, and thereafter, Fobbing's perambulation would have joined their familiar lane (the Billericay highway) before reaching the shady brow of Bells Hill. Below them in a distant hollow of the High Road end, rippled the Crooked Brook[26] over whose little headsprings they had trodden in hours past, its banks now taking up the ancient bounds-line against Vange, carrying it away beyond Whitehall farmstead and draining to a sizeable creek that fed Holehaven's open water.

We have begun to see something of a landscape; its outward places as well as the village itself, over a wide span of time and have observed that the manor lord's estate, his community of copyhold dependents and others, were to be largely embraced within the new structure of a "parish" by the 12th century. But the "parish" in medieval terms was not an administrative unit (as later it would gradually become). It referred merely to the geographical space over which a cleric served in the cure of souls, and from which he obtained means to live and maintain his church. In all things else pertaining to the everyday co-existence of those abiding within the parish, *manorial* governance entirely prevailed, dispensing in normal cases the national justice as well as attending to its own "customary" framework of law. Though by the mid 16th century much of this manorial power had declined, its local courts were still effective bodies, the ancient customs and practices pertaining to copyhold farms in Fobbing, for example, being still maintained far into the Georgian age.

It has already been suggested that the manor house of Fobbing Hall may not have been present on its current site before the late 15th century, while the *Royal Commission on Historical Monuments* appraisal prefers a building date even into the 16th.[27] Its location when compared to the numerous earlier medieval manor halls of this district is unusual in its uncomfortable marsh-edge siting and it is an extremely modest structure besides. These factors may enhance our view that a

---

26 *Crooked Brook* evidently bridged by 1679 when the Court Rental refers to highway leading from "church to Brook Bridge".

27 R.C.H.M. Vol. IV South East Essex 1922, though many of its datings are not to be accepted in the light of more recent studies.

predecessor had stood in some more prestigious hilltop position, for it is hard to conceive that magnates such as the de Camvills, or the far mightier de Bohuns who succeeded them as Fobbing's proprietors, would have been satisfied that their manor house shamed the excellent commerce of the place. Had not this township in the de Camvill's day (1328) been assessed upon its householder's goods among the two most wealthy vills of Barstable hundred?

Its manor lords, as was general along the lower Thames-marshes, were not of course inclined to be resident here and certainly by the Tudor age Fobbing Hall's status in reality had been only that of a solid yeoman tenant's homestead, visited upon required occasions by the lord's steward when coming to take account of his master's assets and to preside over his Court Baron.[28] Indeed, it may primarily have been in the guise of a little courthouse that this building was envisaged when newly erected, albeit with its further convenience as a useful station for the control of cargo-tolls at its doorstep wharf. For this, too, was a manor enterprise through the medieval period and long after.

As to the courts themselves, a few cameos only need be offered at this point to indicate what kind of business they conducted – all typical of their work over several centuries but chosen for reasons of clarity, from rather later periods of operation.[29] The customary regulations to which copyholders were bound varied considerably from place to place, though many practices were pretty widespread – such as the taking of a livestock *"heriot"* at the decease of a copy-holding tenant. At the Vineyard farm we see the possibility of such ancient compulsory gifts being compounded to a money payment, for while in 1700 a usual heriot animal had been rendered, the lord's steward by 1786 could only state that the obligation, though defunct, "does not appear to have been sold off". The heriot had been fairly typically defined by Fobbing Hall's steward in 1650 as "The best Beast Horse or Cow", while copyhold inheritance was strictly limited to the eldest son of any deceased customary tenant. Perhaps, these regulations merely represent a re-tightening (under the lordship of the Whitmores)[30] of systems which had slipped over a period of time, for a century earlier, in July 1561, John Fowlar had been granted dispensation from the court to dispose of his copyholds (Mill Field and Mill Hill) as he desired, by terms of his will after death.[31]

In the event of a minor becoming inheritor of a copyhold estate, the late tenant's wife might technically succeed, as is illustrated in the case of Eleanor, relict of Isaac Libbard, who with June 1768, had "humbly prayed to be admitted

[28] Fobbing Hall TQ78.7199.8388.

[29] Manor of Fobbing and Stanford le Hope, Court Rolls E.R.O. D/DCx M1-4.

[30] *The Whitmore Story,* J. Ayres, PAN. 27, 1985.

[31] Will, John Fowlar, "of Malardes Green" (Romford) proved 26th July, 1568.

R.B.

Bounds ash, Hovels edge

Tenant To one Third part" of a certain cottage with an orchard at the head of Fobbing Hill (for her lifetime) while "afterwards came into the Court John Libbard son and Heir of the said Isaac ... to be admitted Tenant To Two third parts in possession deed and one third part in Reversion ...". The court on this occasion also specified the child's custody to be committed to his mother until 21 years of age. If the language of such late documents implies a somewhat craven attitude upon the applicant's part, we need not believe it in reality, for they were in many instances well-to-do persons of the best village class. Court rolls are invariably laced with legal phrases which pander to the proprietor's self importance, by pretending to a still-medieval power that was long obsolete.

The only other manorial custom specified in 1650 had referred to trees of timber size (that is, not underwood) which, if cut down upon some copyhold premises, must be charged for at one third their market value. But this condition, too, appears not to have been long enforced, for when in July 1735, licence had been granted to Thomas Drew to build a wooden house upon his Vineyard estate, the sole demand would be for the planting of "two Young Trees in the stead of every one", an interesting reflection upon the guarding of landscape resources. The use of the land and traditional rights of access to certain fields was carefully supervised and might at intervals require the action of a Court Baron and its "homage" (or jury of manorial tenants) with their particular local knowledge. In the Maytime of 1657, Richard Doe had thus stood accused because his horseman had ploughed some field across which the lord of the manor "hath free Egresse c regresse to ... the backland unto his ... marsh called Mill hope" – evidently close to the Oil Mill upon Shellhaven creek. Moreover, along this same "Salt Marsh", the culprit had lately cut a ditch, the homage swearing how "the said Richard ... hath taken in of the ... Lord's land more than is his right to have ...".

But not always were matters of legal portent so easy to discern and unravel. Dormant considerations arose from distant years which the active generation of parishioners could not honestly attest to, and during 1743 the keen memory of an old inhabitant called Atkins had been called upon when a knotty question arose about a barn once standing in the Mill field. We do not know the reasons for this enquiry, only that advice was wanted also about a former cottage, since demolished, which had stood nearby as far back as the 1690s. Atkins recalled clearly, because, said he, he had helped rebuild a new tenement on its *very* foundation, having "carted all the bricks from Fobbing Wharf". But the hoary ancient "better remembers it because he has drunk at the Old house before it was demolished" – suggesting it may have been a village aleshop in Atkin's prime. And perhaps today he had earned a refreshing pot in the *Ship* from some grateful party, because of his useful evidence in Fobbing Hall's manor courtroom.

Clay tobacco pipe stamp c.1750, Vineyard farm

In far earlier times before Elizabeth's reign, the keeping of highways passable had been a manorial obligation also, subject to local enforcement through the Lord's Court Baron. With the 1550s however, such matters were to become more centralised within the system of the county Sessions of the Peace (since the maintenance of roads was of far reaching importance). We shall touch on the various records of the Quarter Sessions in due course as they affected Fobbing's sundry anti-social characters, but a single example of highways negligence may be included here because it illustrates a continuity of what had been the age-old manorial method of demanding tenants to provide horses and ballast-tumbrils with labour in attendance, to work at necessary times upon its lanes. During 1641, Fobbing's surveyor of the highways, Humphrey Collett, had been obliged to report both Charles Pitfield, lessee of the Hawkesbury farm, and the Dutchman Giles Vandepett for neglecting to dispatch their carts at his summons. Worse was to follow next season, when the unrepentant foreigner and now Richard Doe also, were not only to refuse their public duty, but made busy "persuading others that they should not come in" with their required road vehicles. Sarah Casterman, another Dutch proprietor, had been happy to go along with this defiance and all would find themselves answering the justices at a future sessions.

Most were ancient highways indeed, essentially the same traffic routes which we travel today, though very different in their scenic aspect. They provided a visual thread of continuity in the landscape, in contrast to our stark modern asphalt which pierces and divides every view across countryside or village. Along the spacious street by St. Michael's, the entire effect in medieval and far later years must have been one of pleasant unity, its (smaller) hummocked burial ground perhaps pale-fenced, but hardly separated in its verdant character from a continuous central green which extended away to the Vineyard's hedgerows. Ornamental gardens were in time to become a norm, fronting the cottages that faced it and all probably nibbled by stealth from the manorial waste. In the early 1760s, Fobbing had probably witnessed its last annual fair, whose suppression, along with many others, was to be sealed with 1762 on the grounds of "unlawful Games and Plays ... to the great Increase of Vice and Immorality and to the Debauching and Ruin of Servants, Apprentices and other unwary people ...".[32]

There was no wish to constantly trim and tidy, because such a concept stole herbage from the free-ranging cottage fowls and made only for domestic want. Its inhabitants were conservationists in a way which has departed from the urban memory; their surroundings teemed with a natural abundance, and their Bible vouched for Man's ascendancy over all living things. At the dawn of our period, the woodlands of Fobbing still knew the roe deer and possibly the wild cat. Pine martens and polecats were hunted to extinction here as late as the Georgian age,

---

[32] E.R.O. Q/SO 10 p. 271.

while the marshgrounds harboured a plenty of otters – killed at whiles because they competed for eels and other fish upon which so many homes relied. As across England, bounties were being offered by Fobbing's churchwardens for otters as late as 1754, in which April three polecats had been slaughtered also. There was a price for the harmless hedgehog even, which was thought to suck the teats of milch-cattle as they lay sleeping in the field.[33] During 1791, a total of 31 hedgehogs had been fetched in for rewards by parishioners, while in 1778 George Ellis had claimed a princely 6s. 8d. for a "Bitch fox". To householders in dire want, such means of earning the price of a loaf, with luck a pair of shoes, were not to be despised. The secretive badger, smoked out and bludgeoned at his hillside sett, might give some family a tasty leg of cured ham as well as providing the hunter with a good, hard-wearing waistcoat front. David Glascock of Fobbing had claimed a shilling in the fall of 1739 for one of these animals.

Fobbing's population during the three centuries or so before 1800 had possibly hovered between 150 and 250 inhabitants, occupying less than 50 or so farmsteadings and cottages. Parson Andrew Agnew had informed his bishop of "about fourty" families within his cure during November, 1723. In comparison with other parishes surrounding it upon the Thames, the place was of middling size. Folk were mobile, and its parish registers echoed a quite normal south-eastern condition – that there was no remarkable continuity here of any surname. The Woods and Dooes appear as the only survivors in a group of inhabitants' names that appears first among the 1539 baptisms, but which has vanished from the record by the period of the Hearth Tax assessment in the 1660s. Such surface checks of course, do not take into account an endurance of the same genetic lines via females of constantly altering surname, but dispersal of persons by migration was nevertheless very much a factor, even though it often involved shifts to places not far off. People like the prosperous Tylfords, Bells and other early Tudor name groups, held property across the boundaries with next-door Corringham and might at times dissolve from the Fobbing record, only to reappear a mile or two off.

Only occasionally do we see sufficiently these cross-parish links, so learning where families moved *from*, or whence they departed. When John James, an East Tilbury husbandman, prepared his will there during March 1643, he showed himself by chance remark to be one of the Fobbing Jameses, a clan which had married-in at St. Michael's with other farming copyholders like the Kents (in

---

33 *Fobbing Churchwardens' Accounts and Rates, 1739-1841.* Microfilm E.C.L. Grays CR18636.

1572 and 1609) and the Sansams and Boones even earlier. With him in the parish to which he had migrated was a servant man called Henry Dore, whom we can fairly assume to be another Fobbing native – one of the Dores of Dry Street. In such surmise, uncommoness of surname can be of real assistance. The unusually branded Charvells of Fobbing, mentioned elsewhere as mid 17th century occupiers of Hawkesbury farm, seem to have had earlier origins at Dunton, where a daughter of John Charvell had been baptised during 1545. They are recorded, too, at Little Warley from 1600 onward. Migration to Vange and Fobbing seems in this family instance, to have come about because both Dunton and the minor Warley were parishes possessing detached marshes near Shellhaven which may have provided tenancies for younger generations.[34]

Of 87 Fobbing household heads questioned on the night of 30th March 1851, a mere 15 were to declare that they had been born within the parish.[35] No public railway had so far reached this district: it relied still largely upon highways of the medieval age in its communications, and yet a slightly greater percentage of these Fobbing people clearly hailed from locations *right beyond* the county borders. As for the remainder – 56 heads – they had been comers-in from other Essex villages, 5, 10, or 20 miles around either as children or during adult years. This picture of movement was probably little different to that of earlier centuries, as indeed Fobbing's burial registers occasionally indicate in their random way: Richard Walker "a devonshire man", in 1544, "a Londoner" called Allum (1567) or "Mr. John Gwin a Welch gentleman", who had died in Fobbing during the fall of 1615. Even back into the medieval age, the place had acquired its foreign settlers, for among numerous lowland aliens allowed into Essex from the new duchy of Phillip II of France, had come Gilbert Godfray, born at Busshe in Brabant and given licence in 1436 to "inhabit the realm peaceably" as a Fobbing parishioner.[36]

Defoe's statement relating to the 1720s, that "not one half of the inhabitants are natives", was near true of this whole Thameside neighbourhood. His further observation, that there must generally be a considerable number of stranger-women entering each community from time to time (arriving from parishes further inland) seems also to be worthy of consideration. One marshland male, the author had heard it jested during the early 18th century, "had had about a dozen and half of wives", rapidly losing each to those "fogs and damps" which prevailed

---

[34] *The Story of the Land that Fanns,* L. F. Thompson, 1957, discussed what he called "Feud in Fobbing" concerning Edward Charvell during the 1650s and an entry *"Sunday 9. Novemb 1657 the Concubine of Edward Charvill was buried."*; a daughter of Charvell married John Drywood, of the armigerous family, of Dunton; Heralds' Visitations, Essex, 1634 p. 390.

[35] P.R.O. Home Office HO 107/1773.

[36] P.R.O. Calendar of Patent Rolls, April, 1436. H.M.S.O.

everywhere along this marsh-edge country.[37] *Anopheles maculipennis atroparvus* was probably the general cause, a wetland mosquito that inflicted its (often fatal) malarial fever and though Defoe's informant, he acknowledged, "fibbed a little" there exists sufficient register inference to indicate certain of Fobbing's males as quite adept in the theatre of wedlock. Three or four legitimate wives might be nearer the usual, but this lowish count pertains to men who themselves might not have reached extensive life spans. Christopher Ford, a labourer who in 1588 had been acquitted of stealing (with a confederate) household things – a hatchet and a hoard of cheeses – was to marry at Fobbing church at least three brides through a dozen years, Humphrey Collett just as many through the 14 years up to 1636.

But these were doorstep incidents. Some ubiquitous blades wed far across the parishes, and even at lax city of London churches, so that a true account of their wife-totals may never be traced. Jacob Samuel the Fobbing wheelwright, who married at Holy Trinity, Minories, in October 1689 was one such. He seems to have enjoyed a double-wedding ceremony there, along with his neighbour, the hoyman Sam Hopkins. The following May, their town blacksmith Richard Upton, would stand at this same distant altar alongside Ann Plant, another Fobbing inhabitant.

If the "ague" dispatched to a considerable extent these changing sexual partners, so did the peril of giving birth. One finds the dual burials of mother and child, as was the case with Alice (Alse) Crosse and her infant William "ye same day c yeare" (1544) or the death of a woman shortly after giving birth, like Margaret Duke, who survived her baby Judith only 12 days in 1595. Occasionally maternity is particularised as the reason for a death. Mary, the wife of "Mr. Martin Masters Shopkeeper of ffobbinge," had "died in Child bed" during January 1637 and the same cause was noted at the burial of Agnes, wife of Thomas Dennis in the spring of 1643.

For the survivor, of either sex, re-attachment was desirable for the upbringing of a young orphaned family, or for plain everyday survival and doubtless various well-domesticated widows sought to tempt helpless males from unnecessary notions of pursuing inexperienced girls from further afield. Three years seems to have been overlong on widowhood's ledge for Elizabeth Larrick, whose spouse had died in 1635. With the filldyke days of early 1638, she would christen her base borne infant, calling the lad after a village widower (Richard Cherbourne) "begotten as she saith by him". Following the Cromwellian protectorate, the first Fobbing weddings were all of women who had buried previous partners, their new bridegrooms, in two cases, apparently single men. Paul Desamoe, a foreigner, "took Widdow Croude to Wife" in the harvest of 1662,

[37] *A Tour through the Whole Island of Great Britain,* D. Defoe, 1724 (Everyman edition, 1966).

while a Rayleigh widower, "tooke Widdow Lister" the February following. In most instances these happy ladies were already pregnant at the ceremony, as some swiftly ensuing baptisms admit. The more lighthearted sexual atmosphere after Charles' restoration was perhaps already sending ripples into the countryside of puritan Essex.

Defoe's keen eye had noted, too, how within these saltings districts "you seldom meet with very ancient people among the poor", while the touring Arthur Young as the 18th century advanced would remark upon pot-bellied children and the sallow complexions of its adult inhabitants. Not only malaria, but smallpox and rat-borne plague were among the constant reapers. Contact deaths are suggested with frequency in the burial registers, typified at the passing of yeoman Christopher Friday in 1607, whose will of 30th May had shown him to be "weak" and followed the decease (only a month previously) of James Evans a "servant to goodman friday". During September 1624 a daughter of a parishioner surnamed Felix had died, to be sequelled a mere two days after her funeral with the note: "There was a fellow lay at ffelixes, was buried". Felix himself would also be dead within the same quarter of that year.

Occasionally, fuller than ordinary details of domestic ties seem to imply fairly strongly that the registering clerk *knew* deaths to be connected. Research among wills may add further credibility to the suspicion of contagious disease. During November 1636, a half dozen Fobbing persons died; a total equal to the whole parish burials in the previous twelvemonth. Among them had been "Goodwife Sarles mother to (Goodman) Cootes wife ..." who would be buried upon 12th November. Two days later, George Harker, a village carpenter and "Soiourner at Goodman Cootes" had gone to the grave.[38] In a memorandum of his intended will, Harker is noted as using the words "that if he did dye of that sicknes", proving some malady had affected him as early as the 2nd of the month. Witness to that document had been the husbandman William Coote himself, who had been present with his wife Ann to hear Harker's feeble utterances. Now "sicke in bodye", the informant Coote would dictate his own will upon the 24th, to be earthed before the month's end, though his wife seems to have escaped the dreadful fate of her companions.[39]

During the last major London plague period, a separate page had been set aside in Fobbing's register – as if in expectation of worse to come – for those "Buried since the 20 January" (1666) and listing 14 dead, some of them now pathetically anonymous: "Snowes wife" or "Stephenses daughters child".

---

[38] One who sojourned, or stayed temporarily.

[39] Actually *"Goodwife Sarles mother to Goodwife Cootes wife ... was buried on the 12th of November"* but plainly an error of gender.

Contagion respected no rank, but the badly housed and undernourished naturally suffered the worst casualties, their cameo pictures unfolding across the register's greasy vellum:

November 1638	*"A poore man that died in Ralph Grubs barne"*
February 1641	*"A girl that dyed in Alexanders barne"*
July 1661	*"A poor boy, a beggar, his name unknowen buried at the Parish charge".*

To Edward Alexander's premises in the first green swell of April 1641 had come another visitor, "an unknowne travailinge woman that gathered scurvey grasse ...". Possibly a gipsy, she had been delivered of a baby that was to die "assoone almost as borne". Gerrard, the Tudor herbalist, had long before found the important medicinal herb mentioned here along the Thames shores, and until the substitution of citrus fruits, scurvy-grass would provide a preventative treatment against scorbutic complaints aboard most oceangoing vessels. Fobbing's saltmarshes were evidently being combed for the plant by seasonal gatherers, for late in 1636 another female had been here at this same lonely task. Sheltering, as so many casual workers must have done, in local agricultural buildings, she "died sodainely in Nordons barne", so that the parish officers had been at a loss to learn her name or usual place of abode.[40]

Data upon health and disease are generally only sparsely available within the parish registers; not until 1813 would even the age of any deceased person regularly feature and to ecclesiastical officialdom the *medical* cause of death was of no consequence at all. An occasional garrulous entry might however, inform of some out of the ordinary physical aspect, or allude to a particularly violent path of demise: 1649 "Tho: Guy sonn of Tho: Guy c Mary ... who was deaf dumbe c Lame was buried ..." or, three centuries on, the killing of a Prittlewell itinerant at Fobbing who toppled to his death from a waggonload of hay at Oil Mill farm. Even more swift seemed the plummet of Edmund Kent during the apple season of 1680, who "fell of a tree & dyed". Kent was to be upstaged in his exit only by the ultimate flash which saw Thomas Ives of Fobbing "killed by lightning" during September, 1743.

Medical practitioners and midwives arose from within each community and not until the high Georgian years would parishes begin to hire at an annual fee some saddle-borne physician of the wider district, to attend their poor. Those with

[40] *Fobbing burial registers 1539-1654:* 4th November, 1636 *"A woman that came to gather Scurvie grasse ...".*

more than basic skills were seldom required, though with August 1768 Fobbing's officers had outlayed a guinea for a surgeon, "for opining of ye Bodye of Young Willows". Whether the child was dead does not appear, but no appropriate burial is registered at this period.[41] Orsett's overseers had seemingly arranged for parish service with a surgeon by late August 1801, when they had paid a villager "Going to fobben for the Docter". Possibly he had been Fobbing's Samuel Shuttleworth, for during 1807 Orsett's medical contract had been with someone of this name (though identified as "of Stanford" at the time).

What barbarous scenes had taken place under the roof of John Coleman of Fobbing when the wife of a man called Haies (from Bowers Gifford) died there "at Surgery" in 1641, few may wish to contemplate. Insensibility by means of alcohol appears a common salve. Where a case looked hopeful, the parish overseers as years progressed might approve a visit to one of the city infirmaries, a service charged to the poor-rate, despite heavy costs. Though her ailment is unspecified, Dame Roberts had been accompanied from Fobbing by one of her parish officers to hospitalisation at St. Thomas' as the roads improved with April 1746, a journey so sluggish it necessitated an overnight stay somewhere "Att the In." A steady horse for the patient had set the parish back half a crown. Mrs. Roberts appears to have remained away nearly 3 months at Fobbing's expense, before being discharged. William Hawkins, a relatively young fellow whose headstone alongside the churchyard wall tells of his death at Guy's hospital during 1876, had known at least the comparative ease of rail travel. For the very poorest by this time, Orsett's infirmary provided some basic cot facilities, though even from here paupers might be sent onward to more specialised centres – as in October 1840 when Edward Lewsey of Fobbing is recorded being discharged from King's College hospital "incurable", Orsett's master of the workhouse being directed by his Board of Guardians to fetch him thither, presumably to live out his few remaining days. He was still however, with King's the following April.[42]

Many inhabitants nevertheless continued to rely wholly or randomly upon native cure-mongers and doubtless the celebrated Joan Bell had been more village homeopathist than malevolent hag. Another of her clan, the widowed Mary Bell had clearly become a healing woman some while afterward, for during January 1697 Bell was to prosecute John Digby and James Read, Fobbing's current churchwardens, claiming want of payment after medical assistance to a parish bastard child recently born.[43] Others sought solace from pain in a simple pot and throughout the countryside it was entirely usual to find decent overseers granting allocations of fortifying wine to pensioners in need of a tonic. William Kie (a

[41] *Fobbing Churchwardens' Accounts and Rates,* 1739-1841. Microfilm E.C.L. 18636.

[42] *Poor Law in Orsett,* 1826-1845, K. Malt, 1973 (Typescript) E.C.L. Grays.

[43] E.R.O. Q/SR 491.13.

'make himself dronke...'

Dutchman?) whom magistrates sent before Fobbing's parson in 1639 to make public apology for a nuisance, would claim "an ague which he hath a long time", adding that he had been advised "to make himselfe dronke and haply might forget himselfe".[44]

With the late winter of 1801, Britain's first census had shown just over 300 dwellers within Fobbing parish. By 1901 that figure was easily doubled as, from 1875, petroleum wharves were established at Shellhaven – to be followed within twenty five years by Kynoch's explosives factory upon marshland close by at Borley farm. Aided from mid 1901 by a light railway passenger service to Fobbing Road, Corringham, many factory workers now sought upland lodgings close to convivial pubs, churches or the social *Institute* which had been founded at Fobbing in the mid 90s. Fields edging the High Road had begun to infill by this, the Victorian twilight. 1881 would see builder William Payne's semi-detached *Bay Cottages,* 1882 his *Avenue Cottages* – a longer terrace row – going up behind them.[45] A small Wesleyan chapel was tucked into the same site for the old queen's jubilee year. Just as the Boer War drew to its conclusion came more terrace rows, at *Mill Cottages*; fourteen no-nonsense three bedroom homes in yellow stock brick,[46] all in the shadow of a rotting wooden smock mill and among the first lucky new places to get their water from a communal standpipe at the rear. Again the distant seaside town had wrought its influence upon rural Thameside, for the Southend Water Company was at this period (1902) sinking deep pumping wells at several points westward to Fobbing with benefits recently undreamed for many habitations along the way.[47]

Mill cottages

There had naturally for generations been fierce contentions over access to sources of fresh water and doubtless, at remote periods, mere ditches or ponds like that which touched the roadside below Wheelers house, must have been in regular demand. During September 1612 one Phillip Brown, "a maker of welles" had died in the parish, while in 1755 tenants of the manor were said to have had "time out

[44] *The Romance of Thameside Taverns,* G. Morgan, 1963 p. 27.

[45] Bay Cotts. TQ78.7167.8419, Avenue Cotts. TQ78.7162.8412.

[46] Mill Cotts. TQ78.7159.8450.

[47] *The Water Supply of Essex,* H.M.S.O. 1916 and *The Water Supply of... Essex,* E.R. Vol. 16, 1907.

of mind" used by right "a certain Publick Well lying near ... the Sign of the Ship". That autumn John England, a prosperous local farming figure, had hindered access by setting up a paling and stile, causing more than a little commotion among cottagers along the street. Presumably an open winch-and-rope affair, this well had stood on the highway waste or verge, as probably did another supply-head a way uphill, mentioned in 1810 as "the Parish Pump" and described as adjacent to "Pump Lane", apparently close to the present Rectory-house garden's south western corner, abutting the Vineyard.

An iron patten-hoop, dug from Probus Hall yard and used through later Georgian times to keep women's feet clear of street-mire and water, reminds of the kind of footwear once so frequently seen at every parish well. Plainly, human beings would always squabble while contending for the pump handle, or in hauling their clanging pails to distant back doors. *"She has been a nuisance for ten years"*, complained Elizabeth Miles, of Mill Cottages, to the Grays bench as late as 1927 after being struck (she claimed) violently on the head by troublesome neighbour, Emily Hills. Hills, it would be alleged, had tried to stop poor Lizzie getting along a narrow pathway from the cottagers' shared standpipe as she carried her brimming bucket away. There was a cross summons for assault.[48]

Though earth-closet lavatories and lamp oil prevailed in Fobbing far into the age of aviation, clean piped water had been a giant boon of the young century. Earlier in this same year, 1927, a daring American, Charles Lindbergh, had been visible, making along the line of hills over Tilbury in his streamlined Ryan monoplane, *Spirit of St. Louis*. The world was arriving from outside, closing in. By now Fobbing's villagers were growing dependent on what Kelly's directory described from 1922 as "a daily service of motor omnibuses" connecting them with Stanford's Tuesday market or with Grays, both picture-house towns where female hearts could throb for the sinuous Valentino and lads rejoice beneath the flickering image of redheaded Clara Bow (*Paramount's* stunning "*It* Girl"). The technically minded tinkered with cat's whisker sets; built their own glossy-valved wireless receivers at home from easy-to-assemble kits. Instantaneous news crackled outward from the masts of the metropolis into Fobbing's parlours and the sane sanctuaries of back garden sheds.

[48] G.T.G. 23rd November, 1927.

Iron patten-hoop, Probus Hall

Less sophisticated pleasures were still enjoyed nevertheless and with mid 1928 the recreation ground, rented annually for some years till then, would be officially purchased by the Parish Council and opened amidst much activity and fun by Nicholas Anphilogoff J.P., a Russian of Greek descent and noted oil industrialist.[49] The great man's comments were disturbing, yet doubtless optimistically meant and hinted at the future preciousness of this four acres of green space. He foresaw surrounding horizons of chimney pots. Fobbing's uplands, he assured, would, in the not so distant future, be *"teeming with houses"*.

Happy with their home plot, the village scouts decided not to go away to camp that season: they'd give the money instead to their ex-army chaplain hero, the Rev. Ernest Gardner, M.C., for his current enthusiasm – the church tower restoration fund. No sense in letting the old thing tumble down now, of all times: not if the mightily well-informed Mr. Anphilogoff had said a town was shortly going to arrive.

The medieval market space

[49] G.T.G. 16th June and E.R. Vol. 49, 1940 (obituary).

4. TREASONING MEN

Sir Thomas Boleyn

Following the de Camvills, who had established early in the 13th century a market and trading fair for Fobbing but who, by 1281, were to find their lands confiscated to the crown for debts,[1] the manor had been absorbed amidst the vast estates of Humphry de Bohun earl of Hereford, Essex and Northampton, High Constable of England. It was so held of the monarch by Humphry at the time of his death in 1298 and, nearly a century on, at the period of the Peasants' Revolt, its lands and tenements were still with this immensely powerful family, the 7th earl (another Humphry) having died during 1372 and his widow the countess Joan de Bohun remaining in possession of Fobbing throughout the insurrection and its aftermath.[2]

There were no males to inherit and thus de Bohun's co-heirs would be his two daughters; Eleanor (who married Thomas of Woodstock, junior son of Edward III) and her younger sister, Mary. She was to become the first wife of king Henry IV and thereby mother of the royal Harry, victor of Agincourt. By that period – in the early 15th century – this coveted empire of manors had descended to a de Bohun grand-daughter, Ann, wife of Edmund earl of Stafford and, during May 1421 the lady Stafford was to agree to a partition of her inheritance into two equal parts, of which (as grandson himself of Humphry, the 7th earl de Bohun) her royal master Henry V would have choice of lands.[3]

It was this division which sets the scene of land ownership as it would prevail through the bloody decades of the closing medieval century for now the de Bohun half-portion (which alone maintained her as "the greatest English heiress" of the age) passed into the family of the Staffords. It represented a huge agglomeration of territories, comprising Brecknock Castle, its forest and other estates within Wales, the castle of Huntingdon, a mass of lands known as the Court and Honour of Hereford, the fee of the earl of Northampton, other estates in Buckinghamshire and a dozen scattered Essex possessions including those of Writtle, Hatfield and its forest on the county's westward border, Ramsden, Asheldham, Chignal, Hallingbury and Fobbing itself. Extensive though they might be, these instruments of wealth and political sway were but a newly grafted wand upon the far mightier landstock of Humphry, earl of Stafford, who by

1 P.R.O. Calendar of Close Rolls (1279-88) H.M.S.O.

2 P.R.O. Inquisitions Post Mortem, Vol. 13, 1372, H.M.S.O.

3 P.R.O. Calendar of Patent Rolls, 12th July, 1421, H.M.S.O.

Arms of de Bohun

mid-century was arguably the wealthiest magnate throughout the realm of England. Among his domains were the Kentish estates that included Penshurst, taken from the fallen duke of Gloucester after his arrest in 1447.

Born in 1402, Humphry had been the son of Edmund (killed in the battle of Shrewsbury) and so came to the earldom as a year old infant. Before reaching manhood, he was to see service in France (1420-21) being knighted there by Henry V. During 1429 he would be raised to the Order of the Garter, the newly created dukedom of Buckingham becoming his in September 1444. A half-dozen years later he was to negotiate (in vain) to make terms with the insurgents of Cade's Kentish Rebellion, an episode tailored by Shakespeare to show Humphry at Southwark[4] boldly confronting the rebel companies after their bloody progress up Fish Street and through St. Magnus' corner, promising the royal pardon to such as should desert their traitorous leader and align under his own banner. Jack Cade's subsequent flight induces Buckingham's command:

> *... go some, and follow him:*
> *and he that brings his head unto the king*
> *shall have a thousand crowns for his reward.*

Buckingham was subsequently to serve as one of the commissioners at Rochester castle for the trial of certain rebels and is recorded in 1458 as having accompanied Henry VI's queen, Margaret of Anjou, at London for the historic though inconsequential "love-day" between the rival houses of Lancaster and York. Shortly afterward, hostilities between the red rose and the white again escalated into slaughter, this time upon the field of Northampton and it was beside the king's tent at that battle, on 10th July, 1460, that Buckingham was slain by Kentish soldiers of the duke of York.

The 1st duke of Buckingham had married Ann, daughter of Ralph Neville of Westmorland, a widow who held Fobbing, among other estates, for her dowry.[5] She in due course re-married, to Sir Walter Blount, Lord Mountjoy, while a young grandchild of Humphry and this Ann – Henry Stafford – would be elevated to the title of 2nd duke of Buckingham not many years after the king's capture at Northampton (during the coronation celebrations of Elizabeth Woodville, the widowed lady Grey and queen to Edward IV) in May, 1465. Elizabeth Woodville had obtained custody of this youngster as her royal ward, quickly betrothing him to her sister (Catherine) one of the several Woodvilles for whom strategic political marriages were to be arranged. But it was to the cause of Richard of Gloucester that the duke of Buckingham attached himself as

4 *King Henry VI Pt. II*, W. Shakespeare, Act 4, Sc. 8.

5 P.R.O. Calendar of Patent Rolls, 9th April, 1461, H.M.S.O.

Badge of de Bohun

opportunity befell. With the death of Edward IV and the murder of the two royal children in the Tower during the spring of 1483, Buckingham's place was foremost in the regard of his newly proclaimed monarch, Richard III. The bard's play makes much of the crookbacked usurper's gratitude as he ascends to his precarious throne, turning to Buckingham with the thought: *"Thus high, by thy advice And thy assistance, is King Richard seated ..."*.[6]

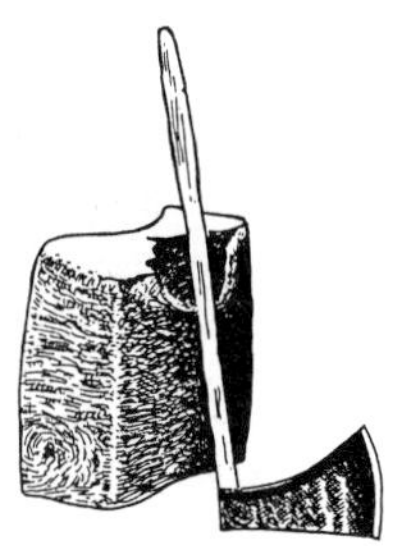

At the subsequent coronation, Buckingham's retinue was said to have "outshone all in magnificence" his horse-cloths embroidered of gold in the burning cartwheel badge and the livery of his retainers wrought with the Stafford knot.[7] In Westminster Abbey it would be he who bore the king's train, acknowledged now as Lord High Constable, the ancient hereditary office of his ancestors the de Bohuns, whose crown-held estates were assured to be returned to the Stafford line in completeness. It was to this jealousy over lost de Bohun lands that Shakespeare again referred in *Richard III*, with the spurning of Buckingham's plea as he begins his slide from the king's favour:

My Lord, I claim the gift, my due by promise
For which your honour and your faith is pawned,

and to which the hunched monarch answers, with dreadful portent:

Thou troublest me; I am not in the vein.[8]

Henry Stafford's course was to hasten for the safety of his family castle of Brecknock, from there to raise a Welsh army in support of the exiled Lancastrian claimant, Harry Tudor, earl of Richmond to whom he had written in September 1483 inviting him to sail for England. In Richard's eyes, his sometime closest ally had become "the most untrue creature living ... there never was falser traitor ...", a price of £1,000 being set upon his head. Buckingham's rebellion dissolved however before the new claimant could effect a landing, the renegade being discovered and captured whilst hiding, it was rumoured, "in a poor hut", from where he was to be brought to trial and beheaded at the market place in Salisbury in November 1483.

---

6 *King Richard III*, W. Shakespeare, Act 4, Sc. 2.

7 General discussion of the de Bohuns and Staffords is based throughout this chapter upon D.N.B. See also *The Staffords, Earls of Stafford and dukes of Buckingham,* 1394-1521, Carole Rawcliffe, 1978.

8 *King Richard III*, W. Shakespeare, Act 4, Sc. 2.

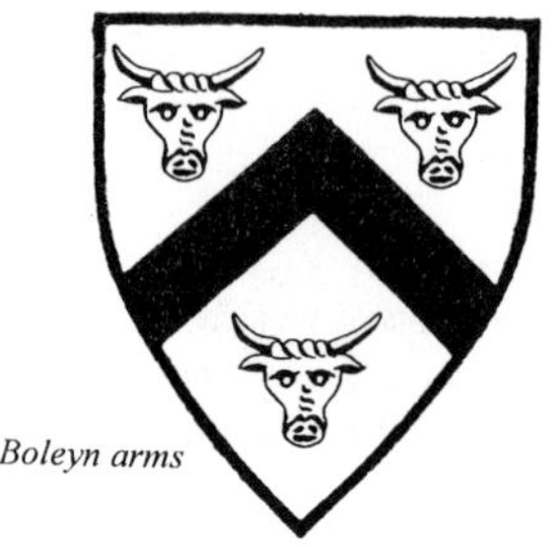
Boleyn arms

Less than two years afterward, victorious Richmond gained the crown of England as Henry VII on Bosworth field, to establish the Tudor dynasty. In consideration of the late duke of Buckingham's unfortunate sacrifice to Henry's cause, his widowed duchess was to retain the vast estates of her late husband. Within a short while she remarried, to Jasper Tudor, the king's uncle, earl of Pembroke and duke of Bedford, while, late in 1485 her young son's right to inherit the dukedom of Buckingham would be given royal approval. This Edward Stafford had been born (in Brecknock) during 1478, being about five years of age at the time of his father's fall from grace. He was dubbed knight of the Garter at the age of nineteen and during the autumn of 1501 was to be sent by Henry VII to meet Catherine, daughter of Ferdinand of Aragon, upon her coming into the realm to marry the ill-fated prince Arthur. She would wed on his death her brother in law, Henry VIII, in 1509, the year in which Edward Stafford, duke of Buckingham, obtained patent to the office of Lord High Constable of England. With 1521, however, the suspicions of his monarch would see Buckingham committed to the Tower "through the artifices of Cardinal Wolsey", says Morant, and ostensibly for having listened to prophecies of king Henry's death, as well as patently toying with notions of his own right of succession to the throne. Thus the 3rd duke of Buckingham suffered an identical exit to his parent, being beheaded for high treason at Tower Hill, 17th May 1521. His corpse was buried inside the Church of Austin Friars, London.

The descent of the manor of Fobbing Hall[9] had passed with these few noble families from de Camvill to de Bohun, to the Staffords who from the mid 15th century had been created dukes of Buckingham, and back (in confiscation) to the crown under Henry VIII. Less than a year after the 3rd duke's execution, on 24th April 1522, the king would grant Fobbing to a gentleman of comparatively modest male ancestry, though grandson upon his mother's side of the earl of Ormonde.[10] This was Thomas Boleyn, one of those loyal henchmen who had served recently upon a special commission for London and Kent which had found the indictment against the treasoning duke of Buckingham. In 1522 also, Boleyn held the office of treasurer of the royal household and was to be given greater estates near Tonbridge in Kent.[11] He was raised to noble rank as viscount Rochford (Essex) in 1525, while the earldom of Wiltshire and of Ormonde were to follow (1529).

---

9 History of the County of Essex, unpublished notes 1700-1730, William Holman, E.R.O. D/YI.

10 D.N.B. Thomas Boleyn, earl of Wilts. Rochford manor, a former de Bohun possession, had been granted to Thomas, earl of Ormonde, who died there, 1515. His dau. Margaret became wife of Sir Wm. Boleyn (Bullen) of Blickling in Norfolk.

11 P.R.O. Calendar of Patent Rolls, 1522, H.M.S.O.

"There can be little doubt", observes his biographer, "that not only his elevation to the peerage, but several earlier tokens of royal favour ... were due to the fascination his daughter had begun to exercise over the King ...".

Anne Boleyn, "lady of the damson eyes" would become Henry's second wife upon the annulment of his marriage to Catherine of Aragon, in 1533. Because of her particular endurance as a folk heroine, Anne's fictional associations with Essex are several, including imagined childhood visits to Fobbing and the eventual burial of her butchered remains here. Born c.1502, she was already a woman, however, by the period of her father's acquisition of Fobbing, while his own interest here was doubtless one of financial kind alone, though Thomas Boleyn's evident concern with the improvement of Rochford Hall manor may have diverted him upon occasions to survey this satellite nook along the coastward highway to the Kentish ferrying points.

Morant's history names Anne's brother, George Boleyn duke of Wiltshire, as holding the manor and advowson of Fobbing during the early 1530s and this may well be the case.[12] For in July 1531 he was joined with his father in the stewardship of Rayleigh, together with certain "other offices in Essex" and would be created Lord Rochford during February 1533. He predeceased his father by nearly two years, being arrested during the spring of 1536 over sundry alleged acts of high treason and of incest with his sister, queen Anne. Two days later, he and four other of Anne's supposed paramours came to their deaths upon the Tower Hill block, the queen's own execution being deferred till the 19th.

Thomas Boleyn died at Hever, his Kentish home, during March 1539, the crown thereafter retaining Fobbing and its advowson through the later Henrican years, from whence they passed, not to Edward VI, but to his half sister the princess Mary,[13] though evidently specific assets were to be leased out to particular officials for their profit. An agreement of 11th March, 1541 had made over to Clement Smyth, Remembrancer of the Exchequer, valuable marshes within the lordship of Fobbing, together with its windmilling concern, all of which by early December 1557 would be leased anew to John Steward for twenty five years,[14] the lessee to keep all in repair and to have sufficient "housebote", or timber and underwood products from the estate, for so doing.[15] A few days only before queen Mary's death in November 1558, the same "divers marshes and a windmill late of Edward, duke of Buckingham, attainted for high treason", were to be made over to George Tyrell esquire, one of the gentlemen ushers in ordinary of

[12] *History of the County of Essex,* P. Morant, 1763.

[13] P.R.O. Calendar of Patent Rolls, 17th May, 1548, H.M.S.O.

[14] P.R.O. Calendar of State Papers Domestic, 1541, H.M.S.O.

[15] P.R.O. Calendar of Patent Rolls, 4th December, 1557, H.M.S.O.

Tyrell crest and knots

the Privy Chamber. Tyrell was to relinquish his present house of Syon in Middlesex and the office of Steward and bailiff of the manor of Isleworth in exchange for the grant of these Fobbing properties, together with title to the manor lordship "and all the lands and liberties belonging" to Fobbing Hall.[16]

The Tyrells of this region were an eminent catholic clan whose genealogy is extensively recorded, though George Tyrell's own descent is not made clear. An inquisition upon the decease of one Humphrey Tyrell of Little Warley Hall in May, 1507 indicates long standing connections in a number of grazing properties including *Slepers* farmstead and *Longhouse* manor in Chadwell, *Inglondes* (Englands) at Childerditch and the pastoral fen called Strincocks in Orsett, while at Fobbing both Wadwyk marsh and grounds called "le Castell" had been held by fealty and a rent of the late infamous Buckingham. Upon the ferny upland ridge around Dry Street and edging Hawkesbury's clays, another Stafford estate farm called *Lesons* (Leesons) had been held by Humphrey Tyrell at the time of decease – some four hundred acres in extent and ranging over the parishes of Fobbing, East Lee and Langdon Hill. All of these would pass (1507) to his twenty four years old son (Sir) John Tyrell, by whose will of February, 1541 Fobbing was to be named as one of those dozen churches (including Chadwell, Orsett and Childerditch) at which his "monthes mynde" should be kept "in dirige and masse for my soule", with a feast in bread, cheese and drink for their parishioners.

Between 1498 and 1516 the Tyrell name moreover had occurred as tenants of quite modest pieces belonging to the abbess of Barking, called Heggemans and Barnfield, situated about Hawkesbury's slopes and Sir John's will would refer to a daughter Mary Tyrell, who had been "sometyme a nonne" of that monastery. To her, he was to bequeath a finger ring "with a safier that my wife hath in keping", some bed furnishings and five marks of money.[17] This period (1541) had proved a traumatic one, since only a year or so previously Barking's great nunnery had been dissolved and its Hawkesbury farmlands confiscated, Mary Tyrell being among those thirty revered but redundant ladies to whom a pension had been allocated by the crown from November, 1539.[18]

George Tyrell finds retrospective mention a little later in the will of John Fowlar of Malardes Green, Romford, proven during the summer of 1568 and referring to "George Tirell esquire and Joan his wife" having granted as lords of Fobbing (at their Court Baron of 14th April 1561) the power to Fowlar to dispose of by will his copyhold estate there; property

[16] P.R.O. Calendar of Patent Rolls, 4th November, 1558, H.M.S.O.

[17] E.A.S. Vol. III, p. 92 *Ancient Wills*, Sir John Tyrell of Little Warley.

[18] A previous Maria Tyrell had been prioress at Barking in 1503, under Elizabeth Green, abbess.

Seal of Barking Abbey

which comprised the eight acre Mill Field and another couple of acres called Mill Hill, though Fowlar apparently possessed some freehold premises also prior to their disposal in February 1564.

A fine of 1565-66 determines Fobbing and other wider estates in East and West Tilbury (the whole worth 60 shillings in rents) to be with Richard Tyrell, Esquire, in the event of whose death they are to revert to Robert, son of George, "with further remainder to Queen Elizabeth". These two appear to be brothers; by 1570-71 Robert, "son and heir" of George and Joan Tyrell quitclaiming the estate jointly with his parents to Thomas Fanshawe.[19] Other properties, the whole with

Grazing verges, Dry Street

Fobbing totalling over one hundred messuages and gardens, ranged by this time as far as Bulphan, Runwell and Wickford. Within a century, the crown was to sell off Fobbing's demesne lands, the manor lordship becoming virtually a nominal title only and, as the antiquarian William Holman revealed early in the 18th century, its courts would thereafter be "kept at Fobbing Hall by courtesy, not of right."

With pleasant verdant prospects over the distant river-curve of Tilbury where St. Cedd had established his first Christian minster amongst the eastern Saxons, Hawkesbury manor had for several centuries been now in Benedictine hands. It was a relatively small estate, probably of only 105 acres or so and (apart from one marshland dairy-wick) was bordered by ancient lanes – the winding Billericay highway and "Dreystrete", which led by ways of field maple and forest ash up to Langdon – the long hill climb. This latter must have been a notoriously miry route and the Lady Abbess' court was to refer during 1455 to the lane's flooding because of an unscoured ditch upon the Hawkesbury side next "Hawkins elme", bringing annoyance to such "people of the lord King" as passed in this

[19] Feet of Fines for Essex, Vol. V, 1547-1580, ed. M. Fitch, 1991.

direction.[20] Again in 1459 the "ladys ditch" was to stir complaint so that Robert Sprever, cultivating these Benedictine lands, would be threatened with a considerable fine of 6s. 8d. upon failure to clear its flow. We know the yeoman Sprever of Fobbing from another earlier source, for upon 29th November 1451 he had been denounced for failing to obey a summons touching his debt to a pair of London businessmen – a girdler and a mercer – for £7. 0s. 0d.[21] Sprever's memory seems to have endured long in *Sprivens Hall* (alias Prosbus Hall) a farm centred in the village street, for his agricultural activities were widespread in these medieval years.

Barking Abbey's manors had embraced all the inland pastoral fens of Bulphan and the lighter creekhead soils of Mucking, the latter well within Hawkesbury's fair-weather sight. Both of these, and Hawkesbury with them, were to be granted a few years after the dismantling in 1539, to another ecclesiastical body which had already long possessed the well timbered manor of West Lee upon Fobbing's high flank – the Dean and Chapter of St. Paul's in London. Upon Hawkesbury's bestowal to the cathedral (1544) it had been straightway leased, together with the ex-Cistercian manor of *Byggynge* at Chadwell and a dairy pasture described as "Lambert Marshe in Fobbyng" to one John Trigges,[22] apparently something of a political opportunist since, before dissolution, he had served the mitred abbess of Barking as her "clerk of the household".[23] This "Lambert" may however be a clerical misreading for "Landsend" which features in other Hawkesbury leases (1521 and 1561) and which lingered as a local marsh name even into the Victorian age as part of the adjacent Corringham levels.[24] By the mid 17th century, it had acquired also the alternative of *"Hawkesbury hook"*, a fresh marsh with salterns abutting upon Holehaven inlet and having a creek wall to southward. That name must refer to the hooked bend of the main tideway here into Fobbing creek and its twenty five or so acres represented a large portion of the overall Hawkesbury manor grounds – whose oak rimmed fieldscape could be distantly seen as a bold north western horizon from its pasture grounds.

During 1649 Hawkesbury manor had been transferred from its short-term lessee, the Rev. Charles Pitfill, to a new name – that of Samuel Moyer Esq., a son of Lawrence Moyer who many years later would serve as a sheriff of Essex (1698).[25] Plainly in Pitfill's day – he had held lease from St.Paul's canons since June 1636 – there existed

---

20 *When Basildon was Farms and Fields,* J. Payne, 1967.

21 P.R.O. Calendar of Patent Rolls, 29th November, 1451.

22 P.R.O. Calendar of State Papers Domestic, 1544.

23 *A History of Barking Abbey,* S. Lethulier, undated c.1750.

24 O.S. 1" to mile, 1843-44.

25 John Heathcote papers: list of leases 1498-1831, C.R.O. Hunts.

R.B.

Hawkesbury

covenants of tenure which harked back to far earlier times, perhaps even to the protestant takeover. A couple of "good ffatt Capons" were to be delivered yearly "tenn Days before Easter" to the cathedral's agent, for example, while the lessee was to receive sufficient wood or timber for repairs to his estate and to its implements, in *cartbote* and *harrowbote*, as well as having bote of fuel for the house. That homestead, the "Mansion Place", was to retain its use as the venue for meetings of Hawkesbury's Court Baron and the Leet Court of St. Paul's – "if the Lord so please".[26]

As to this house with its farming buildings alongside, we shall note it in a further chapter. Adjacent, stood "two Garden plotts" and a small orchard, while skirting all this over the brownish clays and hill-summit sands, were eleven enclosures of arable and pasture all averaging less than seven acres in size. Their names in the mid 17th century are likely to have been already antique: the steep "Hanging Hills", a grazing ground called Meaden hole (Marten Hole?) the Bush field, Black Lands, Small Meals and "ffenney ffield", atop the brook which rilled down the parish boundary line. Though seemingly a compact farm, Hawkesbury was still, in the 1640s and after, rented off piecemeal as had long been the case. During 1454, John Peers had been elected to collect the rents of the lady abbess and in 1458 is found accused of allowing the "ruinous house in his bond tenure called Fullers" to go unrepaired. Long after, in 1598, upon the succession of Robert Breton, these premises of Fullers are described as 35 acres in extent. Another of the Hawkesbury copyholds was the ten acre *Heggemans* mentioned earlier. Cranes (9 acres) and Barleys, a thirty-two acre unit on Dry Street were the others, the latter having reasonably acquired its name from connections with Dorothy Barlee, Barking's last abbess.[27] Totalling about eighty-five upland acres, these small steadings had possibly in the earlier (monastic) period possessed their own cottages.

The nunnery's court rolls for Hawkesbury are scant, being combined with those of its wealthier estate of Bulphan. They make clear, however, that even as early as the 1320s Hawkesbury was being leased as a whole concern, its farmer

---

[26] *A Survey of the Mannor of Hawksbury* ... 1649. C.R.O. Hunts. CON4/2/7/1B.

[27] Dorothy Barlee, last abbess, had also leased Mucking's farmlands to the Tyrell enterprise. She may have been of the family which produced sheriffs of Essex and Herts. in 1466 and 1523.

A prioress

then renting off to other customary tenants of his manor, who were obliged to reap eleven acres of corn at harvest for his benefit "the lessee receiving also from the lady (abbess) in aid of the farm two quarters of wheat and five ... of oats" as well as being given draught animals worth 13s. 4d. and one ox of the same value. On the other hand, Hawkesbury's lessee must upkeep all things upon the abbey's property and, at the end of his term, ensure that ten acres were left "well fallowed and ready for sowing".[28]

A medieval manor was not perforce one continuous grouping of properties, even if sometimes it happened by historical chance to be so. Fobbing Hall manor included some appurtenances in Stanford le Hope (Ivy Walls) and another far flung unit of less than fifteen acres at Chadwell about seven miles off, which came to be pretentiously called the "manor" of Ingelby.[29] In 1502 an inquisition upon the death of William Ingelby, knight, naming his successor as John, aged 24 years and upward, would declare it to be held of the duke of Buckingham "as of his manor of Fobbing."[30] As early as 1364 their lawyer ancestor Thomas de Ingelby – one of a Yorkshire family, lords of Ripley – had acquired this tiny Chadwell estate, while in 1487 the Ingelbys are noted as rendering "one sparrow-hawk yearly" to the Stafford lord of Fobbing.[31] The precise location of this "lost" Chadwell manor remains untraced.

Conversely, there were several more sizeable Fobbing estates which belonged neither to the Hall nor to Hawkesbury. One of these was an appendage of Hassenbrook Hall at Stanford le Hope, to which manor Vange was also by custom attached. At Easter, 1446, William Wetenhale, alderman and grocer of London, was to purchase the main interest in a messuage, eighty acres of land and forty of marsh "in the towns of Fobbing and Fange atte Noke" by service to the king of "one silver needle of the price of 2d.". His wife Alice and a couple of further descendants each called William Wetenhall would succeed to Hassenbrook hall and its extraneous Fobbing parcels by 1468.[32] In view of the proximity of those grounds to Vange, it is conceivable that Whitehall farm, the title of which has never been adequately explained, derives from a vocal delivery of the "Wetenhale" surname.[33]

---

[28] Manor of Hawkesbury, Court Rolls 1329-1357 E.R.O. D/DSg M1 (typescript abstract).

[29] Feet of Fines for Essex, Vol. 4, 1423-1547 ed. P. Reaney and M. Fitch.

[30] P.R.O. Inquisitions Post Mortem, 4th December, 1502, H.M.S.O.

[31] E.A.S. Vol. 24, Archaeological Notes, H. C. Andrews.

[32] P.R.O. Calendar of Close Rolls, 2nd March 1468, H.M.S.O.

[33] Whitehall farm TQ78.7153.8550 (a modern house covers the site).

Edging Holehaven a half mile above the Thames, lay near two hundred acres of Fobbing marsh which would one day be called Borley farm.[34] Attached by title, were a couple of outlying fields at Vange, one of which had been referred to as "Boliffe" as early as 1596, the whole estate belonging to a charitable institution in the city of Norwich known as the Hospital of St. Giles, which drew part of its revenue from Fobbing rents. Founded by bishop Walter de Suffield (1245-57) Norwich Hospital was not only an infirmary possessing some 30 beds for poor sufferers, where "three or four sisters of honest life and of fifty years of age" attended them, but was the residence also of bishops of the diocese themselves. It was conducted under a clerkly "master" until the dissolution of ecclesiastical "spitals", upon 6th March 1547, its ownership and management becoming transferred by the crown to the mayor and commonalty of Norwich. Thereafter it would be known as *"God's House"* or "the House of the poor in Holm Street", though generally Fobbing's officials referred to Borley's lands as of "the Great Hospital, Norwich".[35]

Either for being too charitable, or, like Barking's brides of Christ, too saintly; or as the treacherous Staffords proved, too dangerously ambitious – for one reason or another the holders of almost every corner of Fobbing parish had at some time been struck by confiscation of their property to the king's hand. All property was integrally still the monarch's and could be swept back into crown possession at will, as every man within this region needed no telling. The wealthy rebel William Gildeborne, who had gone with the Great Rebellion, had held certain lands from Joan de Bohun, countess of Hereford, in Fobbing before his execution outside Chelmsford on 5th July 1381. Later in that year a court (at Horndon on the Hill) would list his Fobbing estate[36] – a messuage and part share of "Wadewyk" marsh, another great marsh called "Northope" with a house and curtilage (courtyard or fold yard)[37] upon it and an acre piece by St. Michael's churchyard. A valuation list had detailed movable goods that included over seventy sheep; his whole assets worth £49. 5s. 3d., a mighty fortune in medieval terms. All were confiscated for treason and granted instead to William Geddyng, possibly a crown official; just as Robert Chekeryng, who in 1392 received the property of the rebel Thomas Baker, is identified as "servant of the avenary", a provisioner for the royal horses in oats.[38]

---

[34] Borley farm TQ78.7477.8315.

[35] N.R.O. Norwich City Records 24 (a) 1521-28; 25d (1488-1799). Map MF.NRO 335/1.

[36] P.R.O. Calendar of Inquisition Post Mortem, 1381, H.M.S.O.

[37] Subsequently the Oil Mill farm lands.

[38] P.R.O. Calendar of Patent Rolls, 26th March, 1392, H.M.S.O.

Compared to Gildeborne, Thomas Baker (Bakere) unquestionably prime promoter of the peasants' uprising from Fobbing and in its further stages a "principal leader" of the rebels within Barstable hundred, had only modest land – assets of 6s. 8d. yearly at most.[39] The grant to Robert Chekeryng dates from 26th March 1392 and was made "for life for services rendered without reward", a date by which the excommunicated criminal had been dead ten years or more. Even a century after the rebellion, several old confiscations of outlaws' possessions, such as a Billericay cottage "with a curtilage and 5 acres ... of Thomas Plomer[40] which are in the Kings hand" would be made over to Robert Castell, an officer of the Exchequer. They included Bakerscroft in Fobbing and the document recalls, even in a time that was over the threshold of the Tudor dynasty, that this man had been "drawn and hanged for high treason".

Within a further generation, the 3rd duke of Buckingham's own acts of high treason were to make all of the Fobbing Hall farmlands and profits confiscate, and so thereafter both Gildeborne's and Thomas Baker's became grouped once more with them. From the time of Thomas Boleyn's taking up of the king's grant of lordship (1522) an ordinary process of his assigning periodic leases for these sometime rebel properties began. On 24th September 1562, George Munnes, a parishioner of substance, later referred to as "gentleman", was to marry Mary Tylford at Fobbing. She was of an influential village group of which we shall hear more, and to her at his death in 1583 was to go "Pecottes Croft alias Bakers Croft with all other my lands in Fobbing ...", passing thereafter into his cousin Bingham's family. Few by now credibly knew or cared just where the rebel captain's hedgelined oblong of soil had been. The seasonal plough shuffled its myriads of scarred oval pebbles; harsh estuarine winds redistributed its fawn dust. Old men forgot.

Fobbing Hall

[39] Gildeborne's properties were held of the countess of Hereford, Baker's from the Abbey of Waltham and the same countess (see Chapter 1). No other Fobbing ground is known to have belonged to Waltham and administrationally it may have been grouped with Abbotts Hall manor, Stanford le Hope.

[40] P.R.O. Calendar of Patent Rolls, 1392, H.M.S.O. Beheaded 26th June, 1381. His relict, Katherine Plomer, alias Leders, is also mentioned.

5. "YOKE FELLOWS IN ARMS ..."

Royal politics and internal strife had, as we have considered, proved powerful agents in the affairs of Fobbing's landholding class, but neither could such a maritime spot remain untouched by the wider and ongoing conflict between England and her neighbours. In 1377, an edict telling of "those perils which may suddenly happen" should hostile French vessels sweep into Thames, had commanded beacons to be set up all along the Kent shore, at Sheppey, Hoo and Gravesend and within Essex upon unlocated sites in Tilbury, and at Fobbing.[1]

Though intermittent phases of calm saw a decline of watchfulness, the upkeep of these defensive stations generally prevailed over several future centuries and the choice of Fobbing as a key visual point is worthy of examination. Modern concepts tend to focus upon some kind of blaze being prepared within an iron brazier-frame, affixed perhaps upon church towers, though such a small bright fire in daylight and with even the best meteorological visibility, would surely fail to be observed even over moderate distances.[2] A certain advantage of height gained by church tops such as Fobbing's had to be balanced against the various difficulties of raising fuel supplies by block and pulley for such an operation and of handy storage, not only involving firewood, but combustible liquids also. An outright danger of fire upon a roofing was evident to all.

Yet the indications from later scare-periods like that of the Armada in 1588, would argue that open hill summit positions had really been the ones favoured, at least in rural places such as this, spots where beacons of more purposeful scale could be prepared,[3] with men in readiness under canvas alongside and capable of quite sophisticated control, so as to achieve maximum effect by day or by night. In most weathers between sunrise and dusk, columns of smoke were far more useful than flame, and the addition of substances such as turpentine or pitch, damp cornstubble or leaves, might deepen or lighten the signal in contrast to the sky's mien. The sheer volumes of smoke required would suggest that popularly

---

1 *East Tilbury Fortifications and Coalhouse Fort,* I. G. Sparkes, PAN. Vol. 7, 1962.

2 Wakering certainly used its tower, however, as did Dengie: *The Beacon System in Surrey,* F. Kitchen, S.A.S. Vol. 78, 1987.

3 *Elizabeth's Armada Camp,* R. Bingley, PAN. 29, 1988.

imagined "beacon" turrets such as that of St. Michael's would not generally do, though they may well have served as subsidiary sentinel points in times of alarm. Hawkesbury's crown stood twice the height of Fobbing's church battlements and in all reason it was there that the signal-fires had been mounted, a point supported by the later siting (1639) of the war-beacon for this district somewhat further west along the same ridge, at Langdon Hill.

Juveniles who had witnessed the peasant uprising would, in maturity, have become well attuned to continuing elements of crisis: the Scots, Welsh, French, were an encircling peril by which Essex was not to be left untouched. In 1412 the sundry negotiations with France under an ailing and neurotic Henry IV would bring one swift and effective campaign into Anjou and Orleans, marching with lances and long English bows under Thomas, duke of Clarence, third grandchild of Fobbing's de Bohun lord. A commission of 18th April was to authorise the impressment of 230 mariners for Clarence's fleet of war, most by far from the prosperous woolports of Harwich and Ipswich, others out of Cliffe and Gravesend, but a full thirty to be taken in "Stanvorde and Fobbynge" – all bound away for nearly a half-year's naval service, but doubtless like their combatant passengers, with no promise of wages beyond the first couple of months – save "what the lords of France should pay" as ransoms to the victorious English.[4] In the event, there would be no returning so soon, for Clarence was to continue on into Gascony, to winter in Bordeaux, relinquishing his campaign only upon news of the death of his royal parent, in March 1413. He sailed homeward laden with treasures from the duke of Berry's private chapel at Bourges, including a great gold crucifix and a reliquary which contained one of the iron nails from the true Cross. For Fobbing's lowly sailors there may have been adequate reward in coin from an expedition so endowed with booty; at worst the compensation of red Gascon wines and foreign demoiselles.

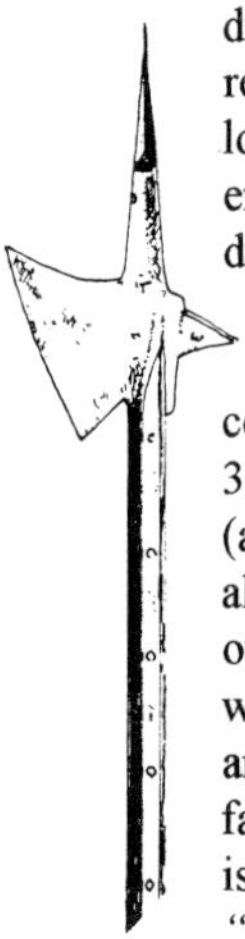

None of these pressed mariners' names has endured, but in contrast complete lists survive of Barstable's "able" contingent for the emergency of 1538-39, mustered before Sir Clement Harleston and John Poyntz of North Ockendon (at Billericay) in readiness for a presumed French invasion into the Thames, where already Henry VIII's blockhouse forts were under development. As with every other Essex parish, Fobbing males between the ages of sixteen years and sixty, would be summoned to the drum and grouped either as archers or billmen – those armed with the black-iron bill, or halbert blade. Three members of the Sansom family and William Spender, who is recorded as possessing his own "harnes", that is, a set of plate-armour, were each noted to be past a reasonable age for service: *"Aged men not Able".* Heading that infirm quartet, Christopher Sansom had retained from bygone times a bill, a salet (or riveted metal helmet) his throat plate,

4 Calendar of Patent Rolls, Vol. 4 (1408-1413) H.M.S.O. p. 427.

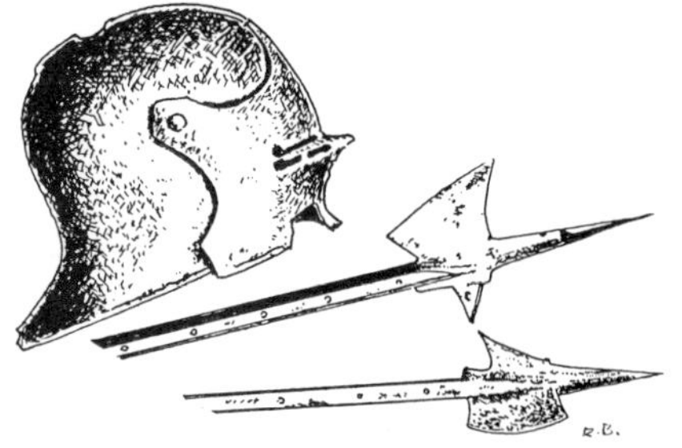

called a gorget and "splynte", armour – for protecting just the thighs and arms. Such antiquated equipment as these elders could offer might have seen service even in the Plantagenet wars.[5]

Of Fobbing's 32 active men, far less than half could provide adequate gear of war. A mere five bows would be found amongst the thirteen parishioners nominated to be archers, only one, John Stnerde (Stonard) boasting "a shefe" (of arrows) to marry to his string. Among the nineteen-strong band of billmen, William Tylford alone wore a harness of armour, but owned no bill. John Peers flaunted a bill and a dagger, William Sansom the elder, a bill and sword, while Richard Egott came to the assembly with a display of black bill, salet headpiece and a dagger upon his hip.[6]

The full identification of Fobbing's mature males mustered under this Commission of Array, provides a welcome glimpse of our resident families at the very moment when, in 1539, Fobbing's parish registers began to be kept; straightway disconcerting, because of the discrepancies which arise. Allowing that about 25 of these men were of sexually active age, we might anticipate their surnames featuring large within the marriage and baptismal record. There appear, however, many grooms and fathers who were not among these rustic warriors: over the decade beginning in 1538, well over a half of the register's male adults fail to match with the military muster list. Evidently, as we suggest elsewhere, Fobbing brides selected (or were sought) from well beyond their own doorsteps.[7] However such a totalling of active men is valuable, suggesting a constant population of perhaps 150 to 200 inhabitants overall during the mid sixteenth century, a little less than the "fourty" families that were to be reported here nearly two centuries on. It would be reasonable to conceive that of this Tudor population, about 5 households inhabited the various marsh dairy holdings, another 10 the northward farms and cottages about Dry Street and Hawkesbury, with above 20 families dwelling in the area of Fobbing's main village settlement, up to the windmill and Whitehall.

The later medieval and Tudor landscape was one from which sufficient images linger for us to trace an overall character; its highways and vestiges of ancient hedged fields still delineate the skeleton at least, even if all but a fragment

5 P.R.O. Commission of Array, Fobbing, E101/59/8.

6 Sansom; Tylford: Joyce Shaw has demonstrated from the 1524 Lay Subsidy how these two clans in their various households controlled the mass of village wealth; *The Survival of the Fittest: Living Standards in the Parish of Fobbing, Essex, in the later Middle Ages,* J. Shaw (Dissertation) 1995.

7 Fobbing Parish Registers: all subsequent register book references throughout this chapter will be traceable by date in E.R.O. D/P414.

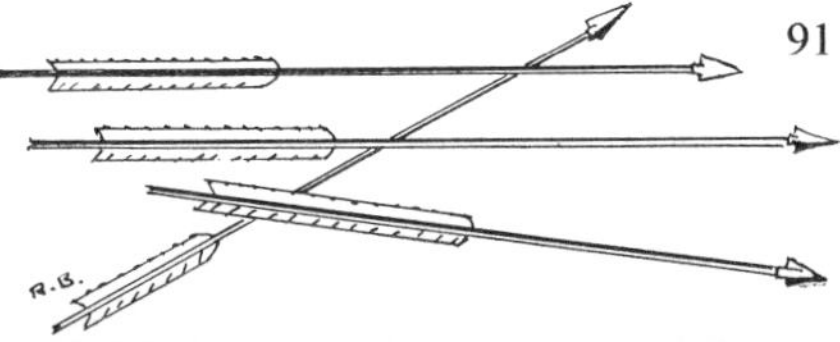

of its farmstead groups have been erased. Barns (structured specially intended to house the intake of the cereal harvest and for its processing by threshing with the flail) represent only a vague feature of the medieval scene and not all farms by any means even possessed such a building. Among the legal transfers of property they do not generally find separate mention until well into the Tudor age. At Fobbing the first is in a fine of 1542, in which William Garlande and his wife dispose of a small acreage of cornland and pasture, a couple of dwellings and gardens with a barn nearby. Several other references in the later part of that century all attach to either very minor acreages of arable, or none. John Sansome's "barn", made over with a tenement to John Trotter during 1594, had been associated merely with an orchard and 2 acres of pasture, and since there is a hint that this was really a carpenter's premises, may represent some kind of woodstore or workshop rather than an agricultural structure.[8]

Hardly a corn barn, cattle house or stable from this period may have remained within the parish, even by the close of the 18th century, so great was to be the Stuart and Georgian farmyard renewal programme. But we may conceive something of their scheme; arranged in courtyard plan around stenchy wintering yards trodden by the beasts, and generally low structures of timber frame and much grey reed thatch. Those tarred weatherboard claddings which we think to be of timeless usage, were hardly known, if at all, in this period, the mainposts and intervening studwork of oak or elm being infilled with buffish clay daub, fibrous with field straw, vetches or even occasional pebbles and puddled onto panels of riven oak laths or halved wands cut from hedgerow and copse.

Thick daub facings, limewashed at whiles, extended to domestic buildings also, even to good yeomen's homes, the earliest of which remaining locally is a boxframe cottage latterly called Copeland cottage,[9] a main street dwelling which has been recently dated upon carpentry evidence to around the 1370s. Carbon deposits upon its oak roof frame indicate the commonplace arrangement of a spacious open-hearthed hall that had no upper-flooring, except in this instance at the northern bay of the house. There, a parlour occupied the groundspace with a solar chamber above it. Access up and down had been perhaps by simple stepladder. Two splendid crownposts of octagonal section provided both a main structural and a decorative feature to the roof-frame within its hall area, their bases set upon massive moulded tiebeams of oak spanning the room's width. These in turn were supported upon curved timber braces locked into each of the plain jowled wallposts. Copeland's total floorspace was comfortably large, about 48 feet long by 18 feet wide, with two arched entrance doors of 40 inches width

---

8 *Feet of Fines for Essex*, Vol. IV, 1423-1547, ed. P. Reaney and M. Fitch, 1964. *Feet of Fines for Essex,* Vol. IV, 1581-1603, ed. P. Reaney and M. Fitch, 1993.

9 Copeland cottage TQ78.7167.8418. The name seems to be recent, but its origin is not understood.

facing each other across its main room.[10] They gave exit to both the street and a westward curtilage or yard. All floors were of earth, but were doubtless made pleasant with clean marsh reeds and kept regularly sanded.

Later the house, like almost all other substantial dwellings of pre-Tudor date, would undergo important remodelling; firstly around the mid 16th century when an entire upper flooring was to be inserted to give extra chambers together with a massive brick chimney stack (7 feet by 8 feet at base) which provided ground floor "inglenook" fire hearths facing into the central and northward rooms. With the 18th and 19th centuries almost all Essex boxframe houses underwent a social downgrading to farm labourers' accommodation, resulting in partitioning into small cottage units. Copeland cottage knew such conversion in late Georgian years, at which time, regrettably, packed earth (of major archaeological interest) within the medieval hall and parlour would be dug away to facilitate the laying of boarded floors. A minor excavation in the early 1990s was, however, able to examine beneath the parlour, indicating that the original ground cill had been set onto the ploughsoil of the 14th century fields, upon the surface of which lay a Scandinavian grey schist hone (a sharpening stone) of early medieval date.

Fobbing Hall and other village houses nowadays known as Fishers, Wheelers and the *White Lion* show a rather different and more complex "hall with crosswing(s)" type of arrangement which replaced Copeland's simple rectangular style of design.[11] This "H" plan concept developed with the 15th century and locally one would expect to find the upper crosswing stories "jettied", or overhanging to some degree the ground rooms – a practice which possibly developed in cities where landspace was at a premium. It gave, however, a little extra roominess at first floor level, where often at this period wealthier occupants elected mainly to dwell. Only the head-high jetties of Fishers are still evident, convenient even today to the passer-by in a sudden rain shower.[12] At the *White Lion* public house and Fobbing Hall, later (especially Georgian) desires to extend ground floor spaces have caused these picturesque overhangs to be tidied away under flush plastered frontages.

Fishers

[10] I am at variance with some earlier mentioners of this building who described it as a hall-house that had formerly possessed crosswings.

[11] Fobbing Hall TQ78.7199.8388, Fishers farm TQ78.7162.8438.

[12] *Local Farm Buildings: Some conversions and demolitions; Fishers Farm, Fobbing,* PAN. Vol. 21, R. Bingley, 1977-78.

Homes like the currently called "Peasants' Croft" (formerly Hillcrest Cotts.) edging the Vineyard, have been radically misdated, for although past alterations would either remove or obscure under black weatherboarding their key features, some remaining closely-set interior studwork upon one (north) wall provides a clue to a Tudor or even earlier frame.[13] This is corroborated by its above-roof chimney work which matches well in its lower courses the diagnostic bricktypes seen at Copeland cottage and Fobbing Hall. An almost identical weatherboarded group was Black Cottages[14] further down Wharf Road – demolished only in the early 1970s, but never internally surveyed by competent eyes. It was considered to be pre-Victorian labourers' housing, but from evidence gathered too late, can be filed as another example of a disguised dwelling of the late medieval or Tudor phase. So undoubtedly was the tenement row of Hill Cottages[15] – with massive internal stack – which stood atop Lion Hill into the 1930s, being removed, it is said, to facilitate the turning of motor buses. By the foot of Bells Hill, a cottage block now lost, but sufficiently attractive to have been captured on various Edwardian picture-postcards, indicates another boxframe house of post-medieval importance which stood within Fobbing – merely yards off the Vange parish boundary. To lose such dwellings is a cultural tragedy, but even to recognise *what* they were in retrospect is important in helping us to sketch out the map of settlement as it stood during the Tudor century or earlier.

Clay tiles had been manufactured within the locality far back into the medieval period and Fobbing Hall, Wheelers, even the older Copeland dwelling were probably so roofed from the start. Brickmaking developed rather later and does not feature through Thameside Essex until the first Elizabethan years. But straightway the eagerness of affluent householders to employ it, is observed, for the innovation of internal hearths and stacks was a great one. Mess, and smoky chambers, and the old peril of uncontained flames were now all at last overcome. Spacious hearthstone ingles under whose timber lintels a whole family might gather for warmth, became a common feature of the yeoman-class home. A culinary aspect of the stack was its built-in side oven and handy "salt-keep" – a small niche at the fireside where this precious commodity, used extensively in vegetable and meat preservation, might be kept in dry condition. The chimney flue itself became both curing space and larder, where smoked bacons or dried fish could be stored at hand, for as yet all hearth fuel was conducive to such processing.

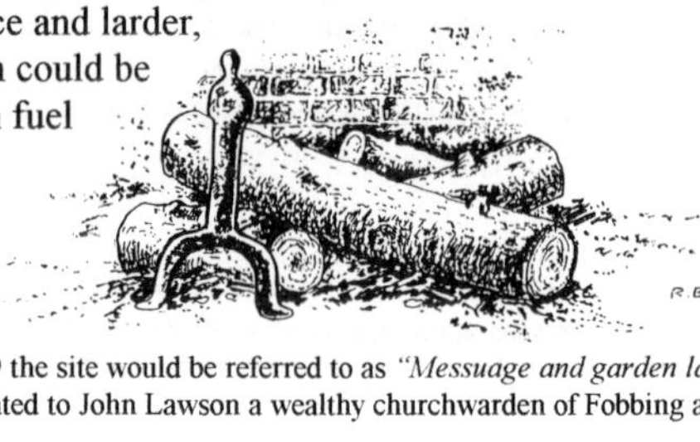

[13] Peasants' Croft TQ78.7184.8387.

[14] Black Cottages TQ78.7190. 8380.

[15] Hill Cottages TQ78.7170.8398. In 1679 the site would be referred to as *"Messuage and garden late the Land of John Seelie ... "* (Celye: related to John Lawson a wealthy churchwarden of Fobbing and resident from late Tudor period).

In time, it became far more feasible to add a large cellar to one's property now that brick had become readily available, and the groundcills of timber barns, and well-shafts made use of this material, too, at an early stage. Indigenous Tudor bricks weathered to a rather dull pink tone. They were made to no standard size, though usually near to a 9" length, and 4¼" wide. They vary in thickness from 1¾" to 2½ inches. Wheelers' diagonal stack,[16] which leans so tipsily above the High Road, the tall range of three flues at the rear of Prosbus Hall, and Fobbing Hall's chimneys, are all of very similar fabric, laid in courses of stretchers with a rather thick and unequal mortar bonding. The *Fishers* farm tudor stacks have been rendered over and so spoiled as a visual means of comparison with other village examples, and the old Black Cottages had (from the historian's viewpoint) received similar mistreatment. At the *White Lion*, an early stack rising aside its south crosswing has unfortunately been restructured with (possibly late 19th century) red brick.

Black cottages

Occasionally, contemporary wills of Fobbing people refer to such homes as we have glimpsed, though almost never can we identify just *which* dwellings are meant. In April 1579, Henry Doe, a yeoman occupying *Hofild* (Hovels)[17] would ensure that his wife "shall have her abode for herself and her two children" (of a previous union) in the farmhouse after his death, "with competent meat and drink". Such provision of shelter was often outlined, in case some inheritor should evict survivors of the family. An Elizabethan parishioner who had occupied Leesons[18] as well as other important holdings over the district, was William Hulke of Fobbing, who would succumb shortly after dictating his will early in March 1572 – perhaps upon the "featherbed in the loft" where (the document suggests) he lay at that poignant hour. Hulke was to leave this desirable item to a daughter, Agnes, together with ten pounds of coin, a cow, household pewter and brass, and a kettle (a cooking cauldron) as well as the guaranteed use of one room in his dwelling, described as "the lower chamber between the doors."[19] In all likelihood then, his hilltop farmhouse was constructed much like the original Copeland, having opposing ground floor doorways leading into the hall. John Hammond, a yeoman who may well have inhabited Fobbing Hall, would bequeath in 1577 to his son Richard not only a farm called Staplers in Stanford-le-Hope but also his

[16] Wheelers House TQ78.7170.8418.

[17] Hovels farmhouse TQ78.7031.8610.

[18] Evidently Leesons, confirmed by burial register of 12th March.

[19] Wills for this parish at E.R.O. begin 1434, though less than half a dozen date from before 1500. Individual serial numbers are not felt to be required: all above are identifiable by surname and date: *Wills at Chelmsford,* Vol. I, (1400-1619) F. G. Emmison, 1957-8.

"copyhold land with a tenement at the quay ..." in Fobbing, while at Michaelmas 1564, a William Hammond and his wife Elizabeth had entered an agreement with Justinian Champneys for a homestall and some 420 acres of upland, fresh and salt marsh in the parish, together with "a free fishpond in Fobbing water", suggesting a tidal trapping system of commercial sort within the main creek area.[20] To Joan his daughter, John Hammond was to leave £20 and a featherbed at her reaching the age of twenty-four, seemingly to be purchased new for her by her eldest brother "out of his farm called Old Hall" (in Corringham) while bedding in the form of a "mattras" would be left by Sarah Smith of Fobbing to her paternal cousin Agnes during 1595. The "saylor" or hoyman John Chrips was to grant his son William two year later, a "halfended bedstead".

If not lavish, domestic furnishings were robust and wrought for several generations of use. Occasionally, as in the household of John Wade – one of those parishoners seen training with his pikestaff about the fields long ago – who had died during the February of 1575, decorative items such as a painted cloth which hung across part of the main hall's interior and another draught proofing drape called "a halling" would be mentioned. There were some chairs, one with a "back" another "with hoops" within Wade's hall, together with two "shelfboards of the largest" and, near to his table, some kind of wooden panelling called a "sealing". A solid table and two trestles to support it, with a plain form for seating, were positioned about the chamber, to which the refinement of a "lockram tablecloth" might be added. This latter would be left to Wade's wife, while a daughter Mary was to receive a single "diaper napkin" amongst other household goods.

William Pittman, buried at St. Michael's churchyard during the fall of 1579, had set aside for his unmarried daughter Elizabeth a similar stout "table and form" with a cupboard and two great chests, of oak and sprucewood, ideal for the keeping of valued clothing or bed linen. Isabel Thornebrowgh (1578) would remember her daughter Phoebe with the bequest of "my wearing linen and my chest." Another chest of imported spruce lay at this time in the home of Richard Boune, a piece inherited from his Hawkesbury farm parent (Boone) earlier in this decade (1572). At Wade's death in 1575 (above) there had been a couple of chests for disposal, one at his bedside, another at its feet.

Two women's wills add to our inventory of Tudor domestic chattels. Joan Spender, after bequeathing in 1544 the modest sum of 4d. "to the holye alter of ... Fobbyng", passed on to her second son Henry one platter and "a candelsticke", while another candlestick, a colander, pewter dish and cooking kettle appeared in the legacy left by Joan, wife of William Bell in 1578. Even if quite richly glazed earthenwares of apple-green and tawny were an everyday feature of most

[20] *Feet of Fines for Essex,* Vol. V, 1547-1580, ed. M. Fitch, 1991.

farmhouses, it is only the more prestigious utensils of metal that find mention in these records, like William Hulke's "best brass pot", his pewter plates, dishes and saucers – the latter pieced out between various offspring. John Wade's brass posnet (small basin) skillets (vessels with legs) and "the other brass pot with the legs sawn off " would be complimented by no less than four "latten candlesticks", that is, of bell metal or bronze. Among the few outdoor hand implements specified were William James' tools, left in February, 1586 to his brother, Miles Boune of Fobbing – 2 axes, 2 bills (for hedging work) and a grass mowing scythe as well as "all my holyday apparel", a pair of "high shoes", and one pair of "low".

Such items of raiment were variously mentioned by male testators, if infrequently with the kind of sartorial detail we should desire. Though Thomas Castle made no will, probate was to be granted during 1590 on the basis of a declaration by some who knew the dead man: "in the presence of Turtulian Bryant (and) Edmund Pettmtann (Pitman?) he did (use) these words followinge Goodman Umffrey I want that you should sell this my Rayment (and) paye my debts as fare as the said Rayment will exstend." Tudor menfolk generally displayed their bodyline from calf to thigh and hosiery items figured in their wills as useful hand-me-downs. Both William Hulke and Philip Frauncis bequeathed sets of hose during the 1570s, the latter granting his father a pair of "close hose and my best jerkin", while to a brother in law called Hare would go the dying man's "best breeches and best short hose". The thoughtful Hulke had allocated to a servant – "Cocker my man" – his "pair of hose and a frize coat", that is, one of coarse woollen cloth, mentioned again in the will of Thomas Gardener of Fobbing during mid-April 1588 in his gift of a "frisse jerkin". Gardener had included also one cloak, the orthodox wear for outdoor journeys, and Christopher Sansom in May 1555 was to remember John Wade, his comrade-at-arms of olden times, leaving

him a valued jerkin and one special garment of rather arresting description, "my vyolet robe". Violet dyes had apparently been familiar in earlier times also, for Alice Spender of Fobbing willed to her daughter in law during 1483 a kirtle of this hue, and a smock, with another violet kirtle (and one of russet) to a woman called Belris (Beatrice?) Bette.[21]

A doublet inherited by Richard Crowe from Thomas Hoode, who had died as the first of autumn's maples coloured his fieldsides in October 1564, was of worsted cloth, while John Pytman would have a doublet also upon his brother's

---

21 *The Survival of the Fittest: Living Standards in the parish of Fobbing, Essex, in the later Middle Ages*, J. Shaw (Dissertation) 1995.

death (1579). "Goodman Burnitt" by the same token was to receive his "best shirt" and another neighbour the dead man's coat. To his sister Thomas Hoode aforementioned would leave four yards of "housewife's cloth". Personal adornment in the form of jewellery finds only scant mention, though the custom of providing commemorative rings appears in the will of Ann, widow of John Roger of Fobbing and daughter of William Hearde, who before Christmas 1584 had provided "my husbands son John a gold ring" with the offer likewise to her sister-in-law (or else 20 shillings).[22] A favoured inhabitant called William Hurte would be remembered by her, too, with a mourning ring as well as the special legacy of a "gold heart". George Munnes had bequeathed to a lawyer relative during June 1580 his "great gold ring of arms", evidently cut with his armorial seal, befitting one who could order his tomb in church to be of "fair marble stone" and upon it "my name graven in brass with the day and year wherein I shall be buried."

The tower of St Michael's which we know today was at this time a rather modern mark upon a landscape where no other architectural structure pronounced itself save the groaning mill, whose dark sails easily overtopped the height of this hillside church.[23] All Tudor windmills were of "post" construction, stabilised at ground by a great buried crosstree of oak from which a central upright arose. Around this was built from some dozen feet above earth, a tall box-shaped house through which its sails were geared to several floor-stages of mechanism, imported Derbyshire mill stones and wooden grain hoppers and a range of further processing machinery.[24] Like all of these workplaces, it had evolved as a property of the manor and had feasibly stood on this site since the medieval age, just at the southward edge of Fobbing's 100 feet contour, a quarter mile upslope of the village.[25] For here both easterly winds from the estuary and prevailing summer southwesterlies could be best harnessed from dual flanks of the village ridge.

Its existence is not hinted however, until the lease of 1541, but thereafter the postmill's historical personnel are fairly frequently detected. A Rettendon widow during 1564 had named her executor as one Thomas Arnold of Fobbing, miller, whose own will happens to survive. Prepared just before Christmas 1566, it contained a worthy list of benefactions to sundry poor Fobbing people whom Arnold knew, desiring also that Martin Kent should "have pasture for his colt till Michaelmas next paying nothing" – presumably upon the mill's surrounding enclosure. Though resident here, where he baptised a daughter Joan during 1564,

---

22 *Wills 1578-1588. Bishop of London's Commissary Court*, F. G. Emmison, E.R.O. 1995.

23 Fobbing windmill TQ78.7148.8455.

24 *Essex Windmills, Millers and Millwrights: The anatomy of a Postmill*, K. G. Farries, Vol. I, 1982, p. 16.

25 *Essex Windmills, Millers and Millwrights: Fobbing*, K. G. Farries, Vol.. IV, 1985, p. 19.

A medieval windmill

Arnold's request that a rector of Great Burstead should "preach at my burial" implies that this tradesman had been a quite recent newcomer to Fobbing. Moreover, during 1575 Joane Jackson of Wickford was to direct in her will that another Great Burstead inhabitant called Harris should "have the lease of the windmill of Fobbing and the letting thereof" though stipulating that some present (unnamed) miller might continue there "for the rest of my years afore any man and shall not pay more than £6 by the year". It seems then that Thomas Arnold's heirs continued to be connected with the milling business for some while.

A windmill's operation was, of course, by no means a one-man task and during the springtime of 1607 a whole trio of Fobbing associates would be described as "miller" in a matter heard at the county sessions. In company with a Horndon clothworker, a miller called John Gudgen would bring his case against Miles Smyth (of Maidstone, bricklayer) and William Johnston – another Fobbing millhand – both of whom would be ordered to keep the peace towards Grace, wife of Nicholas Watson, third miller of the team. Gudgen's own good character was soon to be questioned, however, for not a month later the court would hear how Thomas Ramm, a married parishioner, had taken twenty ewe sheep (allegedly in lieu of some damage owed him) "of John Gudgen of Fobbing miller and wished to drive them into open park" (i.e. to an enclosure). Gudgen's response had been to rescue his livestock and give their drover a sound beating.[26] The outcome is unknown, but doubtless the Justices did not miss the choice rustic drollery of Master Ramm's desire to abduct twenty such creatures.

The John Goodwin to whom, in this same year of 1607, a Fobbing inhabitant called Christopher Friday (his "cousin") had bequeathed a lease of Hawkesbury farm, is plainly our same "Gudgen" of the mill. For in July of the previous year, Goodwin had wed a bride – Marian Dallys – and their child, baptised during 1610 would be registered as a "Gudgein". Elsewhere in the records the surname Goodwin (Goodwyn) is consistent but surely relates to our parish miller, for John Goodwin's will of December 1630 gives that occupation. To Joan, his later wife, he was to leave lands "both free and coppy" in an area near Hawkesbury at Dry Street, John Audley, a neglectful parson about whom we shall learn more, coming to him in his sickness at the millhouse to witness his final

[26] E.R.O. Calendar of Assize Files (1559-1714): all assize file references throughout this chapter will be traceable by year given in the text.

arrangements. Another denizen of the post-mill for a while afterwards would be John Ring, who a confiding line in the register declares: “was buried July ye 11 having been newly married scarse 3 weekes before” (at Stanford, 1636). Seldom more pertinently than for these mealy-coated and industrious men, could the minister have uttered his gravehead obsequy of “dust to dust”.

Some reference to the marsh ground sheep-walks has already been made in a previous chapter and to a slight degree our yeomen’s wills add to this vision of a mixed corn-and-cattle landscape. Livestock was bred without concern for any standards beyond what seemed locally sensible, displaying all the variety of neighbourly interbreeding, in colour, size and form. Of the ungulates, the “great cattle” such as oxen and domestic kine were generally longhorned and so were useful even beyond their intrinsic purposes as draught animals, as milch cows or as producers of beef. Hides, cutler’s bone, blood for pigments such as Prussian blue, and especially horn, used in the manufacture of beaker cups and opaque panels for “lanthorn” windows, were but some of the saleable commodities deriving from the farm beast, animals which tended towards red and black-coated kinds in these times, as the evidence from hair-and-plaster work in the local houses of an early period testifies.

A few wills mention disposal of beasts: Philip Frauncis of Fobbing in the winter of early 1578 had left to his relative “a cow that goeth (grazes) at a spot called Fayers”, adding cautiously “if my wife does not sell them”. There were other cows to be had instead at his farmhouse, should that be the case. Joan Bell’s husband a couple of years previously had left to her “all my cattle and my corn within and without”, that is, both stored in his barn as well as that just spearing the January fields. At Hovels in 1541 the poorly Richard Dowe was to allow his son, Henry, fifteen kine and a bull, together with “all my corne growyng in ffange and holefeld”. Thomas Hoode, buried at St Michael’s upon 5th October 1564 had gifted to Robert, son of John Hoode, four kine (great cattle) and five lambs, while George Munnes in 1580 would put by, till she was of full age, a dozen three-year old ewes and a pair of five-year old “milch beasts” for Bennet Bruer (a great-niece of his liking). They were all somewhat longer in the tooth before Munnes last drew the pleasant beastyard aromas through his nostrils; he died in 1583.

Slightly more full is the detail given by Richard Boune “farmer of Hawksbery” whose burial took place on 19th March, 1572. His wife Catherine Boune was to continue in that farmhouse for five years “from Michaelmas next after my decease, then to depart and have with her 8 kine 20 sheep and 3 horse”. In the event of the lady (who had five children to support from a former marriage) continuing a single widow after this term, the Hawkesbury "mansion house" should remain her abode until the end of its lease from St. Paul's cathedral. Moreover, firewood for her cheer was to be provided, as well as the breeding use of a young bull (for five years) which in due time must be delivered to "Richard my son". To him was also to be given the elder man's "black bullock" at the forthcoming start of the farming year, September 25th.

Death had been busy amongst Fobbing's yeoman this late winter of 1572, striking also William Hulke, whose will hints strongly that the term "kine" extended beyond cows or beefstock, to include working teams of oxen. For his sons Henry and George, after sharing half-and-half in Leesons farm for six years were to separate, Henry Hulke "to depart and have 6 kine and 30 sheep and half the harness thereto pertaining ...". No horses were to be identified in this instance, even though, over at Goldsmith's – another of this prosperous man's farmsteads on Langdon Hill – there had been five horses operating, implying an enterprise there of 200 or so acres.[27] John Hammond's wishes for his son John's inheritance in 1577 were to include a half dozen horses with a cart, to add to what he already had in use over at the marshside property of Old Hall.

From time to time Tudor wills unfold not only connections between human families, but cross-links in the livestock which they own. Two of the above men, Hulke and Doe, referred to wives who had the unusual forename of "Rabage" and plainly, being widowed during 1572, Rabage Hulke[28] had been taken in wedlock once more quite shortly, not least for the handsome dowry of fourteen cattle, sixty sheep and five horses which she would bring from her late husband's hilltop farm of Goldsmiths. Since she was not obliged to relinquish the Langdon Hill lease until 1578 or thereabouts, some of these beasts may well have been still young in the year following when her new husband, Henry Doe, expired. Hence, he assures to her "2 heifers of 3 years old, 1 gelding, 1 mare and a colt which were her own in her widowhood" as well as "all the household stuff and other furniture belonging to husbandry (farming implements) which remaineth and was her own ... and 20 ewes". Rabage had evidently contributed much to the working business during her short while at Hovels.

That "best white gelding" of which George Munnes disposed in his bequest of 1583 to William Bingham "doctor of the laws", who had married the testator's stepchild (Mary Tylford) at Fobbing a decade earlier, was surely no farm-horse, but a good saddle mount for road and country. Other stock, such as fowls and pigs were more seldomly mentioned, though the summertime of 1557 had seen Richard

---

27 William Hulke had also the lease of the extensive Pitsea Hall, left to his sons.

28 Hulke's will indicates her to have been previously the wife of John Ponde of Wickford, husbandman, relative of William Ponde of Langdon Hills.

Lowe devise to his daughter Alys "a rame lambe a ewe lambe c my hogge", while with 1593 a July theft of four pigs from Bulphan by John Baker and George Fawley, both Fobbing labourers, had been alleged.

Forays of rogues beyond their parish bounds combine to illustrate a few other Tudor cases of animal rustling that were dealt with by the assize courts; a drover of Fobbing called Richard Gates would be acquitted of a charge of breaking into the close of Richard Younge of Corringham during August 1593, there to steal twenty-two sheep and lambs of £8 value, while John Hudson (alias Parker) of Chadwell through the year preceding had raided stockfields from Stifford to Horndon, visiting Fobbing in the summer to rid Richard Doo (Doe) of his two cows, worth 60 shillings. Whether by late May 1588 the chances were being whispered of mighty takings in the provisioning racket should the queen's army encamp above Tilbury, who can say? But a pair of Fobbing men – Christopher Ford and John Smyth – were to be charged with carrying off from the dairy store of villager William Nokes some fifty big Essex cheeses. Though the case against both the accused collapsed, someone had benefit of a haul which exceeded in value many weeks' wages for the labouring man.

Those considerable woodlands that had adorned Fobbing's northward countryside at the conquest, were probably all but eradicated by the full medieval years; no more than a few scattered acres could be found upon its Tudor landscape, though each upland farmstead might make worthwhile fellings of tall hedgerow elm and sizeable ash from time to time. An illuminating case of timber theft during 1590 is quoted amongst the collections of F. G. Emmison, elm trees of three Fobbing landholders having been felled and squared ready for removal by a bogus official of the name of Wylson from East Tilbury (perhaps with special inside knowledge from the royal blockhouse there) claiming to be a purveyor of bow-staves to the queen's household. This audacious visitor had even gone so far as to sell off the trees' lops and tops before making ready to depart.[29]

When in 1572 William Hulke had willed "100 oaken boards" to Goodman Hayes of Corringham, they had almost surely been sawn out from timberland beyond Fobbing's edge at Langdon, a resource upon which much of the local woodworking crafts must have heavily relied. A mere two or three village persons may have been constantly employed in the carpentering and cart-building line, folk such as the dimly discerned "Thomas the Sawyer", buried at Fobbing in November 1594 or his contemporary Thomas Boyden, carpenter, who had owned a messuage and garden here – he and his wife, Annys, both dying while the April of 1591 drove its blizzard of blackthorn flowers through the Fobbing hedgerows. The boxframe houses which arose through a broad period of the 1470s to the mid

---

[29] *Elizabethan Life and Disorder,* F. G. Emmison, 1970.

1500s – yeoman class structures such as Fishers and others we have seen – may not have been carpentered initially by village workmen, for houseframing could well involve labour from some ways off. Wheelers especially is suggestive of far-fetched skills, with its curved frontal bracing of plain wealden style. The red-sailed hoys which slid to and from Fobbing manor wharfside, were similarly not the creations of a local trade but were built in yards at Leigh a little downstream, or more distant centres of the shipwrights' craft.

Closely associated with the woodlands in its use of stripped oak bark, was the leather business, which required large quantities of tannic acid for hide-processing tanks. Near the foot of Lion Hill there may have been a penning of the parish boundary stream, used in maintaining a supply of freshwater for this rural industry. A tenement adjacent (on the Corringham side) is identified as "Tannhouse" during 1597, a name which lingered for at least three centuries, while a manor court at Corringham had discussed, in 1507, the unauthorised transfer of a small sheep pasture over to William Heywarde, described as a tanner of Fobbing.[30]

Complete self sufficiency within parish life was no reality and imports from varying distances were the norm, as had been the case for uncounted centuries; in common things such as earthenware pottery, or smithy iron, in much of the people's everyday clothing which derived from sundry market-places, or even the pastor's vellum writing books or Spanish tent wine used in holy communion. Nevertheless local resources *were* tapped to an intense degree, especially by those of the poorer sort. Much attention must have concentrated upon the marshland's abundance of vegetable foodstuffs as well as the great river's wealth of living protein. The fancifully named Turtillian Bryan(t), a literate inhabitant who had married Joan Wade during 1585, was identified in 1606 as a fisherman and many cottagers doubtless took whatever table meals they could from along the foreshore. At Prosbus hall, excavations of plentiful oysters amidst earthenware shards of the 17th century remind of a long predilection for seafoods hereabouts, their shells often finding a secondary purpose for field drains and backyard soakaways. Highly favoured in the medieval economy, eels offered a particularly available diet for those who cared to go with barbed iron spear amongst the ditch reeds. Not only were the levels a wilderness teeming in season with edible fowl and waders, but the skilled netter could take a number of other small species – wheatears, pipits and skylarks, all devoured or sold as pot-meat by the prior countryman. Ready markets for plover eggs, goosefeathers for the bowyer, caged songbirds, or the marketable plumage of kingfisher and the cock ruff were to be found, by which precious pence might be earned in season.

---

30 *The Corringham Chronicle,* J. K. Payne, 1987.

In this age when the consumption of ale, or of beers brewed with the addition of bitter herbs was a universal habit amongst all ages, hop gardens probably existed to some extent in most Essex parishes, declining only with the creeping monopolies of town brewers in the 18th century. Husbandmen operating their own brewhouses at home, cultivated sufficient hops for family needs and for the workpeople's harvesting *largesse*, often along the wet loamy "bottoms" of the parish. Hedgerow survivals of rambling hop bines still appear each summer at Crooked Brook and along Fobbing's other stream edge beneath Lion Hill, though at what exact period they knew pole-cultivation we cannot tell. They occur also at the east Vineyard foot and it is possible that these sandy slopes had been tried for hop-production at some stage after grape cultivation ceased.

The fieldname itself (*le vynyarde*, 1539) may already have been an old-fashioned reference by the Tudor years indicating a medieval vine culture that had flourished during the sunnier climate of Angevin times. As Cobbett pointed out however, "vines may be raised in espalier in a warm situation in any garden on the south side of Warwickshire at the least ... wine made here is very nearly as good as that of France" – a point which clearly rankled back in the 1530s as cross-channel relations strained dramatically and it would be realised that £100,000 yearly in fine gold was draining away to the hands of the French wine industry. "No country robbeth England so much as France", concluded politicians of the period.[31] As a result, a certain amount of fresh interest in the English vine emerged for a while. Whether the Vineyard's south-facing slopes were terraced in familiar continental fashion is debatable: subsequent survey might reveal elements of their profiles, and perhaps postholes also. However, progressive mutilation of the hillside through ignorant "improvement" schemes has already taken place and scant detail may survive for further recording.

Equally debatable despite the fancies of taproom historians, are the names of the parish inns at which the Tudor toper took his ease. Both the *Ship* and the *White Lion* are unrecorded by name for a further century and a half. William Hills, whose will dates from April 1586, had intended chattels for his offspring, though, should they die early, "then I geve ... al the same goodes to the use of the pore ... both in the asspottales in ffobbing and elese wear ...". Here, places of hospitality and shelter rather than infirmaries were meant; inns which provided

[31] "The Agricultural Landscape: Facts and Fashions" in J. Thirsk, *The English Landscape*, Oxford, 1985.

lodging for a resident poor that had no other abode, a system through which publicans well into the Georgian years would supplement their livelihood (through re-imbursement from a poor rate or other charitable source).

The building which nowadays is called the *White Lion*[32] was undoubtedly present throughout the Tudor age however, and was probably one of at least a couple of premises for which John James and John Mott held justices' approval from September 1605, though Mott was to be charged a year or so later as a victualler having no licence to trade. Its heraldic name suggests an early adoption, for which several derivations may equally compete. As a royal badge, it pertains with other symbols especially to Edward IV, who favoured a lion passant guardant, *argent*, royally crowned[33] – usually rendered by sign-painters as white. Through the sisters Woodville (Elizabeth and Catherine) Edward IV's relationship to the Lord of Fobbing (Stafford) was that of brother-in-law and hence indigenous loyalties or military service might logically have led to its adoption as an alehouse emblem. Few published writings upon innsigns have investigated tavern heraldry in terms of their immediate manorial associations and other interpretations of the *White Lion* device are doubtless to be found.

CHIEF OF ANGELS

Medieval or later almshouses barely featured within this region and Fobbing, as we have perceived, was no seat for the kind of paternalistic benevolence which might have fostered them. Nor were there any permanent charities set up for the indigent or sick, though in one case a small but abortive attempt seems to have begun. During March, 1578, Edward Lowe of Vange had expressed a desire that all his lands and tenements within Fobbing and Corringham, whether free or copyheld, should pass to (Margery?) his wife, and then "after her decease, to the poor people of Fobbing for ever ... The Churchwardens ... shall have their letting and pay themselves 3s. 4d. a year for their painstaking". Lowe was to add that a true copy of his will outlining the charity "shall remain in the register book of Fobbing so that the churchwardens may always see ... what they may do." But it seems that here we glimpse the content of a lost memorandum, quilled into the original (destroyed) 1539 parish register, but which never found transfer into the vellum-copy replacement of 1598 which survives today.

---

32 Shards of domestic pottery from the 14th century onward are present at the White Lion site. TQ78.7167.8397.

33 *Boutell's Heraldry,* revised C. W. Scott-Giles, 1950.

'Sick and weak ...'

Prior to the pressure from new protestant statutes, a number of Fobbing wills directed monies to the lighting of St. Michael's high altar, the move after the 1540s being towards granting instead donations to the parish poor. William Batteman, "sick and weak" in May, 1586, was to assure twenty pence "to the reparations of the church of ffobbinge" and, "to the pore of the towne," a sum of 3s. 4d. upon the saint's feast. Richard Lowe (1557) would grant separately "To the church xii d." and a further shilling, for "the pore mens boxe". In only one instance, that of Thomas Hoode, buried at Fobbing during early October 1564, does a list of effects suggest possession of a bible. In this case, Hoode was to leave to Richard, a son of John Hammond, his "Bible of Geneva translation", at that time in the keeping of one Richard Laurens (Lawrence) of Chadwell parish – one of the recently published English versions embellished with figures and verses and remembered, because of its terminology in reference to Adam's apron, as the *"Breeches"* Bible.

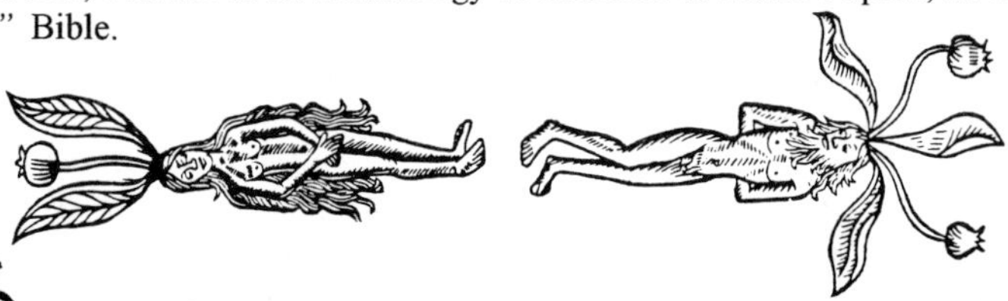

The mere names of the several priests from William Drayton to Laurence Stubs – the last officially catholic incumbent of Fobbing – are almost all that we know of them, and only by relating their terms of ministry to the standing archaeology of the church itself can we advance a few tentative thoughts upon their influences and achievements. What Drayton inherited upon his appointment during 1460 (by gift of Ann, newly widowed countess of Buckingham) was essentially the same edifice in which had worshipped those peasant farmers who had gone in rebellion with the martyred Thomas Baker 80 years before. A remodelled building had been gradually raised through their terrible and turbulent century; it had begun – around the middle of the 1300s – with the swallowing up of its old rounded Norman apse within the scented confines of the priest's new, squared-off chancel. Against its lengthened southward wall, would be created a beautiful arcaded aisle and further chapel,[34] with a square tower (now vanished) of Reigate and Kentish stone upon the southwest.

All of these works would have been at sacrifice to its rector's burying ground and beast pasture – the sunniest and, by Christian tradition, most eligible sector of the graveyard. Under

[34] The dedication of this chapel is untraced: perhaps a de Bohun gift dedicated to St. Martin.

the aisle and south chapel floors must therefore lie the bones of many of Fobbing's pre-Plantagenet community, a village people that had been increasing with more than ordinary vigour over the three centuries since the Norman arrival. In 1086, Fobbing had stood already among the 10 vills of Barstable which possessed the highest density of population (about 189 persons) and by 1377 would show one of the county's most impressive increases (c.338 inhabitants).[35]

In overall groundplan, St. Michael's was, by the latter period, not greatly different in size and arrangement to today, except in its (later re-positioned) tower, the addition of a small timber-framed porch, and a modern vestry room. As its 13th century Purbeck font reminds, not all of the church's beautiful medieval fitments were to be dismantled or disguised with the coming of plainer protestant attitudes. From the 14th and 15th centuries remain, for example, the chancel's elegant stone *sedile*, a recessed seating for the priest's helper during divine service and, alongside, its *piscina*, a sculpted basin with drainage outlet for rinsing of the communion chalice. Other *piscinae* of this period have survived within the south chapel and aisle, indicative of sacred altar positions now forgotten. One other small stone furnishing of catholic installation is a *stoup*, or dip for holy water at the south doorway and dating from the early Tudor phase.[36]

To a casual eye, the outward features of tower and sturdy oaken porch are among the church's most memorable things. They date from someway before 1500; both were probably conceived during the term of George Smyth, who succeeded to Fobbing in October 1494 upon the death of the priest Sampson Alleyn. To both of these men, the living had been gifted by Jasper Tudor, duke of Bedford, uncle of Henry VII and whose marriage to the widowed Catherine, countess of Buckingham, had brought with it the advowson of St. Michael's.[37]

A massive tower of three stages in perpendicular style would now replace its modest earlier counterpart; a great and lengthy endeavour for which some materials would of reason be ransacked from the obsolete fabric. Possibly for years, creekcoming vessels must have offloaded their cargoes of dressed ragstone blocks fetched from the Medway valley, to be dragged as weather favoured by landsledge and labour, uphill to where roped scaffolds of ash or alder wood surrounded the tower's rising masonry. A decade might not be overlong for the completion of this impressive project and many towers were far tardier in their growth. Some East Anglian examples were, indeed *never* finished. It was thought

---

[35] "Richer in land than in Inhabitants: South Essex in the Middle Ages", J. Ward in *An Essex Tribute* ed. K. Neale, 1987.

[36] R.C.H.M. 1922 and updated notes, R. Bingley, 1989-95.

[37] *More about Stifford and its Neighbourhood,* Rev. W. Palin, 1872 (gives succession of Fobbing clergy, though with various errors).

advisable even, not to advance too expeditiously upon any such large building tasks, because lime mortar took so long to reach its final strength and the problems of settling needed careful monitoring. Often, a final joining of nave walls and towerwork was not to be attempted for many years after building schemes had reached conclusion.[38]

By what means all this was financed remains unknown; almost certainly some significant contribution would have been forthcoming from the remote royal uncle and patron, while a local organising of "church ales" must also have assisted – the usual medieval parish merrymakings at which open copper cauldrons of intoxicants were a significant attraction. Surely, too, as was the norm with any ecclesiastical building works, use of travelling proctors journeying abroad to publicise the church's cause, would be made. In all, a realistic portion of funds obtained, must have emanated from the rich grazing of neighbouring marshlands, for as a homespun phrase expressed: *"Where the sheepe hath stood, the land is turned to gold."* As early as the preceding mid-century, Fobbing had been listed with Colchester and Manningtree as a port of shipment for woolbales going from the coastal sheepwalks of Essex and it was fitting that this tall tower of fleece-white should surmount all others visible along the Thames. Yet its very whiteness was deceptive. It could be played upon by the natural elements of light like a screen and when the descending suns of autumn fell beyond London, its western face burned as one great wall of matt rose over the rooftops and surrounding fields.

Its aim was altitude; for Michael, Christian inheritor of the attributes of the banished Mercury, was nothing if not commander of the air, as Durer's woodcut of this same period was to exemplify – the saint's dominion over Satan and his cohorts proceeding out of a great contest ranging through the skies. All across England and France his towers by now dominated dramatic hill positions, often overlooking navigable water or maritime places, for the archangel stood as both warrior and protector, the winged guardian of souls. Thus at Fobbing, a defending company of fearsome demonic stone-masks would glare, with protruding eyes, from high upon Michael's battlements across all quarters of the countryside.[39]

---

[38] *Churches in the Landscape*, R. Morris, 1989.

[39] Grotesque stone-masks: at top stage of tower there are eight, generally now eroded beyond accurate reconstruction. Those on the east are best preserved, but decayed. The illustration is based upon elements of several recorded in varying lights. Also eight smaller masks decorate the turret tower.

Fobbing's roomy two-bay tiled porch was probably wholly of timber in its original design, though nowadays the lower sidewalls are of flint. Its roofing is set upon robust but very plain oak crownposts of cruciform section and its tiebeam braces are simply butted in onto one of the partly dismantled medieval buttresses just above the aisle doorarch. Wedding ceremonies and the religious custom of churching a woman soon after childbirth were commonly events of the porchway before the mid 16th century and this open extension to nave or aisle might serve, too, as a general shelter for the travelling stranger as well as a dry spot for the posting and reading of parochial intelligence. Marriage of couples was not a protracted service in itself and Fobbing's porch must have provided an ample and pleasant space in which to see the normal village ceremony through.

Both catholic advice and common superstition were instrument in the choice of a wedding season during the full medieval period; it was not seemly to marry in Lent, though humanists might reflect how those youthful temptations of each preceding (midyear) hay harvest should render it at times urgently otherwise. A medieval guide to dates for marriage would also exclude December and the first three weeks of May. May figured nevertheless as averagely popular in a mid Tudor sampling from Fobbing, taken through the generation 1539-1568. Strangely, neither January's icicles nor June's hay fevers seemed to make any difference, but it was September and October which accounted by far for the highest totals of weddings – in all likelihood simply because of welcome harvest bonuses reflecting in the couple's economy. December proved especially

Arms of Jasper Tudor

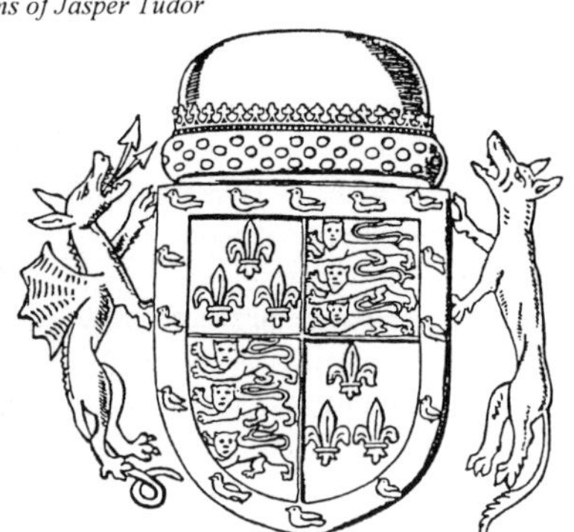

unpopular, March and April entirely non-nuptial. Childless unions were sometimes thought to come about because of a ceremony during a thunderstorm, while a waning moon, even the ebbing tide of Thames, might deter the more diffident maiden from her proposed alliance.

Yet over all this misgiving reigned the ultimate triumph of optimism, deep-cut in oak upon the porchway arch – the bearded, crowned and entirely welcoming countenance of a beaming Christ the King. Beside Him, the dextrous carpenter's blade had wrought another figure, small and strenuous, in mighty tussle with some horrible stub-winged dragon, a beast significantly like that used as an heraldic supporter to the coat of arms of Jasper Tudor, Fobbing's patron. Almost certainly, like the once decorative porch bargeboards that were wrought with more than 30 rose-flowers (as badge of Jasper Tudor's house) all of this wood-sculpture had been brightly painted and gilded for maximum effect. The hero's garb is of the period, with a side-hanging cap of early Tudor fashion. Nearly all localities once favoured their special legends of battles between intrepid males and what – for want of a scientific definition – we will call *"Virgitarian"* serpents. Often, such imaginary monsters were described as "worms" and the example at Fobbing may represent one of these rather than *Satan,* who in popular medieval tradition, had been slain by the sword of the archangel Michael.[40]

Porchway of St. Michael's

40 For example, the famed Lambton "worm" (Durham) or the Brent Pelham dragon (Herts.) see *In Search of Lost Gods: A Guide to British Folklore*, R. Whitlock, 1979. Henham in Essex was briefly famed in a pamphlet by Peter Lillicrap, *The Flying Serpent, or Strange News out of Essex*, 1660.

6. THE VALE OF INTOLERANCE

It is unlikely that any stone wall had enclosed Fobbing's burial acre, even into the 17th century, though at some time the massive displacement of soils that had accrued, together with the incorporation of several thousands of bodies over half a millennium or more, must have required revetment of some sort. Today, one can perceive that the churchyard is a true sepulchral mound, whose turf level lies far above that of the nearby street. As elsewhere, upkeeping a burial ground's boundary was normally the responsibility of sundry parishioners and Emmison's study of Elizabethan misbehaviour touches on the case of one landholder, called Geoffrey Stent, who had attempted to readjust various bushes edging Fobbing's hallowed area, apparently so as to make its hedgeline appear a minister's liability rather than his own.[1] Almost certainly, the eastward skirt of the churchyard was where this felony took place, a part which seems never to have acquired walling.

The individual marking of graveplots was once far less obtrusive than in modern times and though wooden crucifixes are known to have been a feature of pre-Reformation *cemeteria*, the outstanding monument of most sites would have been a plinthed stone communal cross, a dozen or so feet in height and positioned for effect near the south entrance, perhaps overlooking its village market place or street. Few of these "churchyard crosses" were to escape dismantling with the first protestant decades, the greater number being re-utilised elsewhere – not unusually as random building blocks in future renovations of the church itself. At Fobbing the robust array of Kentish ragstone and 17th century red brick which comprises the westward churchyard wall, is supplemented with two larger dressed slabs of white stone, which may well be re-used fabric from the base of a medieval holy cross there.

Multifarious wildflowers and grasses (still to some extent represented) grew across this, the priest's own nutritious acre of gravel meadow and, because it was to his farming detriment to destroy such rich herbage, a fine fell upon anyone who had need to open the earth for burial there. Though of a later date (the mid 17th century) a few receipts at the back of Fobbing's earliest register recall the continued fee for the "breaking up of the Churchyard ground". But the yard's agricultural aspect – a lumpy grass field which united pleasantly with its

---

1 *Elizabethan Life: Morals and the Church Courts,* F. G. Emmison, 1973.

surroundings of wide streetline grazing verges – would be overtaken in time by a more monumental one, expressing the multiple shades of family prestige in its display of bricked table-tombs, or florid, cherub-topped limestone panels, or in simple "headboard" markers of elm, carpentered up in the village workshop for the lesser dead. By 1685 the current parson's disenchantment with clerical life had led to the yard of St Michael's becoming disgracefully overgrown, its fence wanting repair and "Ivey, and Elder, and weeds Rubbish, & bushes" everywhere at hand, plainly no credit to the management of his glebe farm.

It seems reasonable to surmise that 26 acres or so had been granted by some post-Domesday manor lord to establish a glebe farmstead at Fobbing, a modest allocation of lands and by no means a compact one. No marsh grazing had been allowed it. Its farthest enclosures, called "Church Hills" lay a mile off to northward, elm bordered and watered by a small stream that wound on past Brookhouse and Vange edge. West of the sunny Vineyard incline, the priests' land included a piece alongside Fobbing Hill, where until the present century stood Glebe Cottage, whose tangled garden patch is sufficiently productive of 14th century and later pottery to suggest a medieval dwelling plot, not improbably of a relinquished parsonage house.[2] Sturdy strap-handled glazed pitchers speckled in green and sooty cookpots of reddish earthenware proliferate among other finds excavated here by A. Bennett, discoverer of the site.

Perhaps by the 16th century a churchside location for the parsonage house had been established; the suggestion of fabric from this period is present within the north block of Pell House and we may presume this to be the minister's farmstead as sketchily described by Richard Newcourt in 1610,[3] with a barn and stable there at least, a garden "and a Back-side containing an Acre", looking pleasantly out to the Kentish hills across a sail-filled Lower Hope.[4] Both the great and small tithes were customarily the Fobbing rector's; one tenth of all produce or agricultural profit within the bounds of his parish; whether of corn or grasses or cattle, in milk, bacon, on the tenth pig of every litter, underwood and timber, in poultry and eggs, in the pluckings of down for feathering beds and bolsters, in apples to preserve for winter – so the toll of blessings went on. Small wonder the harvest service was a joyous event for any priest to celebrate. Thus, the rectory plot and its range of seemly buildings was to a marked degree, a storage centre, the usual location for the "tithe barn" – though almost any antique corn barn might acquire this tag in recent times.

---

[2] Glebe Cottage TQ78.7162.8390 and T.MUS. Catalogue 2894.

[3] *Repertorium ... an ecclesiastical parochial History of the Diocese of London,* R. Newcourt, 1610.

[4] Fobbing Rectory (now Pell House) TQ78.7179.8397.

Two centuries on, in 1810, a porched ecclesiastical barn would be mentioned, doubtless of boarded timber frame, eighteen feet in width and roofed with thatch. There was a dairy house besides, projecting out from the parson's dwelling, in all likelihood paved with thin russet bricks and slate-shelved for cold cleanliness, a ten-by-twelve space teeming with wide china dishes and churns, horsehair sieves and white maplewood utensils. Fobbing's parsonage house itself was already respectably old, the high-roofed, dormer windowed queen Anne style dwelling which is still *in situ*, with handsome panelled front door and an interior of smallish rooms that were as cosily lined with polished wooden wainscot as any polite church box-pew.

The turbulent fortunes of the early protestant years at St Michael's are well reflected in the trio of rectors serving from 1536, the date of Ann Boleyn's killing, into the age of her daughter, the queen Elizabeth. Upon Thomas Thornham's presentation to the living in August of that year, the edicts of Thomas Cromwell would doubtless normally have found quick effect: with the wrenching out of all offensive trappings of the "old" theology – the great carved rood screen dividing chancel and nave above which had long been set the holy cross, carved and richly painted statues of the virgin and other saints, and the hiding away of its ancient stone stepway to the lighted rood loft above.[5] One high south window, contrived to focus its illumination upon these beautiful images, is still to be seen.

The sacred *mensa*, or high-altar stone, may also at this time have vanished, perhaps (as in so many instances) to be secretly buried beneath the chancel's eastward *sacrarium*. But its destination could eventually have been elsewhere. A brick table tomb that stands outdoors just south of Fobbing's tower seems to relate to a representative of the Button family, lords of the manor during the later Georgian period. Its massive covering is a finely dressed and moulded slab of fossil-bearing limestone and, though now considerably weathered, it is of some beauty and an item of immense original cost. Measuring 47" by 38" and of a depth of 5½", the archangel Michael's pre-reformation altar may be here – more visible than we realise.

Perhaps the small and once richly coloured sculpture in stone depicting the holy mother and child, discovered nearly four centuries afterward during Sedgwick's

Churchyard wall

---

5 E.R. Vol. 49, 1940.

Madonna and Infant, St. Michael's (reconstruction)

restoration of the church and now again exhibited, had been mutilated (by decapitation) during this first phase of sectarian vandalism.[6] In style, it matches a type seen upon Barking Abbey's seal, in use at the time of surrender. The statue's subsequent preservation had surely been due to the daring of some village agent faithful to ousted Romish beliefs, whether in the first phase of Henrican revision, or under the Orders in Council of 1547 (Edward VI) which were to call for the final removal of every image, shrine or picture and all such unacceptable "monuments of feigned miracles" as might remain. Upon each church's walls, ochreous drawings of painted saints, bizarre demons and tortured sinners were to be erased under plasterer's daub and the limer's brush. A truly "pictorial" Bible was to be superseded by blank interiors and the intangible words of a book.

But was Fobbing's St. Michael's, in fact, more tardy than we might presume in its embracing of England's new protestant liturgy? There is strong evidence to imagine so in the connections of Thomas Thornham alone, as well as from other indicators. Oxley's work upon the Reformation for example, points to the open Roman persuasion of a Rochford priest called Henry Canne who, by will of one wealthy citizen in 1541 was to "preach God's Word on Sundays and Holy Days for a year" in several places, including ten at Leigh and five each at Hadleigh and Fobbing.[7] Canne's bequests included 33s. 4d. for priests to sing for his soul: there is no question that this is therefore a catholic document. Nor can we doubt that its devisor named these churches in the understanding that his arrangements would be honoured by the rectors concerned.

Following the downfall of the Boleyns, the manor of Fobbing and its right of advowson had become again the crown's. Vicar also of Horndon-on-the-Hill, Thomas Thornham had been a man already much favoured before his arrival here as Boleyn's protégé, for he was a Prebendary of St. Paul's, the great city cathedral to which, as the second Act of Dissolution took its toll through 1539, the confiscated lands in Fobbing that had belonged to Barking's Benedictine abbey would be

6 *Wallpaintings in Essex Churches,* Rev. G. Montague Benton, E.A.S. New Series, Vol. 20 and *Local Notes,* E.R. Vol. 15, 1906.

7 *The Reformation in Essex,* J. Oxley, 1965.

A Glastonbury thorn

transferred. Unpleasant though events may have seemed, it might be too naive to imagine that the new pastor was unaware of his usefulness in the locality while the monarch's violation of monastic premises progressed.

Folklore has long credited a notion that there had been, at some unspecified time, an outlying commune of Barking nunnery centred upon the Hawkesbury manor farm, an idea at first view having little to support it beyond Stowe's tale of how Jack Cade's rebels – during the violence of 1450 – had broken into some monastery's wine cellar at Fobbing, consuming all its contents. F. Z. Claro, a modern antiquarian and journalist, adds further unsourced yet intriguing aspects: Hawkesbury's summit, he avers, had once been celebrated for its Glastonbury thorn,[8] a variety of the common *Crataegus* of mystical association, flowering around Old Christmastide and by tradition derived from the living staff carried into southern England by Joseph of Arimethea.

In that connection, the secondary name of "Hawkesbury Bush" may be noticed, since in southern dialect "bush" alludes specifically to a thorn-tree; hence a *bush-harrow* in farming, or to receive a *"bush in one's flesh"*. As early as 1649 there had been a *"Bush field"* adjoining the homestall yard, while in 1740 the historian Salmon recalled: *"Some trees here have been a Sea-mark, called Hawksbury-bush"* (that is, a navigational check for vessels in the Lower Hope). A generation on, Chapman & Andre's survey was to hatch-in the hilltop, engraving one significant tree upon it – evidently to emphasise its importance for miles around as a guide-point.

A nun

So much for story and surmise. Diligent fieldwork reveals no continuance of this hawthorn type amidst the dense shrubland which crowns Hawkesbury's rise today, but in view of the ground's disturbance by mineral extraction and the erection of anti-aircraft gun sites, this is barely a consideration. At the chancel's eaves in St. Michael's church is a pair of 14th century sculptured head-stops, one of which is reasonably described as a portrait of a nun. Alone, it provides only a merest additional bearing upon the evidence of a holy sisterhood within these parish bounds. But the papist Thomas Thornham's register entries[9] add a far more potent fragment upon 9th December, 1540, in the burial of "Dame Margaret Sackfeeld Prioresse of Esborne", a Benedictine lady from the recently dissolved

[8] *Old Manor will become part of Basildon's history.* F. Z. Claro, G.T.G. 2nd November, 1973 and *Marshland Villages: Fobbing,* F. Z. Claro, Thames Haven News, May-June, 1960. A springfed pond and depression within the lawned garden, suggest former moatworks: not inconceivably a sacred well site.

[9] Not original, but transcribed from Thornham's paper folio of 1540 into the parchment register of 1598 by his successor Muffett.

monastery of Easebourne, over fifty miles away in inland Sussex and originally founded by Sir John Bohun during the reign of Henry III (1216-1272). Barking was to escape Easebourne's fate a few more years yet, during which time Hawkesbury's house, looking southward across verdant miles to the sacred shore of bishop Cedd's arrival in Essex, remained also a safe haven for the lady prior, under Barking's control. A suggestion surely emerges, then, that the dismantled wealden priory having been abandoned, its occupants took themselves to join with an already long established community upon Fobbing's highest point – so aptly called in these times of opportunism and duplicity, the *"hill of the hawks"*. Dame Margaret Sackfeeld's (Sackville's) interment, if it *did* take place at the parish church, would surely have been in the presence of important Benedictine representatives. But an incumbent's register need not always relate to services undertaken by him, or even to burials within the perimeters of his own consecrated ground. Corpses in many instances found their way to other spots, such as domestic orchards and fields, and Hawkesbury's manor house may well in time yield buried evidence of its pious Benedictine sisterhood.

With Cromwell's mandate, Thomas Thornham was to oversee the preparation of Fobbing's first paper-leaved register, which began with the baptism of Margaret Sansom in early January, 1539 but which appears later to have been destroyed. A special triple-locked coffer to contain these new parish records, the holy vestments and such plate as might have existed, would also have been provided at that time, though Fobbing has not been so fortunate as some other churches in the preservation of its early furnishings. The wooden chest was seemingly non-existent by 1685 when the rector had been ordered to provide a replacement, with the reproach that his "Register booke" be properly kept within it. Plainly by then the several volumes lay elsewhere, at risk of damage or loss.

St. Michael's now began to use its great Bible, printed through the tortured Tyndall's heroism, for the first time in English. Aided during the early 1540s at least by his curate, John Cooke,[10] Thornham's dozen years until his death – perhaps at the start of 1548 – were to be the most changeful thus far in the church's story, though turbulent days still lay ahead for its pastors and perplexing times, too, for its congregation. In May, 1548 came the appointment of John Hopton, whose personal courage, ambition and ruthlessness mark him as Fobbing's greatest and most notorious cleric, during whose initial years the last recorded clearance of trappings of a catholic regime was undertaken. For plainly Fobbing, like medieval churches everywhere, had possessed a ring of bells to its tower which, under Henry VIII had become subject to threat of removal. It was a vogue which did not long persist – the protestant order would be rehanging new bells long before the century's end, even though in 1552 not a single ancient

---

10 "John Coke, curate of ffobbing" witnesses with Richard Dowe, April, 1540.

example was declared to have survived among the inventories of Essex parish churches. On 18th August 1551, a letter to the bishop of London would speak of St. Michael's Fobbing as "in greate ruyne and decaye and the parishioners not able to repaire the same of themselfes without selling somewhat of the churche goodes", to which Privy Council was to respond with permission to sell one bell "to the valewe of xxxl and not above ...".[11] What happened to the others remains unknown, but it is of especial interest that this action should have taken place in view of the peculiar religious position of Fobbing under Hopton and his royal patron, the princess Mary.

King Henry's death in 1547 and the accession of his teenage son Edward VI were not to disturb the protestant continuity. But by odd fortune it was not to the young monarch that nomination of the Fobbing living had now fallen, but to his sister the princess who, of course, never relinquished her Roman catholic allegiance. Sometime a Dominican prior, John Hopton had been appointed confessor and private chaplain to this eldest royal daughter and, while incumbent of St. Michael's would continue in that perilous royal office throughout Edward's five year reign. An outlawed religion therefore continued to prevail over the chancel of Fobbing, though this was probably never manifested to its congregation. In every likelihood, some curate saw to the necessary guise of a protestant performance throughout.

Of Yorkshire family, John Hopton had gone to be educated at the house of the Black Friars in Oxford, making several journeys to the papal city and obtaining while overseas his doctorate of theology at Bologna. With 1542 he would take his D.D., soon becoming rector of a London parish, St. Anne and St. Agnes, which he only resigned on obtaining Fobbing. Great Yeldham in higher Essex was his in plurality until his death.

The year following his induction at Fobbing, pressure had come upon Hopton to conform to the "new liturgy" of the church of England, even to persuade his royal mistress that she should forsake the idolatry of Rome. Officially the princess, however, continued to deny that the Roman Catholic religion was being practised within her Essex residence of Copt Hall, but by late December 1550, Edward VI's journal had noted the issue of letters patent "for the taking of certeine chapelins of the lady Mary for saiing masse". Though seriously endangered, John Hopton's stance remained firm even beyond threats in

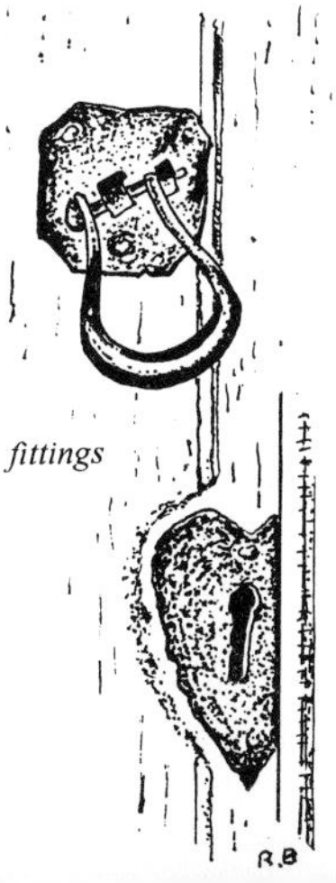

South door, fittings

R.B

[11] *Religious Houses,* R. C. Fowler. V.C.H. Vol. II, 1907.

August 1551, that he and his brother chaplains "must look for puneshment" if they persisted in disobedience. A colleague, Mallet, was to be confined in the Tower for similar intransigence.[12]

Wider political implications, as a promise of outright ideological war with the catholic state loomed, were to prove John Hopton's salvation, for Mary's adherence to the old faith would now slip into an official obscurity till the sudden demise of her half-brother Edward in mid 1553. Hopton had survived, to be rewarded on Mary's accession to the throne with the bishopric of Norwich. Bonner, the notorious bishop of London, whose moated "palace" earthworks still remain amidst old cattle pasture at Orsett a few miles from Fobbing village, would consecrate his appointment to the office on 28th October 1554. Thereafter, John Hopton was to emerge as one of the most ferocious among the Marian persecutors of protestantism, supported by his chancellor, Dunning, who (observed Fuller in his chronicle of martyred worthies) "played the devil himself, enough to make wood dear, so many did he consume to ashes." In Fobbing, parishioners who knew not whom they could trust, would hear of executions by fire of the brewerman Henry Wye of Stanford le Hope, or of Horndon's stubborn victim Higbed, cremated alive in the hilltop market town at winter's end, 1555. The closely guarded cart, conveying yet another tortured heretic of this group, must have passed through Fobbing's northerly highways upon his journey into Rayleigh for public burning.

For such a fanatical creature as bishop Hopton, it proved a personal mercy that his own days happened not to extend far beyond the close of the queen's reign early in 1558, as the young Elizabeth's swift dealing with others of his inclination like the murderous Bonner, bishop of London, well suggests. With 1560, she would grant the gift of Fobbing to the duchess of Suffolk's[13] chaplain, Robert Brown, who obtained dispensation for the holding of two livings and was also vicar of Horndon on the Hill from 15th November, 1565. Brown was probably largely resident at Fobbing, keeping his registers in orderly style and witnessing the wills of various local dwellers. It seems that the temptation of a blank wall, so new a feature of St. Michael's nave in April 1575, was as much to the expressive soul then as now, for in April that year a youth named Lawrence Boyden was to be dragged before an ecclesiastical court (in Brentwood) for having written in the church of Mr. Brown certain "scoffing and uncomely rimes"; some tribute at least to a rough-hewn literacy among the juvenile Shakespeare's south-country

---

[12] D.N.B. *John Hopton D.D.* The possible connection between the Borley farm estate (Chapter 4) and Hopton's becoming bishop of Norwich is at present uninvestigated.

[13] 4th wife of Charles Brandon, duke of Suffolk, associated with S. Ockendon Hall. Distinguished herself by her zeal for the Reformation, "a lady of sharp wit and sure hand to thrust it home and make it pierce where she pleased". (Fuller).

contemporaries.[14] The boy's father, Thomas Boyden, a carpenter by trade, had undertaken to punish his son with a flogging in his parish church upon the next Lord's day in the presence of the warden and congregation. Surely Lawrence would remember this humiliation when his own swaddled offspring was carried there for baptising a half dozen years after.

Parson Philip White's appointment by the queen[15] dates from 7th August 1577. He was a married man and residence within his parish is again proven by several Fobbing documents, including burial details of his children; Jonas in the fall of 1579 and Philip during early 1583. They had been christened together two years after White's institution and were therefore likely twin brothers.[16] At the turn of Michaelmas, 1579, he had been present to witness the dying William Pitman's will, a countryman owning but a cow and a few sheep and who had presumably once enjoyed practice in the nearby archery butts, for he would leave to his brother John a "best doublet ... and bow and arrows". In the previous spring White had attended likewise for the ailing Joan Beeles, witnessing her words of bequest to two village families, the Jameses (her earlier husband's line) and that of William Bell whose name she now bore. When Stephen Suttell, owner of lands in Corringham and in Fobbing, delivered his last will and testament in the February of 1582, Philip White would be identified both as witness and as its scribe – "the writer hereof".[17]

Fobbing householder William Hills had deemed when tying up his worldly concerns in 1586 that his young son should be put "with Mr. Whyt person ... and his stock (finance) with him for the use thereof to bring him up with all in larning both to writ and to read ...", parson White moreover undertaking that when the lad should reach fourteen years, "to bind him prentese in London with Mr Younge grosseour or some other onest and godly mane". There were other more dramatic demands upon Philip White's hours, too; as in 1588, when a summer of menaced invasion under Medina Sidonia and Parma had seen the English fleet gathering downriver, the virgin *"Gloriana"* with her royal armies upon the hills in sight of Fobbing tower and thanksgiving services held in all churches that year's end. A mighty storm had huffed the enemy galleons to ruin: in 1590 another less praiseworthy cyclone ravaged the lofty fabric of St. Michael's and damaged Philip White's parsonage besides. He died during the winter of 1593, bequeathing his estate to Paul White, his son.

---

14 E.A.S. New Series Vol. 20, 1930-31.

15 *More About Stifford and its Neighbourhood,* Rev. W. Palin, 1872.

16 Fobbing St. Michael, parish registers 1539-1654. Originals at church.

17 Wills. Serial numbers are not felt to be required: all are identifiable by name and date: *Wills at Chelmsford,* Vol. 1 (1400-1619) F. G. Emmison, 1957-8.

Despite a laudable record of neighbourly doings, parson White had never been overly estimated by his masters. A mere "ignorant and unpreaching minister", he held no licence to conduct sermons, a deficiency found among many pastors of the time. Not until king James relaxed this attitude to preaching in England, would many churches obtain their high wooden pulpits, with acoustic canopy overhead and hour-glass stand alongside for gauging the duration of each sermon. Certainly by the visitation of 1685, Fobbing's pulpit had been in existence long enough to require a brand new "cusheon" for its parson's comfort.

Within a brief period of six weeks after White's burial on January 31st, his replacement had been appointed; Peter Muffett, who was to work some 25 years among Fobbing's flock, becoming the third successive incumbent to make a home here. Two sons of the pastor and his wife, Jane, came to the ancient stone font during these first years, but shortly died. Other children, Mary and Margery, baptised in the October of 1595 and 1598 seem to have been spared to become the town street's own privileged duo of little Miss Muffetts, though they were to lose their mother during mid May, 1602. Peter Muffett's tidy hand is easily recognised at the very beginning of the oldest parish register, for though the tawny skin casing opens to read: "*A True Regester, of all such, as have been baptized, married & buried in the parish of Fobbing: bearing Date the yeare of our lord GOD on Thousand, five hundreth, thirtie, nyne*" it was under the mandate of 1598 that nearly sixty years of paper records were transferred by him to these vellum leaves. Another innovation which seems most likely to have been of Muffett's term is the attractive group of elm benches with "poppyhead" finials, situated in St. Michael's south aisle, a type of carved design alleged to derive not from the opium plant, but the Latin word "puppis"; a ship's prow. *These* are of acorn pattern.

Muffett was to later remarry, for the will mentions his spouse Mary and refers to one apparently surviving daughter, Margery Clarke. The register notes him last with the line: "Peter muffett pson of ffobbing was buryed on the xxiiiith day of Aprill in the yeare 1617."

"SCATTERED RUDE PAPERS ..."

Many of the sacred days of the medieval church had been swept away during the Rev. Thomas Thornham's term (1536-c.1548) and to engage in frivolities, to partake of sports or other "profane" activities upon those few saintly holidays which remained, became an offence, punishable by amercement for the benefit of the poor. The breach of the Sabbath, even in the performance of essential

Bench finials, St. Michael's

work in many instances, was equally subject to appearance and probable fine, especially after 1570, the year in which Elizabeth was to be finally excommunicated by pope Pius V. A resurgence of anti-catholic paranoia ensued, which to a degree presumed avoidance of Sunday attendance at churches to imply papist inclination, even though this was seldom the actual case. A rich harvest of such wrongdoers tried in Essex ecclesiastical courts is to be had in Dr. Emmison's series of Tudor studies, a few selections of which may add to the perspective of those lives of Fobbing's clergymen already touched upon. Thomas Boyden, a village carpenter previously met with, was one of those accused (in 1582) of a Sunday visit to the premises of Giles Brown in whose unlicenced aleshop in Corringham he played at the "painted cards", participating also in other "unlawful games", while Christopher Seaton, a Fobbing offender of more sober mien had merely been reported for clandestinely dipping his sheep upon the Sabbath "between noon and evening prayer".

Thomas Crowe and George Hulke – the latter a name to be reckoned with among farming folk, part leaseholder of Pitsea Hall and occupying the great estate of Leesons – would together defend their absence from Mr. Philip White's services during 1586 with the claim of "dwelling seven miles from the church", each avowing to have been to Fobbing St. Michael's "often times when he can conveniently come."[18] Possibly Crowe had been a marsh dweller in one of the detached grazing portions of Little Warley or Dunton, in which case his rightful church was indeed a far journey. Yet if master Hulke still kept residence in Leesons, close to Lee Chapel and Basildon edge, the saddle journey can have been hardly more than two miles or so.

When Joan Bell of Fobbing was carried before the court of the archdeaconry, held at Ingatestone upon 3rd May, 1592 for neglecting to receive holy communion, a further aspect of her character had been probed, for a parishioner called Thomas Wapple "did make complaint of her ... of suspicion of witchcraft", an accusation perhaps only brought on because of her apparent avoidance of the "true" religion.[19] Though this Fobbing "witch" incident has been made much of by popular writers on the village, it perhaps serves best to illustrate a sensible caution prevailing in society even during this, the very peak period of mania against the dark craft in Essex (1580-1600). Malicious magic had been subject to a death penalty since Biblical times, though in England persecution of those supposed to perform it was of marked increase following the Reformation. Henry VIII's act of 1542 against the practice of invocations and witchcraft, had been much concerned with its lucrative aspect, in using occult powers "to

[18] *Elizabethan Life: Morals and the Church Courts,* F. G. Emmison, 1973.

[19] E.R.O. A EA/16 f.6.

understand and get knowledge ... in what place treasure or gold and Silver shulde or mought be founde or had in the earthe ...", relinquishing any other malevolent sorcery to further clauses.[20] The whipping up of public hysteria was to largely result from Elizabeth's statute of 1563, framed by her advisor the bishop of Salisbury, who considered witches "marvelously increased" in the kingdom within recent times: *"Your Grace's subjects pine away, their colour fadeth ... for the shoal of them is great, their doings horrible"*.

To what extent a stereotype hag-image was being built into the Elizabethan rural mind is hard to say, but when creating *Macbeth* in around 1606, Shakespeare plainly considered it well within his audience's ken, with murky caves, a boiling cauldron and some fairly vile culinary preferences:

Root of hemlock, digg'd i' the dark;
Liver of blaspheming Jew; ...

Thomas Wapple's accusation of Joan Bell would certainly have been heard, by some parishioners, with a tinge of this theatrical horror, or excitement at the prospect of a charge and committal.[21] Wapple and his spouse Elizabeth had suffered the death of four of their children during the past dozen years or so, their most recently dead infant being Mary Wappell, buried in 1590. Such family wounds might easily turn parents' minds against some neighbour whose acts seemed to have borne malice, or had voiced some painful remark. Nevertheless Joan Bell's general character itself would prove sufficient to clear her name, for having been allowed the usual respite of a month to produce a certificate from four neighbours pronouncing her an honest person "and not at all thought to be such a woman", a Brentwood court dismissed her in the June of 1592.

Joan Bell appears to have been formerly the Joan Sparrow of Corringham who had wed John Bell there during September 1585, the couple thereafter dwelling in Fobbing where they were to be presented by the church court under Peter Muffett's rectorship (in 1588) for having "lived assunder for two years", the evidence inferring that Bell had overstepped the lawful Tudor modicum of wife-chastisement "and that he did use her hardly with unreasonable stripes". In Armada year, perhaps the worst of bellicose English humours were surfacing, but nevertheless the participants were now persuaded to share their matrimonial bed

---

[20] *Witch Hunting and Witch Trials,* C. L'Estrange Ewen, 1929.

[21] There had been a committal for murder by witchcraft in the previous year at Aveley, not a dozen miles off.

again. Failures to co-habit after marriage constituted a considerable sin and another Fobbing pair were reported to be asunder in 1595 when Ellis Wright argued that the bride dwelled in Havering, where he had placed her with a friend (Martin, a relative of *hers*) "by reason of the young years of his wife". A child marriage is here implied, though the archideaconial court would direct them to dwell again as one.[22]

But neither had Fobbing's rectors themselves been always souls above reproach, their parishioners upon more than one occasion demonstrating a preparedness to rally against the clerical view. Robert Brown would be presented to the court by Fobbing's churchwardens during 1576, allegedly for uttering that "a child before he baptized it is not a child of God but ... of the Devil", an orthodox Puritan concept but less convincing for having tumbled from the lips of a cleric already tainted by "unchastity" with the wife of John Perry of Corringham (1563).[23] His successor the Rev. Philip White was to be roundly taken to task during 1580 for the pasturing of "hogs kine" (cows) and horses in the churchyard",[24] which by right was part of his own freehold, to be grazed at will as parcel of the glebe farm. Perhaps the foraging of pigs without the restraint of snout-rings had caused this grievance to escalate, since (as at Little Thurrock in 1650) human remains might easily be "rooted out of their graves by hogges".

If not fetched to answer his accusers in a formal way, one other minister would be severely criticised for outright dereliction of duties. John Audley, A.M., who was to follow upon Peter Muffett's death from 1617, consistently evaded after his initial period the necessary administrational chores of office, bringing a tiresome burden upon those who followed in his chaotic wake. The attractive Tudor baptismal record bears upon its opening folio a retrospective hint of the situation (penned during the late 1630s): *"It is a register as ancient as any is ... if it had been as well kept as it is ancient it might have compared with any ... in England."* Audley it was who spoiled its completeness, as some industrious hand – possibly James Norris, a curate to the later Dr. Johnson – would boldly announce: *"By the great negligence of Mr. John Audley Clerk Rector of this place now deceased this Register hath not beene these 13 yeares written at all; c therefore as we could find them so we sett them downe out of his scattered rude papers ..."*. Baptisms, weddings and earthings had all escaped, and doubtless the parsonage study would be thoroughly turned over following Audley's burial upon the final day of May, 1636, seeking for any scrap or note by which a lost archive

[22] *Elizabethan Life: Morals and the Church Courts*, F. G. Emmison, 1973, p. 162 (misprinted as "Bull").

[23] ibid p. 219.

[24] ibid p. 270.

might be partially restored. Some jottings would be found, but undoubtedly the great mass of data upon Fobbing families has been lost forever due to Audley's lapse from 1622 onward.

The archdeacon of Essex's visitation book reveals a friction between Audley and his parishioners during the spring of 1626, when various folk, "who know best the bounds", refused to accompany their pastor upon his intended Rogationtide perambulation.[25] Parson Audley had duly announced his resolution to beat the bounds the Sunday previous in St. Michael's and yet, at the important moment, William Mott for one had not heard "ye bell towle to morning prayer as in former tymes it used to be, wch was the cause that he did not goe". Evidently then, Fobbing had *some kind* of latten ring, even if only a single bell, remaining after the disposal of its bronze back in 1551. This may imply that John Audley's installation of four bells, bearing Thomas Bartlett's circular cartouche depicting a castle and bells and all dated 1629, may have been assisted with re-cast medieval metal.

Bartlett had supplied several other churches within earshot such as Corringham, West Tilbury and Chadwell, with new bells through these years that Audley was at Fobbing.[26] St. Michael's would wait almost another century for the fifth and greatest bronze: cast in 1724 to complete a quintet of clamour sufficient to inspire the re-titling of a wayside public alehouse a fair mile off in Vange as the *Five Bells.* Within a few years, too, Audley's sole pieces of parish communion plate were to be obtained; a silver cup and paten (cover) of which only the former now remains at the church. It weighs 10¾ oz., is of 7" height and is deeply engraved below its rim: "John Lawson[27] and John Grubb Church wardons Att ffobinge in Essex", together with a date, 1633. The missing cover had certainly been present until 1810, when an inventory of St. Michael's furnishings included it under the description of a "small silver plate".[28]

Silver Communion cup

[25] *Rectors of two Essex Parishes and their Times,* Rev. F. W. Austen, 1943.

[26] *The Church Bells of Essex,* Deedes & Walter, 1909.

[27] The Lawsons were holders of Prittlewell Priory: *The History of Rochford Hundred,* P. Benton, 1888.

[28] *The Church Plate of… Essex,* Rev. G. Montague Benton, 1926. My reading of the cup's inscription differs from Benton's record in several points. Perhaps Benton's information was received via the Rev. E. Gardner.

John Lawson

Ri: Cole Curate.

Not out of character with his several other sins of omission, parson Audley eloped to his maker in timely avoidance of the government's Ship Money demand of 1636; a list headed in his stead by "Dr. Johnson Rector for his Eccles" (ecclesiastical freehold) taxed at £1. 10s. 0d., a sum matched only by that of one other wealthy parishioner, churchwarden John Lawson, who appears to have had connections with the village since at least 1594, in which November he had married Mary Gillet here. This new-come minister was the Rev. Sampson Johnson, a gentleman apparently seldom to be found in his place – for between 1640 and April 1643 curates James Norris and Richard Cole were the active names in matters of the vestry and other recorded parochial doings. Johnson's royalist allegiance as the Civil War between crown and commons advanced, would send him, along with bevies of Anglican brethren, fleeing to exile in Europe, Palin quoting the subsequent sequestration doquet of May, 1645; "Dr. Johnson hath deserted his church at Fobbing and is gone beyond sea, where he employeth himself against the Parliament" – which was to dispose of his rectorial living to one of the now officially established Presbyterian order, apparently Richard Searle M.A., who acted until his death in about January, 1646. Fobbing's patronage had been removed from the monarch's personal gift and was now the republican state's.

For a brief spell from March 1648, Joseph Pease, formerly curate of South Hanningfield, held the incumbency, dying apparently only after a month's office, to be followed by Francis Scott who now assumed his duties over a flock which, if not wholly of Parliamentary persuasion was deeply under its social and military influence, as generally were the country citizens of this strategically significant corridor into London. It is probable that during this bloody period, the munitions drive had relieved many churches of their employable gun-founding metals, especially in the form of the commemorative brasses of medieval and Tudor families, a process easily condoned by new ministers of deeply puritan sympathy. The loss of a handsome Tudor brass effigy from its table tomb just inside Fobbing's south door,[29] may relate to this mid century plundering, just as the removal of iron railings from parson Henry Thompson's vault outside in the churchyard would mark the work of salvage operatives during the second World War.

A brother in law, George Maule,[30] had perhaps been instrumental in Francis Scott's obtaining the rectorship, for though parson of Vange since the late 1630s, Maule elected to reside at a high, mosquito-free location within *Fobbing's* bounds, yet just a short trot from his tiny, low-spired church. During November 1643, we

---

[29] Probably the grave of George Munnes, 1583 whose will of 1580 had directed, "a fair marble stone with my name in brass ...".

[30] *Some Additions to Newcourt's Repertorium,* E.A.S. New Series, Vol. 6, 1898.

find that his sole offspring, Charles Maule, had been born here, "in the mannor house of Hawkesbury", and could only therefore be taken "uppon leave" for baptism over at his parent's hilltop church of Vange, nearer though it might be by half a mile. As pastor, Scott had signed in 1648 the Episcopalian Test, and during spring two years later would be approved upon examination, "an able preacher". One lady at least found his pulpit-manner appealing for a short while – Grace, the widow of a thrice married householder called Humphrey Collett, who had wed her a dozen years before his death in 1647. Hers had been an inspired arrangement, for only a short while previously she had been kept by Collett as his "maide servante". Evidently a woman of strong but shifting passions, Grace Collett would be buried on the arrival of August, 1649, having some while since – as our register tells – *"enjoyned Mr. Scott to preach for her wherever she dyed but removeing to Mr Birds house her mind c will was altered."*[31]

On 23rd November, 1653, "ffrancis Scott minister of ffobbin" was himself delivered to earth, his relict Elizabeth dying in 1660 at Stanford le Hope, having seemingly resided there with a daughter called Susan, wife of Robert Tucker.[32] How Fobbing fared for its next half dozen years is hinted by a signature of John Sandford (of Horndon?) which adorns the vestry's election memo at the spring of 1654 – one of those Justices of the Peace whose part in things clerical would increase under the new system. By Act of 1653, there were to be no weddings made other than of secular kind; the protectorate of Oliver had introduced instead civil ceremonies, to be performed before Justices of the Peace upon evidence (from parish record-keepers, who would be called "registers") that banns had been called upon three Sundays in church – or at some neighbouring market place. Legally, children of these liaisons would for some while afterwards be considered illegitimate, though all marriages made during the Cromwellian years became validated *en bloc* after the restoration of the monarchy.

At a parish meeting early in July, 1654, William Hunter "being an honest man c of good repute among them" (the inhabitants) would become elected "to be the Parish Register" and to have within his keeping the necessary books.[33] Hunter's characterful hand and individual spelling add much to the richness of Fobbing's records and evidently he took to his new job with alacrity, for with his summer appointment a lapse in the keeping of the marriage data from November 1651 was at once corrected. The second volume of parish registers, its leaves bound in white vellum, began with this year, 1654, to continue till 1679-80.

---

[31] A person called Bird was to lease from St. Paul's the 25 acre Hawksbury Hook marsh in 1650.

[32] Both buried at Stanford: Robert Tucker, May 9th 1685, Susan Tucker the following May 12th. Presumably Tucker held some Fobbing copyhold there, conceivably "Ivy Walls". See also *A Visitation of the County of Essex 1664-68*, Sir Edward Bysshe, 1888.

[33] *Parish* Book, 1630-1700. Original at St. Michael's, Fobbing. See also E.R. Vol. XXXVIII p. 157.

Parson Audley's four green-stained bells surely joined with hundreds far across the two counties of estuarine Thames, to tune the coronation of a returned king in May, 1660; along with whom had arrived the dispossessed Anglican, Dr. Sampson Johnson – now eager to retake his rightful place in the rectory. He therefore in effect, was to serve Fobbing twice, though in the sight of his bishops of the Church of England his occupation of the living had been continuous (since the Protectorate and its affairs had been pronounced treasonable and unlawful). Johnson, however, was to die within a few months of his homecoming, bequeathing estate to his wife, lady Rebecca Williams, but having concern also for cushioning the poor-rate by assisting some reduced parochial families. In his will of August 1660[34] he was to provide (for ever) "forty shillings ... to the Churchwardens and Overseers ... to be layd out in Wooll and other fitting materials to set the poore on work ...". Nearby Horndon's[35] textile trade was in distress; within the decade an Act for prohibiting burial in "any stuff ... other than what is made of sheeps' wool only" would attempt to remedy the collapse of a once lucrative and prestigious national industry.[36]

A crippling fine of £5 might be levied upon relatives not providing evidence of compliance and parsons' affidavits are to be discovered in most old parish registers. From Fobbing one example of 1688 may suffice, that of the creek hoyman John Hall, buried upon 30th March in the absence of his own pastor, by the minister of a parish a few miles off. Not for nearly a month did Fobbing's clerk obtain the necessary: "Received a certificate ffrom Mr. Allen Rector of Stanford le Hope dat April 28 concerning his (John Hall's) burial in woolen." Similarly, when in the year following at Corringham, a Fobbing woman called Joanna Blackmore was interred, the details would be approved as having been conducted "according to the woolen Act."

Curates, too, had come and gone, but their speedy disappearances might never be considered remarkable were we to overlook the comments of the ear-bending John Aubrey, whose biographical work *Brief Lives* seems sagely titled so far as his observation of our locality goes: "*At Fobbing seven curates died within the first ten yeares:* (of John Pell's rectorship) *in sixteen yeares six of those who had been his Curates at Lanedon are dead: besides those that went away from both places; and the death of his wife, servants and grandchildren.*" Some indeed

---

34 P.R.O., P.C.C. Prob.11.

35 *Some Background to the Horndon on the Hill ... Cloth Industries*, R. Bingley, PAN. 19, 1975-6.

36 A petition on Johnson's death for presentation to Fobbing of Paul Gosnold is known: *Calendar of State Papers Dom, 1660-61.* It seems not to have been effective.

called the district "killpriest" country, for malaria was its particular scourge and Pell (to whom the neighbouring parish of Laindon-cum-Basildon would also be granted, 1663) is said by Aubrey to have requested in alarm to know if Archbishop Sheldon of London intended he should become resident in his new marshland empire. Upon being assured by his superior that the intent was *not* "that you shall live there: *No, sayd Pell, but your Grace does intend that I shall die there."* [37]

John Pell was a native of Sussex. His taking up of duties at Fobbing had probably been before the summer of 1661, for his first wife, called Ithurniaria, died of fever supposedly contracted there upon September 11th. Some of her husband's correspondence to her survives, described as "contemptuous in tone" and, though Ithurniaria appears to have proved a devoted spouse, Pell is alleged to have considered her "a foolish woman". His writings elsewhere were myriad: political, philosophical, scientific, and the Birch collection in the British Library alone contains 40 volumes of these manuscripts. Pell's loose mathematical papers (he is credited with the invention of the division sign in mathematics) fill more than a dozen books.[38]

The king's choice of Pell for this rectorship is stated to have been founded upon the basis of "some obscure services ... rendered by him to the Royalist party and to the Church of England", during the late period of the Protectorate – yet he had been entirely of the opposite persuasion (Parliamentarian) throughout both the war and interregnum. But in adaptability he was barely different to his celebrated young colleague in a sweeter winding of the Thames, up at Bray in Berkshire. A brilliant mind, great handsomeness, with "dark hair and eyes and a good voice", all had helped John Pell considerably. By his early thirties he was professor of mathematics at Amsterdam and would be appointed by Oliver Cromwell upon his return to England (1652) to lecture in his subject at £200 per annum. Pell's career then moved into its more overt political aspect, for in 1654 he would be dispatched as the Lord Protector's personal agent to draw the protestant Swiss cantons away from French alliance, hoping to lure them into a Continental League headed by England. He was recalled in 1658, subsequently to enter into the ministry, where an ample mathematical wit was not to be left unexploited. His first Fobbing months were evidently devoted to a scheme of reform for the calendar and during 1664 he published *Easter not mistimed*, a letter of support for the new-style of computing the Christian era. By now he had been some while a Fellow of the Royal Society, appearing upon its initial list of luminaries in 1663.

---

[37] *Brief Lives* (John Pell) John Aubrey. Penguin Classics, 1987.

[38] D.N.B. John Pell.

John Pell's clerical sphere might have been more memorable than any of his former realms of activity, and a bishopric was expected for him. Perhaps he was "a man too various", however, for after his second marriage (pre 1669) he sank into indolence and debt, becoming twice internee of the King's Bench prison. He came to his death a destitute creature, while lodging at St. Giles in the Fields, on 12th December 1685, to be buried there in the rectors' vault. *"He was a shiftless man as to worldly affairs"*, said the gossip of him afterwards, *"and his tenants and relatives ... cozened him out of his parsonages and kept him so indigent that he wanted neccessaries, even paper and ink, to his dying day"*.

Born with an enviable fortune of talents and personableness, and favoured by those in power, he contrived to apply his own mathematical device to everything he possessed, till the division was absolute. *"He dyed"*, mused Aubrey, *"of a broaken heart"*. In the last months of Pell's life, even the profits of the living of Fobbing would be confiscated by the diocese to help pay for serious renovations that were needed to the parsonage house. Enoch Hardy, his curate[39] and an old-timer of at least a dozen years survival in this agueish township, was to go with a churchwarden and workmen to look about "and give an estimacon of what the repairs will come to", though it seems that the only long-term solution would have been to demolish and build anew.[40] It was to take the zest of a fresh century to see that dream underway.

St. Michael's north side

[39] Hardy buried in chancel at Corringham on 7th October, 1689.

[40] *Visitations Held in the Archdeaconry of Essex, 1685.* E.A.S., Vol. 21, 1932-34.

7. VAN THIS, VAN THAT AND "GOODMAN PAUL"

We have journeyed with these clerics far into the Stuart century, taking only a circumstantial view along the way of Fobbing's landscape and its folk. At the close of the Tudor years, yeomen's dwellings such as those now called Fishers, Wheelers, the *White Lion* inn, the great brick-chimneyed Sprivens (Prosbus Hall) and Fobbing manor house itself, were already old fashioned laneside features, each with its orderly range of timber framed barns, granaries and cattle byres that are now lost. And though other upland farmhouses of varying ancientness stood, serving as focus to their own groups of workaday buildings, they would be wholly reconstructed due to an advancing agricultural prosperity – homes such as the brick-and-weatherboarded Vineyard, Hawkesbury and, perhaps (nearer the approach of the 1700s) Curtis' farmhouse and Dry Street. At the latter steading, a corn barn of Stuart construction has survived: a smallish three-bay elm structure of suitable capacity to this 100 acre holding, with a central threshing floor (called the *"midstrey"*) and a west facing porched waggon entry. Its roof is of simple queenpost assembly and the barn may be said to be the last parish survivor of a once common boxframe type. The pleasant white-boarded and plain tiled farmhouse alongside appears from its frontage to be a symmetrical, centrally doored affair, though at the rear other elevations strongly suggest that not all of its medieval precursor had been demolished during the time of renewal.

At the village centre, Curtis' farmhouse, too, looks to have been a remodelling of some earlier home, for its internal stack (in which formerly an arched bread oven could be seen) is of considerable width and may be a disguised Tudor survival. But unobscured brickwork within its cellar, as well as some firwood attic queenpost framing, points to a very late 17th century overall restructuring. At this time, it must have been the only brick-cased residence within Fobbing's streetline, an attractive deep red facade which greeted the eye as one laboured to the brow of Fobbing Hill.

A little northward, at Fishers, another rather modest barn survives, converted nowadays to a bourgeois dwelling and possibly of the early 17th century, though some of its minor timbers had been re-employed from an earlier

(Tudor) house. Its basic frame, however, is of a single build and has jowled mainposts – that is, the tree timbers have been set upright in reverse to their growing-stance, with wide heads so as to support the top wall plates and crossing tie-beams.[1] A five bay structure, it had no porch to its central threshing area, both south and northward door openings being of such meagre height that the entry of well-loaded harvest carts must have been precluded. Door widths were also unduly small at under 10 feet, their elm posts thickening at each base and carrying the usual grooves for the slotting-in of heavy boards – a device for retaining heaped grain during the autumn threshing and winnowing processes. This feature has given us the everyday word "threshold" for the domestic entrance.

Upon Hawkesbury summit, the derelict but still existent double-pile manor house of lightweight elm frame, with plaintiled roofing, exemplifies a new "renaissance" fashion of living which had been spreading from the city into Essex during the early 1600s. In appearance, it is paralleled quite closely by the important farmhouse called Polwicks at West Tilbury[2] which had been erected as part of the Featherston's (Hassenbrook Hall) agricultural estate c.1620. Internal stacks warmed each reception area of the Hawkesbury mansion, of which an overall description is given in Seth Partridge's survey, dated to 1649: downstairs, a hall and parlour, a kitchen, brewhouse, milkhouse and two butteries, while above extended "six chambers ... fower small Garretts" (perhaps farm servants' attics as well as sleeping places for its domestic girls). Beyond, to east or to northward, stood Hawkesbury farm's timber framed corn barn, a stable and a hayhouse fronting in the customary way its "ffould Yard" for wintertime sheltering of beasts. Besides a couple of garden plots, there stood nearby a small fruit orchard; the whole contained within less that one hilltop acre.

Fobbing village had by now assumed its present configuration of lanes, radiating as green-verged lines which extended away from the one wide browsing plot lying just outside its rectory gate.[3] Alongside these unmetalled traffic paths, the steaming street beast-yards were open to view. It was still overwhelmingly a world of timber and organically-wrought things, barns wrapped round by foot-wide elm boardings and stanchioned cattle-covers that were thatched in wheatstraw or grey marsh reeds, of daub-plastered houseframes in whose frontages were set shuttered windows of murky green-tinged glass. Outwardly, brick featured as yet only over the yeoman's rooftree in the guise of robust square stacks that had been the Tudor novelty and were now pleasantly weathered into mellow russet tones, though the village harboured by 1646 one of the bricklayers

---

1 R. Bingley, *Fishers farm,* Fobbing: Buildings Record File. T.MUS. 1987.

2 *Polwicks, West Tilbury: architectural notes,* R. Bingley, T.MUS. Buildings Record File.

3 That is, including Wharf Road (See Chapter 3).

trade, Christopher Everard, who died in that year. Doubtless he was an itinerant workman, engaged in the setting up of barn-cills, chimney stacks and perhaps the making of well-shafts. John Bennett (Bunnett) was also noted as of this calling in 1660.

Nazewick sea wall

Across the wide mud creek to eastward of the village heights lay recently reclaimed ground; the island which – somewhat prophetically – is identified in Fobbing's 17th century church registers as "Candy" (1653) and was still so called long years after by the journeying Defoe, where Dutch sea-wallers had become a prominent population since Croppenburgh's 3,000 acre "inning" of its flooded salterns through the 1620s. They were not a sedentary people and their generations would seek opportunities elsewhere as years advanced. Jessie Payne has listed several settled at Corringham,[4] clearly to some extent of the same families that Fobbing was to know, make jest of, and finally accept into their community as most Englishmen in time did. They were, when all was said, nothing but North Sea cousins, of vastly similar understanding.

Usually their surnames alone are distinctive enough to pinpoint them, if not always so conclusively as that of Jobe de Hage who "had a Child named Parnell Christened on Palme Sunday" in Fobbing (1627). There was naturally a tendency for villagers to anglicise alien forenames in the record, and moreover for the Dutch themselves to accept English forms of their homeland surnames too. The Van Raynings would easily transfer to their locally adopted surname of "Raining" and back again at random through the final 20 years of the 1600s and into queen Anne's reign. Those parish literates who maintained at times the parson's registers and other essential files,[5] were fairly often to be found noting the foreigner's presence; in 1642 a son of "John Arnian a ffleminge" and his wife (Grace) surely the same "Arian the dutchman" who was to die "of a fall from his

4 *The Corringham Chronicle,* J. K. Payne, 1987.

5 Fobbing Parish Register: all subsequent register book references throughout this chapter will be traceable by date in E.R.O. D/P 414.

horse" during the July of 1658. His widow would follow him to her grave at St. Michael's with the next October. They had seemingly been originally of one of the Canvey Island groups, for as early as 1628 one Anne Arrians from North Benfleet had moved upriver to marry her Corringham bridegroom, an Englishman. Sarah Skilder was another girl of Netherlands family who would mix with Essex blood when Jeremiah Allis of Stanford le Hope took her to wife at Fobbing in 1707. In all probability she was a sister to the Laurence Skilder of Dunton[6] who five years beforehand had buried his son at Fobbing, being a dweller of either Shellhaven or Oozedam, where lay the detached grazing acres of Dunton parish.

Conversely, Dutchmen like John Eames were to wed local girls. Upon his marriage with Susanne Greygoose in the fall of 1640, some finicky mind had bothered to define him for us in Fobbing's register as "of the towne (there being two other of the same name c surname in the (marsh?) Brothers) which he is uncle to ...". Such pedant scribes are the blessed of all family historians. At a similar period, two "outdwellers" of Netherlands origin would be named in the "Ship Money" assessment (1636); a "Mr. Vanderpitt" and one "Castermann", the former doubtless referring to Giles Vanderputt whose reclamation of Fobbing marshlands has been already touched upon. This influential city merchant appears to have planted relatives nearby at Corringham, for one Peter vande Putt had married a bride in St. Mary's there during 1626, perhaps while the great sea-walling project was being undertaken. Philip Benton, a Victorian antiquary of Rochford hundred, would identify the other non-resident taxpayer as being descended from Geslian Kersteman of Ipres in Flanders, a migrant of as early as 1564 who gave rise to the Kerstemans of *Loftmans*, Canewdon.[7] Both a father and son called Jeremiah Kersteman are found residing at Corringham through the mid 17th century, the younger marrying Judith Bishop there in 1659.

With the Carolean years, a number of other lowlands foreigners were to be active in producing offspring at Fobbing, amongst them the Desamoes, Paul and Sarah, who, having married in 1662, remained together until her death a dozen years later. Thereafter Desamoe would wed a Barking woman at St Botolph's, Aldgate (1677). With the ensuing April at Fobbing "Bolding a dutchman" had been buried, his survivor-partner Frances remarrying straightway to Peter Libert, almost certainly another man of Low Countries stock. The Libberts (variously Libbard) would still be known as tradesfolk of the parish into the 19th century, while a headstone of Isaac Libband, blithely adorned with plump cherubs (dated

---

6 Dunton in this instance meaning almost certainly the detached piece of that parish adjacent to Fobbing marsh.

7 *The History of Rochford Hundred,* P. Benton, 1867-1888.

to 1767) and set alongside the porch, is among the earliest legible graveyard monuments at Fobbing.[8]

More ephemeral on the village scene were the Hansels, John and Sarah (in the 1670s) and a Van Ghissel group, to whom a first reference occurs at the baptising of "Herman van Grinsell the child of a Dutchman Stranger" during the spring of 1685. Subsequent baptismal records identify the father as Peter. There had been passing appearances, too, of "John Bly Dutchman c Sarah his wife", a couple who buried a little boy at the August of 1642, while early in December, 1656, a baptism of Mary ("Mare") Hamplet, the daughter of Cornelius Hamplet, had occurred – surely a Netherlander by origin. Towards the century's end, the passing of one of the parish elders would be observed: "Elizabeth van Rayning a very antient widdow was buried Decemb 26" in 1698, while with May, 1706, another Dutch relict, the widow Sckilder, would be conveyed from the parish for interment at North Benfleet, suggesting that she was being taken to a husband's or kinsfolks' grave.

Dutch integration was wholehearted and valuable to the administration of parish affairs and as early as the 1660s these newcomers had found their place in Fobbing's Easter nominations for leadership. Paul Desamoe would be sworn in as a parish constable less than two years after England's war with the Netherlands and, following a second term through 1671, was to be pleasantly noted after his budget-clearing, as plain *"Goodman Paul"*. Eight years on, George Skilder took up reigns in the senior parish office, as overseer of Fobbing's poor. John Van Rayning was to emerge as another respected village name, serving as churchwarden and in the overseer's role right through the 1690s.

If Fobbing's inhabitants had been once the instigators of national strife, they continued thereafter as mere sideline witnesses to the happenings of a bustling world; in the lower Hope and Sea Reach a youngster called Drake had gained his river-legs; from Fobbing tower in 1576 one could have traced Martin Frobisher's adventurers sailing off to seek a northwest passage into China, in 1620 observed a dumpy *Mayflower* drop down the Hope from Rotherhythe, already

---

[8] Fobbing, St. Michael's: Monumental Inscriptions Recording churchyard, R. Bingley, 1989. A representation of the Libbard stone is on the cover of this volume.

crowded with those who sought refuge in the New World.[9] But few occasions throughout the Stuart period gave sharper sight of England's maritime story, than the several Dutch incursions of 1667, when in both June and July the enemy fleet had blockaded London's river, moving boldly upstream and into the Medway to destroy English vessels of war at will, leaving burning hulks in the very dockyard of Chatham and capturing one first-rate ship of the line complete. Pressing up Thames, foraging parties of Dutch troops had terrified Canvey. Sheep were taken and the smoke from torched buildings must have been observed with dismay from Fobbing township – a half dozen miles away across East Haven's narrow creek. Hawkesbury's tenant, the Vange parson George Maule, was to suffer directly, for his will made in that same summer would put aside goods to be sold for the repairing of his "house and barn lately burned ... by the Dutch at Canvey".[10]

Sometime during 1856, a twelve-pound cannon ball surfaced from beside the porch of St. Michael's church.[11] The Netherland war-fleet had been largely armed with iron shot of this weight, our own navy generally with only six-pounders. Along with East Tilbury (where historians like Holman have alleged Dutch guns had demolished the church steeple during 1667) Fobbing has acquired the legend of being a particular target for naval bombardment upon this occasion. One recent author, unwise to the truth that the surrounding marsh-levels had been embanked well before the mid 17th century, has claimed that the attackers fired at St. Michael's tower from some sea-lane a mere 500 yards away at most. In reality, some three and a half thousand yards must have divided the village hillslope from any navigable channel of Thames, a range over which no gunner would have conceived placing an accurate shot. Nevertheless, the object *does* appear to be Dutch; perhaps a stray ball collected upon the marshland by some ploughman as a souvenir subsequent to the third hostile foray upriver during July. It may eventually have been redeposited near the south porch as a "luck" item, a ward against misfortune, because iron had long been used at entranceways of buildings for purposes of superstition, just as horseshoes are favoured still.[12] In another instance, we know that a cannon ball of iron found during the ploughing of some land near Fobbing Vineyard, probably within the late Georgian period, had been taken to Oil Mill farmhouse by its farm-hand discoverer. There he buried it anew, presumably as a protection for his dwelling, the story of its existence continuing by word of mouth to the people who lived at the farm, down to those who witnessed the old building under demolition through the spring of 1936. The

---

9 *Mayflower* "this leaking, unwholesome ship" (Smith) moved downriver in late June for Southampton, whence she departed 5th August, 1620.

10 P.C.C. Wills, P.R.O. PROB. 11, 1669.

11 T.MUS. Catalogue 359.

12 *The Archaeology of Ritual and Magic*, R. Merrifield, 1987.

remembered object was dug for, and retrieved from Oil Mill's foundations, being passed for safe keeping on to the rector of Fobbing, an ardent parish historian.[13]

By the fourth week of that month (July, 1667) the enemy under De Ruyter had again penetrated the London river, checking out Tilbury's defences, and the capital was in a new wave of panic. Pepys had buried his precious family plate, while John Evelyn dipped pen to bewail England's "dishonour never to be wiped off". On the 29th he had chanced to get down to Gravesend opposite the blockhouse fort and saw downstream five ships of the Royal Navy taking on some 20 Dutchmen "chacing them with many broadsides given and returned" along Hope Reach to Holehaven and on into the widening estuary. One hostile vessel was alight – possibly a fireship anyway – but what became known as the "Battle of the Hope" was being waged: the last seaborne encounter of any scale this far up Thames. Throughout that summer, Fobbing's own small community of Dutchfolk had probably, as had recently occurred in war-scared London, been variously ostracised and pitied. But any rational mind could perceive that they were a reasonable and industrious people. They'd married-in; George Bolding, the widow Casterman. They paid their hearth tax as forthcomingly as anyone else and, like John Wessels of Fobbing, died as unwillingly of plague.

All English counties, and Scotland too, were subject to the hearth tax between 1662 and the late 80s; though not all people therein were liable for contribution. By modern comparison the earlier national methods of revenue collection were more fairly devised to exclude lower income groups entirely. Persons owning a dwelling of less than 20 shillings value were to be exempt, as were all those poorest not contributing to the parish rates. Two shillings for each firehearth or stove was to be required annually, collectable by halves at the usual quarters of Lady Day (March 25th) and Michaelmas and few of the moderately earning population can have seen Fobbing's patronal service of the feast of the Archangel go by, without a mindful groan at the collector's imminent arrival.

Thirty five men and women had been named as heads of household in the primary schedule of 1662. They shared 98 fireplaces. Of the list some 30 are identifiable folk, the rest being persons not yet detected in other documentary sources for the parish and who must therefore be non-resident owners of property here. The widow Casterman (Kersteman) had warranted tax for only one Fobbing hearth, yet would be rated for a further seven at Corringham that year. Shellhaven seems therefore to be the focus of her estate at this time. Not always did the tax-payer dwell in premises where their hearths were situated: Jacob Samuel, the street's wheelwright, paid upon one hearth, but this may relate to a workplace

---

[13] G.T.G. 2nd May, 1936. This evidence is given to demonstrate that cannon balls *were* moved from place to place.

VIRGINIA

forge. If not, he kept a very uncomfortable home for such a valued tradesman. On the other hand, someone who, upon the basis of a single record, might appear an unsupported creature – the "Wid Wood" (Lucy Wood) – possessed seven fireplaces, the highest total of any person other than the Rev. George Mell (Maule) at Hawkesbury's manor house. He enjoyed nine, while John Pell at the parsonage declared only five.

Another widow, relict of the parish windmiller Edward Ford (just dead that January) was still apparently domiciled at the mill house overlooking pebbly Marsh Lane, and declared two hearths in use.[14] Some thrifty folk, of course, sealed up a fireplace or two to avoid inessential bills. Most of the other Fobbing widows mentioned were liable for just a couple of firehearths: widow Norden, widow Gorby (Goodbe, Goadby) bereaved this last winter and whose husband had been earthed "without a coffin" – perhaps for want of a carpenter to hand at the moment – and widow Hall, who remains an elusive figure in the registers, but could be the Frances Hall named upon Fobbing's only trade-token; a copper halfpenny of the mid 17th century. It depicts on its reverse the standard pair of smoking clays which denote a "tobacconist" (a trader in Virginia leaf and manufacturer of tobacco pipes) and hence it seems likely that a small kiln was in operation somewhere locally at this period. An association may have existed between her enterprise and that of Miles Hackluitt of Billericay, for a comparable tobacconist's token of his issuing has been recently chanced upon at the Vineyard farmhouse site.[15] Neighbouring registers, too, perhaps offer a clue to this family's erstwhile movements, for during the years 1643-1651 at Vange, a male named Francis Hall is noted fathering offspring there to successive wives called Joan and Paemitentia.

Not all of this tax-payer group need be considered. Suffice to say that most of the males, yeomen and tradespeople, served at whiles in the several obligatory parish offices ranging from overseer of the poor to parish constable (though such duties were not exclusively in the masculine province). Our lately mentioned Lucy Wood had been appointed overseer in 1664, while earlier, in 1649 the "Widowe Dannel" (Daniel) had occupied Fobbing's post of Surveyor of the Highways. Some offices, such as that of churchwarden, had been of medieval origin, others, like the surveyor's and constable's roles began as manorial duties but would transfer into the parish organisation with time, while the overseer of the poor's duties were essentially part of the new fabric of poor-law administration

14 Possibly Ford would be succeeded by Thomas Baker as miller, for by January 1663-4 a baptismal entry gives *"Edward, the Sonne of Thomas Baker of the Windmill"*

15 T.MUS. Catalogue 2894. *Frances* may, however, really be a male, as in the ensuing sentence re: Vange.

that had arrived with the Elizabethan Acts (1563 and 1602). Initially called "collectors", overseers would be empowered to raise and distribute a local rate for the assistance of distressed parishioners, though following the Restoration in 1660 increasing problems of itinerant claimants and of resident "strangers" were to take the legislation further. Overseers and constables henceforth became able to question the right of any doubtful person's "settlement" within the parish and to forcibly remove those lingerers who had not obtained work within 40 days. With 1697, any party arriving within the parochial bounds must provide a proper certificate of settlement from some home parish, from which re-imbursement might be obtained should the stranger fall ill, or be in need of other relief.

Known collectively as "the vestry", this managing body of varying kinds of officer, acted in collaboration with its parson, being elected by the church-rate payers each Easter – at which householders' meeting also various financial accounts of the previous year's business were to be audited and cleared. Fobbing's paper-leafed "Parish Book" (1629-1700) offers the earliest continuous listings we have of the names and positions of those serving, a scanty glimpse of their transactions and a few more revealing personal memoranda.[16] At times there occurred a pleasant casualness in dealing with money matters, as when, in April 1693, it had been found that overseer John Goodwyn's accounts for payments to the poor and other business on their behalf, had gone awry, though in his favour. Goodwyn was owed no less than £6. 13s. 1d. "towards the payment of wch summ the Parish allows him the sale of six score and ten pounds of flax yarn". Presumably, this fibre came from a parish stock, used to supply needy inhabitants for linen weaving at home.

But not on all occasions were officers' affairs tied up so amicably, nor so swiftly. A long simmering grievance had surfaced during May 1660 at a period of dispute between Fobbing's windmiller, Edward Ford, and two parish constables elected for the previous year – Thomas Cornwell and a butcher named John Snow. The initial contention lay over the great marshland plot of Nazewick lying northward of Fobbing creek, an area farmed jointly, claimed Ford, by a number of men beside himself. Certainly that had been the system during 1636, when the Ship Money assessment had included as one entry the "farmers of a Marsh called Nasse Weekey". Now, the miller complained of having been charged the constables' rate "for the whole ... whereof he holds but a moiety", adding that when he was last constable himself (in 1650) some 22s. 3d. remained unpaid to him at his term's end, which he never received.[17] At Quarter Sessions, the judge was to wash his hands of this perplexing wrangle, ordering "the whole matter to

---

[16] *Parish Book* 1629-1700. Original at St. Michael's.
Microfilm E.C.L. Grays CR18636.

[17] *Essex Quarter Sessions Order Book 1652-1661,* D. H. Allen, Essex Edited Texts, Vol. 1, 1974.

the Justices ... of that division or any two of them ... to settle as they canne". But Edward Ford's death was not far ahead and so perhaps the argument remained unreconciled.

"AND FOR POOR ... WE HAVE MANY"

So far as the needy were concerned, a well-tried system of either regular or occasional payments prevailed. The former had been very clearly the case for "Margaret a pensioner" who died with the hard first month of 1675. In other instances, lean periods might be got through with temporary doles, or allowances in kind in the form of food, clothing, coals, or medication. The natural occurrence of single parent families produced another common kind of burden upon the rates, and illegitimacy was carefully recorded within the baptismal registers, as much for administrational reasons as for the making of any moral point (though by the Act of 1610 an unwed mother might suffer imprisonment unless she could give assurances of her further good behaviour).

A particularly well documented case survives from 1648, when a bastardy order issued from the justices had been preceded by a hearing in which 3 men, including Edward Charvell, a Dry Street farmer and Hawkesbury manor tenant, were to be examined regarding the fatherhood of a female child born to Joan Thorrowgood, a village spinster. William Brackman (Blackman?) junior, of Langdon Hills, would become recipient of this order, presumably on the evidence of dates involved, to become liable for maintenance at 2 shillings weekly for his child and 6d. for Joan. Brackman's contributions were to be backdated to the date of birth (October, 1647) and payable through Fobbing's overseers. Plainly Joan Thorrowgood had been no misused innocent, for the Epiphany sessions sent her "to the House of Correction there to be dealt with according to the laws." When, at a similar period in January, 1649 (1650) the bastard infant Edward Neale came to baptism at St. Michael's, a Horndon on the Hill parishioner had been rather more forthcoming, undertaking to secure Fobbing parish for the infant's maintenance, he being (by its mother's declaration) "the reputed father". Not all single parents, of course, were females, and during 1661 we find a father called Thomas Holloway who appears to have looked after his illegitimate child (perhaps because her mother had died) taking her, "being 11 yeares of age", for a belated baptism at St. Michael's font.

A written observation in constable John Ridley's report for Michaelmas Quarter Sessions in 1649, leads to another aspect of the overseer's many problems: "and for poor children we have many, but they are too small to put out apprentices." This means of solving some of the parish's social and welfare difficulties had various faces, ranging from sending youngsters into training for a useful and profitable trade, to the placing of children in ordinary servitude as domestic skivvies. At best, it provided a continued solution to one kind of poverty problem, especially amongst pauper families burdened by too many offspring – though frequently inconveniencing the better-off rate payers who were obliged by law to accept these waifs into their households. Richard Dow, gentleman of Fobbing, would be fetched before the court in October 1655, having refused to entertain "a poore child ... putt unto him as an apprentice" during the office of Edward Ford and Richard Wright, parish overseers. On the other hand, a parish register memorandum of March 1643 outlines fairly typically a more confident and happy arrangement for the binding of John, son of Mathew Harding, a householder and sexton of Fobbing, to one Nicholas Horsenaile and Joan his wife "till he ye said John bee compleatly 21 yeares of age".[18] No trade is specified, neither do the Horsenailes appear to be Fobbing inhabitants, but generally in these instances the lad's guarantees are outlined, with the provision (upon his future release) of "forty and five shillings in his purse besides double apparell", in other words 2 good suits of clothes, a first and second best.

Girls were alike apprenticed domestically and, as noted, marriage of a serving woman to her master sometimes ensued. Sexual contact, undoubtedly frequent, is not generally visible in the archival record, though one rather later instance does appear – that of Valentine Glascock whose name as churchwarden figures on Fobbing's fifth bell, dated 1724. Despite a local story which insists that Glascock had been induced to pay for this costly item as a penance after fathering a baby upon his servant, Sarah Sharp (1737) the actual hour of temptation clearly postdated the bell's casting by more than a dozen years. The presence of another name upon this bronze (that of John Knapping, overseer) has not managed to associate poor Miss Sharp with any secondary escapade. In fact this churchwarden Glascock of 1724 had been buried at Fobbing in June 1734, and it was plainly his son, Valentine Glascock, shopkeeper, who fathered the bastard daughter.[19] Thomas Garrett in 1614 thought so tenderly of Elizabeth Addams, his neighbour "Mr Lawsons maide servant", as to leave her a cow at his decease.

---

[18] Fobbing Parish Register, 1539-1654. Original at St. Michael's.

[19] *"Sarah Glascock the illigitimate Daughter of Sarah Sharp Servant to Valentine Glascock was baptised"*, 13th February, 1736(7).

It was normal for girls, even of fairly prestigious village clans, to be sent into house-service and the burial registers frequently mention their situation: of Alice Celys[20] in 1643 a clerk noted "she was servant to John Osborne and deceased in his house", while in the late summer of 1661 died "Sarah Reeve a maid servant of Richard Sirrages". Almost certainly a burial of "the maid of Mr Doe" upon Monday, 8th February in 1657 had referred to some domestic menial, for Richard Doe was a respected parish figure, no maiden daughter of whom would be spoken of so lightly. The retention of virginity *was* nevertheless praiseworthy (and rare) enough to find official remark and the funerals of such pristine persons, whether youthful or superannuated, were still honoured by the hanging up of a pair of white gloves in church – a custom today continued in only a few country places.[21] "Susan an ould mayd, was buried on the 28 daye of June" is discovered in Fobbing's register for 1615, in 1627 "Mary Haward a maiden", while "Mris Margaret Coxe", sister-in-law of landowner John Lawson through Anne his wife, would be deemed "a mayden" in the burial record of 1631. Her apparently spousely prefix denoted at this period a mark of social quality rather than mere matrimonial status. With the dangerous autumn of 1636 had succumbed "Jone Thrussell an anciente maid" to be followed a decade later by another: "Mary Wheler an Ancient Maid owner of the house Goodman Kent lives in". Perhaps she was the last unmarried representative of those Wheelers whose name still attaches to one of the township's most picturesque houses at the High Road side.

A few illustrations of cases eventually reaching Quarter Sessions offer a sufficient insight into the duties of both the Surveyor of the Highways and the Constable's offices. Wear and tear by traffic originating outside Fobbing parish brought constant woe and the surveyor's duty to inspect and keep in repair major roadlines must have been a tiresome one. During 1646, the inhabitants of several townships along this madding highway from Rayleigh to Stanford would be summoned for neglect, Fobbing's amongst them, while the year following Richard Backer (Baker?) had failed to scour 40 rods of his laneside ditches in the parish "against the highway to Grays market", presumably along the low brookside grounds near Hovels farm, where flooding could cause travellers inconvenience. Unlawful nibbling of desirable pieces of side-verge might also fall under the

---

20 The Celys were landholders at Prittlewell, relatives of John Lawson of Fobbing: *History of Rochford Hundred*, P. Benton, 1867-1888, 2 Vols. pp. 202, 554-555.

21 *Folklore and Customs of Rural England*, M. Baker, 1974.

suveyor's keen eye and call for a report: as when in 1630 John Goodwin, parish miller, being already warned, continued to encroach upon the King's highway between a certain field and his dwelling house at the village edge atop Marsh Lane.

Such matters would be first drawn to the constable's attention, and if verified, were to find inclusion upon official charge-returns sent at regular intervals to Quarter Sessions by an appointed Chief Constable of the hundred. Briefly, these reports required descriptions of all serious disturbances, and by 1630 listed some 10 broad categories, ranging from rioting and profane cursing, through trade, alehouse and brewing irregularities, to catholic recusancy. Thus, at Midsummer sessions in that year, Charles Segrave of Fobbing would be reported a "common swearer" of whom the parish had previously levied a shilling fine ("given to the poor") while in the fall 1636 Robert Colborne, a carpenter, had been examined for railing,[22] and "abusing with evil words" his churchwarden in the very burial ground of St. Michael's. Absence from Divine service did not go overlooked; the 1630 charge-returns had included a newcomer called John Burton, for "having lived three weeks in our parish and never having come to church."

Christopher Coole (1630) had been summoned before the assize court accused of victualling in Fobbing without licence, his supplier (a Horndon brewer called Wright) being upon another occasion cautioned, but still "hath laid in beer to the said Coole". A more heartless trader was John Adam, reported for "engrossing up" both the price of bread and of butter by arrangements with the "baker to sell no bread but to himselfe" and dealing likewise with local dairy farmers, "greatly by this means oppressing the poor". Sundry folk persisted in operating alehouses without licence, some despite former orders against them. Such was the yeoman John Doe, about whose activities a constable called Wilson testified during October 1627. Already that September a number of aggrieved inhabitants had complained, not only of his selling ale, but of much "misorder" at his premises where "all manner of loose and wandering persons" were to be found "day by day and on Sunday in time of divine service ... guslinge until they be drunk." At the Epiphany Sessions of 1622, two Fobbing tradesmen, thatcher Thomas Butcher and William Tompson, a fisherman, had been named for keeping common alehouses here "for ye space of two monthes" without leave.

An offender against regulations regarding proper apprenticeship is found in 1639, when Humphrey Harvy (one of those modestly-taxed for Ship Money during 1636) was alleged to have carried on the business of a baker, "without having been aprenticed thereto". Already married and a father by late 1632,

[22] E.R.O. Calendars of Assize Files: all references throughout this chapter will be traceable by year date in text.

Harvy's loss of livelihood must have been disastrous, though by 1640 he seems to have adapted to the weaving business. In that year, he and a Fobbing "mariner," or hoyman, called John Clarke, would be found involved in some heated action against carpenter John Coleman, closely involving Clarke's wife Margaret. Both she and Coleman would be ordered to keep the peace, one against the other, at the Michaelmas Sessions.

There was patently no shortage of incident to occupy the constable's unpaid exertions; in 1653 a theft of yard fowls from Nicholas Stonard and in January 1656 the taking of several sheep out of parson George Maule's Hawkesbury homestead, which resulted in the branding as a felon William Clements, a Fobbing labourer. During 1659, one Bartholomew Barnes of the village and Edward Ford had come to blows, the miller suffering assault and beating. Ford himself, as we have already seen, had every reason to believe the constable's office a thankless one, not least for having ended up before the courts several years since, over a matter in which he doubtless appeared the fool. It had perhaps been during his 1650 term of policing, when one Robert Rack, constable of West Tilbury appeared at Fobbing, having apprehended a prisoner "taken in the road there for felony and robbery" and handed over to the miller "safely pynnyoned."[23] Several parties became involved, including Robert Derrington, a tailor called Andrew Coller, and John Bishop, a labourer whom Ford trustingly hired to keep surveillance over his captive while arrangements could be made to transport him back to West Tilbury's Parliament-held blockhouse a few miles up Thames. Yet somehow the prisoner vanished.

This elite parish group was not always literate in the modern middle-class sense, though possibly more could read adequately than could write. Desk education was not yet the norm of youth, yet more than one Fobbing misdoer had in past times saved his neck by means of the ancient legal device called "Benefit of Clergy"; a simple test of reading some Biblical passage and thus proving to be of (theoretically) clerkly status. William Styles, a light-fingered husbandman of Fobbing would do so during 1604. Three years earlier, Matthew Thorpe had confessed at the assize to stealing cloth, a shirt and a sheet, a silver whistle and 5 shillings in money from John Perry at Fobbing and could have been hanged. Though only a labouring man, his ability to decipher a text set him free.

Often, parish officials made their signature by using no more than the capital of a surname – the best some could do with a goosequill – typified in the 1620s by Humphrey Harvy's earnestly contrived , or the laid-back of Thomas Bishop during the next decade. Robert Grubb would scratch as his mark in

[23] Calendared under 1652 Sessions.

Parishioners' signatures

1629 a tee-handled prong, ⅄ strongly suggestive of the implement used for grubbing dock roots in the field. Any distinctive personal graffito would suffice in witnessing the vestry's record of affairs. Occasionally, too, one may detect amongst the fairly competent scribings of the parish register books, echoes of the human voice itself, the ordinary village traits of accent as heard in the 17th century. A deletion of word endings in instances such as "ffobbin" or "Bolden" (the surname Bolding) hint at the easy south-eastern peasant speech, as does a drawling delivery of John Snow's surname in 1655: "John Snoo and Sara more was married". The James family at a similar period were invariably given the Essex pronunciation of "Jeames". Whether the victim of that deliciously inebriated 72 hours called "Thuseday" really uttered it thus, we cannot tell, but he wrote it on two occasions to enliven the chronicle of burials during 1675. Leslie Thompson's engaging volume, *The Story of the Land that Fanns*, covers other local aspects of literacy in depth, but on the whole Fobbing's parish records throughout the Stuart century seldom supply meat for scholastic ridicule.

Witch bottle,

The Ship

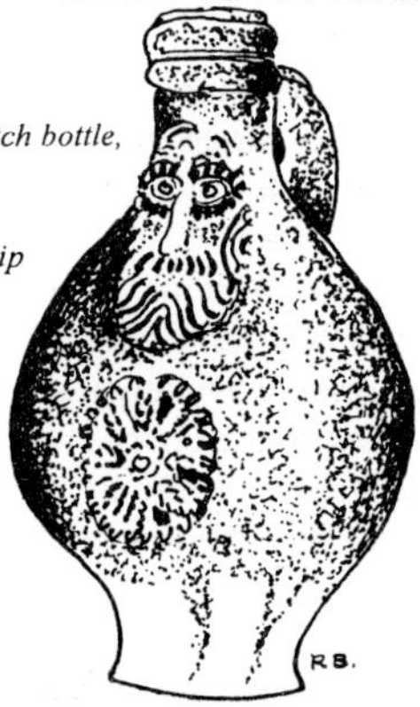

They were superstitious still, and suggestion of witchcraft would have aroused considerable agitation among villagers, even long after the widow Joan Bell's death in the April of 1609. Wards and talismans as protection against evil or ailment continued the norm of farmstead and cottage; the low cattle byres and horse stables made safe with their "hagstone" pebbles and wands of rowan-wood over the eaves. From the *Ship* alehouse at Fobbing comes one of our few tangible evidences of witch-fear;[24] a brown saltglazed *"Bellarmine"* flask bearing a bearded face-portrait and found sealed in the chimney mortar – a typical positioning at one of the vulnerable openings to any house.[25] Though its blackish contents are now unrecognisable, they probably once consisted of human detritus; urine, finger nail clippings, body hair and sharp instruments which were widely employed as a defence against the crone's coming. A latish 17th century date would fit both the weatherboarded *Ship* building and this "witch bottle" and so it may have been inserted at the time of initial occupation.[26]

Invariably, our parish officials represented the section of village society that published wills, for they possessed some wealth of which to dispose. A few of these enlightening documents indicate a concern for the least fortunate and in

---

[24] *Ship Cottages* TQ78.7198.8384.

[25] *The Archaeology of Ritual and Magic,* R. Merrifield, 1987. Bellarmine bottles are not evidence in themselves; it is the positioning within the "openings" of a building which carries significance.

[26] Bellarmine flask. T.MUS. Catalogue 535.

October 1644 the literate yeoman Raffe (Ralph) Grubb would leave "to the poore ... of ffobbin thirteen shillings and four pence", to be paid out within a month of his demise. Grubb himself had served as overseer in the year previous and was amply aware of the cruel social differences which surrounded him, as surely were the five Fobbing willmakers who, between 1612 and 1636, made allowances of 10 shillings each to the needy of their village. A greater sum of £4 had come as a last charity from widow Margery Lawson(e), mother of John Lawson (in whose hands the Fobbing Hall estate lay) during 1617.

To the family historian, wills are among the most fruitful sources for discovery, but here we may just glance at some of their more general contents, particularly referring to the goods and chattels and livestock around the homestead. Beds had long been of prime consideration and in the July of Charles II's restoration year, the sick husbandman Christopher Gowers would pass on to his grandson "my Bed Stead in the parlour wherein I lye together with the pillows Bedd Bolster Coverlett Blanketts and Sheets ...". Gowers' "long table in the Hall" (the great room of his house) and "my long and Short forme by it" were similarly bequeathed. At the prosperous Lucy Wood's death ("old Widdow Wood") in the middle 1660s "two feather bedds of the best" had been put by, together with bolsters, pillow bears (slips) and a dozen each of flax and damask napkins and four "towilles". A table and six joined stools, brass and pewter candlesticks, 12 pewter dishes "great and small" and a couple of pewter salts would be named among this aged woman's effects, as well as a brass kettle, ladle, a brazen and iron pot and spit for the cooking hearth.

Flaxen napkins and a bed had featured, too, in the will of John Mott, made at the new year of 1612 , as well as a kettle (an open cooking pot) and pewterware for the use of his neighbour Harry Bridge, while among the few clothes spoken of were those passed on to a brother of Christopher Friday in the late spring of 1607. He was to receive Friday's "green cloak with the velvet cape ... a payr of cloth breaches which are my best, and my best dubblet." A "best cloake" was to be given also "to my wives sonne John Wrayt" (Wright). One of the sundry Fobbing hoymen whose burial we have noted (March 1688) had owned a minor hoard of silver plate which was to be divided as legacies to his children.[27] Susanna and Mary, were to have £30, and one silver cup and two spoons. A son John, inheritor of "my wharfe house wth all the ground thereunto" (apparently the future *Ship* site) would receive similar silver items. Another daughter, Sarah, on coming to full age, was to obtain her silver as well as "one feather bed next to the best", sheets and the bed's curtain valence, while to Hall's sister, Katherine Wood, he

[27] John Hall, buried 30th March, 1688: see Chapter 6.

By the south porch

wished "the ring my brother Richard bequeathed me". Among the witnesses of this mariner's testament was Enoch Hardy, curate of Fobbing who occupied the parsonage house in the absence of his superior, Charles Wilbraham.

Two Fobbing farmers are found making last arrangements for disposal of lands during 1607 and 1608, Christopher Friday assuring to "cousen John Goodwyn my lease of Hawksberry to enter thereupon at Michaelmas, my wife Jone to enjoy the chamber wherein I live ...". Presumably then, Hawkesbury had been Friday's abode and his intention was to secure for his widow her customary accommodation after Goodwin (the parish windmiller) made entrance. Joseph Trotter's modest 2 acre of freehold and 4 acre copyheld field called "Knight ... howlden of the mannor of ffobbinge" were to become his wife's, "to farm for her life" upon his decease in March 1608, obviously with the necessary agricultural tackle and animals, though these are not specified. Nicholas Alet however showed his affection to a "loveing wife" (Joan Alet) in 1626 with the bequest of his 10 cows, 30 sheep and a riding horse as well as "all her household she brought to me in her widowehood". John Wood received through his mother Lucy's will the old lady's "colt wch now sucketh on the Bay mare", while a few years before in 1660, the sick husbandman Christopher Gowers had bequeathed "my two Cowes and the benefitt of them ... by sale or otherwise to Ellen and Mary Hart my Grandchildren ...". A grandson called Henry Smith was to be helped towards husbandry with "my Mare and Colt my Cart harnesse, plow harness and Colters (soil cutting plough attachments) and all my plow Irons and Implements belonging to a Plow ...". An inference that this testator came from the high northward grounds of Fobbing lies in the fact that both the Rev. George Maule and his late wife's relative (Justinian Champneys, visiting from Wrotham in Kent)[28] had been called in to witness Gowers' deathbed instructions.

A few other livestock emerge in our Stuart wills: Thomas Garrett in May 1614 "did give unto Mr Lawsons children viz John, Robert, Marie, Lidia and Margerie ... either of them a Lambe", while during late October, 1683 the yeoman Robert Wilson marked for Elizabeth Reivall's legacy "one red heifer for the Christmas after the lease of this bargain is out", that is, when his farm's tenancy came to its end.

---

[28] Mary Maule died 4th September, 1659; monuments to both she and George Maule are in All Saints', Vange. Her father was called Justinian, so possibly he, or a son, is referred to.

C Willbraham Rectr.

The brilliant Pell had been rector of St Michael's a quarter-century by the hour of his ignominious death in 1685, his years of absence reflecting a widespread and growing neglect within the Church of England through these (and later) times. Henry Bowyer A.M., his successor from February of the year following, had been vicar of East Tilbury already for almost a decade but died within a short while, to be replaced, during early October 1687, by Charles Wilbraham. Fobbing's register notes in turn Wilbraham's burial, "in the chancell of East Tilbury July the 25th being St James day 1696", though what his previous associations with that parish had been remain untraced. Alexander Thompson, another somewhat obscure minister, continued thereafter well into the reign of queen Anne. It was in all likelihood upon this chain of incumbents that the burden devolved for seeing to certain repairs and improvements which had been demanded at the archidiaconal visitation back in 1685 and from which few churches of the district came through without criticism.

Not a little of the works involved direct cost to the rector's own purse, for there had always been a distinction of responsibility between the chancel and the nave, or *"body"* of the church. The chancel was included in the rector's own freehold, while dilapidations of fabric within the public part of his edifice were a matter for the churchwardens, to be financed from their usual church rates. Within Pell's chancel, then, structural faults had included a weakness in a middle pillar on the south side, while less intrinsic tasks to be undertaken were in the plastering and whitening of its walls.[29] As to the roof "the seeling in ye Chancell is very much out of repaire, it must be mended and most of it made new". Floor paving was ordered to be set even, the much neglected plain-tiled roofs of the chancel, nave and aisles, were to be placed in proper order. Possibly a victim of some past storm, a chancel window was found by the inspectors to be "daubed up" and must now be "beaten downe and glazed" in fitting fashion.

Aside from some regularising of sunken floor paving, the rest of St. Michael's had been maintained in fairly acceptable condition, though builder's work was still required upon various exterior features; one buttress on the westward tower and another "Butterice abt ye middle on ye North side of ye Church." Skimping on expense, brick would be used instead of stone at this spot, and hence today we may not only pinpoint the churchwardens' makeshift effort, but can feel grateful to be able to examine such an accurately dated sample of locally produced red brick of the 1680s. For the architectural historian is able to use this as a cross-reference for dating other structures within the district.

[29] *Visitations Held in the Archdeaconry of Essex in 1685.* E.A.S. Vol. 21, 1932-34.

Various additions and alterations to interior furnishings had also been required, though most was in proper order here: "There is a Bible and two Comon prayer bookes, a booke of Homilys ... of Cannons, and a booke of Articles. There is a Table of ye degrees of marriage ... hung up in ye Church" (i.e. the nave). High on the walls, "The Comandmts and Sentences of Scripture ..." were to be renewed, for presumably these great lettered boards had become illegible. A lead lining for the medieval font was needed, "and the Cover of it must be kept hansome, and a pulley to be made over it to draw up the Cover ...". Clearly, public baptisms had to some extent been held elsewhere than within the church of late years (under curate Enoch Hardy) and this laxness was to stop. It would be conventional during the late Stuart period to find a communion table guarded off from the congregation – a feature not yet effected at St. Michael's. Now, a rail must be provided "and plac't ab't ye Comunion Table", while for its surface there should be, as elsewhere, "a carpett" (or covering) "of greene Cloth". Various unseemly desks nearby were to be placed further away, including that which had been "for ye use of ye Clerke".

Heygate's dialect poem *The Old Essex Clerk*, albeit of a later time, provides an amusing account of the Parish Clerk's activities; armed as he sat beneath his parson's pulpit with a "white wand to keep the young folks still".[30] A half guinea fee would be paid in the spring of 1748 to John Libbard, parish clerk of Fobbing, for performing exactly this disciplinary role – "his fees for keeping the boys in order at Church."[31] Through medieval times, this office had frequently been filled by men in holy orders, though with the Reformation it would become increasingly a lay-duty, performed by any inhabitant of the parson's choice and embracing matters such as bookings for marriages and christenings, seeing to the bellringer's gratuities, and sexton's work. He usually led the hymns and congregation's responses in service time. Few have been identified from St. Michael's: Matthew Harding had probably been parish clerk in 1639 when, as "Sexton of ffobinge," his name heads "a note showeing the rates due" from various parishioners, while during 1679 one called Gower(s) had held a tenement and an acre of land "near the Church". The year following, in late September, he removed thither entirely, the burial register giving "Roger Gowers, clerk of ffobbing" as a final memorial to his calling. Such a useful aide to the minister naturally managed to devise a tidy income and in 1693, under Charles Wilbraham, the clerk Henry Downing was to "have for the future twenty shillings a year allowed him out of the Overseers Rate" – an interesting reflection upon the dispensing of monies from the poor's kitty rather than out of the more appropriate church funds.

---

30 Reprinted in *Stifford and its Neighbourhood,* Rev. W. Palin, 1871.

31 Fobbing Churchwardens' Accounts and Rates, 1739-1841, Microfilm E.C.L. Grays, CR 18636.

8. KING GEORGE UBER ALLES

William Atkins was not of the village elite: he was one of those ordinary hundreds whose name inhabits Fobbing's registers for a while, raising no initial chord of interest. Atkins merely existed. Yet by chance, a day or so before Christmas in 1743, a manor court enquiry found a niche for him simply because he was very old and could clarify points of legal importance that had slipped out of local memory.[1] Atkins had been born around 1653 under the protectorate of Oliver Cromwell, yet here he remained, "above ninety years" in age, a lowly subject of the second Hanoverian King George, with a mind as nimble and responsive as parson Agnew's iron weathervane upon the grey church top. As a lad, Atkins had heard Dutch guns bombarding along Thames; he remembered the last extraordinary storm of the old century, when a fifty-six feet long whale had been driven up-river, swimming its way amidst the great sailing vessels to London. Twice, in 1690 and 1736, he had witnessed these wide marsh levels consumed by silver tides: he could relate stories of the fearful hurricane of November, 1703 when Fobbing's high elms were torn from their tethers and how a morning in the Maytime of 1715, the countryside had turned black as night, so that the yard-fowls took up their roosts at noonday.

Atkins had outlived a fair half-dozen of Fobbing's rectors and could recollect totally the time when the handsome, dark eyed, Mr. Pell had maintained his particular leave-way through the lord's ground, from his parsonage to a certain marsh spoken of as *"Black Shipp"*. That was during the late 1670s, when he had laboured upon his own little copyhold called "Reames". Years later, while a young married fellow still, he had rented another modest couple of fields of Mr. Robert Grey; *Little Broad Gates*, and gravelly *Sheepstealers* alongside the main street.[2] For forty years, Nathaniel Goodbe's daughter Mary had been his companion and spouse, till Andrew Agnew put the old lady to rest in her woollen

---

1 Manor of Fobbing and Stanford le Hope, Court Books, 1743. E.R.O. D/DCx M 1-4.

2 Rental of Fobbing Hall, 1679 *ibid.* *"Black Shipp"*, poss. plural of "sheep".

shroud, 10th March, 1727. Ancient Atkins well remembered. At the August of that year, Gravesend town was seen ablaze against the dark Kentish hills and they had heard of two hundred or more houses in the place consumed before sun-up.

He had witnessed plenty of the parish flock go beyond that final gateway into St Michael's mould: humble and high: James Cooper, an anabaptist, whom they had planted for his unorthodox opinions in a dark spot "behind the church" during 1733; poor Mercy Fitchet, so strangely united in death with her lover Mathew Lance, a married man who had fathered upon her a bastard babe some half dozen years before. He was buried on the turn of March, 1703, and Mercy gave up the ghost straightway, to become the very next entry in the minister's book of vanished souls.[3] Atkins had put his own little boy to the grave this same September – his third lost child in a row – and had heard the Great Hurricane howl across the sad spot before ever it grew a tussock of grass.

Only in recent times was gone Mr. James Foxon (quite a tempest himself at moments) a great yeoman of Braziers Hall beyond the windmill. More than once had Foxon been hauled to the assizes for his turbulent ways: as a parish officer in 1704 he had taken strong exception to a certain order signed by several neighbouring magistrates – Dacre Barret of Belhus and Nathaniel Grantham of High House in West Thurrock – "tearing and trampling under his feet" their precious instruction and uttering "contemptible words of the ... justices". Others present had agreed how Mr. Foxon had "stamped upon it" in his rage, declaring "I value it not a farthing". Such lively incidents would be cherished long about the place, this one volatile yeoman contributing a goodly share. Again, in the fall of 1706, James Foxon, gentleman, would stand to answer the accusations of William Mount, for beating and wounding him in the highway at Fobbing, Foxon's wife Sarah and John Saunders, and Martha Norris, too, each allegedly collaborating in the assault.[4]

It was a joy of old age to reflect upon the endless conflicts and passions which lay beneath the surface of this mundane place. The Sarah Foxon who had momentarily appeared so unladylike in a shameful street affray, lay now in her cold church vault beneath a few respectful lines.[5] Two or three generations on, and her very identity would be forgotten. But the creaky William Atkins could recall this woman's influential role in the history of those manor lands which had been sold off from the lordship back in the early 17th century to John Wood and

---

3 Fobbing Parish Registers: all subsequent register book references throughout this chapter will be traceable by date in E.R.O. D/P 414.

4 E.R.O. Calendar of Assize Files: all subsequent assize file references throughout this chapter will be traceable by year date in text.

5 *History of Essex: Fobbing,* unpublished Ms notes, W. Holman, E.R.O. D/Y1.

ANCIENT BOUNDARY. Dividing fully-urbanised Corringham and (foreground) rural Fobbing, the eastern boundsline of the manor and parish lands here follows a
1 small stream ditch, hemmed with pollard oaks, dogwood and hazel.

Photo author.

DISCARDED HIGHWAY. Evidently part of the late prehistoric-Roman trackway system, Mill Lane nowadays lingers as a pleasant public footpath, a westward
2 parallel to the High Road. The view looks north from Waterworks Lane end.

Photo author.

SEPULCHRAL MOUND. From its extension burial ground, St. Michael's churchyard is observed in this 1920s image as a prominently domed enclosure of ancient meadow, possibly utilising a sacred pre-Christian site on the hill's shoulder. 3

Edward Smith coll.

BLEST NEST. Most prestigious of village homes was Fobbing's rectory house, really Queen Anne and Victorian buildings set side by side. The attractive diapered red-and-black brickwork was repeated in its high streetside garden walls. 4
Here, parson Ernest Gardner absorbs south-corner sunlight with a book.

Gordon Hales coll.

A COMPLETE RURALITY. A duty constable (Frank Eagling?) crosses the
parish edge by Fobbing's *'Peculiar People's'* chapel c.1906. Old copyhold homes
5 fringe his way: the *White Lion* retains its agrarian aspect. Hill Cottages tops the
rise: to right, stackyard and barn of Sprivens Hall huddle St. Michael's church.

Gordon Hales coll.

THE 'WARE' POND. A mighty-wheeled timber carriage fronts Dan Raison's
weatherboarded builder's shed and Wheeler's back garden plank-privy overtops its
6 meadowside hedge, c.1910. An essential natural water supply for homes and
passing workhorses, the pond's name had possibly derived from the word *'weir'*.

R. Eaton coll.

FLOODED MARSHGROUNDS. All Fobbing generations could recall at least
one inundation of the levels. Here, 1928's January waters are seen from the East
Vineyard, behind Wharf Lane's Black Cottages and overtop the creekside quay. 7
Standing clear is the curve of the Corringham Light Railway embankment.

Winifred Tinworth coll.

ROOK'S-EYE VIEW. An east wind cuts over St. Michael's tower. Curtis'
farmhouse gables lie below; to left Prosbus Hall and Hill Cottages (rear) enrich the
long streetline, seen as far as the Avenue. Even in early spring, deep hedgerows 8
and great elms beyond Payne's Cottages render the upland ridge pleasant.

Roy Eaton coll.

STOCKYARD DANDY. Born c.1844 Emma Ann Rush (right) lived with her parents at Fobbing's Oil Mill cattle farm from maybe the late 1850s. Here, she extends an affectionate palm to husband Samuel Charles Jiggens (a decade her senior) who had begun life at Great Leighs, Chelmsford. Moving down-county to Fobbing, in time he and Emma would occupy her parents' marshland abode.

9 *Cardy family coll.*

WORKADAY SHEPHERD. Simon Gilder (1849-1936) was a typically mobile herdsman. Born at Finchingfield, he had come to Shellhaven homestead by the 1880s and later occupied Slatey House. Subsequently Gilder dwelled in Vineyard Cottage, where his picture (with English sheepdog) may have been taken.

10 *Thurrock Museum coll.*

HALL WITH CROSSWINGS. Fishers farmhouse in the High Road (west side) was a minor yeoman's home of c.1470. An excellent example of the 'hall house' style with both wings intact, it was partitioned to three cottages during the 18th century and was photographed here while still labourers' accommodation, c.1915. 11

Jack Brown coll.

FRAMED FROM THE WOODLANDS. The small late Tudor-Stuart barn at Fishers farmstead, before conversion to a modern dwellinghouse. Jowled mainposts of elm, a 'queenpost' roof assembly and low midstrey doors are visible. 12

Thurrock Museum coll.

TUDOR PERMANENCE. Yeomen's houses of timber frame like the Kentish-
style Wheeler's, hugged Fobbing's streetlines, changing their outward features
13 only slightly through five centuries, even though downgraded to cottage status.

Roy Eaton coll.

WHITE LION. Depicted here under the Seabrooke's brewery banner, this was
another 'hall with crosswings' of the 15th century, though its lineage as a public
14 alehouse is not proven before the mid-Georgian years. Adjacent is the Rust
family's Victorian barge-tackle and sailcloth store, of stuccoed yellow stock brick.

Gordon Hales coll.

VINEYARD FARM. Church, stable, and old lynchet fieldbanks of High Road houseplots lie to eastward behind the stoutly timberframed farmhouse. Its sloping, intensely cultivated kitchen garden is adjoined by Harry Hockley's (Glebe Cottage) streamside dairy pastures. A commercial viewcard, postmarked during 1907. 15

Simon Carter coll.

HIPPED ROOF AND WEATHERBOARD. Wooden rain guttering, a once familiar building feature, is seen on this probably late 17th century pair of plaintiled cottages in Wharf Lane (east side). The next-door Brick Cottages have survived. 16

Jack Brown coll.

17 CREEKSIDE ALEHOUSE. Possibly a remodelled Tudor building, Ship Cottages had been in use as a drinking place from the early 18th century until transfer of its licence to the Victorian *Dock House* at Thameshaven. Upslope, unsightly telegraph posts bring significant visual downgrading of a once scenic streetline.

Gordon Hales coll.

18 RECYCLED FOR EFFECT. An 18th century dwelling, later lavishly ornamented with waste green or black bottle bases, this distinctive double-gabled house in Wharf Lane (north side) was associated with the Rust family of publicans and carpenters, keepers of *The Ship* nearly opposite. 'Glass Bottle' remained till 1960.

Thurrock Museum coll.

HAWKESBURY MANOR HOUSE. Modernised with verandah, windowbays
and pebbledash coatings over old weatherboard, the basic mid 17th century
double-pile structure still shows its essential features in this 1930s snap of the 19
south front. Its light timberframe was constructed of elm under a plaintile roof.

John Dowson coll.

DRY STREET FARMHOUSE. Out on the northwest parish edge toward
Langdon Hills was this symmetrically-fronted home of simple boxframe and
weatherboard. With the 1820s, local Wesleyan Methodism focused here under the 20
Wrigglesworth family, one bedroom becoming called the *'Prophet's Chamber'*.

Photo author.

21 EWEN'S STORES. Formerly John and Ellen Halston's, its Georgian windows facing the parsonage offer a characteristically wide range of goods from tinned foods to galvanised footbaths. Right alongside was an open butcher's stall.

Roy Eaton coll.

22 GEORGIAN FORMALITY. Brickhouse in the High Road (east side) typified the 18th century southcountry vogue for warm redbrick facades with symmetrically placed sashlights and central doorways. Its rear wing – perhaps of an earlier date – was pantiled and weatherboarded. Demolition came with the early 1960s.

Roy Eaton coll.

QUAYSIDE IDYLL. The sailing barge *'Eliza'* of Rochester sits, prow-to-shore, offloading at high water in the lay-by of Fobbing Wharf. At left, are the earthen seawall and off-street alley opposite Glass Bottle House. *'Eliza'* would be lost in the estuary, mid October 1909, bound for Maldon with a cargo of sludgecake. 23

Thurrock Museum coll.

WATERFRONT DECLINE. The post Nazi-war years were to see Fobbing's navigable tideway dammed off and its quay – which had represented the village's picturesque 'entrance' point – sadly decayed into a ramshackle 'back-end' to the village. Later, cattle would browse the hollow channel of its dried-out creek. 24

Thurrock Museum coll.

25 TWIGHLIGHT OF HORSEPOWER. Walter Partner, who worked for westcountryman Clem. Hawkins of Whitehall farm, is the *horseman*, pausing at the tail of his wooden beam plough, with '*Boxer*' and '*Major*' in the traces. Though a drear-day, the background of Whitehall Hill is discernible above the marshes.

Thurrock Museum coll.

26 INDUSTRIAL GENERATION. John '*Borley*' Meen (1846-1911) was nicknamed after the farm on Holehaven creek. Also bailiff at Shellhaven house, he is seen here c.1897 with wife Martha, daughter Eva and six of his sons, another being killed at the Kynoch's jetty in 1902. The new industries fed them all.

Maurice Meen coll.

ELEMENTARY EDUCATION. Reputedly pictured during 1887, waspwaisted Miss Harriet Milne gathers thirty-five of her pupils at the church porch – a mere half the number recorded in Fobbing's censuses as 'scholar' during 1881 and 1891. 27

Lily Sadler coll.

POSTWAR RATIONALISATION. At back of Fobbing's schoolhouse just before closure and the move to Herd Lane; old style pinafores prevail, while grey jumpers and knicker-shorts are the lads' roughhousing kit. Bobbed-haired Miss Florrie Skills (left) and Ruby Broad lead fashion into the new *'jazz-age'* of the 1920s. 28

Roy Eaton coll.

VICTORIAN SPECULATION. The popularity of cheap yellow brick brought a townish mood to the rural High Road after 1880: Payne's '*Jubilee*' chapel, the
29 Avenue and Bay Cottages are pictured from the (later) Recreation Ground field. Ugly post-and-wire fencing creeps in, replacing ancient living hedgerows.

Roy Eaton coll.

MARSH HOMESTEAD. A foggy profile of Harry Jiggens astride nag, c.1910, gives rare backscene data on vanished Oil Mill house: seemingly 17th century, but
30 with Georgian leanto. Earlier windows were maybe not replaced till the Victorian.

Bob Cardy coll.

BOOTED CUTIES. Within the parish bounds stood the Kynoch's explosives factory and township. Social activities for its women employees included soccer. In this 1918 lineup, 'B' shift's team provides a daring glimpse of knee. 31

Jack Brown coll.

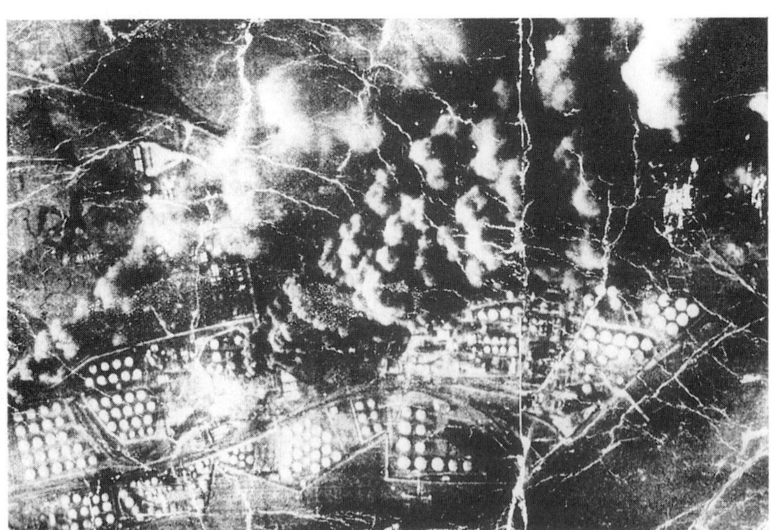

HERMANN'S EAGLE-EGGS. Shellhaven's bomb-blasted oil-holders cascade plumes of burning fuel during the first days of September, 1940 as a prelude to the battle of London. Goering's warplanes, flying cross-channel from the *Pas de Calais*, could see Fobbing's smoke columns clearly; a beacon of Nazi triumph. 32

Thurrock Museum coll.

John Goss

Mr. Lawson – the latter whose name still adorns Fobbing's bright communion cup of 1633. He died during 1640 at Dagenham, his corpse being carried home for burial. Thereafter, Fobbing Hall was to come into the Gosse family, considerable farming folk in their day, who had moved into the parish before the early 1660s when Mr. Thomas Goss of Fobbing had been interred at "Stanford Green". An overseer of the poor in 1667 had been John Goss, after whose death in 1685 his widow would re-wed to a Dutch parishioner John (van) Raining – though meanwhile the old manor lands were to be sold from Goss to Henry Saunders.

Several daughters were present in Saunders' household, his bride Sarah Dry becoming in time widowed and marrying this fiery young bachelor, James Foxon of Brentwood, with whom she'd dwelled at Fobbing from about 1698. At once he was to be found creating little difficulties for officialdom: in early December of this same year Horndon on the Hill's overseers had begun proceedings that would fetch him to court for having turned William Townes, an apprentice "out of his service, being legally hired". The March following saw the baptism, at home, "by reason of its weakness", of Sarah and James Foxon's first baby, James, an infant who nevertheless survived some way into his junior years. Of the family step-daughters, Sarah Saunders was to marry at London during 1703 Peter Willoughby of South Ockendon, who soon purchased from the other Saunders sisters their various portions of the estate, so becoming master of Fobbing Hall and its farms right into the mid 18th century.[6]

Such were the dry bones of their story, these few eminent names that figured transiently at the head of village affairs. Parson Agnew's bells had joined with literally hundreds around for the royal progress up-river to Gravesend of the new "furrin" monarch during 1714; it was Mr. Foxon's wedding year also, for Sarah Foxon having died near eighteen months previously, he had chosen secondly Dorothy Allen of Stepney, marrying her away at the London parish of St. Dunstan's in the East. She would bear him several children, including Anna Maria and John Foxon, a boy who was to inherit with the years a few manor copyholds including Red Marsh (Redmers) and a parcel called the Frith, near Fobbing quay. Mrs. Dorothy Foxon would outlive her husband, who died 15th August 1737, seeing her distant connection, Peter Willoughby, relinquish his freehold of Fobbing Hall to Mr. Robert Johnson, a wealthy innholder of Low Leyton though a mere beggar on horseback compared to those princely Boleyns who had possessed it a couple of centuries since.[7] The dance of time disposed of all things, and placed new figures in the superior box-pews of St. Michael's.

---

6 Essex Freeholders, 1734 E.R.O. Q/RJ 1/1. Holman shows that, though Fobbing Hall manor lands had been sold from the Whitmore estates, Sir George Whitmore retained its *lordship* till 1682, when it was purchased by Sir Thomas Davall.

7 Manor of Fobbing and Stanford le Hope. Court Books, 1735, E.R.O. D/DCx M1-4.

The *Royal Commission on Historical Monuments* mentions a forged iron weather-vane[8] set upon the tower of Fobbing church, decorated with the initials "A.A.". This mechanism (now vanished) must have been put aloft in the time of Andrew Agnew M.A., Fobbing's minister from 1710 to 1729, whose grave-slab is to be found within the south aisle. In all likelihood, Agnew had moreover been responsible for creating the handsome steep-roofed rectory which today represents a northward block to "Pell House". Its symmetrical facade is in conventional queen Anne character, of red brick with some blue-black headers and having at one time a central panelled door under its pleasant canopy. The sashlights are regularly arranged and set flush to the brickwork. It is of two main floors with attics and dormers, the claytiled roof being of extraordinary height and steep pitch, suggesting remodelled elements of an earlier rectory building.

Fobbing's parish register contains a pair of memoranda (penned by curate Thomas Spencer) relating to the customary ceremonies by which Agnew had taken office.[9] On 23rd February, 1711 the Rev. John Johnston, vicar of Grays and chaplain to Tilbury fort had been present to perform the Induction of "Mr. Andrew Agnew Clerk into the Rectory & Parish Church of Fobbing ... with all the Profits and Emoluments thereto belonging", while upon the Sunday following (25th) Andrew was to deliver prayers before his gathered congregation in both the morning and afternoon, "& also 39 Articles of Religion after some part of ye Divine Service was read", declaring his unfeigned assent, and confessing "to all & everything contained and prescribed in & by ye sd Book of Common Prayer ...". Among those attending to hear his oath and declaration were village leaders like James Foxon master of Brasiers Hall (Great House) the yeoman John Goodwin and Robert Wildes, publican of Fobbing.

Agnew's response to the bishop of London's "articles of enquiry" during November 1723 avowed him to have been a fully resident pastor, inhabiting the neat new house, having no other benefices and serving (he said) no cures elsewhere.[10] Like some, in other words, he did not play saddleback curate around the countryside. Nevertheless his name not long since (1720) had been listed among those acting as curates to St. Mary's Corringham, in whose register the actual course of events is clearly noted: "For diverse Years past ye Cures of Corringham and Fobbing have been supply'd by one and the same Curate who read prayers and preached at each place alternately every Sunday." As for his own flock, the forty or so dispersed families posed certain embarrassments. Some quite

---

8 R.C.H.M. South East Essex, Vol. IV, 1922. During 1922 also, the weathervane, bent by recent gales, would be removed to a workman's yard at the High Road, never to be reinstated. Its small turret spire remained only a few years more.

9 Memoranda at rear of Fobbing Parish Register, burials (1680-1736).

10 Response to Articles of Enquiry November, 1723 by Edmund, bishop of London. G.L. Ms 25, 750/1.

Andw Agnew

nearby dwellers were outrightly resorting to Corringham of a Sunday, others "who live out of ye village" resided closer to other parish churches than his own by a mile or more. "My parish tho' small yet very narrow is of a considerable length", explained Agnew, defending his Sunday laxity in providing but a single service instead of the two required by his bishop. The sacrament was administered "Thrice a year", but catechising of the youth he saw to "in ye summer season only" because so many of his young flock had "far to come". It all smacked of going with the drift of things.

It was a century in which, across England, the Established Church lapsed often into a forgetfulness of purpose and country parsons, like the literary Sterne, or Dr. Derham of Upminster, could turn to favourite private studies, to the natural sciences, or to the antiquities of place. So came William Holman, a minister of Halstead during Agnew's later years, stepping the riverside parishes to scribble manorial gleanings for his invaluable *"History"* into which all future Essex antiquarians must delve for reliable morsels. Possibly Andrew Agnew entertained and accompanied this great enthusiast upon his visit round St. Michael's – "Pleasantly situated on a rising Ground ..." and with its "Square tower of Stone Embattled", entering the limewashed interior to record – with surprisingly modern concern – the sharp chiselled memorial slab to Sarah Foxon and her 14 year old offspring James (1712 and 1713) as eagerly as the chancel's 14th century marble tablet, cut "in Saxon letters in Old French capitals" commemorating Thomas de Crawdene. William Holman's Fobbing notes seem to have been gathered sometime during the mid 1720s, after the fifth bell of churchwardens Glascock and Knapping (1724) had been installed.

There is little to discern of Agnew's personal character in the registers, records which he generally himself attended to – a series of neat and diligent entries with marginal surname index, hinting at a north British fondness of order. He appears to have had no close family at Fobbing, performing his last baptism (of Betty, child of John and Ann Marrett of Whitehall farmhouse) on 6th November, 1729 and dying upon the 24th. Will Blake, Corringham's curate, was to record the event, affirming our rector's burial in legal woollen and seeing thereafter for half a dozen years to parish duties on behalf of the absentee Richard Rudge, M.A., Fobbing's first appointee under its German patrons, the Electors of Hanover, whose induction to St. Michael's came on 17th February, 1730.

By 1736 another joint-curate would take the place under his wing – Richard Ockleshaw, married to Arabella, an "affectionate Wife & Faithfull Friend", whose plain floorbrass epitaph is set in the Baud chapel at Corringham. During November 1746 Ockleshaw had delivered his burial-rote as the Sexton's shovel clattered over Fobbing's oldest inhabitant, William Atkins, and he would remain

R Ockleshaw Curate

the curate in office till the mid century's appointment to the benefice of Dr. Lucius Henry Hibbins, LL.D. A casual air had maybe lingered long enough, allowing carved graffiti to spawn upon Rudge's church door – a very handsome gothic outline with flying flag above and the bold cypher T S is dated 1734 – while even the baptismal register carries its stigma of some quiet tipple whilst catching up on parish bookwork: *"wrote with port 1740"*, it confides, and powerful port it must have been, to have coloured the page so well.

With Lucius Hibbins, Fobbing had obtained, once again, a fully resident minister, Justice of the Peace for Essex, a clergyman of evident forcefulness and individual opinion. Hibbins (Hibbens) would be inducted to his rectory (that is, the living, not merely its attractive house) by curate Ockleshaw upon Friday, 30th March, 1750, doubtless later that year to feel some annoyance for having come into the expense of chalkstone and timber piling for seawalls upon his glebe farmland just at the hill's foot "near Fobbing Barrs". The marsh bailiff, moreover, had reported 60 rods length of ditching to be attended to along Hibbins' property; all were matters carrying substantial fines to the Court of Sewers if ignored.[11]

The rector's lawyerly handwriting is distinctive among the Georgian register entries, but lacks intrinsic character, though the occasional remark suggests an aspect or two of his personality. Following the baptism of a bastard son of a woman called Sarah Crispe in late July, 1753 some offence seems to have been exchanged at the interrogation about her infant's paternity. Hibbins had evidently felt sufficiently piqued to add in his register beside her name – "young impudent Whore of this Parish". Were that her true vocation, Sarah was adept at skipping its inconveniences, for no other children of her name can be traced in all the district around. It had been an unusual week for the parson, since his only other baptism would be that of a blackamoor servant belonging to "Mr. Philips, Brewer of Ratcliffe Cross", perhaps a colleague of Richard Philpot at the *Lion*. Christened in the name of "John", this black slave would also be noted as having assumed the English surname of Stanford. Few negroes can have been met with in deeper country places at this time, though London's African population was already considerable by 1750.

At a similar time, late in 1751, Lucius had prepared his church records for a forthcoming change from the old (Julian) calendar to Gregorian style. Long before there had been a brief attempt to organise things this way, for an entry in

[11] Court of Sewers, Fobbing Levels: Order Books, 1729-1934, microfilm E.C.L. Grays, CR.22919.

Fobbing's register of 1677 notes simply "beg^{n} at Jan", meaning that the regular fashion of starting the English year upon Lady Day (March 25th) was to be ignored. However, this innovation was not to survive far into the 80s. But with 1752 law dictated a January start, Hibbins explaining in his baptismal book: "By Act of Parliament ... the first day of next January will be the first day of the year 1752." Just to ensure the message got home, his burials register would phrase it another way, "... the commencement of the year was changed from the annunciation of the Blessed Virgin Mary and set back ... so that there will be no January February or March MDCCLI but on the First Day of the present January commenced the year of our Lord – MDCCLII."[12]

The session's files for 1752 introduced a little more scenery relating to Mr. Hibbins' activities as a county magistrate.[13] In early June of that year, one of the frequent notices relating to a local outbreak of distemper among horned cattle had reached him from Orsett, so that he was obliged to investigate any untoward movements of beasts within his jurisdiction. Almost straightway Hibbins was to learn of a drover, one Stephen Revell of Great Easton, with half a dozen bull calves intended for suckling and sale, having arrived at the *White Lion*, to which house he hastened "to see What Certificates the said Stephen had ... or by what Authority he drove and jobb'd them." Richard Philpot, victualler, had been present as witness and so possibly had been Thomas Offin, Fobbing's butcher, who testified to events shortly after.

At the same time (June 9th) Jacob Bunnet was to record precisely the "Species of the Six Calves Stopp'd this Day at Fobbing": three were "Red Ones – a bout 3 weeks Old", a couple "Creme Colourd" and one brown, these all of a fortnight's age. Revell, being questioned, had avowed that all were his own property, "*by him bought of Robert Pegg of what place he knows not but the said Pegg is a Jobber as he believes and he bought some of them (but can't tell which) of the said Pegg at Nayland ... and others of them (but he can't say which) of Henry Bolton of Debenham ...*". To all this was added a certificate which the drover Revell produced, signed by a constable for the Land Tax in Suffolk a week or so previously but referring to four animals only, and stating three of them to be "*Red & White Cow Calves*" intended for sale "*att Clenchford market ... Taken from ye Cowes & herd Entirely free from ye infection & Distemper which is now ... Raging amongst ye Horned Cattle for forty Days Last past* ... (and) *have not been to the best of my Knowledge & belief within one mile of any infected Place.*"

[12] Dates throughout these chapters have been adjusted where applicable to the current (Gregorian) calendar years.

[13] E.R.O. A.F., depositions, 1st, 9th, 10th June, 1752.

The matter was becoming both complicated and suspicious, since the calves concerned failed to entirely tally with those upon this Suffolk doquet and Hibbins was not satisfied. There should, objected the parson, have been fresh certification applied for by Revell "on coming out of Suffolk into this County". At this, Revell had apparently lost his equilibrium, in the words of the *White Lion's* proprietor crying, "that he knew what to do as well as the said Justice and he did not care a Fart for him ... nor a thousand such Fellows." Thomas Offin's account of the alleged outburst would be less exact, but he was able to confirm Revell's having "abused and insulted him (Hibbins) in the Execution of his Office in a very scandalous manner ... as was not fitting a Common Person much less to a Magistrate doing his Duty ...". Since the reverend gentleman took both depositions and wrote them down himself, the variation of description may have been purposefully contrived. In due course, one Aaron Lockwood of Hitcham, a Suffolk jobber, would testify that the calves belonged to himself and his partner Robert Pegg of Nedgen, and that Revell was his servant, apparently droving them for sale by consent.

Unlike some proximate parishes whose churches drifted into neglect during the Georgian years, Fobbing looks to have done what it could, as its earlier churchwardens' accounts (surviving only from 1739) occasionally reveal.[14] Rudge's chancel had undergone "Tylers" work in 1741, but not until the late decade would there be a bustle of improvement about the whole building, heightening after Hibbins appeared on the scene. With March 1749, Elizabeth Turner took payment of £1. 4s. 0d. for window glazing, while during drowsy July the township's aptly named brewer, Richard Philpot of the *White Lion*, was to be reimbursed 30 shillings for beer, seemingly to encourage workmen in *"doing of Bell".* Through 1751 an interior purge is reflected; washing surplices and "the church linning" (linen) the purchasing of "ten Ells of Holland" at £2. 10s. 0d. for a surplice whose making up had cost a further half-guinea; a couple of dozen "Hassaxs" and – in the waning year – "a new cloath for the communion Table." That spring, under the churchwardenship of Richard Boon, Hibbins' improvements had run to some minor lath-and-plaster repairs, also suggesting perhaps an accumulating decay. For with the mid 1750s carts would go rumbling off towards the Grays chalk pits fetching quantities of lime – a half dozen journeys in the fall of 1754 – and others for "hart Laths" of softwood, "for ceiling the church". These wardens' bills however, appear to cover only a parish outlay in farming vehicles at more quiet times of the agricultural year and it may be that a suitable arrangement had been made with Fobbing's nominal manor lord, whose Davalls estate in Grays included all the resources of chalk for builder's lime that one could require.

---

[14] *Fobbing Churchwardens' Accounts and Rates, 1739-1841.* Microfilm E.C.L. Grays, CR 18636.

Under Richard Ockleshaw's curacy, a village wife called Mrs. Cock had been paid "for Ringin" (1740) and much was made throughout his time of the bells' music – saluting coronation anniversaries of monarchs, or the news of distant victories. Good sums were given to Fobbing's bellmen; through the 1740s each ringing day earned them a collective five shillings, at Christmas, November 5th (the preservation of king James) and again upon 29th May (recalling the safe concealment of young Charles after Worcester in the branches of an oak, hence "Royal Oak Day"). Late in Lucius Henry Hibbins' rectorship, in 1758, it became politic to add another token of respect, for "ye King of prusias birth day" (January 24th) since Frederick the Great had proved England's closest ally in the late intercontinental war against Austria and the French.[15]

Springtime's parish business meetings continued in St. Michael's and though until Victoria's reign there was to be no separate apartment built, a "vestry room" certainly existed, simply employing space within the broad south chapel. Late April, 1747, was to observe Fobbing's churchwardens clearing debts after a recent vestry dinner (its small annual perk for those unsalaried parishioners who, as officers, had guided matters through another year) for which Thomas Offin, grocer and butcher, supplied thirteen shillingsworth of beef. Thomas Merris, "for dressing the Victuals and beer and punch" would present a bill for £1. 3s. 10½d. Formerly a Vange inhabitant, Tom Merris is believed to have wed Richard Philpot's sister Sarah, having therefore connections with the *White Lion* at this date and strongly inferring that the vestry feast had been held on these premises. During 1741, Merris had been victualler of the *Crooked Billet*, Stanford, an outlying property of Fobbing manor.

Perhaps with something of an impish notion that his magisterial presence should continue to influence village decision-makers at their Easter meetings, the "late most worthy Rector" Lucius Hibbins was to direct his corpse be buried "in the Middle of the Vestry Room" – an obligation duly attended to three days after his decease, on 30th June, 1759. Presumably his chilly cavity of repose was not to be within the flimsily screened area whither Fobbing's gentlemen withdrew to make use of the "chamber pot for the Vestry" purchased for 6d. back in March, 1752. "*The Grave's a fine and private place*" considered the poet Marvell, but for the late Reverend Mr. Hibbins, it seems there could be no permanent guarantees.

His will had been witnessed a few weeks previously by a Fobbing curate called Rogers, John Libbard the parish clerk,[16] and Richard Philpot. Hibbins' wife Elizabeth, who had "departed from and sold her Paternal inheritance to pay ... Debts wherewith I and my Estate were encumbered", was to be provided for with

---

[15] *Fobbing Churchwardens' Accounts and Rates, 1739-1841.* Microfilm E.C.L. Grays, CR 18636.

[16] Libband: variant of *Libbard, Libbert* (Chapters 7 and 8).

properties that would be sold off in Shropshire.[17] Old legal friends should have gold rings each for mourning, while a debt of £1,000 to another lawyer, Randal Wilbraham of Lincoln's Inn, must be settled. Lucius Hibbins' relationship with his offspring had evidently been tense, and though, at the last, bequests had been rather aloofly set down for both, he was evidently unsure whether one, the "unhappy ffugitive Son ffrederick George" might still be living. The other object of a somewhat grudgingly granted bequest had been his "undutifull and unnatural daughter Henrietta Lucretia", whose filial failings we shall never discover, though just for a moment, these dreary pages of probate hint at the kind of human passions upon which Hogarth or Henry Fielding had engaged their delectable skills.

Fobbing burial ground still played its part in the glebe farm system, its regular mowings haycocked for use in the rector's stable nearby on the north side. In June 1739, John Poleand (Poland) had pocketed his eighteen pence for a churchyard scything; in March ten years on John Libbert (Libbard) would have double this amount, a three shilling payment still pertaining through the mid 1750s. Evidently that seasonal task went with the church clerk's office. Libbert, village carpenter and coffin maker, is seen also engaged upon improvements to the church fabric during the winter of 1754-55, noted for its great March snowfalls throughout England. That August his own son, just reached manhood, was to be buried, John Libbert himself dying in the May of 1761. To his wife Martha, had been assured a room in which to live in their copyhold premises, daughter Elizabeth Libbert being granted accommodation at the western end of his woodworking shop, "as far as the back of the chimble" (chimney). Libbert's garden and a grove (orchard?) of trees was to pass to his son Isaac, whose cherub-topped monument of 1767 is still discernible next to St. Michael's porchway.[18] Sheds, sawpit and timber yard, all stood at the streetside above the public house of Richard Philpot, right within the morning shade of one spreading tree that made a bold island in the highway atop Lion Hill.[19]

Substantially wrought medieval and Tudor countrymen's homes needed no replacement until fashion put them quite beyond the pale of acceptance and so they overwhelmingly sufficed in places like Fobbing far into the Hanoverian century. Even then, there was little entirely new building and not until the very end of the Georgian years were many timber frame homes relinquished by the aspiring farmer and his wife. A sudden downgrading of the

[17] P.R.O., P.C.C. PROB. 11.847.

[18] Monumental Inscriptions, St Michael's, Fobbing, R. Bingley, 1981-89.

[19] Chapman & Andre (map) Plate XXII, 1777, surveyed 1774-5.

John Libbard

"hall house" through the 1780s to the 1820s typifies our whole Thameside district. Fobbing Hall, Fishers, Copeland, Whitehall, each was to be lath-divided into two or three smaller tenements for the field labourer's or stockman's family. So were other buildings known now to us only from photographic evidence, such as the five-unit boxframe row called Hill Cottages – demolished around 1930 at Lion Hill's summit. Obviously a humbled hallhouse of apparently medieval date, the group can be identified in a rental of 1679, lying near to "Spreevers ... adjoyning the two high Ways". In the possession of farmer James Greenaway of Prosbus during 1820, it had been by then already remodelled as "4 tenements and a public oven" – offering an insight to the little township's way of providing for those poor who still knew no sufficient home means of breadmaking.

To workfolk who had been raised in crumbling rural hovels, these converted houses of an olden time must have seemed lordly quarters, even if extravagant comforts such as inglenook hearths had been bricked up and good breadovens plastered over. Such things were discouraged, since their requirement of log-fuel could only tempt the agricultural man into hedgebreaking, or to stealing the field stiles. Domestic cooking *was* managed nevertheless within these constricted new fireplaces. At Copeland, sooted potsherds from the present garden soil tell that even into the twentieth century a Georgian open-hearth culinary method tarried still.

But not all smaller homes were partitioned hand-me-downs. Plough surface gleaning at a dwelling plot aside the public footpath behind Mill Cottages indicates by soft red bricks and other ceramic debris, that there had been a quite modern cottage provision here around the start of the 18th century.[20] Among its household pottery fragments were late Georgian "combed" wares from the English midlands, used extensively around Fobbing and much liked for their yellow-glazed cooking dishes with chocolate coloured trailings over the shallow interior. Such items gave a cheery contrast to the somewhat monotonous range of heavily rimmed platters and pancheons of orange-red hue which were the Georgian woman's commonplace crocks. For those in the middle social scale, plenty of pleasant white pottery with blue designs of "Dutch" inspiration were available also. A specially pretty vessel handle of this sort, dating to c.1740, comes from the yard of Prosbus Hall.

---

[20] TQ78.7145.8452. This thatched roofed wooden cottage was burned down April, 1935. Though called "Old Mill House", it does not appear to have had any connection to the mill estate other than a general proximity.

Andrew Agnew's response to his bishop's questionnaire of late 1723 establishes that no charitable foundations provided any hospital or donation within the parish, for the assistance either of church repairs or for the help of the poor. Another nearby parish was however to operate in future times its own benefaction within Fobbing, where a corner of rented ground with a cottage called "Vine House" (on the south of St. Michael's churchyard) helped pay Stanford le Hope's vestry for the maintenance of needy inhabitants.[21] Since, in 1768 this property had been owned by Sir Mathew Featherston,[22] squire of Hassenbrook Hall, a clue to the charity lies in that quarter.[23] Stanford's overseers nevertheless seem to have possessed no record of it in later years, save that Vine House had been "destroyed by fire" and its insurance of £1000 invested in consols sometime in the 19th century. It would be still an occupied cottage at the 1851 census, when Charles Malin, a Stanford native and farm labourer had newly settled there with his young family.

While leading lights of the 18th century sought sizeable mansions elsewhere, their lesser farming counterparts and tradespeople whose livelihood depended more directly upon village contact, were to build at home, though only to a minor extent. Their dwellings, of red brick and symmetrical neatness are largely vanished now from the landscape, though Byrons farmhouse remains (Fobbing's store and post office) behind blank renderings of stucco. It is however, still recognisable by its mid-18th century facade; a central doorway, double dormers and with a single storey brewhouse of typical form alongside. Upslope, the now demolished Brickhouse abutting Wheelers Lane[24] is a rather similar (though earlier) structure, with symmetrical sash windows, a pair of wide, central, canopied doorways, endstacks and a couple of dormer windows to its plaintiled roof. Here, a lead Sun Fire Assurance mark (No. 174156) long survived, relating to a policy of 11th March, 1760 when the recently widowed Ann Green had paid £100 premium upon "her new dwelling house ..." and a further £40 for farm sheds adjoining: a timber carthouse, stable and cowshed, all tiled and a fairly safe risk in their assessor's eyes.[25]

F. Z. Claro, who knew the building before its demolition in the early 1960s recalled a number of lights (2 upon its frontage) that had been blocked so as to avoid window duty (a tax which pertained all through the Georgian period to

---

21 *Reports of the Charity Commissioners 1819-1837,* parish of Stanford le Hope.

22 *The Uppark Papers,* Calendar of muniments relating to Thurrock properties, Typescript, T.MUS.

23 E.R.O./T/B 56.

24 Brickhouse site TQ78.7167.8425. Its boarded rear wing was pantile-roofed.

25 *Sun Assurance Policy Books*, March, 1760. G.L.

1852) and this observation seems to affirm that Brickhouse had been set aside for tenure of other village families at some date.[26] Fobbing's court rolls prove the point and offer some explanation why. As only daughter and heir of Mary Clifford, who had died during June 1759, widow Green had inherited Brickhouse as a copyhold of the manor, her official admission at the court being dated almost 2 years later, in 1761. It was to be described then as a cottage "now used as two Tenements", explaining its unorthodox double entrances, for clearly it was not to be needed as the lady's main home. According to Claro, Ann was soon to remarry to a West Thurrock parishioner,[27] while Brickhouse and other rented cottages in Fobbing, inhabited by William Higgs, a grocer and flour-shop keeper in 1766,[28] and John Hill, added to her financial support. Joseph Green and Ann had been married since the early 1740s, burying an infant, John, in October 1745. They emerge together as witnesses in a small domestic drama during the spring of 1752 that may have centred upon an earlier cottage occupying the Brickhouse plot.

On Sunday the 23rd, Ann had noticed that a pair of scissors with a silver chain attached, was missing from their hanging-place in her home and at once her husband suspected whom the culprit might be. Richard Right (Wright) "a strolling Boy" had been playing on the premises with the family's servant lad that day, a character whom (Joseph Green deposed) "had been pilfering and stealing up and down ... the Town of Fobbing all this present Morning". Consequently Green somehow arrested his youthful suspect and "found upon him his Wife's said Scissors but the Chain was off from Them". Right provided a glib story: he had received the shears, he said, from a maid servant at the *Cock and Pye* alehouse in Stanford as an exchange "for a knife she had of him", denying at first the presence of any silver chain, though subsequently admitting having "dropp'd it at Corringham". Later, the boy admitted "without persuasion" before Lucius Hibbins J.P., to having stolen the implement and its silver attachment from the Green's abode, adding in his defence that he had "been brought up to begging and strolling ever since he can remember."[29] His destination would presumably be the House of Correction.

The Clifford family, into which Ann Green was born, figured moderately around the earlier Georgian years. John Clifford, farming the Prosbus (Sprivens Hall)[30] acres as customary tenant by 1740, had married at times two girls called Mary, the first dying aged only 17, on 11th May, 1731. Her headstone, sculpted

---

26 *The Days When there was a Tax on Light and Air,* F. Z. Claro, G.T.G. 29th May, 1962.

27 Ibid.

28 At the Epiphany sessions, 1763, Higgs was to answer for using "a false Ballance wanting half an Ounce".

29 E.R.O. A.F. *Deposition of Joseph Green & "Voluntary Confession" of Right*, 23rd March, 1752.

30 Prosbus (Sprivens) Hall TQ78.7164.8392.

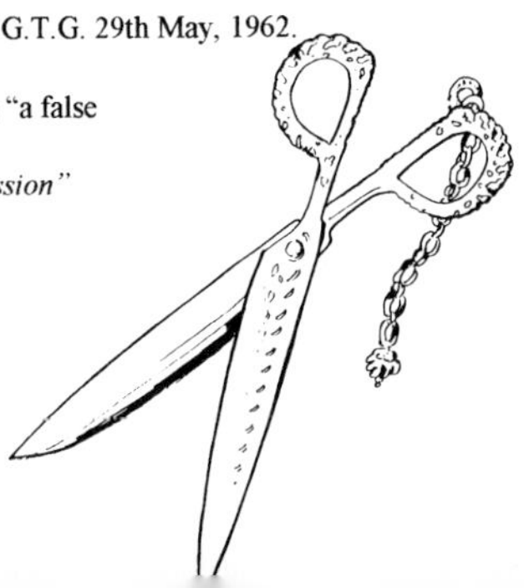

with skull and bones (so extensively featured through this century) is dimly legible near the church door. A few years before his own death in 1745, Clifford had added to his holdings the tenement called "Harrises", which appears to be that same block already glimpsed, the Hill Cottage group that would pass after the second Mary's decease to Ann Green and which, to add complications, is termed "Clay Hall" when insured for fire in March, 1741. The Sun policy which embraces this block had been issued primarily for Prosbus Hall, upon whose pleasant facade of red brick with occasional blue headers the lead mark (No. 87172) remains.[31] Though in the tenure of Clifford, its landlord was Alexander Masters, a Smithfield ironmonger seemingly descendant from Martin Masters, Fobbing shopkeeper, who had paid Ship Money tax in the time of Charles I. The line had become, in time, city based, for Martin Masters the elder, a London draper, held East Hill, one of the fields overtopping Whitehall (in 1738) when his under-age son Alexander was admitted to the land at the manor court. Now, in 1741, the young man's property included all Prosbus Hall's 150 acres, the copyholds of Rogers (a Fobbing manor farm) in Stanford and the *Crooked Billet* pub there while, fronting Clay Hall, lay another Masters asset, which this policy calls "the sign of the White Horse". Its description as "timber and tiled" assists our supposition that this must really be the present *White Lion.*

If dwelling houses built by the Fobbing middle-class were few, none can have vanished with greater local regret than Wharf Road's "Glass Bottle" cottages, a pair which reputedly bore the date 1783 upon one chimney stack.[32] Outwardly they were of "red and black chequerwork bricks" beneath a gabled plaintiled roof, having internal stacks at either end. A pair of central street-facing doors with small Georgian canopies were matched by ground floor sashlights that had dripmoulds above. Their glazing bars were somewhat thick, suggesting a rather earlier period than claimed, while an extraordinary appearance had been effected by studding the entire facade of the building with some hundreds of dark bottle bases.[33] Semicircular panels of waste glass likewise filled the fanlight spaces above each doorway. The result was to create a masterpiece of rural vulgarity, in all likelihood around 1830 when, one imagines, a single handsome house had been converted into "semis". An obvious source of materials lay at the *Ship* just a few yards away, and since Glass Bottle, or Bottle House, had been in the possession of the Rust family of publicans, this inspirational flight probably emanated from one of them. A number of tin-glazed pictorial tiles have survived from a mid-Georgian fire-surround at the house, each representative of Biblical and other scenes,

---

[31] Sun Assurance Policy Books, March, 1741. G.L.

[32] Glass Bottle TQ78.7197.8383.

[33] *Fobbing Loses its Glass Bottle Cottages,* F. Z. Claro, G.T.G. 3rd June, 1960.

John Clifford

including the women of Samaria at the well.[34] Such an image might have been selected because of the communal manor well which once gave animation to the street just outside through every season of Fobbing's year. A few of these mauve-tinted tiles are now with Thurrock Museum.[35]

Farmyards altered their appearance only in detail through the Georgian age, elm frames and boarding, with thatch, being still relied upon, though in draught-horse stabling some rebuilding with red brick made an impact in later years. Among surviving examples is the attractive two-horse stabling at Vineyard farm with its typical vernacular flooring of flint boulders – matched nearby at Prosbus Hall. There, the excellent late Georgian stable is of timber and board, its hardstanding of flint complemented by a neat centre-walkway of paviour blocks in hard yellow-grey fabric which were the product of country brickyards around the 1830s. Stables were changing in this period from rather tall thatched sheds with hay-tallets (lofts) above the stallage, to longer, single storey ranges, with either pantiled or slated covering and separate half-doors at intervals along the facade. A pantile roofed redbrick row of c.1840 at Whitehall farm illustrates this style ideally, its doors all set to the north. Another local aspect of animal housing can be seen there, an internal insulation of the "cold" tiling effected with bunches of wild marsh reed packed against its roof-batons.

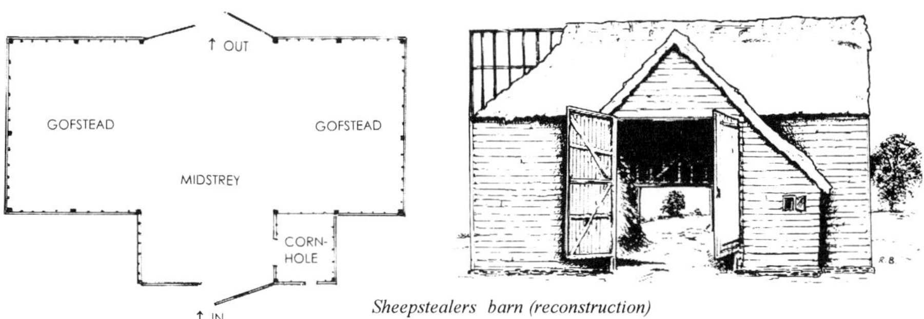

Sheepstealers barn (reconstruction)

For several hundreds of years through post-medieval times, barn design varied only moderately and the most expert eye can seldom date a weatherboarded example with any closeness from exterior look alone. All were lofty – the tallest of the yard's structures and had great doorways sufficient for the access of a team of horses drawing waggons loaded to perhaps thirteen feet in height. In harvest, these buildings were to be packed almost to their rafters with sheaves of cereal (called the "mow") with a generally central passageway or "midstrey" between

[34] Probably early 18th century Lambeth potteries ware.

[35] T.MUS. Catalogue 483 (though affixed as a wall decoration during the early 20th c.).

Threshing with flails

remaining as the only clear space. Here late autumn's threshing took place with the hand-flail, separating the grain initially from its long-straw. Secondly, came the winnowing, which cleaned off unwanted husks and dust by tossing it in the air upon shovels within the windy area created by opening the barn's broad doorways. Once "dressed" in this way, the corn or other fresh seed was ready for measuring, sacking and lifting to the security of the locked granary. Stubby "knee" supports under each tie-beam, bolted through with iron, were the constructional norm from the late 18th century onward and this technique is present both at Curtis' and at the Whitehall barn of c.1840 which is similarly of five bays' length.

Dismantled following the great storm of October 1987, Curtis' barn had been positioned like so many, to shelter house and stockyard from the unkindest quarter. Its porch faced north and the great elm frame stood upon a plinth of yellow stock bricks (from the Ingram brickfields at Little Thurrock) implying a date similar to that of the granary alongside.[36] This was therefore one of the last local barns to be set up before corn threshing became an outdoor process undertaken by steam machinery.

William Atkins, who introduced this chapter, must have used the five-bay barn upon *Sheepstealers* ground. Though burned by its owner during the summer of 1966, a chance surviving photograph indicates that it possessed a light timber frame and that its west door was built only to half-height (for the outward passage of empty harvest waggons). Dating in all likelihood from the earliest Georgian phase, a significant feature was its single 'corn-hole', built against the winnowing porch – a small, sealed room into which grain could be shovelled, away from yard fowls, and to free working space within its great doors.

From the corn-barn's winnowing area, grain proceeded to a free-standing box-granary out in the yard, placed well within surveillance of farmhouse windows. Like the fine example which attracts the eye inside Curtis' farm entrance, these black weatherboarded buildings were set a few feet clear of the ground upon a series of mushroom shaped stone "staddles". For the preservation

---

[36] *Brickmaking in Little Thurrock,* A. Benton, PAN. 29, 1988 n.18.

of the farm's dressed corn and other threshed seed was of crucial importance. It must be kept both dry, in a clean and airy environment, and safe from predatory vermin. This raising upon staddles provided a sufficient draught beneath for good keeping, as well as a simple security against rodents. Elm framed, the Curtis' granary is dated upon a tie beam to 1837 and it is partitioned within to a series of eight cubicles or bins, each numbered neatly with raddle-paint.[37] Moveable retaining boards at each area allow for the stacking and organisation of grain, beans, or other seed which, through varying seasons, might be drawn upon for animal fodder, as a cash resource at market, or for sowing the next year's crops.

Curate Jerome Alley in 1810 was to mention in his description of Fobbing's glebe lands some other familiar farmyard features: the dairy, a hen house of seven by eighteen feet attached to the parsonage tithebarn, and the odorous piggery, almost as large again set alongside his little nag-stable.[38] Occasionally from the Georgian newspapers we observe the predations of horse-thieves sidling amongst these farms, both George Smith at Hovels and a farmer called John Clark losing animals[39] during 1827, a year in which Fobbing seems to have quite effectively targeted. That 11th March, a Sunday night, Fobbing farm upon the Billericay road would be deprived of "an Aged Horse full 16 hands high, knees broken, black legs, small star in his face, and what is termed a roarer." This superannuated steed appears to have been a creature whose worth lay in the affections rather than the farm economy of Mrs. Ann Rand, widow of the late Robert Rand, for in offering ten pounds reward should the felon be apprehended, she was to append the temptation of a three guinea bounty for its quiet return *without prosecution.*[40] Something of the farm's condition in these austere agricultural times may be inferred from the theft on the same occasion of "an old TAX CART, with the off shaft broken and tied with a cord." Her husband had laid under St. Michael's turf a half dozen years now and farm tenants everywhere had felt the pinch of failed corn prices since the late war. Perhaps as a result, things were becoming a little less shipshape about the widowed lady's homestead and yard.

Hovels farmhouse, 1825

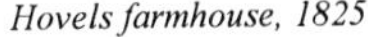

[37] Curtis' farm granary TQ78.7176.8397 is set upon 14 outer staddle stones.

[38] *A True Terrier of all the ... Glebe Lands ... belonging to the Rectory of Fobbing,* Jerome Alley 28th June, 1810.

[39] *The Brooks Scrapbook,* undated, newspaper cutting (1827) PAN. 27, 1985.

[40] C.C. 16th March, 1827.

9. MIDDLIN' SORT OF FOLK

Given a diagonal sunbeam across the russet table-tomb fronting Fobbing's oak porch, one can discern sometimes the first few phrases of a longish inscription upon its limestone cap: "MRS ANN BUTTON wife of Mr ZACH BUTTON of Mucking Hall in this County ...", leading us to a village family which soared higher than any through the Georgian years.[1] Its genealogy is fraught with snares, for several generations of Fobbing namesakes preceded the yeoman Zachariah Button who, around the mid 1790s was to create his fanciful gothic "castle" called *Belmont* upon the beautiful heights above Grays. His ancestor had been Zachariah, a migrant carpenter settled in Fobbing and who, upon his death in 1692, was to leave worthy £40 legacies to each of his daughters (Elizabeth and Frances) and his remaining goods to another Zachariah, his only surviving son.[2]

In turn, the October of 1704 was to witness the burial of that successor Zachariah, described then as "yeoman", who had married Mary, "kinswoman" of the Glascock family, carpenters and grocers at this time. His farming activities involved property held of the bishop of London in "Laindon" (Langdon Hills) a leasehold which was to pass, by will proved in 1706, to another son called Zachariah.[3] To other children (Mary and John Button) sums of £100 each would be set aside. The testator had arranged also with John Goodwin to execute the trust of a further £100, which Button the elder had been keeping in faith for the children of Samuel Hopkins, a recently dead village hoyman. At an earlier period, in 1700, Zachariah and Goodwin, as "neighbours" of the declining George Wildes, had agreed responsibility for the overseeing of his two maiden girls, who were to be "maintained and kept at schoole, as long as shall be needfull". Perhaps no formal education was here meant, but useful domestic instruction which might fit them in time to find suitable farming husbands. W(h)ilde's estate was to go both to his widow Anne, and son Robert (a Fobbing publican of future years) though he

1 Monumental Inscriptions, St. Michael's Church, Fobbing, R. Bingley, 1981-89.

2 Elizabeth married at Fobbing in November, 1752 the farmer Arthur Piggott of Lee Chapel. Their son Zachariah Piggott later resided at Mucking Hall.

3 Langdon Hills Parish Registers 1686-1752 E.R.O. D/P234/1/1.

plainly feared disagreement might flare between mother and offspring. In that event, Thomas Emersham of Vange, gentleman, Zachariah Button and Goodwin, should have power to see any dispute "wholly determined".[4]

The Langdon Hills register as well as the above connections, suggest that the farm there was never a Button home and at young Zachariah's decease (during the summer of 1727) his will confirmed it to be in the hands of a tenant. The burial was at Fobbing, Zachariah's still modest estate now devolving to his son, another of the same distinctive name. A second boy, Francis Button, and daughters Mary and Elizabeth also featured in this document – both girls to appear again among the beneficiaries of their children's uncle's (John's) will, made upon his deathbed at Fobbing during 1734. This John Button had wed twice, first (1724) with Elizabeth, the widow of a Dutchman called John Vramoutt (Vromout) and quite recently to the spinster Grace Sawell, a lady who was not to survive more than a few months after her marriage at St. Michael's upon 19th April, 1733.

Yet it was she in the long term who most favourably influenced the Buttons' social advancement, for the Sawell clan figured prominently in agriculture and other business ventures along these saltings parishes and John Button's will points out that his nephew Zachariah – a minor – was to be placed in the guardianship of his "friend" Francis Sawell of Pitsea "till he come to the Age of twenty one Years". Maturity cannot have actually been far off, for the youthful Zachariah would marry during August 1736 in the church of St. Mary Queenhythe, London, a girl called Ann Johnson of Mucking. Their first child, John, was to be born there[5] the year following, in future times to become a noted agricultural magnate and master of Stifford Lodge. Among a half dozen or more other babies baptised at the parish church standing just opposite their tall Jacobean gabled house of Mucking Hall, was another little Zachariah (born c.1739) who would one day also gain a significant fortune. Of the several other children of these parents who died in infancy no burial details are to be found at Mucking, though at St. Michael's Fobbing a December entry of 1746 notes "Mary Button an Infant from Mucking". Plainly (from tombstone evidence) *three* of the youngsters' corpses were brought home to their father's parish, while during September (1752?) their mother Ann was to be placed in the churchyard vault here also. It seems remarkable that a woman of such caste as she, should go without a line in Fobbing's register of burials.

---

4 Wills: individual serial numbers are not felt to be required: all in this chapter are identifiable by surname and date: *Wills at Chelmsford,* Vol. II, 1620-1720 and Vol. III, 1721-1858, F. G. Emmison (1959-60, 1969).

5 Mucking Parish Registers E.R.O. D/P 108/1.

Your very Hble Servt.
Zach. Button

Through these mid-century years the Sawells and Buttons had remained closely involved together. With February, 1769 old Zachariah had gone to join his wife's remains in Fobbing yard, leaving the Mucking Hall estate and his Langdon Hills property to Zachariah, a man now approaching thirty years of age. Within a short while he had brought as his bride to Mucking Hall, Sarah Sawell, nine years his junior and who, as sole heiress, would soon bring him the sizeable inheritance of her parent Francis Sawell of Pitsea. By 1771 their first child was on the way and as the decade advanced Zachariah's schemes for developing a landed estate of considerable proportions began to unfold. From Sir John Van Hattem during 1777 he was able to buy the valuable Peverell manor westward of Grays township, a few years later adding to it the lordship of Walton Hall at Mucking – purchased from the hard pressed young buck Sir Harry Featherstonhaugh[6] whose Essex farms surrounding Hassenbrook were now being relinquished. For Zachariah Button, ancestral roots, however humbly they had begun, must have counted for a good deal and possibly he coveted the lordship of Fobbing more than any; a prize for which he would have to wait until he was approaching fifty, in 1786.

Since before the time of Sir George Whitmore (who had disposed of Fobbing manor in 1682 to Sir Thomas Davall senior) the demesne lands had been separated and sold off from the title. By will of Sir Thomas in 1714, his son Thomas Davall, M.P. for Harwich, was to inherit,[7] marrying Lydia Catherine Van Hattem, yet dying soon after in 1718 without having produced heirs to his estate. Lydia would subsequently re-marry to Henry Brydges, duke of Chandos, though, by the terms of her settlement, she was to retain both the Fobbing and her Grays Peverell lordships in her own right. These at her decease passed to her relative John Van Hattem, whose name first appears heading the Court Baron of Fobbing during September, 1752, while a memorandum by its steward of December 1786 confirms the conveyance of "Sir John Vanhattem Knt ... of Fobbing with Stanford le Hope and his lands called Little Illford Marsh ... unto Zachariah Button Esq ...".[8] By now widowed and residing at Grays, where Sarah Button's plain mural monument (1781) had been erected, he was to serve as Justice of the Peace, Deputy Lieutenant and, through 1792-93, as High Sheriff of his county, filling his fifties with the planning of *Belmont* and planting its small but picturesque hilltop park. Here at last were the refinements of a suitable country seat, with an outdoor hothouse and fruit trees, classical "temple", and good stables; indoors, elegant rooms including an oval library with Gothic book-cases and mouldings.[9] Little more than a century had elapsed between this refined old gentleman's twilight and

---

6 Protector at this time of Emy Lyon, the future Emma Hamilton: *Beloved Emma*, F. Frazer, 1980.

7 P.R.O., P.C.C. PROB11, Sir Thos. Davall, 20th April, 1714.

8 Manor of Fobbing with Stanford le Hope, Court Books, 1653-1910, E.R.O. D/DCx.

9 *A Picturesque Object: the story of Belmont Castle, Grays,* T. Carney PAN. 28, 1986.

the Fobbing carpenter's bench, where his ancestor had toiled with spokeshave and adze amidst his elm shavings. Zachariah died in November, 1805.

Fobbing's lordship through the further Georgian years was to remain with the Button family (another Zachariah) though he would subsequently change his surname by licence to Cox. The Court Baron, which by ancient courtesy had apparently continued to be held in a room at Fobbing Hall, would be advertised in August, 1821 in a more convivial venue – "the house of Mrs. Rust, known by the sign of the White Lion" – where the various customary tenants of the manor were required to appear "to do their suit and service". Quaint medieval parlance would be practised still, though evidently Fobbing Hall had fallen into decline, by now considered unworthy for anything beyond labouring families' accommodation (presumably for workers hired by Henry Sackett, current tenant of its farmlands under the Baker estate of Orsett). For ever since the mid 18th century the Orsett squires had owned Fobbing Hall and in this line it would continue – to the Victorian Bakers and Wingfields and their inheritors, the Whitmores of Shropshire. Within the estate records of the Orsett enterprise, it was to be generally referred to by the title of "Fobbing Farm", a name otherwise more frequently attached to Leesons (or Whitbreads) upon the heights towards Basildon.[10]

One other yeoman family is of especial record in its local prominence. Just as the Buttons had been village newcomers toward the close of the 17th century, so appeared the Longs as migrant copyholders at the latter part of the 18th. Their arrival at Fobbing in the 1780s had come about through a progression of minor chances, which illustrate rather typically the intertied genealogy of this agricultural tribe. William Green, whose kin we have already observed, left by his will of July, 1732 a farm of scattered crofts, lying both in Fobbing and at Corringham, to his daughter, who had married Edmund Byron. Thus, the farmhouse and yard overlooking the head of Lion Hill came to acquire the name of *"Byrons"*, sustaining it even into the modern period. With the death of Elizabeth, Edmund Byron's attorney was to come to Van Hattem's court (June, 1774) begging in the required archaic style for admittance of the widower in his own right, but further proposing that the lands should be made over to the *use* of one William Towers, a greatly respected farming magnate of East Tilbury and one who rented widely through our saltings district.[11] In reality, Towers had been operating already at Fobbing upon the Byrons' behalf for some years.

---

[10] The will of William Whitbread, gent., made September, 1659 refers to "Leesings" having been purchased from John Petrie (Petre) of the noted recusant family. It would be bequeathed to William, third son of the testator's late brother, Henry Whitbread.

[11] Manor of Fobbing and Stanford le Hope, Court Rolls, 1774 E.R.O. D/Dx M1-4.

East Tilbury was also a stronghold of the Skinners,[12] of whom Joseph Skinner – occupier in 1751 of the unextensive but productive loams of Becksland farm – died in that mid-decade at the young age of thirty eight, his wife having borne him a batch of girls. Of these, only one (Elizabeth Skinner) was to survive to maturity. During May 1759, with her mother's remarriage to the most eligible bachelor of East Tilbury, William Towers became this Elizabeth's stepfather and since there was to be no issue from his union with the mother, the young lady eventually found herself possessed of sufficient a fortune to attract a good yeoman husband. During the very summer that Byron (and Towers) had been admitted to the Fobbing property, Elizabeth Skinner was to be married in her home parish to a young up-county man from Writtle, called Charles Long. With the decease of William Towers in 1780, it was Long who was to continue cultivating the Byron acres in his stead.

A trio of sons of Elizabeth and Charles were all to pursue the agricultural line, the elder (Charles Towers Long) at Stisted, his brother William in their father's old home village of Writtle.[13] But it was the second boy, Henry Anthony Long, who would remain to build his fortunes along Thameside, reaching far from Fobbing in his operations by the 1820s with the important holdings of Bluehouse farm and the Hall in West Tilbury. Of Henry's sisters, one was to wed Alexander Cole, an East Tilbury friend of the family, another (Mary) George Curtis of West Thurrock further upstream. It had been a century of opportunity for these agriculturists of the London periphery, with their mixed cattle and corn enterprises centred upon useful creeks of shipment. Almost 20 years of war and a vastly increasing city's demands for produce had set most of the greater farmers up in a way to ride the short post-Napoleonic phase of depression. By the 1830s a long remembered *"golden age"* which would endure almost fifty years, had begun its course. The Longs and Curtises proved to be but two of those closely joined groups who gained full advantage from the times.[14]

Circumstances have preserved the Curtis surname in Fobbing village's main working farmstead up to the present. A number of 18th century men of agricultural prominence at West Thurrock were to be concerned in Fobbing, perhaps with an eye to its extensive grazing grounds. Notable amongst them were the Englands, and as far back as 1655 an infant of John England "liveing in Cande Iland" had been baptised at St. Michael's. Later, in 1734, a John England would be listed as freeholder of a Fobbing estate valued at £30, doubtless the "Wharf House" near where, during November 1755 England had illegally stopped the

---

[12] East Tilbury Parish Register 1754-1783 (Marriages) D/P 92/1/5.

[13] Manor of Fobbing with Stanford le Hope, Court Rolls, 12 September, 1815 E.R.O. D/Dx M4-7.

[14] *Their Very Life and Existence*, E. H. Rowley, unpublished account of farming, based on Orsett parish, 1957. E.C.L. Grays.

public's passage to a well "where all the tenants come and dip water," alongside "the sign of the Ship".[15]

This John England was never a Fobbing *parishioner*, but resided until his death at Bunting's, one of the Grantham estate farms in West Thurrock, which in due course would also become a Curtis tenancy.[16] A reasonable business association between England and the Curtises is suggested, for it was in the very same period that Richard Curtis had moved to Fobbing, marrying Mary Kent of Horndon on the Hill here upon Michaelmas day, 1753 and baptising twin infants, Richard and Sarah Curtis, during the February of 1761. Meanwhile, with 1754, John Curtis had wed in West Thurrock, bringing his wife Mary to Fobbing by 1759, when its registers record the springtime arrival of their son William. The attraction to this new parish appears to have been the uptaking of John Digby's former lease (from the Great Norwich Hospital) of the desirable Borley marshes edging Holehaven's water, offering ideal wharfage facilities, nearly 200 acres of which lay in Fobbing. Thirty years later, John Curtis would be operating the Nazewick pastures to the north of Fobbing creek mouth.

During the later Napoleonic war years Henry Anthony Long and Charlotte Curtis – a West Thurrock daughter of John and Mary Curtis – were to wed, Long by now working (as well as Byrons) the near 150 acres of Braziers which draped the pebbly hillcrown above Fobbing village. Curate Jerome Alley was to baptise their eldest child, Henry Charles, in January 1811, though noting his birthdate as somewhile earlier, during July, 1809. With 1815, the year of final victory in Europe, was born George Long, though his parents were to await the birth (c.1823) of their third boy, Wellington Surridge Long, before honouring the British hero of Waterloo. His initials remain, to puzzle many a village browser, upon the wooden Paynes Cottages, close to the original family farmstead.

But by this period, a move had been made to a more commodious brick house, Corringham Hall, rented by the Longs from the Orsett (Baker) estate, and where during 1827 Herbert Clarance Long would arrive to complete a male succession of four farming heirs.[17] Corringham Hall (425 acres) was to be the largest of the Long family's holdings lying beyond Fobbing's fringe, the others including a tenancy of Bush House's near eighty acres and various outlying enclosures belonging to both Byron's and the Vineyard steadings which were upon Corringham territory. Within Fobbing by the later 1830s, Henry Anthony

[15] *Essex Freeholders Book, 1734* E.R.O. Q/RJ 1/1 (John England, aged abt. 36. Fobbing Estate £30).

[16] *Buntings Farm, West Thurrock, Essex in 1761,* O. Turner, PAN. 3, 1958.

[17] P.R.O. Home Office HO.107/1773 (1851 Census).

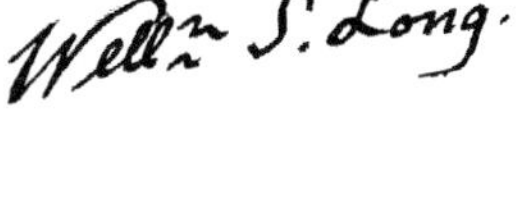

Welln S. Long.

Long was to be listed as *owner* of Hovels[18] (136 acres) Vineyard farm, Great House lands and Brook House – a small stream-pastured holding – and a 70 acre portion of Great Ilford's levels. All told, it was an estate of well toward one thousand acres. The Vineyard, he had purchased freehold during August 1834, following the death of Harriet Drew, last of a London family whose customary tenancy had begun just a century earlier upon the surrender of Richard Grey, last of several Greys (Thomas and his son William) who had occupied Mucking Hall during later Stuart years.

It had been during the time of Thomas Grey, in September 1703, that the parish of St Nicholas, Laindon – having consulted queen Anne's Commission for Charitable Uses – undertook a hearing "against John Dodd and Thomas Grey, concerning the gift of 4l. per annum from certain lands lying in the parish of Fobbing and recovered their right to the said gift." It appeared that an unknown benefactor at some unspecified period in the past, had laid the above rent charge upon the Vineyard farm, as a financial assistance to the Laindon poor. A handsome gilt-lettered board outlines these details still, upon a tie beam above the nave in the church of St. Nicholas, Laindon. Under Henry Anthony Long, this Vineyard charity would continue to be dispensed in coals and clothing to their needy inhabitants through Laindon's overseers.[19]

There were other assets within the H. A. Long concern that were not directly agrarian; for example, through his wife Charlotte had come a property still referred to at that period as the "*Grove*" opposite Byrons farmhouse, where the carpenter John Libbert's garden and worksheds had stood.[20] An advertisement put out by Henry Anthony Long, encouraging some useful tradesmen of the saw and plane to set up business there during 1825, identifies its late occupier as William Rust, who had died just that April. If ever family dwelled under a misnomer, it was that of the Rusts, since as both village carpenters and publicans it had a vested interest in keeping every village blade *oiled* to perfection.

Subsequent to Libbert's decease back in the springtime of 1761, Fobbing's recently arrived carpenter would be Leonard Rust, whose earlier namesake had married Mary Fitch at Great Leighs, Chelmsford, in 1688. At St. Michael's Fobbing, Rust was to wed

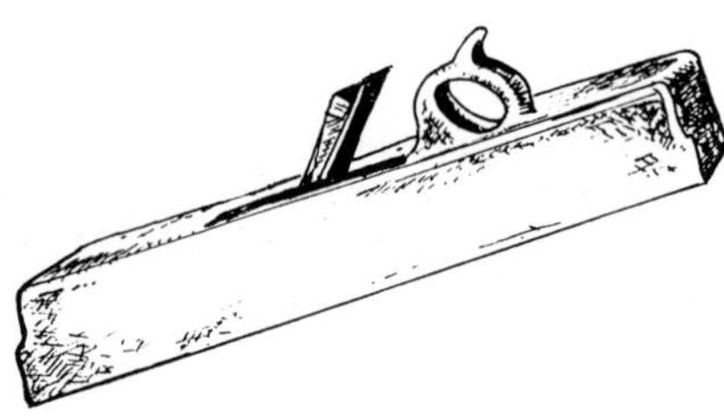

[18] Probably purchased 1825: *Hovel and Brook house Farms in the Parishes of Fobbing and Vange ... the property of Henry Long Esq. and Jane his wife,* 1825 E.R.O. D/DB.

[19] *Report of the Charity Commissioners,* 1819-1837.

[20] Grove and yard TQ78.7168.8398, currently a car parking lot for the *White Lion.*

on 22nd October 1763 the nineteen-years-old Martha Murdock, daughter of a Sandon farmer – again indicating his connections with the Chelmsford district. This couple it was which founded the industrious and celebrated village tribe whose surname tarries in local memory even to this day, not least for its connections with the sailing barge trade.

Leonard Rust's presence was swiftly felt and by 1767 he is noticed serving as a juror upon the Court of Sewers for Fobbing level, before 1773 taking up lease upon the Rev. John Ryley's glebe. Richard Philpot's pub, the *White Lion*, was to be briefly licenced under Leonard's name during 1769-70, though it would be many years yet before alehousekeeping became the Rust's major concern and in later life he took over instead the *Ship*, dying there sometime after mid summer, 1798.[21] To Leonard and Martha there had been a number of offspring; Leonard and William (baptised 1764 and 1766) both to become carpenters up at the *Grove* yard, and Thomas, a bargemaster who, after his mother's death, would continue as tenant of the *Ship* inn at Wharf Lane's foot. Bankruptcy was later to cloud his affairs. Thomas' marriage (1817) had been to the widowed Sarah French, his sister Elizabeth Rust having also found a spouse with this same local family – John French, farmer of Langdon Hills. During the fall of 1819, only two years after Elizabeth and he had united, French shot himself and was buried at Fobbing, aged thirty-five.

Through the juvenile years of this generation of Rusts, the *White Lion* had known various ownerships, that of Philpot reaching back before their father's arrival. Richard Philpot may have had brewing links with Horndon on the Hill[22] but had married in Fobbing during 1730 to the spinster, Elizabeth Knapping, serving in course of time both as Marsh Bailiff (1763) and churchwarden and dying around the year 1778. Some while beforehand, he seems to have stood aside, to put in various licensees: Joseph Mulley would be present late in 1766, from 1772 James Frost, whose widow Rebecca took the helm awhile toward the end of the 1780s before remarrying to Thomas Turner. Thereafter, under a new owner called Henry Reach, Turner was to act as innkeeper (1789) his will of 14th September 1797 bequeathing "the White Lion Inn and the Farm Lands ..." to Rebecca, upon condition that all profits and produce should be directed to "support clothe educate and bring up my Daughter Mary to the good liking of my friend Mr Thomas Wood of Great Bursted." The girl was to have besides, his "large Mahogany dining Table, Mahogany Card Table and great armed chair". Kept upon the small farmstead at back of the *Lion*, was another gift for young Mary Turner; her father's "colt called Jolly" in which she perhaps found comfort through the few years before their departure from the place at the century's end.

---

21 *Alehouse Recognizances* 1769-1805, E.R.O. Q/RL Vol. 24-59.

22 *Brewing, and Philpot the Brewer,* R. Bingley, PAN. 29, 30 and 31, 1988, 1989, 1990.

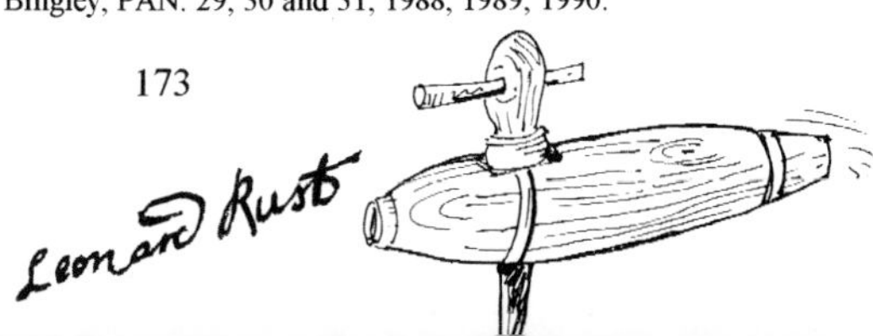

John Quilter held the licence through the months of uneasy peace between Britain and the *First Consul* in Paris (1802) but as renewed hostilities with the French fuelled discussion around the *Lion's* cavernous brick inglenook, so stepped up John Gillman, son of a farming clan long known round about and who appears to have been captain of Fobbing's bell-team. Hard upon the news of Trafalgar, the churchwardens had paid him "for three Ringing Days", a fifteen-shilling windfall which he maybe distributed in kind rather than cash. As landlord, he saw the long war through to Napoleon's flight and exile, handing over a not inconsiderable half-guinea to Fobbing's fund "for the British Prisoners in France" during 1815, perhaps collected among the *Lion's* clientele.

William and Ann Parsons replenished the parish pots for a few subsequent years, by the autumn of 1821 the *White Lion* premises coming at last to William Rust (1766-1825) though his wife Sarah looks to have been its effective manager as well as seeing to the village store which also operated from this building. A communicative woman, she speaks to us personally from a little paper memorandum[23] found during 1960 amongst lumberwork in the *Lion* beer cellar. "*This partition was put up by William Rust the tenant of this house under Mr Ind, brewer of Romford in the year 1823. He at the same time carried on the bisness of ganarl shop carpenter and undertaker on these premises. Please to excuse the spelling as I am in haste. Sara*". Mrs. Rust's charming testimony to her spouse's activities could have added his time upon parish concerns also. He was churchwarden in 1822, the date upon which his two brothers, Leonard and Tom, impishly conspired to decorate the Fobbing bell-stage stonework with their neatly graved initials.[24]

William's death shortly after left Sarah to carry on his victualling business, though now with the aid of a mature family – all females save for another William (bapt. 1808) who would subsequently remove with his wife Rebecca to follow the carpentering trade at Barking. Of the girls, Sarah remained single, while Martha was to marry James Challis, a farmer of Havering atte Bower, who now assumed the copyhold of the several Rust tenements at Wharf Lane. Her elder sister, Elizabeth (bapt. 1801) would bide with her mother into her 30s – becoming something of an attraction around the hostelry – until parent Sarah's decease (at the age of 68) in November 1834, a year previously noted as the time of a notorious fracas at the *Lion.*

Wm Rust

23 *The White Lion Story*, F. Z. Claro, G.T.G. 21st May, 1976. Original apparently lost. Framed up for public view, this item was stolen shortly afterwards from the bar.

24 As churchwarden, the care of the fabric of St. Michael's was his especial charge for this year.

Doled out by a country press under the headline *FREAKS OF THE WEDDING DAY*, a scandal had unfolded of how Miss Elizabeth Rust's suitor, William Bogue, having been "wounded by the bewitching glances of the landlady ... immediately took out a patent from the office of Hymen to restrain her from operating on other hearts without his leave and license". To what extent his darling humoured this arrangement we cannot tell, but all looked fair until the marriage feast itself, when inferences arose as to Lizzie's former association with one of the male guests. A dreadful fight broke out forthwith between Bogue's friends and the associates of a man called Labor. Later, "others of the *crew* of the belligerent Lion" (Cawston, Hills and Dunton) were to arrive outside "armed with horns" – a pair of cattle horns which in country lore widely proclaimed an act of cuckoldry – to taunt wretched bride and groom alike. At this, the distracted husband is reported to have "Caught up a poker and struck them about the jaws". All would be summoned to answer the Billericay justices over this affair.[25]

Whatever Elizabeth Rust's attractions, any vanquished suitor surely had more to rue than the loss of feminine favours. *"Captain"* Bogue had acquired, as victor, a most enviable commodity of which he remained master some 14 years until his death, aged 58 in 1849. His headstone near the rectory wall remembers him simply as "Lighterman of this Parish", though an inventory of his assets taken soon after makes plain the wealth he had derived from the Rust conquest; including six sailing barges and the manifold luxurious comforts of a thriving public house.[26] Somewhile before his demise however, another face had been installed behind the pump handles and it was he – bargeman Samuel Wade – that Elizabeth would eventually take for her new husband. She was then in her fifties. By mid century, her elder maiden sister Sarah was dwelling with them, "assistant" around the house, helped further by 16 years-old Sarah Kemp and young George Bridge, the *Lion's* ostler-lad. As late as 1874 (a widow once more) old Mrs. Wade still oversaw her smoky stone-flagged bar room, with its smart array of beer engines, stone liquor jars and the ribbed window blinds,[27] loud with talk of quoits matches, and horseflesh and knuckle fights and the ever important river trade. But it would never again resound to such commotion as she had herself sparked, half a lifetime ago, as the blushing bride of *Captain* Billy Bogue.

Once an attractive hipped-roof building of timber-frame and weatherboard, the *Ship* alehouse continues in folk-fantasy to be the very marshland inn to whose dim light the escaping Magwitch and Pip were drawn in *Great Expectations*, an

[25] *The Brooks Scrapbook* undated, unsourced newspaper cutting, PAN. 27, 1985.

[26] *Inventory for Administration,* W. Jeffries, auctioneer 1850. Photocopy T.M.

[27] ibid.

idea much propagated by the late F. Z. Claro.[28] In 1679 the premises had been listed as "late called the Kingshead ... lying near Fobbing Key", operated by John Bundock,[29] its customary tenant (and mariner or hoyman besides) while a manor rental of 1713 would note it as "the Ship late Watts". Tobias Surry, as copyhold tenant, at this time owed three years' quit-rents upon it. Surry is known to have been resident in Fobbing since 1692 at least, serving at that time his obligatory year as constable along with Tom Knapping, his will of September 1723 referring to a brother (in law?) Samuel Bunnett, who was to receive twenty one shillings "to buy something as a memorial of me". Valentine Glascock the elder and curate Will Blake would be his witnesses. Another alehouse keeper here was Henry Crow "at the Ship" during mid 1755, while, with the earliest Georgian licencing records (1769) Elizabeth Waterfall (Waterford) would be already present as widowed successor to a former husband, Robert. At a Christmas sessions three years earlier, Robert Waterfall had been accused of deficiencies in his measures, for one quart mug at the *Ship* lacked "half a Quarter of a Pint", a serious defect indeed. To this "Mr. Waterfall" Fobbing's churchwardens had entrusted nevertheless in 1768, the bellringers' ten shillings.

Elizabeth Waterfall was to deal out the topers' fancy at the *Ship* till 1776 when William Dickens succeeded to her victualler's apron – perhaps as her new husband, for with 1780 an Elizabeth Dickens figures upon the yearly recognizances for a further few years. Timothy Pierce (1784) would now occupy the premises until, with 1793 (another date in which the churchwardens paid out "at the Ship for ringers") Leonard Rust commenced his family's extensive sojourn there, Tom Turner of the *Lion* acting as his surety to decent behaviour. Broadly from 1798, the widowed Martha Rust kept the business going under her own name, right until her death at the age of 72, in 1816.

The John Wilson formerly of the *Five Bells* at Vange, who as publican tarried a few seasons up to 1819, was a close relative through Martha Rust's daughter Sarah, wife of Wilson Simons. With 1820 however, the county magistrates were to approve Thomas Rust, bargemaster of Fobbing, Sarah's youngest son, for the *Ship* licence, which he held for upwards of a dozen years. Possibly due to difficulties which crippled many farming men during the early 1820s, Robert's financial affairs collapsed and he was officially bankrupted some years before his death,[30] aged 51, in February 1833. The Rusts hereafter were to

---

[28] A topographically untenable idea. Claro seemed attracted by the fact that a *William* Dickens had been licensee during the 1770s and went so far as to compare samples of his and the novelist's handwriting, as if to prove relationship. G.T.G. 27th December 1968.

[29] Fobbing Hall manor Rentals, 1679 E.R.O. D/DCx, M12-21.

[30] Declared bankrupt, sale of goods 12th June, 1828. A share of his property in Fobbing wharf would be purchased by Robert Partridge, publican of the *Cock* at Orsett.

William Dickens

trade only from the *Lion*, though the *Ship* would make its way successfully under Billericay Brewery ownership for another half century or so, largely in the hands of a Finchingfield native called Hezekiah Wash.[31]

Wash's daughter Emma would marry a waterman named Thomas Ellis, son of Ambrose Ellis – who was to emerge in future times as one of the most notable sailing barge masters of the Essex shore. As was generally the case, the *Ship* had served also as a village provision shop to some extent, though a young lady's preference for the description of her father as "draper" upon Emma's wedding lines in 1869 may represent a prim use of the term *"ale-draper"* for the keeper of a common beerhouse. Married twice, Hezekiah Wash died in July, 1879, his second wife Sarah – born at Stanford about the time of Waterloo – keeping his wharfside tavern under her own name until its licence became transferred in 1885 over to George Ockendon's *Dock House* upon the Thameshaven marshes.[32] Old Sarah Wash would live on till the reported age of 84, dying in the Essex Lunatic Asylum during October, 1891.[33]

A few Georgian wills enhance our picture of the time. Before Christmas, 1723, Joseph Eve – farmer of lady Davall's marshes – had taken as his bride Agnes Johnson, though leaving her widowed by the mid 1740s. She, in turn, prepared her will early in 1746. To their son John Eve would come Agnes' "red Trunk and the Things therein" – a charming collection of petty heirlooms, mostly of silver, including a punch ladle, porringer pot, a cased watch, some spoons and "a silver Tooth pick", besides table linen and her "China punch Bowl". There was a box moreover, "with one pound one shilling and Ten pence in it" for the young man, and a wainscot chest-of-drawers. To his sister, Elizabeth Eve, befell a similar cabinet in walnut wood and, suitable to this high-period of Chinese voguishness, some tea-drinking things, a half dozen of silver teaspoons, tongs and a strainer.

William Turnedge, yeoman, whose will, proved in October, 1744, had been witnessed by John Clifford of Prosbus and wealthy Benjamin Jocelyn, was another possessor of a silver watch, which would pass to the use of his first son, a younger brother receiving his father's clothes. Even so late as 1821 "wearing apparel"

---

31 P.R.O. Home Office HO.107/1773; RG9/1074; RG10/1655; RG11/1755.

32 G.T.G. 5th September, 1885 (incorrectly states licence transfer to "Tilbury Dock Station", meaning Thameshaven dock).

33 G.T.G. 24th October, 1891. Her reputed age in this source does not agree with the various census return evidence for Fobbing.

figured importantly, placed above the china, furniture and property left by the Fobbing farmer James Greenaway to Frances his wife. Household stuffs, with an important feather bed, blankets, hanging curtains and "Vallence" had been earmarked by Henry Fletcher (a butcher in 1696) to Frances his daughter during the summer of 1705, with "every thing standing in the Hall Chamber" – an apt reminder that, even by the period of queen Anne, most prosperous folk still inhabited homes of entirely antiquated kind. Their structural village surroundings were everywhere tinted with the medieval mood.

In response to his bishop's enquiry during 1778, Fobbing's parson had ruefully reflected upon an inclination here to adultery, though perhaps this was merely a facet of the world's general failings in which he showed a specially sharpened interest. Having outfaced the scandal of fathering his servant's baby, Fobbing's shopkeeper Valentine Glascock was to bury his legal wife Martha, who had succumbed in childbed as 1744's reaping of the fields drew near. Perhaps somewhat to assist in his bringing up of a juvenile family, he had taken as *"housekeep"* Mary Attridge, leaving to this helpmate all his goods and naming her during May 1766 executor to his will. Only one witness had signed the document and its legality appears on that ground to have been disputed by relatives. With 1769 however, probate would be granted to Valentine's intended beneficiaries upon the affidavit of James Eades, miller of Fobbing, who declared he knew well the shopman's writing and could swear the will to be of the deceased's true hand.

Similarly, Arthur Smith, another tenant of the "Lady's Island" or Little Ilford grazing grounds, would leave in 1752 his worldly goods entirely to Elizabeth Vincent "my housekeeper", while Samuel Keys (apparently an agricultural labourer) having provided in his will of 1732 for two sisters, by legacies of £5 apiece, would grant the residue of his effects "to my fellow Servant Ann Parnel ... of ffobbing". Though rarely did the cottager aspire to dispose of his goods through formal probate, the humble were not always so clearly separate as we may suppose. Men who held good farms might well be in touch with relatives whose lives were less financially enviable. Abraham Boone, a churchwarden during the early 1750s and who farmed both at Vineyard and the picturesque meads of Brook House, put aside when in a "weak state" and ready for death (in 1762) welcome sums of £10 each for a couple of Essex nephews who were both labouring men. Also to be helped was his niece Amy, though she had set herself up more easefully, by marrying a Wickford blacksmith Thomas Newcombe.

Wills[34] frequently expressed concern for the "education" of the young, generally by means of training at home for a life of usefulness and proper

---

[34] See Note 4.

Christian morality. Tobias Surry, victualler at the *Ship* alehouse, would look to his wife Sarah for "the bringing up of Susanna Cary and my daughters" (Elizabeth and Sarah) providing them with meat, drink, lodging and "schooling", during September, 1723. Likewise, when the yeoman John Goodwin had fallen "very sick and weak" in the February of 1720, he had arranged fortunes of over £300 each for offsprings John and Martha, charging the elder to provide for his sibling one year's "boarding scholing" with six months' school tuition for another Goodwin child called Thomas.

Thomas Coleman, a farmer and blacksmith of Fobbing would be especially concerned to ensure the "Maintainence & Education of my natural daughter Sarah now living with me" (May 1795) directing all of his agricultural and smithing assets be sold at public auction for the benefit of his widow and child. Resident for 20 years already, Coleman had mended iron locks at the church and had been called in for "fixing the Bell Claper" upon occasions by St. Michael's wardens during the same decade.[35] Named also in Coleman's will was his brother William, of the same clamorous trade, over at Benfleet forgehouse. Less confident of how events might turn in his absence, was Thomas Lucas, another Fobbing yeoman who, in 1727, was to leave household items and estate to his spouse and his mother (Elizabeth Lucas) to pass after *their* lives "unto my two Nieces Martha ... and Judah Nobbs". A cautionary afterthought had induced; "and I do hereby order that my ... mother should not imbezell any of my said goods", a supervisory chore with which he would burden his "good ffriend" Valentine Glascock the elder.

The younger Glascock's business in Fobbing had been of a general shopkeeping sort, ranging from dry foodstuffs, sugar and fruit, to ironmongery – for example mops and brooms had been supplied by Valentine to St Michael's church during 1761, while 5 years afterwards a check of weights and measures would mention Glascock's "Grocer & Flower (flour) shop". The family line was surely the subject of female village interest and conversation as this Georgian century advanced, for in 3 generations dual births had been witnessed, first to the carpenter John Glascock's wife during 1694, then secondly to Valentine and Sarah ten years later. This couple had been the shopkeeper Valentine's parents, though both of those boy-twins had died somewhile before his own appearance about the springtime of 1708. Regrettably, the older Valentine, buried early in June, 1734, was not to have the uncommon delight of seeing his son and daughter-in-law publicly cap their clan record when, with May 1740 were baptised "Ann & Jemima Twin daughter of Valentine Glascock & Martha." The springtime in 1743 brought Martha Glascock another round of neighbourly congratulations with

[35] Fobbing Churchwardens' Accounts and Rates 1739-1841, (1778-1779) Microfilm E.C.L. Grays, CR18636.

Valentine Glascock

“Valentine & Orsyn, Twin sons” appearing at their parish font. A next pregnancy was to kill her.

The parsonage

HAPPINESS IS ... FOBBING PARSONAGE

The inception of the third Hanoverian George’s extensive reign introduced to Fobbing John Ryley (9th March 1761) a rector who held the living forty years, though shedding his responsibilities to a chain of curates after 1763. He had evidently ordered a clarification of the marshland parish limits for tithe-gathering purposes in that year, Holy Thursday seeing nail-booted parishioners going the bounds, marking spur-gates and posts along the curling salt fleets by Shellhaven and Borley farms. At St. Michael’s, moderate sums would be spent upon reparations of weather’s toll; in 1780 and the year following a glazier called Thurogood attended to winter’s damage and, with March 1788, charging for a “bushel & half of Coles ... for Sodering the leads” upon Fobbing’s steeple. Whether a small spire existed at this period is questionable: Chapman & Andre’s map of the mid 1770s implies none, though during 1781 a survey by Thomas Marsh was to sketch St. Michael’s tower quite dominantly spired. Most likely, the south eastern stone turret alone was so heightened, as is seen in photographs into the early 20th century, for during August 1798 a baptismal register memorandum had noted: “The Roof of the Tower ... was cover’d with new lead the plumber had £16 & the old Lead for compleating the same”. Other cladding jobs through the mid-90s were to involve the purchase of well over a thousand “plain tiles” from a supplier named Brand at around three shillings the hundred,[36] while a further 3,600 were to arrive through the first clement months of 1806.

Following Leonard Rust’s period as tenant of Ryley’s glebeland, curate William Thomas looks to have farmed on his own behalf over the last decade of the Georgian century; a field sportsman besides, since in 1800 Thomas is noted as a three-guinea game licence holder.[37] No general firearms licence was at this time required and numerous village flintlocks were present for the shooting of species not legally designated as “game”. Upon 3rd May, 1801 the Rev. George Burrard,

[36] ibid.

[37] Game Duty Registers 1784-1806, E.R.O. Q/RTg2.

A.M., would come to the benefice of Fobbing, another absentee whose name,[38] despite a longish incumbency, was to evade the painted list of rectors in St. Michael's nave; a fellow of Merton and chaplain-in-ordinary to the King.[39] George III's gift, besides Fobbing, furnished him with 3 other royal livings, all apparently in this same year. They were Saltfield and Yarmouth, both upon the Isle of Wight, and Middleton Tyas in the diocese of Richmond, Yorks. Doubtless Cobbett would have welcomed an opportunity to have his say upon the circumstances by which such a system of plurality flourished.[40]

Soon disposing of curate Thomas, parson Burrard installed various successors including, from November 1808, Jerome Alley, whose preparation of a manuscript terrier (ground-survey) of his master's glebe in June 1810, is of continuing topographical use. Lands, parsonage house, church,[41] and inventory of its furnishings, would all be described for the first time, it seems, since Agnew in 1723 had reported no terrier in existence. There was some precious social detail, too: Alley's salary stood at £80 per annum, a very reasonable stipend, and his duties had included the overseeing of a small school for the education of ten children – another innovation since Agnew's day. Four only of these scholars were Fobbing dwellers, parson Burrard financing the embryo institution to the tune of £10 in schoolmaster's pay, another £8 being found for him from the rates. Three years earlier Burrard had apparently dispatched no reply to his Archdeacon's circular for gathering information upon provision of schooling in the diocese. But at that time (1807) Corringham had reported "a day School ... of about a dozen and a half" (scholars) and doubtless there were growing pressures towards establishing a basic educational facility for suitable children in the years immediately following.

A fresh energy looks to have pervaded parochial matters around this time; after a long absence from the church's furnishing, the autumn of 1805 was to bring delivery of a gaudily coloured royal *"Court of Arms"* at the cost of over ten guineas, a sculpted work of heraldry far finer than the conventional arms-boards found in most rural churches.[42] Regular arrangements had begun for day-treat outings to Brentwood aboard the big red-wheeled carts of local farmers, to witness the bishop of London's visitation and, during 1803, some eighteen folk had journeyed there. 1809 had seen the parish pay fifteen shillings "for carrying the Children to be Confirmed & Eating & Drinking." As ever, for many the religious

---

[38] Also much mis-spelled in various records; as Buzzard, Burrand, etc.

[39] *Clerical Guide,* 1822 (G. Burrard).

[40] *Cobbett's Legacy to Parsons,* W. Cobbett, 1835.

[41] Alley measured the building: Church 50 feet long, 45 feet wide: Chancel, 30 feet long, 20 wide: Tower 22 feet square.

[42] Fobbing Churchwardens' Accounts, 1739-1841, Microfilm, E.C.L. Grays, CR 18636.

aspects of such country trips were secondary to scenic and prandial pleasures; just as Sunday's confinement, while interminable sermons droned, must have offered

at whiles certain covert joys. From this period come the mild treasures of pocket knife art which still decorate Fobbing's polished bench-seats: a sinister gallows-tree and anchor, the deeply hulled sailing brig of about 1800 and swim-headed Thames barge, so familiar to every creek-lingering lad.

A black marble slab by the chancel arch remembers the Rev. James Wright, rector of East Harling in Norfolk and Hinderclay, George Burrard's curate till his death in October 1818 and to be followed in the curacy by William Rose Stephenson, newly installed that February as rector of St. Mary's at Corringham. George Burrard's resignation led in 1822 to J. H. Randolph's appointment as rector of Fobbing,[43] a family surname which cannot have been unhelpful to clerical advancement since it was that of a recently deceased bishop of this diocese. A Prebendary of St. Paul's, Randolph remained with Fobbing until 1839, moving thereafter to the living of Sanderstead, Surrey.

Hone's yearbook of 1832 has been often quoted for its praise of the rectory home-plot in Randolph's day, with its "fair garden, very sweet ... and proper for pleasure or pastime", wherein the (anonymous) correspondent might be found "holding converse with nature ... never beyond the pale of happiness, which I hold but another name for Fobbing parsonage."[44] An engraved block of the west frontage, embowered in climbing plants, shows formal lawns and pathways, with a genteel group comprising a bonneted female and children beneath shady boughs at the street entrance. From this elegant space, one might experience at varying intervals the allegorical extremes of a village world: street brawls spilling up from the *Lion* curtilage, or the decent tone of fiddle-and-woodwind[45] accompanying a rustic congregation at their hymning just alongside.[46]

Church musicianship at least could be rendered a little more harmonious, and with 1843 the Soho firm of Bevington and Sons[47]

[43] *The Clergy List,* 1846 (J. Randolph).

[44] E.R. Vol. 49 p. 33 Hone's Year Book, 1839 (suggested wrongly dated by some years).

[45] The usual church band or *"choir"* consisted through this period of a range of strings and woodwind instruments (e.g. *The Melstock Choir,* T. Hardy).

[46] *Old Country Life,* Chapter 10 "The Village Musician". Rev. S. Baring-Gould, 1890.

[47] *The Barrel-Organ in Fobbing Church,* anon. typescript description T.MUS.

Bench Graffiti, St. Michael's

would be directed to transport one of its famed barrel-organs to Fobbing, an ingenious Gothic cased instrument of eighty-six pipes and over 7,000 mechanically operated pins which could turn out any of thirty-six tunes – from the 148th Psalm, *Hanover*, Sicilian and Portuguese hymns, to Rousseau's *Dream.*[48] A dubious story of its heyday persists: *"I did hear tell"*, one aged informant told an Orsett writer, *"they was having a service in Fobbin' church and they came to the end of a hymn and they couldn't stop their barrel organ nowhow, so as they had to cart it out into the churchyard before the parson could say the prayers".*[49] A race more logical, less servile than these east Saxons, might have thought instead to carry out the parson.

Fobbing's population by comparison with its neighbours was by no means small at the close of the Georgian period: in 1831 there had been just under four hundred residents,[50] compared to 234 at Corringham or Stanford's 330. The greatest close community was in Horndon on the Hill, with slightly above five hundred folk. Fobbing had never found argument for taking advantage of the Workhouse Act of 1723, which *enabled* the setting up of poorhouses under vestry management, and the parish overseer's records, dating from 1739 onward, contain no specific details of how Fobbing's rates were disbursed in the area of financial relief. Among the churchwardens' accounts for May, 1825 is found a solitary payment of two shillings when "a distressed Family" had been given assistance.

The Poor Law Amendment Act of 1834 was to bring the concept of a workhouse close to all, for there could be no opting out of the system from here on. Fobbing was now to be grouped with 18 contiguous parishes, extending eastward from Aveley and the Ockendons to embrace Langdon Hills, Stanford and Corringham to form the Orsett *"Union"* under control of a Board of Guardians selected from each of these localities. Charles Greenaway, tenant of the Borley marshlands, would be elected by Fobbing as its representative during 1835, in 1837 George Spitty, landlord of Whitehall, taking over his office. For these first few years, sundry tenements in Orsett and at Grays were to be utilised, accommodating (March 1836) 116 paupers, only one of which had come from Fobbing parish. Far larger numbers of inmates had arrived from South Ockendon (16) West Thurrock (25) and Orsett itself (17). With 1837 would be constructed a gaunt yellow-brick *"Union House"* upon fields beside picturesque Orsett post-mill, through whose portals by the following spring had passed 130 of the district's poor, eleven of them taken from Fobbing. Visits by friends were

48 *Ted Smith's Labour of Love*, S. C. September, 1990 (re: restoration of barrel organ).

49 *Essex Folk*, E. S. Knights, 1935.

50 *Answers to the Population Act (1831).* Memo at rear of Fobbing baptisms register 1783-1811.

generally allowed upon Mondays and Fridays between 10.00 a.m. and twelve and inmates might also go by arrangement to see others outside.

"Outdoor" assistance for those who struggled to remain in their village cottages prevailed also, though not always providing a less painful solution. Fobbing's overseer had been reprimanded by the Board (5th October, 1837) for the "highly reprehensible" neglect of a cottager called Rainbird, who had fallen into "sudden and urgent necessity." The village officers would be advised to give "better attention to their duties" in future. Again in the area of outdoor relief the Board's attention was turned in the fall of 1840 to the situation of pauper Mary Gladwell, "deserted by her husband and having four children, some of them supposed to be illegitimate." A grant of 1s. and 6d. weekly and 4 loaves of bread for three months would be granted in this case.[51]

During 1836 the tender of John Burles of Fobbing windmill had been accepted by the Guardians, for providing "Bread & Flour to be delivered in Fobbing, Corringham, Stanford le Hope & Langdon Hills," over a six month period, while the summer of 1838 was to observe a local overseer granting John Causton help "in kind" to the value of half a crown. For this, the Orsett Union Guardians would approve repayal to the Fobbing funds by their relieving officer. But there were less direct aspects of assistance, too, apparently arranged so as to give a modicum of respite to villagers not of the poorest sort by any means. In the spring of 1847 the vestry, "in consequence of the present high price of Provisions," was to excuse about a dozen of its poor-rate payers from their May charge. These included two cottage widows, Mrs. Wright and Sarah Causton, Josiah her labourer son, and smallholder James Frost.

As occasion befell, the Orsett workhouse master boxed up his dead, dispatching them along country highways back to their parishes of settlement for burial, by convention to be put in the sunless north side of the church ground: in March 1841 at Fobbing, Sarah Todd, "Union House," aged 13 years: during October 1866, John Brand, still in his middle thirties. An analysis of the first generation at Orsett workhouse indicates some 25 Fobbing persons expiring while inmates of the institution between 1841 and 1871, only nine being aged above 65 years. One antiquated resident there had been Sarah, former wife of the deceased and bankrupt Wilson Simons of Fobbing wharf, who in 1847 at the age of seventy-nine would be conveyed back in a plain deal coffin by horse wagon for burial, having previously reverted to her maiden name of Rust. Her niece (Mrs. Elizabeth Bogue) dwelled cosily without imaginable want in the *White Lion.* Ten years into the young queen's reign, could it be that those caring *"Victorian*

---

[51] *Poor Law in Orsett 1826-1841,* K. Malt, 1973 typescript, E.C.L. Grays.

values" had not yet finally ripened and that family responsibilitv was sometimes so imperfectly demonstrated? It looks that way.

By what custom across the centuries of ecclesiastical dues-gathering, the rectors' tithes had been collected at Fobbing, we cannot see: methods varied considerably between parishes, but in general a process of physically taking away one tenth of each farm's produce in corn, grasses, wool, milk, and so forth, had prevailed since the Saxon era. In numerous instances, a rector while resident in one locale might hold the right to tithes of parishes far distant and the will of Lucius Hibbins (1759) for example, had declared his ownership of "Great tithes of the several townships of Stoke Newton, Aldon and Woo Rowton and Stokesay" (all close to Ludlow, in Shropshire) besides those he had formerly enjoyed in Fobbing.[52] Practicalities of collection, storage and sale might well therefore be left to some advertent agent, a curate perhaps, or trusted farmer, but naturally at times (many times) dispute must arise over exact yields of crops, or over field measurements, or numbers of cattle upon the grazing pastures. Litigation between cleric and farming parishioner became frequent. Harvest-time frauds amongst men who (perhaps as religious dissenters) strongly resented giving up their produce to the established clergy were evidently commonplace and certain parsons had long seen the wisdom of settling for overall monetary payments based upon a rent charge *per acre*.

This system was to be taken up across England and Wales with the Tithe Commutation Act of 1836. By the early 1840s, most parishes had moved by public meetings and the preparation of meticulously surveyed "tithe-maps", to their individual agreements. For the first time in history a relatively complete record of farmstead acreages, enclosure patterns, land use and field names came into existence. It contained a register of ownership and tenancy, as well as the land's valuation and it remains the most important single source of topographical information for every district in England.

Parson Randolph's departure (1839) occurred during these significant deliberations, his successor Henry Thompson M.A., being finally awarded in 1841 an annual rent charge for Fobbing, in lieu of tithes, fixed at £761. 9s. 4d., a very comfortable stipend.[53] Of the parish lands (2,632 acres)[54] about half had been

---

[52] P.R.O., P.C.C. PROB 11.847.

[53] Based upon the current early Victorian agricultural wage, an equivalent of about £30,000 per annum in modern terms.

listed as arable, the remainder pasture or meadow, a little woodland, public roads and "waste." Thompson's own glebe freehold was, of course, not liable to the payment, except by such tenant as might from time to time rent it from him. Some 19 other farms would be identified lying wholly or partly within Fobbing's boundaries, aside from which a few other businesses can be traced from the map and its matching (numbered) schedule of 1839.

Within the main street, almost fronting the churchyard, lay widow Sarah Sparkes' shoemaker's shop, in the occupation of William Austin and the nearby bakehouse, operating under James Shuttleworth, whose business had probably supplied bread since the previous century. For during 1797 a certain Samuel Shuttleworth had been the last Fobbing person to persist (despite a wartime tax) in the old-fashioned custom of wearing his hair "powdered" with flour over a larded foundation.[55] Despite this outmoded trait, Samuel was no old-timer, for he and Mary Shuttleworth would produce several children between 1796 and 1810 and at his death in 1814 he was still only 57 years of age. James Shuttleworth's bakery would add considerably to the modern interest of the street corner atop Wharf Lane with a new building scheme about the mid century: a sash windowed residence in orange brick, with its tall chimneyed pantile-roofed bakehouse and cart-pony stabling alongside.

Closely associated with this enterprise was James Sawell's smock mill a half-mile off near the village brow, managed at this time by his lessee, John Burles. In November 1825 Burles and his wife Harriet had baptised a daughter Fanny, soon to be followed by a bevy of little sisters of patent uselessness to their father's trading aspirations, while another daughter would later give birth at Fobbing to an illegitimate female child, in 1843. Fobbing's windmill has been closely documented by K. G. Farries, supreme historian of the industry in Essex, but to his work a morsel or two of Georgian detail may be added.[56] A parish constable of 1700, James Grove(s), was ten years later to appear at the Chelmsford sessions accused and found guilty as miller of Fobbing for using false weights, while "Old James Groves", whom the burial register names on 11th January, 1719, is presumably that same character. He may have been soon succeeded by John Pain, miller, whose will of October 1732, though lacking in occupational interest, identified a kinsman called George Havinson of Southminster and refers to the ownership of copyhold houses there. Windmillers were generally ubiquitous men, the density of operation in grain-growing counties such as Essex giving ample

---

54 Actually 2,932 acres as a parish total, but some 300 of these were tidal waters, part of Thames (reaching to mid-river and therefore contiguous with Kent) the rest in Holehaven and Shellhaven creeks.

55 Hairpowder duty returns E.R.O. Q/RT p. 4.

56 *Essex Windmills, Millers and Millwrights*, K. G. Farries, Vol. 4, 1985.

impetus to mobility. "Henry Naish Miller", buried on 26th March, 1756, was a subsequent occupier of Fobbing mill, which throughout these times had evidently been of post construction as sketched in an earlier chapter. During the year prior to his death the inspecting official had pronounced his steelyards and measures true and fair.

James Eades, who as windmiller had certified the handwriting upon Valentine Glascock's will (1769) had been resident in Fobbing some dozen years already and during 1757 John Van Hattem was to allow him the shooting of all game upon his manor grounds. A couple of years after, his first son (to the former Dorothy Offen) would be baptised by parson Hibbins. Disastrous wintertime flooding all along Thames early in 1760 was to see Eades engaged, along with Richard Curtis and the publican Philpot, as juror for the Fobbing levels, while with 1766 an examination of weights pronounced him an honest trader. A rating list containing only "Mrs. Eades" and dated 1771 implies his decease, while in the same year occurs an inference that the *Lion's* proprietor, Richard Philpot, had taken up residence at the Mill House.

Chapman & Andre's large scale mapping of our district, published during 1777, had shown the post-mill here, even sketching its open lower framework of angled stanchions in some detail. Farries indicates that a replacement windmill (a smock) had been constructed by the dawning nineteenth century, a modern Georgian type in which only the upper section – usually of "boat" design – turned into the wind's direction. It had found mention as a post-mill during 1792, working with a single pair of French stones and in 1796 was to be insured "for a mere £50 and the millwright's work for £50", the latter premium relating to its machinery which would reduce to £30 in 1799 when James Hills of Corringham operated the venture.

Subsequent to the regime of John Burles, whom White's directory lists in the trade as late as 1848, Fobbing's miller would be Charles Spencer Boorman, born in the mid 1820s at Snodland in Kent and who, with his brother William, had set up at the Mill House by 1851, where they operated a bread business also. James Shuttleworth continued to advertise his older-established bakery as well, his widow Charlotte keeping its ovens going into the 1870s, by which decade both windmill and the Wharf Lane bakeries came into the hands of Benjamin Frostick. An *Essex Weekly News* advertisement of 1878 observes the new master seeking "a respectable lad who can mould and serve customers with a horse and cart: good character required". Boorman's windmill at a similar date is found equipped with *two* pairs of French stones and a fifteen-bushel oven, though by now

Fobbing's milling power was peripheral to that of his large steam-powered operation alongside the railway station in Stanford le Hope. Few of the now obsolescent wind systems would long survive this kind of technological competition; by the early 1890s Fobbing's sails had ceased to turn and the Mill House was in the tenancy of a village sawyer called Tom Lindsell, evidently an employee of William Payne's carpentry and cottage-building business five minutes downhill. Things were looking ripe for development, here where the neglected windmill field edged its elmy lane.

Afar off at Dry Street,[57] a Wesleyan Methodist ideal flourished under the rooftree of farmer William Wrigglesworth and Hannah his wife – north country people by birth, but surely junior kinsfolk of Benjamin Rigglesworth of Langdon Hills, who as early as 1768 had acted trustee to the fortune of Sarah Sawell, bride of Zachy Button. William's wedding to Hannah Plummer had been at Thormanby near Ripon during April, 1823 and he is said to have been "turned out of his Yorkshire holding", for having entertained nonconformist services at his home there.[58] The couple seem to have migrated south with the Michaelmas of that same year, for their child William would be baptised in the established church, at Fobbing, late in July 1824.[59] A second son, John Burnett Wrigglesworth born around 1827 does not appear in its register and the parents were probably by now worshippers at Henry Smith's Orsett meeting house some seven miles distant – at this period the only centre of Wesleyanism within the neighbourhood – served by ministers travelling from Dartford and Gravesend in Kent.

Though not naming the Wrigglesworth involvement outright, Fobbing's curate, William Rose Stephenson, would be seriously concerned by mid 1829 about the nonconformist presence at his elbow. Unlike other ministers locally, his reaction to a diocesan enquiry of that summer as to what religious activity (other than C. of E.) pertained within each parish, went far beyond the bland official requirement. Stephenson waxed even so courageous as to point out the ineptitude of the questionnaire's approach, "There is no place of worship, except the Churches" he informed, "But this reply ... will not convey a statement of all the exertions which are making by persons not connected with our church".[60] Last summer and the present, he explained, there had been preaching out of doors at Fobbing and at Corringham, currently, "in a Barn – *& chiefly by a Woman*" who had in attendance two or three men that were visitors from Billericay. "I know not how to describe the religious demeanor of these persons", continued the curate,

---

57 Dry Street farmhouse TQ78.6967.8674.

58 *When Basildon was Farms and Fields,* J. Payne, 1987.

59 First rated, March, 1826. Fobbing Churchwardens' Accounts and Rates, 1739-1841, microfilm E.C.L. Grays, CR18636. By 1829 he had become parish overseer, serving several terms through the 1830s.

60 E.R.O. Q/CR 3/1/90.

adding only a horrified reiteration of the prevalence of "Female Preachers" before extending his observation to Stanford le Hope. There, Sunday attendance was flourishing at "a private House ... supported by a Society of *Independent* dissenters called "The Home Missionary Society". The tide of prodigal expression was all about him, so it seemed.

With November, 1834 William and Hannah would inaugurate Dry Street's own licenced meetings – addressed on that first occasion in the westward front parlour of the farmhouse by John Haswell, superintendent of the Southwark Methodist circuit. Directly above, a bedroom which, with time, was to acquire the name of the *"Prophets' Chamber"* would be allocated for the many subsequent visiting preachers who journeyed from the Kentish side by ferry; walking the Tilbury turnpike each Wednesday to take services and sleeping overnight at East Tilbury and Stanford villages prior to Friday's arrival for the Dry Street gathering.[61] Growing up at Ingrave near Brentwood at this period had been the young workman William Payne,[62] drawn initially to Stanford le Hope, then after some years to Fobbing as a carpenter in 1861 – a time at which the new widowed Hannah Wrigglesworth still carried Wesley's bright banner upon the parish fringe – supported now by her farming sons. Both were already well known to Payne, for the three men had been instrumental together during September 1855 in leasing land for the building of East Tilbury's Methodist chapel.[63] William Wrigglesworth junior appears to have been of fairly worldly attitudes, setting his eye upon a widow 10 years his senior who (in 1851) was living with her teenage daughter as "Housekeeper" to the unattached Elnathan Fisher, master of Fobbing Farm, a mere few fields away. Sarah Joshua was 39 when Wrigglesworth married her upon April 1st, 1854. Perhaps only she and Mr. Fisher could have said whether the date of transfer had been an appropriate one.

At Fobbing, William Payne had first set up under John Wright, a carpenter with no sons of age to assist him and whose copyhold cottage on the *"Grove"* corner the newcomer rebuilt, occupying it during his first year there. It still bears his name with the date (1861). This was to be a changeful and cruel period in the household; Payne's wife Louisa was to give him five children, the youngest still an infant when she died, the eldest but nine years old. Swiftly remarrying, his second spouse, Charlotte, must have succumbed at the birth of their firstborn in January, 1863. William Payne was to bury this baby also that spring, after a respectable interval fetching over his threshold the Caroline with whom he would establish a successful second family – Walter and Lydia being conceived in her

---

[61] *Methodism in Thurrock,* K. Ward, PAN. 7, 1962.

[62] P.R.O. Home Office HO.107/1773.

[63] *The Methodist Church, East Tilbury 1856-1956,* R. Collier, 1956.

William Payne

years somewhat beyond forty.[64] Through this while, Payne and Wright advertised separately in the wheelwright's and carpenter's businesses, William Payne's housebuilding activities eventually proving more profitable. A wall letter box would appear affixed to his cottage frontage during 1871, though as yet no rural sub post office had been granted to the village.[65]

Mailing facilities had nevertheless been long available to the place, dependent through the 18th century upon the usual "post boy" horse-riders delivering bags from London to offices at townships such as Romford and Grays Thurrock. With late 1803, transport of mails between the city, Billericay, Leigh and the fast developing seaside of Southend, was running upon six days per week, and daily to many of the smaller villages such as Orsett, Tilbury and Horndon on the Hill.[66] This latter spot – 5 miles off and served from Romford's office – would remain Fobbing's postal focus from which foot postmen ventured to carry (and collect) the penny-post across the farmsteads and village centres. With the late 1850s, the management of sorting and delivery was to come closer, to Stanford le Hope, a railway station village which now provided telegraph links and a money-order service. From here Herbert Massey began a daily delivery service by donkey cart covering villages as far eastward as the *Barge* inn, Vange.[67]

During 1890, William Payne was to be appointed "Receiver of Letters", by 1895 gaining preferment as Fobbing's first rural sub-postmaster. Close by upslope, smart yellow cottage terraces of the early 1880s bore his own builder's signature "W.P." In 1884 Payne had housed in one of them an aged acquaintance whose family and grandchildren were now all passed away. Her name was Mrs. Hannah Wrigglesworth. Three years previously, the census had noted, somewhere just at hand, a *"Mission Room"*, perhaps an iron hut which answered the Wesleyan purpose awhile, for it seems to have occupied the same laneside corner on which William Payne was to erect his superior slate-roofed chapel during jubilee year, 1887. His personal triumph had been to nurse the Wrigglesworth dream and transport it from its outback location right into Fobbing's hub: a plain, solid brick-and-matchboard cubicle for the righteous,[68] whose Sunday reverberations of *"God and Sinners Reconciled"* could be heard upon any favouring breeze right down to the rector's front porch.

64 *Memories*, G. M. Hunwick, PAN. 11, 1967.
65 *The Story of East Thurrock's Postal Service*, F. Z. Claro. G.T.G. 14th March, 1969.
66 C.C. 21st September, 1803.
67 *The Posts of Essex*, L. Johnson, Postal Hist. Soc. 1969.
68 Chapel TQ78.7166.8415.

Fobbing porch, Fred Roe

10. PASTURES NEW

Harvest flagon, Fobbing

By mid 1881, the widowed queen Victoria was approaching her Diamond Jubilee. Nine times since the beginning of this century a census had been taken of the people, documenting a nation's structure with growing accuracy. With 1851, the kind of detailed household questionnaire that was to prove of real value to historical and demographic understanding had been formulated.[1] Allowing for a little error, some outright deceit, a certain natural amnesia and a modicum of cussedness amongst those involved, whether in gathering or in answering, there remains today a valid micro-biography of nearly every English resident then alive for us to study.[2] Formal education for everyone had begun by 1881, but it had not yet achieved anywhere near its best effect. The household head (usually male) and perhaps his wife were to be interrogated by some journeying official (the enumerator) and their responses placed upon his draft census forms. Although individual addresses were not often written down, it is normally possible to reconstruct the route followed by an enumerator through his locality, simply by pinpointing at intervals certain known spots, such as a public house, a railway cottage or some outlying farm.

In selecting 1881 for a brief glimpse of Fobbing parish, we have the advantage of being able to scan back and forth across both earlier and later census lists, comparing family evidence and so perceiving aspects that are stable within the Victorian parish as well as things which are undergoing change. More than this, it coincides with a time when common printed sources such as the trade directories published by Kelly or the Post Office had become highly reliable in their social information and so expand our view of the census evidence – at least so far as the commercial and farming classes are concerned. This decade, moreover, would bring for the first time an increased reporting from within the district via the *Grays and Tilbury Gazette* newspaper,[3] previous county journals having reached toward Fobbing generally only for tit-bits of misdemeanour, or to carry the occasional trade advertisement and auction notice.

Even with this infant paper (1884) Fobbing lay rather eastward of its real focus, though at least by now the *Gazette's* news-sleuths had the facility of stout iron safety-bicycles for missions over the unmade gravel roads which led this way. And Fobbing held a special cultural trophy to itself which editors of Liberal

---

1 P.R.O. Home Office HO.107/1773 (1851 census).

2 Forms were completed in most cases during the 19th century by oral interrogation and filled out by an enumerating officer.

3 *The Grays and Tilbury Gazette and Southend Telegraph*. 1st issue 24th May, 1884.

inclination could hardly ignore in an age when the "regional novel" had become so popular through creators of fiction such as Blackmore and the Rev. S Baring-Gould. For in 1860, the Rev. William Heygate of Wakering had given Essex his historical romance of the 14th century rebellion, called *Alice of Fobbing, or the Times of Jack Straw*. No other Thameside village was to bathe in such direct literary glory, though the book itself never found a popularity much beyond its county of inspiration.

The population census of Sunday, 30th March 1851 had been accompanied by a questionnaire to all ministers of the Church of England, requiring details of seatings for each congregation and attendance figures, the latter statistics which were soon to shake the establishment out of its long-held belief that protestant Christianity was alive and healthy throughout the realm. At Fobbing, Thomson was to inform of total space for a congregation of 225. There were 75 "free" seats and 150 "other", that is, places which remained exclusive to certain property holders or their kin, such as the manor lords of Fobbing Hall, or of Hawkesbury. The agricultural poor were still at this period effectively only admitted to the lower end of the nave in many country churches, at least upon occasions of full congregations. But such events were infrequent, and Thomson's average of attendance revealed St. Michael's less than half-filled for his afternoon service, and with only 58 present to hear him in the morning. On March 30th itself, his response would be similar, declaring 120 (afternoon) and 60 (morning) though there must have been a considerable group of ardent worshippers participating *twice* on that day.[4] Nevertheless, we may conclude that somewhere above one third of Fobbing's total population (of 429 persons) had been to a service on the Sunday in question and that they were perhaps fairly regular churchgoers.[5]

From the historian's viewpoint it could have been more beneficial had the authorities obtained their statistics not from the parson's view (however impeccable) but by adding a declaration to each personal return: *Did you attend a place of worship last Sunday?* With a refinement or two, this would have answered all, as well as enabling us to see in hindsight just *who* these devout parishioners were among any particular

Cottages, Bells Hill

[4] P.R.O. HO.129/7/198.

[5] Fobbing had recently come into the diocese of Rochester (1846): since the Saxon era, all of Essex had been within the see of London. Further change would follow; in 1877 into St. Alban's diocese, later (1914) to the newly created diocese of Chelmsford.

community. To what extent was religious commitment related to class, or to mundane factors such as how far a cottager lived from the church? None of this, alas, is revealed in the census as it stands.

One of its real advantages however, is what can be detected "between the lines" about the previous geographical movements of most people – including those many immigrant farm labourers who, by 1881,[6] had settled themselves at Fobbing, often simply by the chance of having applied for some hiring and so obtaining a place in which they *happened* to remain. At Oil Mill farmhouse (by then divided up as a couple of tenements) dwelled Samuel Jiggens, 47 years-old and a native of Great Leighs near Chelmsford. Ten years his junior was Emma Jiggens (née Rush) – perhaps the magnet which had drawn him to seek employment on Thameside – a Vange girl to whom he had been married above 16 years.[7] Their eldest children, William, a farm hand, and Louisa Ann Jiggens aged 14, had both been born at Corringham, while 8 years old James (a scholar) was a Fobbing born baby. Other youngsters aged 5 and 2 were of Stanford and Corringham birth, maybe suggesting recent shifts of this family to very local farms, or perhaps, indicating Emma's return to her mother's home for the delivery.

George Hills, living at No. 2 apartment in Fobbing Hall, was a farm labourer of 44 years of age and had also migrated some miles from his Nevendon birthplace. In this case, Hills had married a fellow parishioner called Sarah, now aged 39. Their son, too, had been born in Nevendon before the move. He was 18 years old and working now as a "Waller" upon the Thames embankments and sewers. This family appears to have made just one shift – direct from the Nevendon area to Fobbing during the mid 1860s and here all their three subsequent children were produced. George, aged 14, was in farm work, Elizabeth a scholar, 8 years old, while Edward Hills at 4 would not yet be quite ready for Fobbing's church school.

Simon Cardy, living in a cottage at Dry Street (in Fobbing) was a younger farm worker, aged 32, who, with his 30 years-old wife Eliza, shared a story similar to that of the Hills, for both had first seen the light of day up at Bures St. Mary in Suffolk, where they still lived after marriage. Their 12 years old son had been born there and not until c.1875, a half dozen years ago, had they apparently made a move into Essex; to the Colne Valley. In 1880 their youngest child, Daisy Cardy, would be born at White Colne and so this family had somehow struck out for a new life at Fobbing only during the past year. A clue to migration might lie in the 1881 census enumerator's *next* stop after Dry Street, a mere two calls away.

---

6 P.R.O. Home Office RG11/1755 (1881 census).

7 A frequent cause of alliances established miles from home, lay with girls situated in domestic service, who met up with farmhands in a fresh locality, but eventually married them in the female's village.

For at No. 1 Fobbing Farm cottages, was Vince Coker, a rather older agricultural labourer, dwelling with his wife and 16 years old niece. All of *that* trio were natives of White Colne, so the Cardys and the Cokers had probably known each other before and kept in touch over the jobs market.

These are merely random images of inward movement, but since Fobbing's population cannot be seen to increase dramatically during the fifty years between 1831 and 1881, then *outward* flow must have been significant also. In the earlier of those census-takings, there had been 391 resident people present in the parish, thirty years later only 393, though intervening counts had seen rises to nearly 430. With 1881, Fobbing's total was up to 429, but against this (roughly 10%) increase, we should be aware of a few chance omissions of folk such as bargemen overnighting in other hythes, moreso of the seasonal variations at times of enumeration which might increase the numbers of labourers present as temporary lodgers. Generally, the census took place in early spring, however, before the largest movements of itinerant hands (June's sheep shearers, the July reaping men) were underway.

The contraflow of families going *from* Fobbing is typically observed between 1881 and 1891, a period which still preceded any sizeable industrialisation of the marshes, but one in which depression-farming had seriously begun to bite. Fobbing's population would drop numerically by only 20 overall through that decade, and yet the visible changeover of surnames was to be dramatic. Out of just 100 village households, not less than forty family units departed for pastures new, to be replaced of course by a fresh bevy of surnames – mainly agricultural workers, as had traditionally been the case. Only a few "modern" occupations featured, such as police constables or Thameshaven customs officials. Though not nearly so marked, well over one-fifth of family surnames present at the 1851 enumeration would have vanished by the census of 1861. Some deletions were obviously due to death, but most by far can be accounted for by movement to fresh hirings upon other farms.

The Bakehouse

Occupying Fobbing bakehouse in 1881 (3rd April) was a recent arrival – following on Boorman's relinquishing of the business – Joseph Fincham. Just in his early twenties, he was a native of Ramesden Crays, where (in the same year) farmer Jonathan

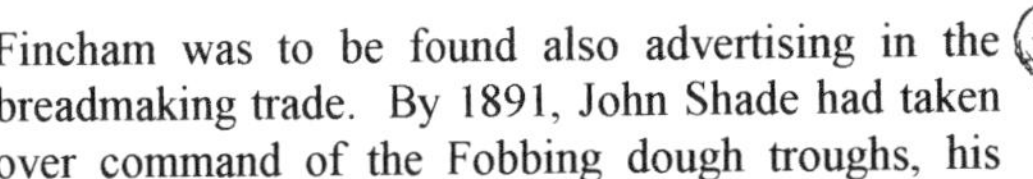

Fincham was to be found also advertising in the breadmaking trade. By 1891, John Shade had taken over command of the Fobbing dough troughs, his wife and youthful boys being from Great Burstead, but *he* specifying Ramesden Crays as the home parish. By making such geographical connections across various census years, the reasons why village surnames appear and depart can often be gauged. Among this "trading and service" class (1881) the floury Fincham stands outside the norm however, for being born *within* the county. Most had migrated *much* further, as the enumerator's northward round, crisscrossing Fobbing High Road, was to confirm: farmer John Halston's grocery store, managed by his Surrey spouse; the rectory house of Mr. Thomson opposite – a Hertfordshire gentleman with a daughter born in Switzerland – or the Norfolk cornmiller Harry Lloyd. Beyond, on Bells Hill, was to be found an elderly blacksmith, whose accent had been received from a childhood about Bury in Suffolk during the late Napoleonic years.

Agriculture and its associated trades accounted by far for the work of the majority of families, though in most households only the *husband's* employment would be stated upon an enumerator's form. There was a strong presumption at the hiring of any married farm labourer, nevertheless, that his spouse and children of responsible age, would undertake fieldwork also: providing a considerable but generally "invisible" supplement to the cottage wage. On the surface, 1851's figures had recorded 127 agriculturally employed at Fobbing (farmers, stockmen and agricultural labourers) with a further 20 men engaged upon associated rural crafts such as wheelwrighting, milling, smithy work or haybinding. Of the former group, we might add another 60 "unseen" pairs of hands in the guise of wives and elder offsprings.[8]

By 1861 (7th April) those *listed* as farming people had significantly dropped to 84 persons,[9] the rural crafts to a dozen, while with 1871 a mere 53 were described as of agricultural status (though rural craft-workers had risen to 17). Much has been made of this apparent massive decline, suggesting a shift from the land towards industrial jobs.[10] But agricultural depression had not yet (quite) surfaced in south Essex, nor was any industry yet locally established to a significant degree. The figures are simply misleading. In 1871 especially, Fobbing's enumerator was downright erratic in his recording, the description "labourer" often sufficing when patently the named household head is an *agricultural* employee. A further 30 men may thus be added. Besides, with the

---

8 The farmers' declarations of numbers of workers employed are of limited use in this observation, because they often included workers from several parishes.

9 P.R.O. Home Office RG9/1074 (1861 census).

10 *A Study of Fobbing in Essex 1841-1871*, D. Carney, 1978. E.R.O. Typescript.

arrival of 1881, a full 104 farming people are again seen, with no less than 24 engaged at the country craft skills – at the very period when the social historian might anticipate the corn-depression to be baring its teeth.

To some extent it must be remembered also, farm labourers did not always live in the parish where their daily toil took place: there was undoubtedly a moderate exchange of workmen between Fobbing and Corringham, Vange and the Basildon farms. Fluctuations are therefore bound to occur over the census years as such movements took effect. But this is not to say that an overall decline was not in the making. Attractive employment markets *were* opening; a few which may surprise those who imagine that the agricultural hand could use no other talents but those of the plough and reaphook. That James Halston of Fobbing Street who, in 1851, had answered to the farm-labourer tag, was to rise to "General Dealer" within one decade, his son John William becoming a farmer of 140 acres and keeper of the main village shop. Here, the humble official status of Halston (in 1851) conceals an important point – that he was a nephew of Jane Shuttleworth, widow of Fobbing's prosperous former baker. Another case of escape from the land was Alf Gladwin's (Gladwell) who had shifted from agricultural labouring at the mid century to working as a bargee by 1861. A shepherd at the 1871 census,[11] Jacob Jaggard, would appear soon afterward in the capacity of wharfinger, presumably managing the business side of Fobbing quay.[12]

Despite a continuous activity geared to Fobbing creek and its wharf, the shipment trade was naturally one which involved crews from various other parts of Thames and the eastern coastline. On average, only five village household heads are named as bargemen over the census years in question; three in 1851, during 1861, 1871 and 1891, seven and in 1881, eight. To some degree the parish registers (especially baptisms) not only corroborate these family identities but reveal also the parenting of Fobbing children by outsider-watermen who were presumably occasional callers at the wharf: James Howard of Hullbridge in 1828; Thomas Ellis from Stepney (1870) in 1872 the lighterman George Wennel of Wakering in Essex.

But the familiar *Fobbing* bargee names during this late period were Bandick, Nunn, Scott, Stammers, Wells and Wilson. Plainly George Wells, barge-going spouse of Susannah (she, a native of Fambridge on the Blackwater) had been absent somewhere (on board?) upon the night of 2nd April, 1871 and thus the census omits any suggestion of the

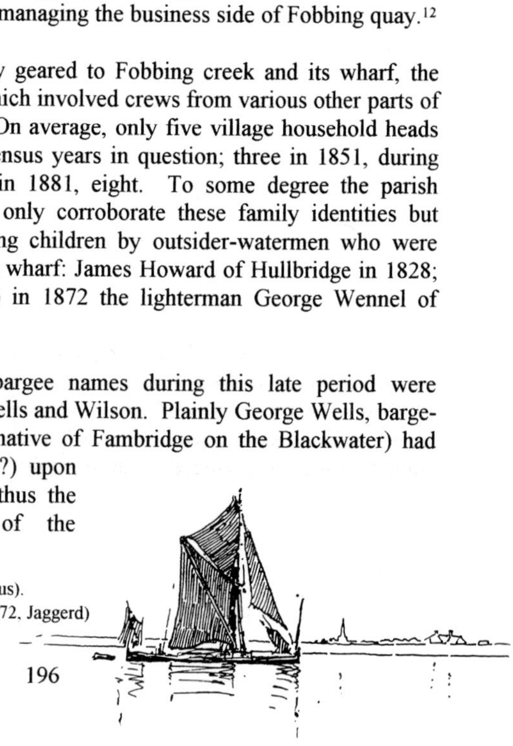

[11] P.R.O. Home Office RG10/1655 (1871 census).

[12] Fobbing Baptismal Register 1813-1874 (1872, Jaggerd) Microfilm E.C.L. Grays CR18645.

D. Maxwell

household's connections with Fobbing's waterside trade.[13] A couple of doors away were Richard and Hannah Stammers, both in young middle-age and originally from Tillingham on the Dengie coast. Their older children, Eliza and Emily, were natives of other small hythe townships – Burnham on Crouch and Benfleet, while nine years old Margaret had been the Stammers' first Fobbing baby. Migration down-Essex through pursuit of the family's line of work speaks from the census form in this example with entire clarity. Relying upon the 1881 evidence alone, we would label James Bandick a farm labourer, living then at No. 1 Brickhouse, in the High Road. A decade earlier Emma Bandick, aged 27, had kept census night with her two youngsters, her husband being away, and so going unrecorded. Yet other sources such as baptismal entries of the family between 1866 and 1872 *all* mention him as a regular bargeman, who had come from Rochford to Fobbing because it was his bride's native place. Fobbing quay and its couple of nearby mariner's alehouses had evidently much to answer in the everlasting push and pull of human circumstance.

Both James and Henry Nunn were Eastwood people (a parish adjoining Leigh) and each had married East Tilbury women. They captained vessels from the 1870s onward, James surviving almost to the end of the Thames sailing barge era, dying in 1935. Among their generation was also William Scott, whose first child to his wife Martha had been born during the 1850s downriver at South Benfleet. At Fobbing, this couple had occupied one of the weatherboarded Hillcrest Cottages atop Wharf Lane[14] where James' occupation – dependent to some extent upon the Medway and Greenhythe cement boom – caused him to evade *every* Fobbing census.[15] By 1891, his widow is found making ends meet as village laundress, "specially appointed," it is grandly told, "to do the Rectory washing". F. Z. Claro's anecdotes, collected from descendants, attribute this accolade to her ability to wash and iron the Rev. Mr. Thomson's cravats entirely "to his satisfaction". Martha's younger son, Harry, and her daughter, seem also to have found employment at Fobbing rectory as gardener and domestic servant, while Thomas and John Scott continued (1891) at the waterman's trade.

These coastal mariners were not normally vessel owners themselves, but operators of a fleet that had centred on the family of Rust at the *White Lion*, listed in 1850 upon the death of Captain William Bogue as "6 Barges with Boats as rigged and in decent repair", to which inventory was added the vague extras of "things in the Store House" – presumably related tackle such as pulley blocks,

---

[13] Occasionally in various censuses, a woman would declare herself "Bargeman's wife" – like Hannah Wilson in 1861. Also at home, aged 24, was Thomas Wilson "Bargeman's son".

[14] Wharf Lane was not so named on any early census, but this is the general term used before 1920.

[15] That is all *Fobbing* census-takes of the second half of the 19th century.

cordage, cabin ladders, sails and sundry mending requirements.[16] In 1871, a young Billericay born sailmaker (James Wiseman) had been resident upon the premises, while the store building itself still forms a significant roadside feature of the public house. Brick built and slated roofed, it dates perhaps from the 1840s and must have contained both workshop and upper storey sail loft. Just prior to his decease, Bogue had been occupier also of Fobbing wharf (rented from its owner, Abraham Daniels) and this long standing tenancy was to continue under Elizabeth Rust's next husband, Sam Wade, into the 1870s. A prayer book, said to be dated by inscription to 1865 and bearing the name of Elizabeth Rust, would remain with Fobbing relatives and contained a list of names which are patently those of sailing barges operated by her kin, the *Neptune, William, Bodsey, Sophia, Susan, Mary, Benjamin, Avis* and *Foundry*. A few decaying wharf-timbers today indicate the quay's location, edged upon the west by an extensive dry hollow (once of rectangular form) the "lay-by" in which Fobbing's barges could be turned upon the flood ready for their downcreek departure to the Thames.

As the London, Tilbury and Southend railroad proceeded eastward towards Benfleet – initially, in the mid 1850s, a single track line – plain company housing was to be erected alongside the Fobbing crossing of the High Road,[17] accommodating at first migrant plate layers. Among these newcomers of around 1856 had been Richard Connoly of Tipperary and his Irish spouse Bridget, while with 1861 Fobbing railway gatehouse would be in the charge of a Northamptonshire employee called Joseph Reynolds. By the 70s and 80s, this little enclave featured rather more *local* operatives, attracted in from Vange, Rochford and the Hanningfield districts to enjoy the relatively secure existence offered by the L. T. & S. R.

At the southernmost parish tip, Thameshaven's branch-line terminus and steamboat pier had accrued around them a personnel which was distinctly foreign: present in 1881 was a resident customs crew that included William Coles, "outdoor officer" and his wife, both old natives of Dorsetshire; a Cornishman named William Stone (driver of a stationary engine) and his Pembrokeshire partner Amelia (a dressmaker). Other westerners were the Hawkes at No. 2 Station House and Devonian Harry Jones, victualler of the clapboarded *Pig and Whistle* beerhouse at Shellhaven creek edge.

---

16 *Inventory for Administration*, W. Jeffries, auctioneer 1850. Photocopy T.MUS.

17 This name is currently in use; possibly it was Vange Lane, or Basildon Lane prior to Post Office systematisation.

It was within the surround of this rough and ready tavern that Fobbing's illegal fist battles had latterly occurred, a premises which – although in one local writer's testimony termed "a very ancient public house" – had presumably sprung up only with the coming of the cattle-landings and railhead. In 1851, among a workforce of builders and painters, had been a plasterer called Benjamin Howlett whose Kentish wife Elizabeth (widowed during the January of 1856) would by 1861 set up as "Innkeeper" at the *Dock House* (a lessee of the railway company). She was assisted there by her son in law, John Sylvester of Dalston, Middlesex. Evidently, *he* had been from the family of an older John Sylvester who, during 1839, occupied William Wingfield's Shellhaven farm. A much worn headstone of 1864 in Fobbing churchyard bears faint traces of the younger man's name. Elizabeth Howlett continued until c.1870. Alongside its official title had appeared the alternative *Pig and Whistle*, under which sign William Lockley was advertising in Kelly's by 1874. The recollection of W. G. Styles tells of it as open to trade "every day and night when the ships were unloading merchandise", while F. Z. Claro's images add a touch of atmosphere: "Unless you were well known when you called, it was as well to keep quiet. There was an open fire in the tap room where customers could cook their own food and a large frying pan, which could hold great gammon rashers, a dozen eggs and sausages, perks from the ships on the tideway ...".[18]

Such was the place, though *which* premises of *two* we do not know, for Styles tells of *The Old Pig and Whistle* being "only about six feet away from the sea wall but in view of the danger of the bank being washed away a new sea defence was built."[19] A subsequent rebuilding of the pub sited the *New Pig and Whistle* near to the London, Tilbury and Southend branch line. Chance agricultural migrations as ever played their hand, as in the case of the widowed George Ockendon of Rayleigh. He had been sent to Fobbing's Borley farm as overseeing bailiff around 1880, having not long married a teenage West Tilbury girl and by 1886, under the banner of Messrs. Seabrookes' the noted Grays brewery, was following a fresh calling as publican of the *Pig*, where he remained past the mid 90s, to be succeeded by George Partner at the century's end.

A long-surviving system of providing manorial (later parish) constables from within each community was to be overtaken with the first Victorian years by a uniformed county police force (1840) though in fact Fobbing did not discontinue for some while its annual

[18] *Thames Haven News,* Summer, 1957.

[19] *Marshland Memories,* W. Styles, PAN. Vol. 29, 1988.

election of unpaid parishioners to the obsolete post. Placed within the Brentwood Division, the village was thereafter to see an occasional top-hatted presence from the Orsett station but recorded no resident policeman until the census of 1881, when William Webb, a 26 years old married constable from Nazing was to be found stationed with his wife and baby in one of Fobbing's cottages called "Challaces Farm" (Prosbus Hall). His successor a decade on, P.c. Walter Fisher of Lexden, had clearly served previously upon the Grays establishment, for it was there that his child Dora had been born around 1887. She and an elder sibling now went as scholars to Fobbing C. of E. school. Within a year of this April census, parishes eastward of Orsett and Stanford le Hope were to be placed under a new separate Division – Grays – comprising thirteen beats[20] of which Fobbing's was not noted as the calmest since it extended across the tough cattle-wharves and spirit-landings alongside Ockendon's beer saloon. Yet the milder upland, too, provided its steady flow of incident: labourer Henry Clifford – drunk and disorderly in November 1892, refusing to quit the *Lion*:[21] the grim mischance involving 10 years old Fred Wakeling at Hovels who, finding a loaded shotgun at the barnside, blew half his jaw away and would be rushed to Gravesend (the nearest hospital) where his life was despaired of.[22]

That summer, (1895) a pleasant June evening at dusk, P.c. John Bigg, Fobbing's blue tunicked trouble-shooter, would be called out to confront a gang of village youths making disturbance "at the top of the hill" – a well known consortium comprising the Laver brothers from Copeland cottage, the Avenue's Arthur Ockendon, David Mann and Jimmy Strutt. There had been some cursing, but, even worse, "one of them was trying to play a mouth organ".[23] Not all Victorian self-made entertainment came free, as subsequent draconian fines of 9s. 8d. each would demonstrate.

There was always a quota of large village families, but these were not typical by any means. Dorothy Carney's study of Fobbing through the years 1841-1871 reveals a high percentage of young, or youthful folk:[24] out of a population total of 428 persons in 1841, some 140 was of children aged under ten. More than a half (228) of all inhabitants here were beneath 20 years in age. The following three censuses to 1871 dipped only slightly, still showing the parish to contain almost 50% of junior people. A comparison of the 1851 and 1891 recordings – covering the Victorian generations quite widely – reveals, in both surveys Fobbing parents having to support at home an average of only three

---

20 *The Essex Police,* J. Woodgate, 1985.

21 G.T.G. 19th November, 1892.

22 G.T.G. 16th March, 1895.

23 G.T.G. 6th July, 1895.

24 *A Study of Fobbing in Essex 1841-1871*, D. Carney, 1978. E.R.O. Typescript.

offsprings. During 1851 a rather greater proportion of couples actually had children with them; 62 couples from 87 houses; in 1891 only 49 couples from the 94 occupied premises. Such momentary sampling naturally does not reflect the whole number of children born over the years to each parent group, since some at any enumeration might have recently died in infancy, or grown sufficiently to leave home. Others were yet to be conceived. Six viable pregnancies would be about the normal Victorian woman's experience.

Of the three children observed in each parental household, a considerable number were of an age beneficial to the family income. Teenage boys were still normally dwelling at home, though sisters of comparable years might be absent in domestic service. But the bringing home of pence began far earlier than this. At Hawkesbury Bush, George and Amelia Partridge – a couple in their mid-thirties during 1851 – registered a 5 years old son George as employed already upon farmwork. So was the 10 years old Charles Bridge, child of a youngish widow at the High Road, while his near neighbour John Baker (aged 13) appeared in the census alongside his namesake father, as a shepherd. Of the four children of Golden Fretton, another cottager along the village street, three sons like himself were working as haybinders – their ages 16, 13 and 8 years. In every previous instance, the male parent had been either an agricultural labourer, or a stockman. By contrast, households like that of James and Emma Heathcote (baker) or Abraham and Sarah Crooks (blacksmith) could manage to keep their boys of similar age as scholars yet awhile.

During the 1851 enumeration, nine of Fobbing's parent groups had listed 5 or more young ones (their own children) still living at home. A couple of those had as many as 8 offsprings in their cottage. The increase of this kind of situation by 1891 was considerable; some 11 parent groups now looked after more than 5 youngsters, of which 3 had 8 or 9 children. Significant amongst the latter was William Wright, a boot and shoe maker in his late thirties, living in one of the black boarded cottages opposite Shade's bakery. Arriving in Fobbing around 1890 (a Wethersfield native) he had been a highly itinerant tradesman, for each of his nine children – aged from 16 to only 1 year old – had come into the world at a different parish. His eldest were all working at farm jobs or were in family service, another 4 being yet "scholars" across at the churchyard edge.

In this instance Wright's family was possibly better equipped to manage than, say, the Hollidays, who succoured a lesser tribe of 6 youngsters upon Lion Hill. Jonas Holliday, an East Horndon born agricultural labourer, had remained fairly stationary at

Sheepshearing

Fobbing over the past fifteen years or so, where every one of his youngsters had been born. But all save Samuel, age 14, were still under earning age in this census year of 1891.[25] Over the parish stream that April, Richard Rushbrook, "Master Potter" of Haveringham in Norfolk, had made his first appearance, having recently set up with his brother a brickmaking factory edging the "hopes" below Vineyard farmstead.[26] Small wonder the Hollidays saw in this new industry a brighter future for their boy than upon the farmwork at which his parent Jonas had toiled. Young Samuel was already familiar with horse-work and by the spring of 1893 would be employed in operating Rushbrook's clay-pug mill, driven by a shaft attached to a steady lead-animal. There, aged 16, he died with his head crushed between the mill edge and his horse mechanism, as an April inquest at the *Lion* was to tell.[27]

Fourteen children would be listed as scholars in 1851, though no schoolhouse had yet been purposely built, nor was any person specified in the census as a teacher. A single entry amidst the churchwardens' accounts for April 1838 had allowed two shillings to a person called Freeman "for teaching school", while a decade later White's directory was to identify mistress Catherine Harrison at a "parish school supported by the rector." Presumably this was for elementary instruction only, for during 1847 an "Infant School" had been mentioned, excused its payment of poor rates.

The Rev. Henry Thompson, M.A., had succeeded Randolph in 1839, dying aged 67 at Fobbing during early March 1850. Sometime during 1853, the incoming minister, William Stephen Thomson, would see the opening upon the churchyard's edge of a first purpose-built schoolhouse, a tiny brick place with slated roof, said in later years to have been designed for 69 children. Regrettably, Fobbing's following census was to omit any useful reference as to which children were in education; but with 1871 only 23 youngsters would be declared by their parents to be at a place of teaching.

Occupying *Glass Bottle* house in 1881 was a young schoolmistress from Euston called Emily Thompson – perhaps, despite a variation in spelling, the relative of Fobbing's rector – while the number of scholars had leapt to 76 children, plainly due to the important Education Act of 1880, which required school attendance for the nation's young up to the age of ten at least. A whole *sixth* of Fobbing's population was now in formal education, a picture which prevailed also a decade on, when 68 youngsters would be identified as classroom-

---

[25] P.R.O. Home Office RG12/1380 (1891 census).

[26] Rushbrooks' claypits extended onto the Fobbing marshes near the wharf, and other minerals were perhaps dug adjacent to Fobbing Hall.

[27] G.T.G. 8th April, 1893.

The Schoolhouse

goers. Miss Harriet Milne, a mature spinster who would soon perhaps be jostling the various gentlemen serving upon Fobbing's vestry to thoughts of building extensions,[28] appears by this date (1891) to have been using part of her schoolhouse as living quarters. Parent of one of the aforementioned village pests, Mr. D. Mann would be present with parson Thomson and the Wesleyan builder William Payne in May 1895, to vote power to the school's management committee for raising the necessary finance. By late November, Payne's son Walter was to be granted a £3. 0s. 0d. payment covering his duties in collecting subscriptions to a building fund which, with mid January 1896, was to flower in bricks-and-mortar: a good additional classroom adequate for some 45 infants, bringing the total child capacity up to 107.[29] Actual attendances seldom however averaged above 40.

Construction had been undertaken by the same Walter Payne (carpenter, of Bay Cottages) and Daniel Raison, a builder who since his marriage to Rebecca Rust, great grand-daughter of the Georgian Leonard Rust, had resided in Glass Bottle House. Both Payne and Raison would sit to hear, early in 1897, their perturbed rector's reaction to a seeming calamity; for the much-praised school extension was settling badly and must be watched awhile "to see if it come over any further". In the meanwhile, the pair were to take down its small bell tower, perhaps in the hope of alleviating some pressure upon their new building. Those juvenile imaginations that nursed images of an absolute collapse were nevertheless to be disappointed and within a very few years the educational side of Fobbing life was to expand in an unanticipated way.

The late 1870s would be long remembered throughout south Essex, as the first phase of an agricultural crisis which was to have painful and protracted effects. The decline of the "golden age" of corn farming had come with suddenness, brought about by the cheap and rapid importation aboard steam vessels of prairie wheat from the American states. Though, to some extent, local farmers had been preserved from immediate financial ruin through other, more diverse aspects such as livestock grazing and market gardening, the long term

[28] Fobbing Vestry Minutes 1862-1923, Microfilm E.C.L. Grays. CR18645.

[29] Fobbing Vestry Minutes 1862-1923, Microfilm E.C.L. Grays. CR18645.

effect was generally disastrous.[30] As tenants' rents failed, so landlords such as the Whitmores of Orsett, owners of Fobbing Hall, became severely pressed.

Alternative uses for farmland were obviously attractive and where these involved outright disposal by landowners for industrial development, the appeal of cash gains was strong. With the autumn of 1896, the Corporation of Norwich, as trustees of its Great Hospital, relinquished their Borley (Bawliff) farm to the Kynoch Explosives works for the establishment of its great 200 acre factory. Hutments appeared shortly after, by late November the embryo plant being announced as already in operation, though in 1897 suffering initial setback when the Fobbing seawall gave under an especially high tide, causing serious flooding over the whole levels. An early newspaper account had defined the Kynoch enterprise as already "a household name with military men and those ... who delight to blot the life out of living creatures in the name of sport". But here was employment at a time of disintegrating hope around the local farms and by February 1898, candidate for county elections Mr. Morley Hill was selling to a substantial audience (at the Fobbing Institute) the notion of Kynoch's arrival as "the panacea of the evils of agricultural depression", and opining upon the local authority's manifest responsibility in making up the roadway towards Iron Latch.[31]

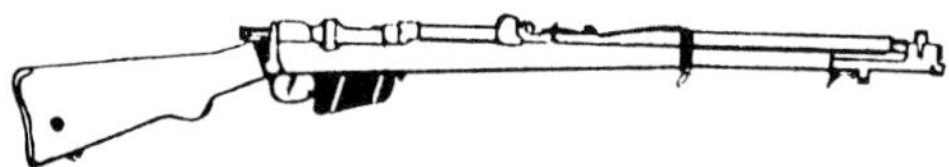

A commemorative dinner held that April had heard its speaker refer to the Thames Explosives Works as "a bleak place at present in which to live", though the full future programme of site-development would surely improve matters.[32] A few brick houses for some managers and initial operatives had been already erected: with 18th November, 1899, Miss Katherine Chamberlain, Company Chairman's daughter and niece of Joseph Chamberlain (current Colonial Secretary) would bring a touch of elegance to these wastes of bloody purpose, by officially naming Fobbing's new satellite community *"Kynoch Town"*.[33] Some while anticipated, the South African war had commenced some weeks earlier and few Victorians would have felt uneasy at the whiff of family nepotism which the charming V.I.P. brought along as she undertook her tour, laying the foundation stone of a new schoolhouse for 40 junior children and 24 infants. Suddenly, the ecclesiastical parish of Fobbing, possessed upon its soil *two* centres of education – the upland and the marsh.

---

30 *A History of the Orsett Estate 1743-1914*, E. J. T. Collins, 1978.

31 G.T.G. 26th February, 1898.

32 G.T.G. 30th April, 1898.

33 *Coryton: The Story of a Village*. W. Scott, 1981.

Gateway decoration, Kynoch's

With the start of 1900, the district's weekly *Gazette* could headline "*PLENTY OF WORK*": every department at Kynoch's was in "full swing", operating both day and night.[34] Somehow, the great sculpted company lions which posed regally atop its entrance pillars seemed especially appropriate to a determined imperial mood. Subjection of the savage symbol of Africa into an ornamental species was (after all) the name of the Chamberlain game. Beyond its gate, the Kynoch factory opened into two distinct areas: a plot containing its chemical processing and sundry workshops and the danger zone which bordered Holehaven creek. Here were manufactured guncotton, black and smokeless gunpowders, cordite, highly sensitive nitroglycerine and .303 cartridges for the regulation British infantry-issue rifle.

One contemporary account would tell of a "subdued sense of discipline" within every stage of manufacture, "the underlying sense of danger, and necessity for absolute care, with which even the most thoughtless employee is impressed while engaged on his or her work. For at Kynochtown ... the workpeople are of either sex. Probably on the whole something like ten per cent are women or girls, whose deft touch and quickness of hand render them specially fitted to deal with such branches as the blending of the cordite and other stages in the process ...". There were lines of females to be seen, quietly engaged, "all uniformly clothed in scarlet dresses, the colour denoting that they are employed within the danger zone ..." and from whose busy fingers the explosives would pass onward to their test-laboratory chemists, or to the marshland ranges, "where the actual velocities and pressures have to come within certain definite limits".

By the new century's beginning, a labour force of some 500 would be employed; many living within the wider district, giving a useful opportunity for villages nearby to make a side-line at renting spare rooms. From a population of 409 in 1891, Fobbing's figure would rise with 1901's census by a further 250 residents, while Corringham's expansion was to be even more impressive in its surge from 269 to 582 persons. From Kynoch's wharves, a whole fleet of dark-sailed barges was engaged in shipping explosives up-river to the government arsenal at Woolwich. Old Borley farmhouse and its cluster of wooden agricultural buildings had changed its guise into the company's general store, serving workers with everything "from a pin to an anchor, or from a pair of goloshes to a suit of clothes, with a helmet to complete the outfit if needed."[35]

[34] G.T.G. 13th January, 1900.

[35] G.T.G. 2nd June, 1900.

Oozedam farm, D. Maxwell

Cycling down the trampled Fobbing-marsh manorway that early June of 1900, reporter's notebook at the ready, the *Grays and Tilbury Gazette's* representative could enjoy tender green expanses of an ancient marsh, where bulky longhorns and recently introduced Ayreshires browsed the middle distance towards Kynoch's perimeter fences of barbed wire. Far on his left appeared the russet-hipped roof of Oozedam homestead amid a sombre burst of elms; back nearer the village height the clean yellow blot of Slatey House farm, its low stockyard wall fronting the creek's winding gully of mud.

It was sheepdipping time; the month of shearing, a bustling season for shepherd Simon Gilder, born in Finchingfield a half century ago and who now lived here with his wife – Wrighty Garnish, once known as housecook to the Longs up at Old Hall. Age old occupations like the handsomely bearded Gilder's still went on. A few blazing summer weeks and the scene of panting flocks out among their arid, tawny-brown sheepwalks would take on a kind of biblical *persona*, a landscape where the prehistoric herdsmen of Abraham or Job might have passed with dusty robes and crookstaves; familiar and seemingly eternal. But the baked clay road under swift pneumatic tyres, led far away beyond, to somewhere else; where nothing would ever be so pastoral or so certain again.

Fobbing manorway, D. Maxwell

11. GROWING PAINS

Leafing through the marriage-lines of St. Michael's from 1900 on, one can perceive in the occupations of its newlyweds, a half-century's story told outright. *Horseman, wheelwright, dairywoman, brickmoulder, munition-maker, oil-worker analytical chemist*; a rural countryside was slipping away, even though for many years it would be easy for the village to pretend that those distant marshland structures – so often screened by veils of hilltop elm – were really something of a separate universe. The mid-year of 1900 had issued nevertheless a forecast of future perils – one flash of lightning from out a violently stormy afternoon sky, which struck clean into the open hold of the ship *Helena*, a sailing barque berthed upon the Thameshaven jetty.[1] Owned by a Bremen firm, she had arrived from New York laden with a shipment of inflammable naphtha oil, of which some 2,800 barrels were still on board at the moment of combustion. Four German seamen were to die, the cargo bays "a vast cauldron" of fire. Retelling the saga long after,[2] one old worker would claim, "the only course was to batten down the hold ... although men were below, it had to be done." Despite the reasonable request for a delay of inquest to allow a German consular presence, the matter would be hurried along with unseemly disregard for the foreigner. It was the year of Kaiser Wilhelm's expansion of his fleet under the Navy Bill and weightless seeds of enmity between both countries were already blowing on the wind.

The great queen whose accession back in 1837 only our parish ancients could now recall, had died in January 1901, to be mourned in every continent, a year which took to his grave also Henry Long, oldest of a family that was Fobbing's largest combined landowner. A lifelong bachelor whose figure, cantering over the neighbouring farms, had been familiar throughout Victoria's extensive reign, he had some while before celebrated his 92nd birthday.[3] Long "would mount his horse without assistance and continued to visit the London Corn Market up to the last",

---

1 G.T.G. 7th July, 1900.

2 *Marshland Memories,* W. G. Styles, PAN. Vol. 29, 1988.

3 G.T.G. 3rd August, 1901.

observed a newspaper obituary, recounting a paternal consideration for his workers that was reflected in the infrequency with which "he found occasion to dismiss any of them". With 1905 his younger brother, Herbert Clarance Long, both churchwarden and a manager of Fobbing's parish school, was to be buried also, ending the male succession to a substantial cluster of farms; Oil Mill, Great House, Vineyard, Sprivens Hall, Curtis' and Byrons, as well as others beyond the parish edge. If distant yet, a gradual break-up lay upon the horizon.

From the top of a village hierarchy, other hoary headed Victorians were tumbling; for on 12th January 1902, in his 85th year, the Rev. William Stephen Thomson passed away in his rectory room, following long incapacity and several days' unconsciousness during which his physician "tried to arrest the progress of the fell destroyer." Graduating long ago in 1839, Thomson had served as English chaplain at Heidelburg prior to his appointment to Fobbing in 1850. His body was to be taken to Chorley Wood, Hertfordshire, for burial.[4]

A month to the day had separated the old parson's decease from that of his erstwhile competitor, William Payne, the former carpenter who for almost half a century had headed the district's Wesleyan Methodist movement. A summer's evening meeting[5] at the Jubilee chapel (which Payne had been instrumental in setting up during 1887) was to be held in early August, 1903 to unveil his brass memorial tablet as "founder of this place of worship". Not all, perhaps, remembered him afterwards with

Payne's Jubilee Chapel

4 G.T.G. 18th January, 1902.

5 G.T.G. 15th August, 1903.

affection – his annoyance with villagers' behaviour had brought cases before the Grays justices more than once, including the silly affair of James Bandick, accused in the fresh February of 1888 of throwing a snowball at the new chapel's door during service.[6] Payne had already on one occasion before gone out and "spoken to men" about such disturbances, finding, he said, that "they have only sworn at me". Fitting enough, then, that his final oak-mounted plate should boast, *"I have fought a good fight."* His earthly tormentors would be hard pressed to find a snowball where *they* were going.

Old rivalries with the village next door could be put by for the sake of sport, if for little else. Fobbing's and Corringham's combined football club was having notable successes just now, roundly beating a Tilbury Fort eleven in February, 1902, "a pleasant game" confided a quaintly unhysterical reportage of the period, followed by a sing-song with soldiers at the nearby *World's End.* At home that April the F.C.F.C. beat again a visiting team from "Clapham Crescent", Clapham being the home of the Ewens (brother and nephew of Eleanor Halston of Fobbing's store) future shopkeepers here. A handsome score of 7-1 had been contributed to, perhaps, by one of the Surrey side's backs departing the fray with "a severe kick on the ankles".[7] The generally more passive game of quoits brought *White Lion* regulars victory through 1903, even against exponents from the Little Thurrock *Ship*, a distinguished, even famous, bunch at ringing the pin over an 18-yards distance.

Down in Shellhaven house, a quiet drink at home brought John Meen, farm bailiff, into court with a plea of guilty to having sold beer without licence to two lodgers, apparently "working men" from Kynoch's adjacent factory. Their real identities as constables Mott and Cameron were, alas, soon revealed.[8] An 18 gallon cask of liquor on the premises, explained Meen, had been required for his half dozen sons (all munitions workers) because his farmhouse water was "not fit to drink". It was somehow difficult to do right where water was concerned. That hot July, 18 years old Charles Sargent of Fobbing, was to find himself on a charge of indecent exposure for bathing by the creek wall, where, Edith Taylor (married woman) testified, she had appraised his exposed person. Those long Edwardian summers here on the muddy downstream end of Thames

---

6 G.T.G. 3rd March, 1888.

7 G.T.G. 1st March and 5th April, 1902, 3rd October, 1903.

8 G.T.G. 31st January, 1903.

were a world away from Henley regatta. Sargent's injudicious dip got him 14 days hard labour.[9]

Meanwhile, in July 1903, Fobbing Parish Council would meet to discuss applications to the Orsett Rural District for an extension of the Southend Water Company's 3 inch main (already serving the High Road) to supply the few dwellings down as far as the foot of Wharf Lane, an improvement which in the autumn of 1912 the 30 or so cottages northward from Bells Hill would be also hoping to obtain. However, £360 for the 1,317 yards of piping up to Fobbing farm was considered to be beyond financial resources for the present. Luxuries such as plumbed bathtubs were still not yet part of the Fobbing experience, but one serious fire within the village had already shown what a valuable property-insurance the main might represent. During September, 1907, three 40 feet lengths of leather hosepipe had been purchased, with branches and jets, from the celebrated suppliers Messrs. Shand & Mason and soon a volunteer fire team would be getting its red-painted fire-box for storing the new equipment, set up by permission of Sarah Long against the weathered brick wall of Byron's farmhouse.[10]

A decade later, on Saturday 8th December 1917, this same widowed lady would find herself grateful of its proximity, when her nearby cattle yard of Sprivens Hall – tenanted by west country migrant Clem. Hawkins – went swiftly up in flames. It was mid-afternoon, and though many helpers arrived quickly upon the scene, and Kynoch's up-to-date horse drawn engine appeared soon besides, the great timber-and-thatched barn, granaries and a loose-box stable would be rapidly consumed.[11] A vehicle shed containing governess cart and harness were also incinerated. Alongside, corn ricks would somehow be saved and mercifully all horses released. John Ewen's grocery business next door had escaped but narrowly. In our own time much of Spriven's ancient barnyard plan can still be glimpsed as hummocks of grassed brick and summer parch-marks, beneath pleasant orchard trees.

Huge developments had suddenly threatened to engulf countryside edging the highway from Southend, called variously the Vange Corner and Vange Park Estate,[12] yet entirely within Fobbing's boundary, where something close to a thousand building plots were on offer by speculative

---

9 G.T.G. 18th July, 1903.

10 Fobbing P.C.C. 1903-1936.

11 G.T.G. 15th December, 1917.

12 Sale Cat. Messrs. Deeley & Kesterton, Vange Park Estate, June, 1902.

businessmen from 1900: a characteristic result of the last decade's depression that had rendered void so much South Essex arable land. Near Hovels farmhouse, a roadside hotel was now proposed and a terrace row actually appeared fronting London Road. Fancy postal addresses were being dreamed up, such as *Palm, Fern* and *Ivy Road, Mount Drive* and *Hovels Chase.* Few of these ever came to domestic realisation, except for a cluster around Vange Park Road and the surrounding landscape would in time assume a guise of ramshackle cottage independence. Yesterday still decided the look of tomorrow, and a dormant medieval factor awoke and played its bony hand, as fields surrounding Mill Lane (originally villein furlongs attached to Hovels farm) became available as new "plotland" dwelling areas. Inglefield Road was to be the result, a significant feature in the extending of Fobbing's village periphery as the century advanced.

Plotland bungalow Inglefield Road

Following Thomson as parson, John Edmund Sedgwick's rectorship embraced a fairly brief period until 1907, during which years nearly £2,000 had been expended on serious structural faults in the church fabric.[13] Cracked walls were filled, new pillars skilfully inserted "instead of some old ones which had long been shored up with oak beams." After several months closure, a special re-opening service would be held and Sedgwick's important archaeological discoveries made public – Fobbing's ancient rood staircase, a mutilated effigy of Madonna and Child, as well as the baptismal font's original shaft and pillared support (for some reason previously obscured within "a heap of plaster"). He had been concerned also, to purchase land for an extension of St. Michael's overly-pressured burial ground and on Friday, 5th July, 1907 the bishop of Barking would consecrate a meadow alongside Fobbing schoolhouse and southward of the red brick churchyard wall for that use.[14] This same day, he was to install Sedgwick's successor, the Rev. Arthur Banan who, from 1887 had held the chaplaincy of the Scilly Isles. Banan would soon be campaigning for yet further church improvements, approaching Scots-Canadian millionaire

---

[13] E.R. Vol. 15, 1906.

[14] G.T.G. 13th July and 20th July, 1907.

A. E. Banan

Andrew Carnegie for means toward a new organ costing £300 from Walmsley's at the Lea Valley works in Maidstone. Come November, the old stone edifice stood packed with those who had gathered to hear Banan's "capital instrument" (with its 20 stops and "a full compass of pedals") din out from the southern chapel. In true style, Carnegie had matched local donations pound for pound.[15]

Along by Bells Corner, hastening to Southend's hotels, burnished motor cars and their goggled passengers were occasionally observed. This July, it had been possible to trek over to Langdon Hill and witness a whole cavalcade of internal combustion machines on trial up the demanding wooded steeps by Goldsmiths farm. But the pneumatic-tyred bicycle was as yet the best most might aspire to, and those cottage breadwinners were lucky who could afford to get to their factory jobs by pedal-power. February, 1907 had seen Fobbing's police constable, Frank Eagling, investigating the theft of a cycle lamp and pump from Kynoch's premises, property of George Wells, of 9, Mill Cottages.[16] As proved so often the case, the dastard's trail led him to Digby Road, Corringham, where the iniquitous seemed somehow to flourish.

But cycling brought to this landscape folk in search of more cerebral rewards, too: long skirted scenery seekers, Norfolk-jacketed, tripod-hoisting photographers; a host of knickerbockered collectors, chaining the miles in search of picture postcards at rural post offices and village tearooms. From the pages of an *Essex Review*, an early Edwardian had urged the tourist's inspection of the village and its neighbouring settlements while yet unviolated by the debasing influence of commerce. "*If only it were better known, Fobbing should become as favourite a centre for painters as Rye ... or even Newlyn. Alas! this charming scene, so delightful to the eye, is not fated to last much longer.*" There were summery photographs of the wharf, a barge *"with tawny sails, brailed up and stowed"* and (to prove his point) the *White Lion* overhanging a delicious rural lane.[17]

William Payne's middle aged daughter Lydia had taken over as rural sub-postmistress soon after the century turned and, with January 1909, Fobbing's Parish Council would consider a letter from the Grays

---

[15] G.T.G. 9th November, 1907.

[16] G.T.G. 9th February, 1907.

[17] *Vanishing Essex Villages,* E.R. Vol. 11, 1902.

postmaster suggesting her office duties be trimmed, so as not to exceed a recommended 8 hour-day. The nearest money-order and telegraph service lay in busier Stanford and merely stamps and parcels would be dealt with out here – henceforth between 8 a.m. and noon and 3 p.m. till 7 in the evening every weekday. A morning service only would prevail upon bank holidays. Council members conferred and concurred. The village wall-posting box outside her white boarded cottage was still being cleared twice daily; once on Sundays.[18]

From now, beyond the threshold of war, the outward scene of village trade was to alter little. Cottages such as that opposite Charlie Shade's aromatic bake house and stables did a little confectionery business from front rooms, but the continuing general store and drapery was facing Mr. Banan's high garden wall,[19] a stuccoed and pantile-roofed building run by the widowed Ellen Halston (d. 1911) from behind attractive double frames of multi-paned windows. John Halston, her husband, had served here too, amidst the shelves and matchboarding, back into the 1860s.

Though modestly enlarged to accommodate some 89 scholars, the low-eaved parochial school continued a comfortless progress. Its couple of rooms (29' by 18' for 52 children, and 18' by 18', holding above 30) were supplemented by small cloakrooms and outside lavatories with "mud playgrounds" for the separated sexes. During January 1907, the weather had become so severe that ink froze overnight in its desktop pots; in March 1909 the main room, housing Standards I to VI recorded a temperature of 40 degrees at 11.30 a.m., this with an open fire burning. Ten degrees less would be recorded on one bitter occasion. Roy Eaton's vignette of the children's difficulties and successes through this time deserves a full reading, yet to poach a few of its Edwardian images is perhaps permissible. The June pea harvest, hop picking in Kent and even alleged blackberry gathering during early October, provided seasonal excuses for poor attendance, in November 1911 "a party of shooters" employing 4 boys as

---

18 Fobbing P.C.C. 1903-1936.

19 *Directories of Essex;* Post Office, 1866, 1870; Kelly's 1878, 1895, 1906.

beaters. The teachers themselves during the fall of 1912 were to be ticked off by a superior for being "somewhat slack" in their timekeeping.[20]

On the credit side, July 1905 had seen a "Tea and Prize Giving" at which eleven medals would be awarded to pupils "who had made perfect attendances during the year." In June 1914 youngsters Mark Outen and Mabel Charlton were off to the Crystal Palace at Sydenham, where a recently deposed king Manuel and queen Victoria Augusta of Portugal would present their prizes for an essay upon *"Kindness to Animals"*. But if Manuel's far realm had collapsed in chaos to the revolutionary hordes, an invincible royalism continued at Fobbing, England. The king-emperor, Edward VII, died and the village school closed for his funeral in the cuckoo-loud days of 1910. Each 24 May, upon Empire Day, national songs were to be shared, a rousing talk might be given "on the greatness and unity of our Empire" (1907) to be followed by "marching around the playground with the Union Jack in front."[21]

Leaning out of smoke-smudged train windows, could be seen military men who had known Zululand and Afghanistan; red-tunicked, mustached, chinstrapped faces pushed into helmets of blue cloth that was spiked and starred with gaudy brass. Along the London river swept novel wonders of empire on canvas wings; Farman seaplanes of the Royal Naval Air Service. It was hardly more than a decade since the American Wrights had lifted to air at Kitty Hawk, when, on May 20, 1914, Nazewick farm's 253 level acres went onto the market, suitable (suggested the sale catalogue's boldly-inked frontice) for marsh grazing, or perhaps the erection of a factory; alternatively "for an Experimental Flying Ground."[22] A new national idea was being felt even here, among the mundane literature of country estate-agents. People were wondering if there could be a future in this exciting aviation business. Above all the imperial pink there appeared suddenly a lot of blue for the taking, and the far sighted were asking the question: *whose?*

To a half dozen servicemen of the parish, August 1914 had brought the optimistic dawn of a war which effectively did (for them) "end all wars"; one, J. R. Cowans, killed in France during September 1918, is not recorded upon Fobbing's unimposing marble plaque within St. Michael's

---

20 *Fobbing Parochial School,* R. L. Eaton, PAN. Vol. 12, 1968.

21 F. Z. Claro, G.T.G. 23rd April, 1976 (photo of schoolhouse).

22 Fred Taylor & Co., *"Narswick"* Sale Catalogue, 20th May, 1914. As early as 1911, the village might have seen aviators in training at nearby Blue House farm, Pitsea (G.T.G. 27th May, 1911).

church, though his graveyard memorial is nearby. For the first time in modern memory, a modest danger from hostile action would touch village lives, heralded upon Christmas morning, 1914, by the drone of a solitary *Albatros* bomber bearing the black cross of Germany upon curved wings defiantly over Thames. It was a day of alternate brightness and haze. Dinners were delayed as the land guns of Purfleet 10 miles westward and other estuary stations spattered shells into a misty sky. One bomb was heard to fall over the river on Cliffe in Kent.[23]

The first late summer of the conflict had raised a terrifying issue regarding Kynoch's alleged part in polluting a brook dividing the two parishes, branded "the stink stream" by Corringham's rector, who claimed its "deadly germs" had been directly instrumental in a sudden and massive child mortality. Five youngsters of Fobbing Church of England school alone had succumbed to diphtheria between mid September and October 14th, and he minced no words about the death of a little girl, daughter of his friend Clement Helecke of Fobbing. She had been "murdered", his Deanery magazine column claimed, along with 16 others, by these waters' filthy state, pointing out that both parish councils, and the District too, had attempted without effect to get it cleansed. "A few hundredweight of disinfectant might have stopped the evil", he felt, "if only the company's Birmingham headquarters would do something".[24] Presumably, the cause lay in sewage disposal from a new "Colony" of hutments for munitions women, on Herd farm's westward slope.

The sudden influx of migrant parishioners brought both problems and pleasures, engagingly outlined in Winifred Scott's *Coryton:* a book which provides plenty of technical and social detail upon this aspect of the century's story.[25] Though Fobbing's industrialised marshgrounds had been (for civil purposes) transferred to Corringham parish during 1889, ecclesiastically they remained unaltered. All the accompanying residential development of Kynochtown (later called Coryton) including its new school (1899) likewise fell within Fobbing's parochial bounds, as indeed would the future *Shell Cottages* to southward. The local newspaper, the *Gazette*, adds to Mrs. Scott's wartime scenario with incidental reports – like that of a Kynoch's workman lodging during late 1916 at "Glass House" *(Glass Bottle House)* in Wharf Lane and found in illegal possession of a pair of army boots, reputedly purchased from a soldier of the Suffolk's, from the factory. There are contemporary references, too, to the servicemen

[23] G.T.G. 2nd January, 1915.

[24] G.T.G. 6th May, 1916 (re: Summer, 1914).

[25] *Coryton: the History of a Village*, W. Scott, 1980.

'defiantly over Thames'; an Albatros

themselves, who were manning Kynoch's military blockhouses and the oil depot's riverward walls. The 3rd Border Regiment is named on station in the midsummer of 1915, when Pte. Fred Pounder fell over Thameshaven's sea wall on sentrygo and was found dead there the following morning. Pounder would be buried by his companions at Fobbing's churchyard. Another soldier victim came from the Manchesters; May 1st 1916 had seen Pte. Joseph Statton patrolling the workers' passenger line when he was struck and killed by its small steam-loco driven by Thomas Johnson. By 1917, hundreds of operatives, living as far away as Southend, would be described by the press as coming each shift by motor charabanc via the *"Bells"* and Fobbing's long leafy street, to connect with the C.L.R. platform terminus at Digby Road.[26]

Arthur Banan, Fobbing's parson, and other local clergy had been guests at Kynochtown during October (1915) when a gay military concert presented by the 20th Bn. London Regt. included a topical farce based upon England's ever present wartime spy alarms.[27] It featured one Taggie Murkyn – "a detective of the humourous kind" – called in by the firm of *"Flynochs"* to identify a suspected German agent in its midst and provided a certain Lance Cpl. Lowry with ample scope for his thespian talents in a much applauded love scene as "Flo, the Flynoch Flapper."

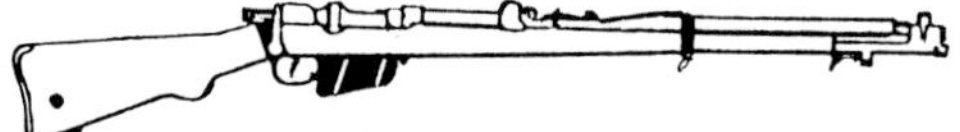

Everyone had an idea of what action to take should the Kaiser's army invade. There were printed instructions, issued by the Orsett Petty Sessions Emergency Committee, and "Local Helpers" had been sworn in (for Fobbing: John Ewen at the stores, Clement Helecke of Kynochs and Nazewick's farmer George Vicary) who already knew their organisational drill thoroughly. All parish civilians were to become refugees; those from Fobbing to evacuate their homes and get as best they could with bundles and "prams" up the High Road and Bells Hill, onto Dry Street and thence over Langdon top, to congregate (with other incoming parishioners) on Childerditch common bordering the clay fens about 8 miles to north-westward.[28] Farmers likewise, having slaughtered all livestock except breeding animals "of great value" and leaving carcasses with broken skins to decompose, were to hurry their prize beasts (branded with an "F") in the same direction, avoiding such roads as would by now have been commandeered for military use. Just what plans of disposal for the

---

[26] Corringham Light Railway: ceased operation 1952.

[27] G.T.G. 30th October, 1915.

[28] *The Flight that Never Was,* R. Bingley, PAN. Vol. 18, 1974-5.

thousands fleeing from Thameside, might lie beyond that makeshift camp for displaced persons none could conceive. Nor need they. The *Boche* and "Tommy Atkins" were going to pursue their tussle over metres of Flanders mud, not in the cosy home counties. And so there was work. Plenty, at all hours, with a munitions plant at full stretch alongside Holehaven creek and oil and spirits needed for all the newfangled ways of continental death.

Fobbing's own rustic bombshell soon rocked the houses, with tantalising divorce details early in 1915. Edith Jane, middle aged wife of parish baker (and recent churchwarden) Charles Gentry Shade, had conferred the connubial favours upon a long term working employee of her husband's at the bakehouse.[29] A letter to the usurper of Mrs. Shade's affections, Arthur Macaulay, would be produced in court, containing the telling endearment – "My darling boy ...". Latterly a teacher at the nearby church school, she had now fled with her lover to an address in Folkestone. Further down Wharf Lane another anxious household that summer heard of Pte. J. Quy, killed with the Suffolks at the front line, when a shell burst upon a communications trench.[30]

War had brought a first taste of blackout regulations to the district and a Zeppelin raid upon Maldon during the April of 1915, followed in May by another sinister intruder (LZ.38) scattering bombs over Southend, told the reason why.[31] Though slow moving and without sophisticated navigational means, the German dirigibles were yet able to operate at heights that mocked the sluggish climbing capability of Royal Flying Corps machines. They were hydrogen-filled and vulnerable, yet early reports had spoken of an outer safety envelope of inert gas, so that it came to be conceived that only bombing from *above* might fetch a successful kill.[32] Nevertheless, the ensuing year was to bring encouragement, when L.15 entered over Thames on the night of 31st March – to be fixed by searchlights and seriously damaged both by overhead fighter engagement and the Purfleet ground battery. Much of this drama was to be seen from Fobbing; at Kynoch's explosive plant, workers waited out in the open, the Zep. passing directly above them and dropping "a sort of lighted parachute" whose explosive device "just missed the cordite incorporating room".[33] Extensive leaks caused L.15 to nose-dive shortly after turning away over

[29] G.T.G. 13th February, 1915 and *Fobbing Bakehouse,* R. L. Eaton, PAN. Vol. 16, 1972-3.

[30] G.T.G. 14th August, 1915. Wharf Lane was the correct roadname at this date.

[31] G.T.G. 15th May, 1915 (raid on Southend 10th May at 3.00 a.m., seen and heard in Fobbing).

[32] *Zeppelins over England,* K. Poolman, London, 1960.

[33] *Kynochtown in Wartime,* J. H. Freeman in *Corringham* ed. I. G. Sparkes, 1965.

Holehaven for the coast, her frame finally buckling and bringing her down in the Thames estuary; a suitably aquatic demise since the Zeppelins were a naval craft of war.

With September, Lt. Leefe-Robinson's destruction over Cuffley of Zeppelin SL.11 was to be rewarded with the Victoria Cross. Along Thameside's villages, only flashes of heavy gunfire and a "brightness" were to be noted as the giant burned, descending over a distant Hertfordshire countryside. It was in the way of a tiny but tangible revenge for the daily losses of youth everywhere. Another Fobbing lad was gone (in "the great advance") during these last few weeks; Pte. Brown, Royal West Kents, of *Kings Terrace*, near the *Five Bells.*[34]

Within another month, in the starlit dark of September 24th, and while many were preparing for bed, began the Zeppelin fight that was to engage the attention of the whole district, a drama closely observed, its grisly aftermath discussed into old age by many local residents. Commanded by Lt. Peterson and with a crew of over 20 on board, L.32 had approached the coast over Dungeness, following a course northward above the darkened weald to cross Thames near Dartford at a height of about 12,000 feet, where the now celebrated Purfleet gunners were again on alert. Searchlights soon "enveloped the Zeppelin with a coat of phosphorescence, and this the monster tried to throw off by emitting a thick black vapour", told one newspaper report, describing a further "dash for the fleecy clouds", where she lay, "stealthily and snugly, an elongated patch made picturesque by the elements." Artillery positioned upon both sides of the river opened up, while another local witness would claim to have observed "a white flag fluttering" from the German craft after some minutes amidst this terrible barrage of shot.[35]

R.B.

[34] G.T.G. 5th August, 1916.

[35] G.T.G. 30th September, 1916.

Lt. Sowrey's biplane, based at Royal Flying Corps station, Suttons farm, Hornchurch, was now seen (allegedly taking off from Long Reach marshes, Purfleet) whose incendiary bullets were eventually to strike one or more of L.32's hydrogen compartments, so that her silver framework was already turning a "lurid red" as she moved north-eastward, losing height, over the fenland and towards Billericay. It was a huge, erupting conflagration which illumined the fieldscape over many square miles and in whose radiance hundreds of cottagers and industrial operatives cheered and chorused and banged household utensils in excitement at the deserved deaths of hated men. Safely distant from their worksheds, Kynoch girls taking refuge on the night marshes saw it define Langdon Hills and Hawkesbury in dense silhouette as it met the earth. This was Friday night. That weekend, Snails farm at Great Burstead was to be deluged with the cloth-capped curious from every parish within foot's reach or cycle ride, ogling the tangled mesh of scorched aluminium that towered in strange impotence over withered hedgerows.[36] In a nearby barn were the brittle remains of nearly 2 dozen German airmen, their buttons and unmelted accoutrements already plundered and dispersed as souvenirs by the crowd.

Effectively, the Zeppelins' days over England were ended, but an air war was yet to be played out with intensive attacks by conventional army aircraft – notably the impressive *Gotha* class biplane bombers, whose twin 260 hp Mercedes push-screw engines gave a speed of around 70 miles per hour in minimal headwind and carried a 3 man compliment of pilot, navigator/bomb aimer and forward gunner. London's eastward A.A. defences lay under the Thanet and the Thames and Medway Commands, the latter having established gun stations by early 1917 along the Essex riverline at Bowers Gifford, Canvey, on Fobbing's Hawkesbury Bush top and Tilbury fort among other places.[37] A first incursion in this significant year of *Gotha* activity had come during late May, when 91 persons were killed in an attack on Folkestone, while on Wednesday 13th June "An air raid by German aeroplanes" was to find children at Kynochtown's school

---

[36] Agricultural workers still refer (1995) to the crash site as *"Zep Field"*.

[37] Hawkesbury artillery site TQ78.7001.8690 at *"Gun Meadow"*, in current use as fieldname of Dry Street Farm, where circular concrete gun-platform still defies the plough. This measures 10' diameter, with fixing bolts and 11" metal traverse-plate. Apparent horseshoe gun-platform also upon Hawkesbury summit, 20 yards northeast of trig-point stone, at TQ78.7050.8670. At TQ78.7040.8682, upon north side of Hawkesbury Bush Lane hedgerow, vestiges of another position, thought to be searchlight station.

dismissed to adjacent villa homes at 11.45 a.m.[38] It proved a far-off London action, on a morning already hazy with heat and the youngsters would have to wait for Saturday, July 9th, before perceiving something more memorable.

Described with picture-house panache by a neighbouring weekly press as "a gigantic spectacle ... greatest ... ever witnessed", events had begun when a formation of 22 raiders appeared out of the north east, roaring citywards but rapidly to be engaged by "British pilots rising and darting at their opponents" while factory sirens blared and aerial machine-gun fire mingled with the greater barrels' thunder from surrounding land positions. The defending machines were probably Sopwith *Strutters* and *Pups*. Through this, the *Gothas* would nevertheless proceed undaunted to deliver successfully upon their metropolitan targets, returning later (about noon) along what laconic Essex yokels now termed "the owd Zepp. route" for home. Behind Fobbing ridge, Hawkesbury's battery had hurled its twelve-pounder shells as the hun departed Essex airspace, but to no avail. For the second time in a month London's skies had been violated, 57 deaths inflicted today alone upon its people. That night, East End mobs began breaking and looting the premises of traders whose names appeared to be of German origin and 10 days later England's royal family – until now the house of *Saxe-Coburg-Gotha* – tactfully assumed the surname of "Windsor".

For youngsters at Fobbing's churchside school, October 2nd had brought a welcome afternoon's liberty (right in the conker-harvest) due to another air raid, while a more alarming incident on 18th December at about 6.30 p.m. was to see "several bombs dropped" on the blacked out Kynochtown area, shifting tiles and breaking a couple of windows at its smart brick schoolhouse. Night raids over the estuary would continue far into this late year, reviving during the spring of 1918 – the ultimate and most massive on Whit Sunday when some 43 hostile 'planes (a number of the 9 crew Straaken *Giants*, but predominantly *Gothas*) drew to the skies over 80 defenders from the (newly formed) Royal Air Force scrambling from various flying fields around London. Taking off at intervals the German 'planes had operated widely spread, bombing at random, so that a game of hunting the enemy by moonlight soon developed. Word images from the Thameside district's press spoke of an "interesting three hours", the battle illuminated by a "medley of light ... pale, relentless beams ... the

---

[38] Log Book, Kynochtown School, 1900-1929. E.R.O. E/M7.

flashing of bursting shells."[39] Flying one of Suttons farm's big-snouted *Camels* was 44 Squadron's Capt. D. V. Armstrong who, sighting a lone *Gotha* over Orsett, had attacked for 20 minutes with amazing aerobatic technique until spent of ammunition, to be followed up by a Bristol fighter of 39 Squadron, which at last put the enemy down in flames at East Ham. Both upon the ground and in the blue, London's defences were a last breaking the confidence of Germany's one invincible *Gotha* crews and the Kaiser's cruelly mauled air fleets would not appear again after this date.

A TIME OF FORGETTING

As the Great War drew toward its end, government moves to terminate the Kynoch explosives operation were met by protests from the inhabitants of Fobbing and surrounding communities, as well as several trade unions, on the basis of its painful consequence upon local employment.[40] Closure would come a year later, in January 1919. Serious domestic shortages induced the Essex War Agricultural Committee to invite formation of Food Production Associations and during February 1918 farmer Clem. Hawkins took the chair at the *White Lion* for a public meeting which resulted in 20 applications for vegetable allotments on land which he himself was to rent for the purpose.[41] Mature women over 30, till now deprived of suffrage, obtained the vote. As nesting rooks racketed amid the great elms backing Wharf Lane that mid April of 1918, a reaching spade in the extension-churchyard sought contact with recently-dead Daniel Raison's coffin lid and his wife Rebecca was lowered into the same toffee coloured ground. Old Mrs. Raison had been the last representative of the Rust family, which had actively fingered the Fobbing pie ever since the 1760s.

At Kynochtown that May, Charles Cox of Fleet Street found himself whisked into custody, having attempted to evade army conscription, claiming he was merely "waiting to be called". It would be found he had twice or more ignored draft papers and was duly handed over to a military escort.[42] With November, the Armistice brought an end to active slaughter,

---

39 *The Gotha Summer*, C. White, 1986 and *"Gotha Hunting in the Moonlight"*, G.T.G. 25th May, 1918.

40 G.T.G. 18th May, 1918.

41 G.T.G. 23rd February, 1918.

42 G.T.G. 11th May, 1918.

though the conflict was not yet to be officially concluded. However, Sunday 16th July, 1919 would see at last churches throughout Britain holding their services of thanksgiving for a terribly won peace.

Bloodlust nevertheless still revealed its vile head and in September 1919 Edwin Flavell, licensee of the Seabrookes' brewery *Dock House* on Fobbing marsh, would discover an atrocious attack upon his stabled mare.[43] A boatswain of the S.S. *Vitruvia*, anchored at Thameshaven, was soon apprehended, his arms still "a mass of congealed blood" from the blade's work upon what the prosecution described as "the rear portion of the animal". Such perverted mutilation of horses was by no means a rare kind of crime in the former rural society. A little more than a year later, the slaying at the fo'castle of S.S. *Yamhill* of a seaman called Crawford by the Serbian Peter Kristio was to be reported. Both had returned to their vessel "a little drunk" and were playing at cards when Kristio struck with his jack-knife. The killer received a mere 3 years for manslaughter.[44]

In June 1921, the local licencing committee would consider the *Dock House* question, referring to ship's crews resorting to its bar as "very rough and disorderly", though recent military commanders stationed on Kynoch's had observed Flavell's premises to be "conducted in an exemplary manner". Concerned about persons smoking, Alfred Adams, London and Thameshaven Oil Wharves' manager, felt the place "a public danger", pointing out that the capacity of present storage tanks nearby had reached a half million gallons, one half of which represented petrol.[45] There were about 36 houses quite close by, 15 of which had been "recently erected". Though the licence was to be renewed, a mere 6 weeks later saw the *Dock House* proprietors fined for again permitting drunkenness amongst seamen. The place was clearly under the eye of Fobbing's ubiquitous cyclist, police constable Sach.

Environmental hazards were being underlined. For some time, back into the war years, the oil industries' obnoxious windborne smells had served as a matter of concern, though "suffered in a patriotic spirit" (quipped a local newspaper in April, 1922).[46] Now, the County Medical Officer was actively investigating chemical odours which "penetrated the house" and seemed to be affecting residents' throats. But this was a mere background irritant compared to the nightmare possibility of industrial disaster, which, in the late summer of 1924 sadly struck the family of

---

43 G.T.G. 4th October, 1919.

44 G.T.G. 4th December, 1920 and 5th February, 1921.

45 G.T.G. 18th June, 1921.

46 G.T.G. 8th April, 1922.

15 years-old Frank James Jiggens, patrol leader of the 1st Fobbing Scouts, choir member at St. Michael's church and company messenger boy at the Shell-Mex fuel depot.[47] Besides young Jiggens, killed instantly that 28th August, a tanker-lorry driver called Herbert Raveling had died of burns when "a fountain of petrol" at the wagon loading bay rained fire upon them both. Fobbing's khaki-clad troop under scoutmaster Roland Smith and Miss Nellie Ewen's cub pack would honour their pal at his Corringham funeral on September 2nd.[48]

With early November the Boy Scouts gave their felt hat brims another steam press, this time for the burial of Arthur Banan, rector, who had died in his early sixties after 17 years amongst his flock.[49] From Herd Lane came, in crocodile fashion up Lion Hill, teachers and scholars alike for the service – for this last couple of years had seen the closure of Fobbing's own little schoolhouse at the churchyard's edge. Just before Christmas appeared news of Banan's successor, straight from the tough streets of Canning Town in East London, former scholar of Keble College, holder of the Military Cross, the Order of the Nile (4th Class) and the Territorial Decoration, lately chaplain to the 54th East Anglian Brigade in Palestine – and a man who announced at once a keen interest in work with the Army Cadet Force. *This* was the Rev. Ernest Gardner, a mentally and physically sizeable character in the Conan Doyle mould – "a regular Hercules", wrote Donald Maxwell after meeting him a few years on, the "right stuff" to lead Fobbing on the way it would surely have to go – towards another taste of war with Germany.[50]

But the meanwhile was optimistic and progressive, a time to "*Charleston*" – for youthful fun and forgetting. Young flappers' hemlines, old gentlemen's eyebrows, and (soon) the national birthrate, went up. And so did the number of motorborne holidaymakers calling at the miraculous "Vange Wells" alongside Hovels farmhouse – inspiration of an ex-Islington publican and newly styled "farmer" Edwin Cash of Fobbing, who had erected in ironwork and plastered brick, a domed pumphouse of plebian-Paladian at the hill's foot there.[51] Its "magic" waters were now obtainable

---

47 G.T.G. 30th August, 1924.

48 Scout Troop photo, G.T.G. 26th June, 1978.

49 G.T.G. 15th November, 1924 and 20th December, 1924.

50 G.T.G. 11th April, 1925 and *A Detective in Essex,* D. Maxwell, 1933, Chapter 3, "The Clue of the Hidden Creek".

51 Still visible as a vandalised ruin alongside Martinhole Wood TQ78.7009.8623.

CASH'S VANGE MEDICINAL WATER

ABSOLUTELY PURE AS IT COMES FROM THE MAGIC WELL.
IS THE MOST WONDERFUL DISCOVERY OF THE AGE.

THIS WATER has effected most marvellous cures, to numerous sufferers all over the British Isles.

Unsolicited Testimonials may be seen at the Registered Offices of the Company, 2, Foster Lane, Cheapside, London, E.C.2.

Nothing Added Nothing Taken Away

SEE "LANCET" ANALYSIS AND REPORT, DEC. 9th, 1922.

The GENUINE VANGE WATER bears Mr. CASH'S PHOTOGRAPH & SIGNATURE on each Bottle.

REFUSE ALL SUBSTITUTES.

at "all Chemists for 2/3d. the bottle", claiming to cure tender stomachs, rheumatic troubles and nervous disorders alike.

Alongside the Southend road, a massive placard announced "THE VALE OF HEALTH". Dr. Thresh, consulting M.O. to the County Council, had visited only the year previous (in May, 1923) declaring to gathered members of the Essex Field Club how "Many waters in Essex contained the necessary sulphate of lime whereas the real Vange water contained all the necessary sulphates for water of the highest medicinal value." The misleading title of "Vange Water" had simply come about because of the wells' proximity to the failed Vange Corner Estate and few travellers to or from Southend's beaches knew, or cared, how Fobbing was being deprived of its due advertising glory.[52] Before long anyway, rumours were afoot that drainage from the Langdon Hills tuberculosis hospital (upon higher ground a mere mile away) was filtering into the Hovels farm stream and closure orders were to follow.[53]

As the twenties advanced, the parish council, sitting as ever in Fobbing's decaying schoolhouse, debated means of providing improved dwellings for expanding local families. A village meeting on 24th April 1926 had assessed that homes were, in some cases, "very badly needed" and a year later a suitable piece of building land for the project was being sought. Six 3 bedroomed council houses of brick with cement rendering and capped with cheery orange pantiles would

The pumphouse

[52] G.T.G. 19th May, 1923 and (advert.) 21st July, 1923.
[53] *The Vale of Health,* L. Fox, E.C. Vol. 8, October, 1960.

be under construction during April 1928, set along the High Road at the village fringe and abutting Marsh Lane. Rents were being heatedly discussed by July, having been pegged at 11/6d. weekly, with an additional quarterly water rate of 13/5d. Both sums, felt Fobbing's councillors, were excessive, and the water company was to be approached with their opinion forthwith.

The rectory lawn dimpled this June beneath many heels, and teacups clinked amidst happy chatter emanating from the founding assembly of the Women's Institute.[54] Monthly meetings for its 20 or so members would thereafter normally occupy the schoolroom, a couple yearly to be held at the Shellhaven recreation hut. That autumn, the ever growing concern over village amalgamation into some form of Urban District surfaced anew, Fobbing voting to join with Corringham and Stanford le Hope; though by 1930 a revised concept of an Orsett Urban District would look more appropriate. It was within the old Orsett Rural District Council after all, that their parish had long existed.

June 1928 had seen very happy celebrations for the opening of the village recreation ground – called *"Wheelers Meadow"* – to which chestnut fencing and oaken gates would soon be added, while in February 1929 the parish committee approved an order for 6 Lombardy poplar trees from Waterer's,[55] the south-country's most prestigious nursery, as a final touch to the highway frontage opposite Payne's *"Jubilee"* chapel. It was a typically suburban piece of thinking. On August 22nd, 1929, a letter had been read from one resident arguing for a signboard to be erected near the Mill House, requesting "motorists to Drive slowly through the Village". Fobbing was still, after all, a place worthy of a lingering look, though that wasn't the plaintiff's point.[56]

Convenient but ugly, tarred road surfaces had already arrived, and during the busy summer of 1930 a "traffic line" would be felt desirable at the top of Lion Hill; and, near the bend of Wharf Road, a *"Dangerous Corner"* notice. The highway authority's repairs of this section of the ancient street had brought a nasty retort with the spring of 1931 from the tenant of Vineyard farm, grousing how waste soil had been dumped at the entrance to his meadow. After attending a patient in the farmhouse, the doctor had required assistance to "pull his car out of soft clay". Human muscle would be in demand awhile, for all the coming powers of science.

---

[54] *Short History of Fobbing and Corringham Women's Institute*, anon. Undated, c.1960.

[55] Fobbing P.C.C. minutes, 1903-1936. 3 remain; 1 fell in a recent gale, February, 1997.

[56] Ibid.

The dying twenties had put Corys, Shell-Mex and LATHOL onto the telephone, and so by 1929, was Sid Wise at the *Haven Hotel* – an upmarket replacement (1924) for Seabrookes' much maligned former *Dock House* pub. Around the village, hard headed traders like butcher James Ewen and Gilder the builder were also obtainable via the enticing switchboard chatter of Stanford's exchange. Fobbing rectory, on the other hand, didn't feel quite ready for such anonymous contact with the outside world just yet.[57]

Many parish hands, including the rector's, got busily warmed one January evening of 1930 as flames licked in the dark over old farm buildings at Great House. Just leaving a Wesleyan concert at Payne's chapel, people "rushed down the narrow cattle-track", women and girls setting up a bucket chain from the farm pond downslope while Corringham's hose-cart followed along within 20 minutes. Fobbing's Waterworks Cottage hydrant mercifully stood only a few hundred yards off. No loss of livestock was reported, though a byre would be destroyed and the corn barn damaged. With relentless bites, time was gnawing away at the toothsome timber fabric of an earlier village world. Again, at winter's end in 1935, the local press offered news of: *SMUGGLERS' HAUNT BURNT DOWN*, identifying the Old Mill House as the latest victim of fire, "believed to be more than 400 years-old ... an old wooden farmhouse with a thatched roof ... at the back of Mill Cottages". Its octogenarian occupier had fallen to a doze at his hearth when the chimney caught alight and neighbours had luckily seen the roof burning in time to save both the old fellow and the family's household goods.[58]

Street furniture seeded itself along green, plantained verges, 1930 having brought in a year of perplexing options with regard to highway lighting; beneficial to pedestrian and motorist alike. It had been straightforward at first; the Electricity Company would lay a supply and erect 6 curly-topped standards through the village centre at £3 per annum per lamp post, giving illumination from a half hour after sunset to 11.30 p.m. during each period October 1st to the end of April. Fobbing agreed at once, only to learn in June that the Gas Light and Coke people were about to insert *their* main and could, of course, offer street lamps at very competitive rates. Corringham having settled already for *gas*, impishly enquired if the Fobbing flock would like to share expenses at the parish edge, by contributing part of the cost towards altering an old Kitson lantern at Lion Hill foot over to *gaspower*. No, retorted Fobbing, an *electric* standard for this spot was already envisaged – perhaps Corringham

[57] Post Office directory of Essex, 1929.

[58] In Mill Lane (F.P. 23) now ploughed over: TQ78.7145.8452.

ratepayers would bear half *that* bill instead? Over such practical matters, some arguments for a central Urban District control, were beginning to cast their little pools of illumination.[59]

In man's battle against the forces of darkness, none must be forgotten. Giving way to reason, Fobbing conceded that *gas* offered a better bargain for the London-Southend road and Bells Hill residents, though in the same year (1931) continuing to add some swan-necked electric lamps opposite the church gate and partway down Lion Hill, at Hockley's Lane.[60] Just as in the Elizabethan years (1590) sharpsters were on hand to take advantage of the moment and in June, 1930 the case of petty crook Charles Mayes of Thames Ditton made news, his game a familiar one of pretending to be a works employee, taking money ahead of proposed services. In the name of the County of London Electric Supply Company, Mayes had conned Marianne Chappell out of cash for wiring her premises, assuring that the Company would be laying on power across fields near Bells corner free of charge.[61] That fall, having approached the relevant authorities regarding a sub post-office at their end of the parish, Bells Hill folk had obtained a reply from Southend headquarters in October, 1930 confirming that "suitable premises" would be looked for. Soon, Boreman's confectionery shop set up its wire grill and took the challenge on, adding to a series of services around the junction which by now far outclassed the "old" part of Fobbing; Sid Lockhart at the Bells Hill grocery stores, Ben Franklin (family butcher), T. Leonard Chappell's thriving roadside garage and one-legged Joe Judd's "Fobbing Tea Rooms" just adjacent. All were present by the early 30s – Judd's a roadstop where the latest dance band recordings cheered weekending bikers and the lucky minded could manipulate tableside slot-machines of chrome and plastic beauty. The police sometimes gave it a look-over, cruising by.

At a more celestial level, Ernest Gardner's enthusiastic collecting for the fabric of his historic church had borne first fruit; the crumbled tower strengthened back in 1928 and now, with the census year of 1931 – after "hanging mute for nearly thirty years" – all 5 antique bells recast, retuned and resounding sweetly again across Fobbing's parish fields. Everyone was working hard to pay off the debt

Ernest Gardner

59 Fobbing P.C.C. 1903-1936.

60 Hockleys Lane, a now defunct title. The lane led to Henry Hockley's dwelling, Glebe Cottage.

61 G.T.G. 25th June, 1932.

before the June following, the parochial fete on Wednesday 22nd of that month producing a less dulcet tune – that of an escaped pig (a sideshow prize) which interrupted the opening ceremony, to be chased by howling Fobbing scouts until neatly caught in mid-squeal by an agile Mrs. Scott. The delinquent was to be carried back to its pen "protesting loudly".

Not long prior to the Reverend Gardner's arrival, in 1923, Kynoch's somewhile abandoned marshscape had been taken over by the Cardiff firm of Cory Bros., for further oil storage and refinery purposes, under the local management of John H. Freeman. He and the rector were soon to become close allies in the cause of church and village, Freeman's carpenters manufacturing St. Michael's new organ screen from redundant bellframe oak during 1932's winter, setting to work afterward upon converting Sprivens Hall (formerly partitioned as 2 cottages) into a comfortable "Club House" for community use by Fobbing's youths.[62] Through unhappy chance, both men were destined to lose close female associates in Harriet Maria, Gardner's mother who had lived in Kent though frequently holidaying at Fobbing and John Freeman's wife, Jessica Louise. It was to these ladies that a sixth and seventh bells would be dedicated during 1934 and 1935. An eighth followed by Christmas 1935, intended, reported an ephemeral *Thameside Mail* newspaper "to be a general memorial to the dead of the parish", while May 1936 found the Essex Bellringer's Association visiting to demonstrate the miracle of Fobbing's completed octave. So wholehearted had been people's response to Gardner's appeal that funds topped his target by about £70, leaving monies not only for weatherproofing the tower roof,[63] but for the future installation of electric lighting at the church.

Mr. Nicholas Alexander Anphilogoff, Russian-trained brain behind the London and Thameshaven Oil Wharves, had attempted expansion onto Canvey during April 1930, to meet a resounding veto from the island's councillors and not until 1936 would a House of Lords ruling overturn their decision and grant him his desire. "Miles of docks" had been his dream for a whole waterfront and the best professionals were being appointed to his side. In July 1928 had come "the youngest Chief Fire Officer in the British Fire Service", 25 years old Charles Tozer, fifth generation of a family long famous in the Midland brigade.[64] Anphilogoff's empire west of Holehaven was already said to be the world's largest, with tankage for more than a million tons. But Fobbing was used to nabbing its share of press

---

62 G.T.G. 6th February and 13th February, 1932.

63 In the spring of 1934, jackdaws intruding in the tower roof had caused the discovery of unsafe timbers under its leadwork.

64 T.M. 11th July, 1928.

superlatives. Structural engineering in-the-round was not limited to the oil empire alone, it seemed and along the ancient eaves of the *White Lion* next midsummer a local reporter could count 17 mud-made house martins' nests, crammed in less than 30 feet. One of the many out of work that season (1932) was Mark Cain of Wharf Road, who, by chance of unemployment, became village hero of the hour for rescuing a drowning girl, 11 years old Alice Blackburn, who had been bathing in Fobbing creek.[65]

At Shell-Mex and B.P.'s open day for traders during early May, 1933, "a bewildering mass of details met the eye", Public Relations Officers explaining that within the site (100 acres or more) stood 160 tanks holding 67 million gallons of products and somewhere near 26 miles of pipes along which travelled the company's exports and imports.[66] A diesel ship, the *Fjordaas* from Norway, would be observed discharging her 16 tanks containing 11,000 tons of benzene. The local press thought it marvellous. Filing through laboratories, they were to behold a range of derivatives of crude oil; kerosene, gasoline, wax and lubricating oil distillates; from crude petroleum came cooking and signal oils, kerosene for tractors and spark ignition engines, petroleum jelly, diesel, domestic fuel and furnace oils, aviation, racing and medical spirits. Residents could hardly avoid getting educated, with this kind of fare in their district newspaper of a Saturday.

Equally eager-eyed this year had come a contrasting tribe of bespectacled, brown brogued antiquaries from the Essex Field Club, bussing out from Pitsea to the *Five Bells*, thence hiking with haversacks, guide books and linen-toughened maps "up the steep lane which gives such commanding views over the Thames Estuary," to examine Fobbing's timbered cottages and wharf.[67] The Rev. Gardner's personal invitation had tugged them thither for a September pilgrimage into peasant country, to enjoy again his fairytale visions of John Ball and Jack Straw. But there were modern matters looming always. As a New Year dawned, the rector worried himself over what the proposed Urban District might bring, fearing that Fobbing's identity and voice should be lost if the place became merged with Corringham. "I have kicked against it verbally", he told the Old Folks Dinner gathering in February, 1934, "and your Parish Council has kicked ... officially". But come it would with the mid-decade. There was the forthcoming Jubilee to deal with too, 1935's spring

[65] G.T.G. 13th August, 1932.

[66] G.T.G. 6th May, 1933.

[67] G.T.G. 16th September, 1933.

witnessing national rejoicing at 25 years of the king's reign. Recently laid tennis courts on Fobbing's recreation ground were to become a dance floor, a bonfire sparkling alongside, with another blaze set going by boy scouts on the steep hill's edge. George V's historic wireless speech was to be broadcast outdoors for all to hear and residents aged over 65 would receive gifts; a decorated canister of tea for the females; to the menfolk "a Jubilee pipe of the value of 2s."

The little irritations of existence proliferated: messy people in *Avenue Cottages* (July 1932) were causing annoyance on allotments opposite by dumping household rubbish and Mr. Maklin their landlord would have to speak to them about it: from December 1933 the red-biked rural postman was to take a longer weekend and residents must put up with having their second delivery "about noon" on a Saturday instead of at 6 p.m.[68] One man's social improvement, as ever, was proving a fellow creature's woe. There had been a brutal crime that summer, too, when Lydia Payne, well into her sixties, suffered a night-time attack by some unknown assailant as she entered her post-office cottage, never recovering health and dying the following late February in Orsett hospital.[69] Details of her physical ordeal were not published. Miss Payne had been a dedicated Methodist worker, long known for "unobtrusive generosity and kindness".

In the same month of 1934 passed Henry Hockley, cowkeeper, milkseller and latterly poultry-farmer, an "outstanding character in the village life" who had worked the church grounds from *Glebe Cottage* (where he had been born) for some 40 years.[70] Late 1935 would see two further aged men depart, in September 86 years-old Simon Gilder of the Vineyard Cottage, long a shepherd of the marshes, and the month following Tom Scott, 76, former bargeman. Though latterly dumb and paralysed Scott had once been adjudged the strongest man of Fobbing, who could "pick up a sack of corn in one hand." When Fobbing wharf's trade in corn, hay and straw dropped off, observed the old fellow's obituary, "he made Greenhithe his home", moving back to his native parish in retirement.[71]

---

68 G.T.G. 3rd March, 1934.

69 G.T.G. 3rd March, 1934

70 G.T.G. 24th February, 1934.

71 G.T.G. 14th September and 5th October, 1935.

Another capital idea had hatched under the rector's balding pate, and seemed by the declining winter of 1936 to be moving to fulfilment. Gardner's notion was to purchase, from the former Long estate, what his researches claimed to be "the vineyard of the old priory of St. John" – a tilting couple of fields next the glebe which would be handed over to the church authorities in trust as a place of public pleasure and escape. Duly, on 12th September, the bishop of Chelmsford was to attend "to take seizin of the property" on behalf of his diocese.[72] Such was the quaint phrase of olde England picked up by the local paper (anticipating the event) for its Saturday edition of June 13th. A few pages on, a double column advertisement invited readers to come along for a "Blackshirt meeting" at Bridge Road Senior School in Grays the next Tuesday, where Mr. William Joyce (Director of Propaganda for the British Union of Fascists) would speak upon the aims of his party. Thurrock's newly created Urban District, not 3 months old, was unwittingly entertaining the future world's first radio traitor – *"Lord Haw-Haw"* – in its home town.

[72] G.T.G. 22nd February, 7th March and 13th June, 1936.

12. LOOK FOR THE SILVER LINING

George V had died that early January: the following filldyke month observed Fobbing's Old Folks joining Mr. Gardner in a toast to the late king's memory at their annual dinner – and raising a second glass to his popular son, Edward VIII. Their loyal cup would avail him little in the cooked-up crisis of love and kingship ahead. But at hand other phantoms were hovering, for parish councillors could well foresee the environmental horrors promised by a recent acquisition of Fobbing Hall by Mr. F. W. Surridge, whose waste-dumping schemes for its creekside marshes were being murmured. There had been some typical associated attempts to close old footpath ways through the hall's grounds and towards Marsh Lane and Pitsea, plainly to divert public observation of an imperilled area. Strangely, Gardner did not appear to see the obvious, and during February had assured a worried parish meeting of "his confidence" that proposals "would do nothing to mar the beauty of the village." Surridge meanwhile was applying for similar tipping consents on Vange marshes and had already begun the desecration of whole landscapes a few miles south-westward around Mucking creek.[1] Thankfully, his Fobbing application was to fail, while the somewhat more ambitious territorial aspirations of Mr. Joyce's superhero would shortly see it shelved for good.

With April 1936, village residents learned officially of a War Office intention to establish searchlight and artillery posts across the levels on the Dutch island of Canvey. If for the unbeliever the writing was not yet on the wall, it would soon be patent in the skies, for during 9th-11th August, 1937, Royal Air

[1] G.T.G. 28th February, 1937.

Force defence exercises about London were to include 5 mock sorties attacking Thameshaven. At 10,000 feet, their light bombers and hopelessly obsolete biplane fighters seemed "mere specks" roving the daytime heavens. After dark, over 30 searchlight beams, piercing upward from many directions, declared it was not only on Canvey that Royal Engineers installation teams had been at work this recent twelvemonth. Everyone watched as "officially destroyed" attacking 'planes fired green rockets into the space of night.[2] Back on earth, the A.R.P. was being formed and that month public press announcements prepared civilian homes for a "blackout" through the dark hours of November 4th-5th, not a very well-considered Whitehall choice in view of what England's juvenile fire-raisers generally had in mind for the time of year.

Technology had featured in this year's coronation celebrations. There was a feeling that nothing ought to be spared in providing a good time for the kiddies, because the barrel of fun might just be running dry. As it turned out, Wednesday May 12th was plentifully moist and afternoon rain poured on Fobbing as elsewhere, so that the children's sports programme had to be relinquished. An entertainment committee avowed that all 120 young folk of school age should nevertheless have their souvenir book – (*"George VI, King and Emperor"*) and the babies a colour transfer printed portrait mug and plate, all presented at eating time[3] under pattering canvas and after a drumhead service on the "Rec."[4] Fancy dress competitions amused parents and later, as evening befell, Fobbing's traditional Vineyard bonfire went crackling away delightfully to the sound of community singing. St. Michael's ragstone and rooftiles had been wonderfully floodlit with electric lamps and "fire balloons" were to be released in spectacular display from the crenellated "beacon" turret. For the elder folk, next day brought an outing to the *Regal* cinema at Stanford to see a newsreel show in "natural colours" of the royal enthronement and ceremonial parade – quite a miracle of speedy film processing and distribution – before returning villagewards to a nice tea.

As hoped, electricity had been wired in during the past year at St. Michael's and a faculty obtained for shifting Banan's pipe organ down to the west end, blocking the big tower's base from the church nave.[5] Ostensibly, it allowed the beautiful south chapel to be enjoyed again, but possibly the Rev. Ernest Gardner's warrior mentality was already one jump ahead of political events and making quiet provision. Bitter cold and occasional snowy flusters saw Christmas approach with

---

2 G.T.G. 14th August, 1937.

3 G.T.G. 20th February and 8th May, 1937.

4 "Rec.", universal rural term for recreation grounds. Recently, Fobbing's "rec." has become referred to as "the park", which it is not.

5 G.T.G. 17th April, 1937.

picture-card promise and the rector could report that his new *"Aladdin"* radiators had solved a long-suffered heating problem ("without knocking the old fabric about") though areas under the east window were as usual "receiving the full blast of the wind". The A.R.P. classes found good attendance and he had hopes of a new year first-aid meeting.[6] Mr. Alf Waylett of Mill Cottages and Mrs. (Ada?) Baker of *Belvedere*, High Road, had passed their Air Raid Precautions exams by mid January, 1939 and the parson's latest youth project was moving ahead, soon to find name as the Stanford le Hope Company, 1st Cadet Battalion.

But escapism tarried yet. A television van was touring Thurrock to demonstrate that dubious electronic bauble, hopefully to retail a set here and there within the 25 miles receiving radius of London. February, too, sent aero-enthusiasts outdoors one thrilling Thursday to wave home Alex Henshaw as he sped atop far oil holders in his white Percival *Mew Gull*, dropping into Gravesend from the England-to-South Africa (and back) record of 4 days 10 hours 21 minutes. "THAT'S THE CAPE – THAT WAS!" quipped a Shell advert in the ensuing issue of *Popular Flying*, showing the hero in amiable handshake with the nozzle of one of its aviation fuel pumps. Very soon, Henshaw would be joining Supermarine as production test pilot for Mitchell's lithe and lethal *Spitfire*, which had come on-stream to the R.A.F. only months previously.

At April's annual meeting of the London and Thames Haven Oil Wharves Ltd., presided over by Sir Vernon Thompson, a recent company offer to store "petrol acquired for the nation's use during wartime" would be discussed. Government's answer had declared the Thames area "too vulnerable from the air", though LATHOL naturally argued it better to take that risk than suffer a shortage of supply in the event. So ran an open press reportage, for home and foreign intelligence to swallow or not. At intervals through spring, motor trucks began delivering thousands of buff coloured boxes, with instructions for use enclosed, to Urban District A.R.P. centres and Fobbing families bravely tried on their gas masks, breathing pristine rubber as small birds grew tuneful in the hedgerows. In Vineyard cottage, the domed *"tin hat"* of Bob Scott, Air Raid Warden-in-charge for the parish upland and marsh grounds, sat like a relic of Agincourt, awaiting its new day of active service. Behind big cool leaves of the lime tree fronting Brickhouse, pleasing patterned Georgian brickwork had been horribly daubed with white paint, a dominant "S.P." marking one of the village points where a stirrup pump (for dousing incendiaries) could be found.

Through the parson's involvement, there was to be a rather dashing exhibition of soldierly youth right there on the Vineyard that last pre-war summer, when 30 Scottish lads (aged 12 to 19) of the 1st Anti Aircraft Divisional Signal

---

[6] A.R.P. Air-raid precautions. G.T.G. 14 January, 1938.

Percival Mew Gull

Corps made an August camp; an impressive sight in their "swirling kilts and colourful dress". A couple of military field days were arranged and Fobbing could hear for a while about its lanes the young corps pipers pumping out nasal homeland airs.[7] From afar, they might at moments have been mistaken for something else. A fortnight or so on, Prime Minister Chamberlain's Sunday morning broadcast which everyone by now expected, gave out its depressing ultimatum and the Stanford and Shellhaven sirens were unleashed for a first time under conditions of war.[8] The Celtic pipes had seemed a preferable agony.

Fobbing's public air raid shelter, ready within a week, found ample praise at once in the local news; an ingenious adaptation of the stoneflagged space under St. Michael's tower "specially sandbagged for the purpose" and capable of protecting 30 or 40 persons.[9] Perhaps a little naively, Ernest Gardner was to expound how "a bomb would have to penetrate three feet of concrete covered with asphalt, the steel girders holding up the bells, and two lower floors before it could reach the people ...". But as a protection against high explosive sideblast and splinters, it certainly appeared substantial, the great Walmsley organ now acting as a fourth wall and sandbagged like the rest of Gardner's fortress to a height of 8 feet. Night as well as day, the church's north and south doorways were to remain open for "prayer and refuge". Some affinities with 1938's studio sets for John Ford's tropical disaster movie, *"The Hurricane"*, can hardly have been missed by grimmer humorists among his congregation.

Food production figured large again nationally, local War Agricultural Committees pressing for wholesale ploughing of grasslands for cereal growing, though "Billy" Wilson, of the Rookery farm at Mucking, held doubts over these "sticky clays of Fobbing and Dunton", advising them best left alone and fearing hardship for the farmers of such waterlogged soils. Late November saw swastika-tailed seaplanes openly operating in Thames waters and laying magnetic mines against shipping, while land defenders stood impotent – ordered to hold fire for fear of explosion on oil installations. By the year's close, a dozen vessels had been fatally mined in the estuary, among them the Shellhaven-bound tanker *Arinia*, her cargo of spirit to be seen burning beyond the Canvey horizon for two days before she broke up and sank. Sixty men had died in this one explosion.[10]

"A good company of personnel", chatted the minister in his magazine column, "are working hard to make their aid post in the Rectory as ready for an

---

7 G.T.G. 19th August, 1939.

8 Within weeks, the nearer air raid siren would be operative at Corringham, installed due to "faint" local perception of the above location.

9 G.T.G. 16th September, 1939.

10 *Local Shipping Companies in World War II,* G. Jenkins, PAN. 35, 1995.

emergency as possible", while Fobbing's "comforts for the troops" fund had been set up a little before Christmas by the village branch of the Women's British Legion, just celebrating its third anniversary of existence. Evicted from their now commandeered schoolroom, the W.I. bewailed lost teacups and cutlery – "wrecked" by khaki clad vandals. Monthly meetings moved to members' homes for the duration.[11]

"DECENT CIVILISED WARFARE"

Over late 1939 and into a freezing January of 1940, Fobbing folk hugged the evening wireless and tuned with fascination to the B.B.C.'s weekly serial *"Shadow of the Swastika"*, outlining the barbarian saga of Hitler's Third Reich. Most parish families were in regular employment and had felt able to contribute to the £14. 0. 0d. quickly raised for relief of a swiftly vanquished Polish people.[12] Now back at Herd Lane after the rather subdued yuletide break, excited schoolchildren pulled on scarves and played normally through dinnertime on January 11th, as a preliminary Ack-Ack reconnaissance by German aircraft took advantage of modest visibility to scout above the winding estuary. The day following, 3 hostile warplanes drew some informative plots from riverside gun emplacements, the youngsters carrying on their classwork. There were as yet no school air-raid shelters available anyway. Heavy snowdrifts in the late month, with splendid playground ice-pools "twenty yards across" soon replaced any youthful concerns of a Nazi menace.[13]

At home, gas respirators hung with kiddies' coats at garden doorways, newly issued ration books added to a sideboard clutter of torches and ministry pamphlets, and by February the district council was offering everyone the first domestic Anderson shelters, on hire-purchase terms if required. A 4-person dugout could be bought for £6. 14s., about the price of a good Raleigh roadster bike – 2 weeks' earnings for the farm worker. On February 25th, clocks were put forward; daylight extended until 7 p.m. In comfy Fobbing Hall, a Wednesday "working class" for local seamen had been arranged, the Rev. Mr. Gardner (historian by training) expressing a surge of gratification that "the old Manor House" and its family should be "taking this lead in the life of the parish." If confident that the British Expeditionary Force would prevail, the parson's view nevertheless held a note of caution – "as Hitler sees his hopes of victory vanish ...

---

11 *Short History of Fobbing And Corringham Women's Institute.* Anon. Undated. c.1960.

12 G.T.G. 27th January, 1940.

13 Log Book, Herd Lane School, Corringham. Xerox copy. Original with E.C.C.

he is likely to snarl and bite like a mad dog", warned Gardner,[14] adding that "though in decent civilised warfare Fobbing should be safe enough", the wisest precaution should be to "turn to God".

The black-out winter crept on without serious disturbance and by the first month of spring Churchill's forlorn sacrifices to a Norway campaign[15] were being beaten out of the cold lands with terrible casualties that were not to be disclosed. Any talk "in the news or on the air" of making a peace with the *Fuhrer*, thought the rector (side-stepping a gospel ethic or two) was entirely futile. Not only Hitler, but Stalin alike, would have to be "crushed" before there could be any possibility of securing a Christian future here at home. As allotment soil warmed and beans spiralled first inches toward the clearing sky, a motley flotilla of small boats, paddle steamers, posh upriver launches, Pickford's lighters, strings of London refuse barges, passed with the downtide beyond Holehaven mouth, and out toward the harried beaches of Dunkirk. Soon, restrained B.B.C. news announcements would tell Fobbing listeners what valour had gone forth along this grey shoreline: remoulding the reality of an army's continental defeat.[16] Meanwhile, the district's newspaper could report Fobbing church full for late May's *"National Day of Prayer"*.

Only a couple of pay-days ago, Anthony Eden's appeal for a force of civilian soldiers had crackled through the wireless valves. A Local Defence Volunteer unit[17] would be quickly organised within the Grays Sub-Division under command of Orsett's Capt. J. C. Chaplin. Just in receipt of their .303 rifles, Shellhaven's unpractised volunteers were caught early on the hop by a visiting general officer, for whom a passable parade was somehow effected; the men in A.R.P. issue steel helmets (property of Shell-Mex Ltd.) with varying suits or sports jackets enhanced by hastily stitched on medal ribbons from the Great War.[18] An official historian would record their platoon commander's appearance on this panicky occasion, laden under service Webley revolver and bands of .45 cartridges, as "a cross between ... Balkan bandit and a Texan cowhand". The L.D.V.'s ephemeral hour passed by the middle summer and, as members of the reorganised 3rd Essex (Home Guard) Company, platoons would be formed for Stanford le Hope (No. 4 embracing the Corringham and Fobbing section under Lieutenant Frost: No. 5, Thameshaven and No. 6, Shell-Mex Ltd.). Fobbing's parish territory was therefore to include 3 platoons serving within Britain's important H.G. "Estuary Sector". On Germany's waveband the ridiculous accent

---

14 O.G.R.D. February, 1940.

15 At this point of 1940 Mr. Churchill was 1st Lord of the Admiralty.

16 *Dunkirk: The Necessary Myth,* N. Harman, 1980.

17 The L.V.D. would be retitled "Home Guard" as from July 1940.

18 *Warmen Courageous*, P. Finch, 1951.

of *"Lord Haw-Haw"* was soon heard to crow over an "England feverishly preparing for a war of armed civilians ... exercising with umbrellas", most recognising his jibe as a painfully close caricature of the truth.

From highway corners, direction posts had been dug up and lorried away to council yards. Anti-paratroop training and night watching for surprise enemy landings came into full swing. Small arms drill and aircraft silhouette recognition were drummed home at *"Battle H.Q."* (Stanford Co-op Hall) and Volunteers left cottages for their workplaces with rifles slung and 10 rounds about the person. In Fobbing churchyard on Tuesday, August 9th, the Stanford Company would assemble for the funeral of Pte. Richard Stanley Coffey of Mill Cottages, a fairly recent newcomer to the village from Upton Park and Bulphan, Home Guard colleague and victim of a cycle accident on the village hill.

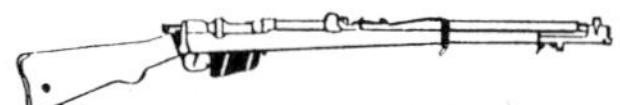

The Royal Air Force had withdrawn from Nazi occupied France on 18th June 1940. At about 11 p.m. that same night, over Thameside, occurred "the first serious air raid" as viewed by one local record keeper – though merely part of diverse attacks by *Luftwaffe* formations between Yorkshire and the south east.[19] Villagers waited on tenterhooks as high explosives thumped over westward farmland fringing the oil depots,[20] a few cattle died and drowsy scholars, kept from their beds by the din from anti-aircraft positions, nurtured hopes of a deskless morrow. Weatherwise, a perfect season was emerging, during which the Rev. Ernest Gardner threw himself yet more deeply into home-front administration, as secretary of the Lord Lieutenant's appeal for recyclable kitchenware – "a *blitzkrieg*" (he called it) on all vessels from aluminium saucepans to kettles and jugs. If neighbouring batteries of the 17th Light Anti-Aircraft (Royal Artillery) knew how to send metal skywards at a stupendous rate, so (more noiselessly) would the aproned amazons of eastern Thurrock. They had Southampton's *Spitfire* factories in mind and dutifully surrendered through early summer 25 tons of scrap, realising £55 for the rector's kitty. Against such a patriotic background, it was perhaps not easy, nor unbrave, for 27 years old George Hills of *"Myrtle Lodge"* in the High Road to state before a South East Local Tribunal his reasons for objecting to "all forms of military service." A carpenter at the oil works, Mr. Hills had attended Fobbing Methodist meetings since the age of 12 and believed armed combat to be "against the Christian faith he upheld". With practised deafness, the panel arranged forthwith that "mister" should not be his continuing form of address.[21]

---

[19] Log Book, Herd Lane School, Corringham. Xerox copy. Original with E.C.C.

[20] Engineer's Report, T.U.D.C. District Council Engineer's Report, 1945. T.MUS.

[21] G.T.G. 29th June, 1940.

From up-Thames Essex, the showery morning of July 10th heard *Spitfires* of 74 (Tiger) Sqdn. based at Hornchurch throttling high away beyond St. Michael's tower, Merlin engines fading south-eastward as they closed to the defence of shipping convoys around the North Foreland.[22] In future reckoning, this would be considered the start date of the Battle of Britain, a contest of eagles which was to send village eyes aloft on constant thrilling occasions over ensuing weeks. For the *Luftwaffe*, the battle's official commencement was to be placed far later, on August 8th – with the period 18th August to September 6th representing its severest phase of fighting. Adolph Hitler had as yet proscribed all bombing over London, though the pre-noon of 13th August saw attacks well up the estuary, upon Sheerness and R.A.F. Eastchurch on Sheppey, where 5 *Blenheim* fighter aircraft were destroyed on the ground. Two days after, a bright-skied Thursday, came the approach of more high enemy formations above the river – the air a maze of giddy contrails as North Weald's *Hurricanes*, together with a couple of Hornchurch *Spitfire* squadrons, strove to turn the advance of 88 *Dorniers* backed by fighter *schwarms* of over 130 *Messerschmitt* Bfs. as they struck again onto Rochester and Eastchurch 'drome.

Effective though the local air-raid sirens might be, their slow-wavering cry was already proving a serious irritation. The rector's own fatigue was telling: the strain upon him of these months is proven in the disintegrated penwork of his church registers, worsening through to late 1940. A *"banshee"* was how he described the sound,[23] akin to the shriek of some supernatural being, and Gardner's bishop, too, thought it a psychologically disturbing noise for the authorities to have approved. Something perky and defiant was his lordship's preference. Aloof to the nervous sensibilities of Britain's already overworked chicken population, he had suggested Government adopt a rousing *"Cock-a-doodle-doo"* blast instead. Essex pressmen were glad of the bishop of Chelmsford's bantamweight jests from time to time.

---

[22] *The Battle of Britain,* R. Townshend Bickers, 1990 (Map) pp. 110-111. Forward field, Manston, Kent. Hornchurch 14 airmiles away (about 4 fighter minutes) – Eastchurch 20 airmiles, about 5 fighter minutes.

[23] O.G.R.D. November, 1940.

At 12.10 the following afternoon (Friday August 16th) the distressing *banshee* wailed anew and, at Herd Lane, Fobbing's and Corringham's little bare-kneed Britishers shuffled across the playground for cover, within minutes "quite happy ... singing and laughing" inside echoey concrete-topped blastwalls of brick, their teachers (observed the school log) "very smart and cool".[24] They were confined an hour in the shelters as Goering's bombers weaved through flak[25] and clean-winged fighters toward their target of Tilbury a few miles upriver, where, amid fairly minimal commercial damage, 5 dock employees would be killed. With Thursday 22nd, infants were just on their ways home, the older children still at classwork, when another air-raid warning sounded, apparently causing distress among a few mothers, though most "were sensible". Some young parents had barely known time to grow up and make homes since the final *Gotha* raids of 1918. Now, here they were, seeing another slide into state-approved insanity. The school record was starting to treat the unthinkable as normal. Matter-of-factly, it closed the week's affairs: "Over 40 Heinkels came over ... They were dispersed by anti-aircraft gunfire, and went away".

It was to be a bad 48 hours of more mass attacks at night. Due to navigational error, *Luftwaffe* crews, detailed to strike Thameshaven's storage tanks, off-loaded instead onto civilian areas a few minutes westward, at Stepney and East Ham, even into the city itself. *Reichsmarschall* Goering's telegram to all bomber units would demand on Sunday the names of captains who had violated their *Fuhrer's* orders concerning his proscription of London. They were to be demoted to infantry regiments. Through the dark of August 25th-26th, R.A.F. Bomber Command personnel reluctantly actioned Churchill's directive for reprisal missions onto civilian quarters of Berlin, escalating the war into a total dimension.[26] "Fobbing should be safe enough" had been the Reverend's words, and that weekend it was; but by strange irony its chance deliverance had served to set cities on fire.

Monday saw a notable absence of youngsters arriving through the school gates. Most lads well realised that enforced sanctuary during air raids left much to be desired – just when the heavens were so perfectly full of skyborne heroes, the staccato prattle of .303 Browning machine guns. Long after, 85 Squadron's commander, Peter Townsend, whose Hawker *Hurricanes* had come winging down from Debden the previous week to their new Croydon base,[27] would reflect on days like these and recall: "up in the sky, we fighter pilots could see more of

---

24 Brick shelters were being erected at the school from 27th March, 1940. Described 6th March, 1941 as "dugouts". Electric lighting installed 20th March, 1941.

25 Flak: anti-aircraft shell-fire – abb. German *Fliegerabwekrkanone.*

26 *Battle over Britain,* F. K. Mason, 1980.

27 *Duel of Eagles,* P. Townsend, 1970.

England than any of England's defenders had ever seen before ... Yes, it was a help to have England there below." Below, that first day of the week, August 26th, the fields of Whitehall, and Curtis', and Great House were being reaped of wheat as red-necked agricultural men, turban-headed girls, and farm dogs, cart horses and tractor-binders moved amidst a tawny summer's dust. It was the finest harvest weather since 1921.

Between 2.30 and 3.00 p.m. a force of German aircraft of Kesselring's K.G.2 (*Kampfgeschwader*) and K.G.3 was approaching north-westward toward the Dengie peninsula of Essex, its purpose to destroy R.A.F. stations at Debden and Hornchurch. At 18,000 feet over the North Sea, they split formation, one half of the 80 *Dornier* 17 bombers proceeding for each target escorted by 40 twin engined *Me* 110 *"Destroyer"* fighters and swift 109s. At Debden, severe damage was sustained before defensive measures by Bader's Czech *Hurricane* Squadron (its first combat) could be brought to bear, though most of the hostiles had made away westward of Chelmsford without attempting their strike.[28] Kesselring's southerly attack roared meanwhile over Canewdon to be met – with better timing – by both 65 Sqdn. *Spitfires* (Hornchurch) and *Hurricanes* of No.1 (Canadian) Sqdn., a tiny total of 19 defenders which swung the mass of Dorniers away in a spectacular hairpin over Holehaven and Canvey Island. Though more than three miles above the pattern of ancient countryside, the tangle of dogfights grew very imminent ("a battle overhead", noted Herd Lane's log-book) as aircraft curled through sky, switched and broke for advantage, square-winged *Me* 109s already dangerously edging onto homeward fuel reserves, but resolute in the protection of their slower-paced companions.

Far away, under warm cloud, *Hurricanes* of 85 Squadron – distinctive with their white-hexagon badges – had scrambled at 14.50 hrs. and, led by Peter Townsend, were leaping upward from the chalk-scarred Surrey hills to confront the dark formation of 'planes somewhere above Maidstone. In further minutes, Pilot Officers Allard and Worall would send one *Dornier* lunging across two counties to thump, more or less intact, onto Rochford aerodrome,[29] another not far from Eastchurch field. Amongst the melee now taking place at about 20,000 feet above Sheppey's runway, P.O. John "Paddy" Hemingway's plane received hits from a familiar yellow-nosed Bf.109, the German's fire crippling his controls and forcing him to bale out after making away northward, his doomed *Hurricane* in wild vibrating throes. Those watching from the Essex hills noted the pilot's 'chute

[28] *The Battle of Britain*, R. Townshend Bickers, 1990.

[29] Rochford forward base, 10 airmiles away, 3 fighter minutes.

unfold and his approaching aircraft angling down atop Thames at 40 degrees before its duck-egg blue underwings folded on impact and one brief fuel-explosion told its destruction among the scented sea-asters edging Fobbing creek.[30]

It was 15.25 hrs.: Tortoiseshell butterflies quivered in disturbed air and sought other flowers. Black ooze steamed awhile above a smothered kernel of heat. Down Marsh Lane, over the near pastures of Nazewick, men and truant youths hastened, eager to hold pieces of the battle. A couple of miles off at Pitsea, the young Irishman Hemingway – one of Townsend's most valued and experienced flyers – was being offered a cigarette while contemplating his survival after a second "brolly-hop" in recent days.

Along Fobbing's levels, War Department diesel-diggers were ripping trenches to prevent the possibility of landings by enemy gliders. At August's end the sorry news of John H. Freeman's only son was received.[31] He had been killed in action while serving as 1st Radio Officer aboard a merchant vessel; his age 19. In time, the church would have a coloured glass window to the young man's memory. Still at home, the miracle of safety endured. Thameshaven's vast *laageren* of oil tanks had not been damaged and, as August's page was torn from fancy cottage calendars, minds registered a nearing anniversary. The first year of war against fascism had been gotten through without dreadful scathe, though the bombers were ever overhead.

With Tuesday 27th, after six hours of raiding through the darkness, Herd Lane noted its children "All tired and worn out". Shrapnel from anti-aircraft fire had dislodged a few tiles over the weekend and on Monday 2nd September the school stayed closed "to paper the windows against blast." At home, rumours of Tilbury's death toll were filtering in – the previous day's pounding of a marshland community, which all the villages round had witnessed being crumpled as sticks of H.E. whined down through a pleasant sabbath sunlight. Exhausted squadrons of 11 Group seemed no longer capable of inflicting adequate injury upon their foe and homecoming *Luftwaffe* personnel could now claim "enemy resistance easily countered". This Monday, after escorting K.G.3 above the Thames, Major Walter Grabmann was to remark – "There's not much doing over there any more."[32]

---

30 Incident reconstructed on information from R. Pickett, Thameside Aviation Museum. Excavation of site during 1988 recovered one of Hemingway's Browning .303 machine guns, gunsight, control column, pilot's seat and various other instruments. Crashpoint TQ78 7371.8490.

31 G.T.G. 31st August, 1940.

32 Grabmaan: his *Me* 110s had been a notable force in the conquest of Warsaw, September 1939. *The Luftwaffe War Diaries,* C. Bekker, 1972.

JOHNNY HEAD-IN-AIR

Thursday September 5th was another balmy summer's day, grey-silver barrage balloons floating lazily from their upriver barge tetherings. A slight westerly breeze huffed Fobbing's high, droughted fields, quivered leaves on slender young poplars facing Payne's chapel. "Fair. Warm", wrote local farmer John Lindsay in his work diary.[33] From a couple of miles distant, he would note a morning raid at 10 a.m., his expectant eye upon the camouflaged ranks of oil holders out beyond his grazing pastures at the bright tideway's edge. One *Spitfire* of 41 Sqdn., piloted by Sergeant Carr-Lewty, was sighted hurtling low for a forced landing almost at once, ploughing hillslope pebbles just westward of Lampits Hill, Corringham. At about 15.00 hrs., the sirens alerted Lindsay again and within minutes Canvey and Bowaters farm gun-crews had begun assailing oncoming bandits, approaching from the estuary and stepped between 12,000 and 15,000 feet.[34] At Observer Corps post "P (for Peter) One" on the valley shoulder above Orsett village, spotters were counting the now easily recognisable *Gruppen* of *Heinkel* 111 and *Junkers* 88 bombers with their menacing top cover of clip-winged *Me* Bf.109s.

The German onslaught developed "with remarkable suddenness", observed a district press writer,[35] describing the cessation of groundfire after only a brief barrage as *Spits* and *Hurris* came "streaming across to the attack" and identifying correctly the inclusion of "the Polish Squadron" (303, Northolt, eventual top-scoring fighters throughout 11 Group) with their red and white diced national markings. Scrambled from Hornchurch came 41's *Spitfires*, soon to be cruelly culled from the blue, as – in the later recollection of P.O. R.W. Wallens – "B Flight was overwhelmingly attacked by 109s", the Hornchurch defenders in power-climb "line astern and open echelon port" to a head-on confrontation ("a desperate manoevre that could age one very prematurely").[36] Pilot Officer John Mackenzie remembered: "we were climbing up but the 109s came right down and got us ... it was a shambles. If ever one got beneath a fighter squadron it must be a shambles." A New Zealander by birth, this officer used the word in its correct English sense – a slaughtering place.[37] Leading 41 into the fight was "Robin" Hood, who, as his 'planes broke formation, was thought to have collided with

---

[33] Walton Hall, Mucking, farm diary. Photocopy T.MUS.

[34] *"Bandit"*, R.A.F. radio-transmission code for hostile aircraft.

[35] G.T.G. 5th October, 1940.

[36] *Flying Made My Arms Ache*, W. R. Wallens, 1990. Forced landed at Crawford's farm, Stifford Clays.

[37] *Five Fighter Pilots 1939-45*, Sqdn. Ldr. J. N. Mackenzie, D.F.C., N. Shanks, 1987.

F/Lt. "Terry" Webster's *Spitfire*, reported falling over Nevendon around 15.07 hours. Neither man survived, and in total the squadron was to see four of its aircraft lost during this single fearsome sortie. Wallens himself, raked by Bf.109 cannon fire which wrecked his instrument panel and severed radio contact, attempted to struggle away back to Hornchurch base, finally bulldozing fields a few miles short of his goal. He would be lucky enough to reflect how "one bullet had neatly removed my right earphone", another his wristwatch glass.

Today, the *Luftwaffe* target was clear below; effectively struck in a storm of falling explosives and incendiaries from *Ju* 88s that lasted no more than thirty seconds. At Canvey's jetty, Ack-Ack crews observed "salvoes of bombs dropped in a line west of No. 1 gunsite and ending at Thameshaven." The crouched bomb-aimers had literally struck oil, a whole marshscape behind them breaking into flame as a first petroleum tank ruptured, black, raging columns billowing up into the eastward heavens. Over twenty H.E.s of 50 to 1,000 pounds had rained upon the Coryton area alongside without more than moderate human damage, while 3 other bombs fell across and behind Shell Cottages, blowing in windows at the firm's admin. offices. Incendiaries and H.E.s from a delivery which had found success on LATHOL's tank storage, struck nearby boiler houses also, all at about 15.18 hrs.

Canvey's soldiers pinpointed meanwhile what they pronounced to be a Messerschmitt Bf.109 swooping within machine gun range from northwest, and fired "Two short bursts" from 600 yards, claiming the 'plane "straightened out for approx. 1 mile and crashed in river". It was 15.25 hours.[38] Real credit for this kill lay with R.A.F. fighters overhead, though, throughout these perilous moments leading to the half-hour, individual victories were naturally confused. Somewhere "over the estuary" Sqdn. Ldr. R. G. Kellet of 303 (Polish) Sqdn. had cut down a Bf.109, as had the Czech J. Frantisek, a sergeant-pilot of the same squadron. Flying its first combat mission today was the unique 4 cannon *Hurricane* of 46 Sqdn. in which F/Lt. Alex Rabagliat made victim of yet another Bf.109 over the Thames at around 15.30 hours.

Towards Bowers Gifford one of these carcasses would be reported by the A.R.P. burning out near Chalvedon Hall (15.25 hrs.). Ten minutes on, over Benfleet, P.O. "Lulu" Lovell from Hornchurch (41, *Spitfires*) was baling out, while above Burnham and Billericay 3 *Hurricanes* of 73 Sqdn. were all similarly lost. The Polish flyer W. Lapowski (of 303) was to return to Northolt base with a broken arm after parachuting onto Hawkwell three-quarters of an hour after the

---

[38] *The History of the 17th Light Anti-Aircraft Regiment 1938-1945*, Lt. Col. H. S. Eeles, O.B.E., M.C., T.D., undated, c.1946.

siren's warning had first sounded.[39] Safe too, for another (though distant) day was Wallens, dragged by a couple of passing motorists from beneath the jammed cockpit canopy of his "lovely Spitfire" which lay forlornly grounded under a tree at Stifford, his rescuers driving him off to Orsett hospital for treatment to a badly cannon-shot leg. Too many defenders today had been stripped from the sky and the scales of salvation, which depended no longer on aircraft production, but upon well tried fighter pilots, tipped a little further against an English survival.

That Thursday night's communiqué from Air Ministry was to evasively tell of the afternoon's "large force ... all engaged by our fighters and driven back". Bombs had been dropped "on an industrial installation on Thameside. Some damage was done." Still untouched by intentional raids, Londoners could view the not so faraway pyre of an oil kingdom alight, its inky pall drifting high above their onetime cockney playgrounds of Canvey and Southend. Despite "desperate efforts to localise the outbreak" from 2 direct hits by H.E.s upon a single tank, a second holder would soon be on fire. For all the presence of every available brigade from surrounding localities, the countryside as night closed, lay bathed in the candescence of dreadful leapings of flame. Spasmodic air activity continued, the raiding *Luftwaffe* making for "the targets the fire gave them" (recalled a mid-month *Gazette*) their 'planes passing over "singly or in small groups" and attempting on occasions, it was claimed, to machine-gun toiling fire-fighters pouring their liquid blankets of Foamite into the roaring conflagration.

Friday the 6th brought no respite. Before many had breakfasted came a first air raid, another at lunch time, while around 15.30 hrs. radars[40] were picking up a fresh wave of determined invaders approaching the eastern coast. Croydon's

---

39 Brentwood Division air raid reports (Constabulary) November, 1939 – January, 1941.

40 Though "radars" was not in current use by 1940. The system was called then R.D.F.: Radio Direction Finding. King George VI and queen Elizabeth lunched at Bentley Priory (Fighter Command H.Q.) on this day, observing events from its underground operations room through the heavy midday attack.

111 Squadron *Hurricanes* had again raced airborne on this occasion, ordered over Thameshaven to intercept, though losing contact with their quarry due to "smoke and haze" – pollution was pouring up seaward to a height of some 10,000 feet and building all the while. Nevertheless, *Reichsmarschall* Goering's eagles were to ascertain faultlessly their objective, delivering another swift and crippling blow.[41] "In two minutes there were five columns of smoke", wrote one observer, as holder after holder was blasted open.[42] Obeying the siren, 17-year-old Maurice Meen had left off loading cylinder oil onto a Cory railtank waggon, yet even so was taken by surprise. He thought the hour "half past five-six o'clock", when "All of a sudden there this *roar* of aircraft ... coming *downriver* from the direction of Thameshaven to Coryton. So I belted into the shelter again, you know ... low level attack ... these were Messerschmitts, 110, twin-engined fighter bombers, that's what they were ... perhaps 50-60 foot up." When the young man emerged, only minutes had passed, but "all hell had been let loose ... Shell was alight, *we* (Cory's) was alight – it was quite catastrophic."[43]

Lindsay's farm diary fixed the time of impact with a touch of rural Essex: "T.H. sit ablaze at 6". Powerful gusts laid flat the purple crowned marsh reeds, rucking suddenly the surfaces of watery channels. Steel splinters whirred, puncturing other tanks, severing air, embedding in random obstacles. Somewhere out on the grass levels, 67 year old cowkeeper Sam Jordan thought to make from Cory's middle gate to his corrugated shelter and was razored instantly dead by metal flashing to meet him.[44] Further bombs from diving runs rocked the ground, and witnesses safe on village heights could count a seventh and eighth inferno send its oily plume upward, pumping coils of black down the valley. They were clouds that "veiled the sun" told a graphic press account afterward, adding that by now the R.A.F. had got its defending squadrons over "and as one watched the fires so the sounds of the bursts could be heard above". One *Hurricane* of 111 Sqdn. (F/O Bowring) was to be sighted in the clearer west, going silently down over Dartford at 18.10 hrs., the only British loss of this Friday afternoon's combat.[45] Tired flyers of 66 Sqdn. (Gravesend) had been granted a day's furlough and were out together on a betting spree at a nearby greyhound track, from where they followed "a terrific dog fight" going on over LATHOL's furiously blazing tank

---

41 T.U.D.C. War Damage report, Sheet 1,920; Cory's Works. T.MUS.

42 G.T.G. 14th September, 1940.

43 Oral evidence: tape recording, M. Meen with R. Bingley, 27th October, 1995. Some witnesses to this phase of attacks, insist that *Ju* 87 Stuka dive bombers were present. But Thameshaven was beyond their fuel range and *Stukageschwader* had been withdrawn from the English campaign by mid August, due to heavy losses.

44 O.G.R.D. December, 1940.

45 *Battle over Britain,* F. K. Mason, 1980 is source for the wider daily record of events in this chapter. Gravesend airfield 7 airmiles, 2 fighter minutes.

farms. "You know", said one, eyeing the darkened sky, "I can't help feeling this is a case of Nero fiddling while Rome is burning."

But through all there had been only limited loss of life; old Jordan, and Sub-Divisional Officer Tom Farrow – killed by an explosion while fighting fires which had engaged over these 24 hours a force of some 2000 men and 500 pumping units. Pte. Alfred Smith of the Thameshaven platoon Home Guard (a LATHOL works manager) was to be subsequently awarded an M.B.E. for special bravery. In company with helpers unnamed, Smith had striven to open valves of a burning tank in a compound that was 2 feet deep in water "with blazing oil on the surface". His citation would add: *"Visibility was practically nil ... and the approach to the tank was hazardous by hidden bomb craters and ditches. After pumping started the head of spirit and flame jets ... were reduced. Valuable plant and material was saved"*. Other M.B.E.s would go to Acting Chief Officer H. W. Heptinstall of the Thurrock Brigade for leadership in fire fighting operations and Air Raid Warden John Wynne Roberts of Fleet Street, Coryton.[46]

Among the first fourteen of the king's newly instituted George Medal, issued for air-raid gallantry, was that awarded to George Howe of the Cottages, Thameshaven, manager of Shell-Mex and B.P., who with "conspicuous bravery" at the site of pierced tanks, had stoically worked "within a compound of blazing spirit", opening valves to transfer stock. Another was to go to Southend's Chief Fire Officer, Percy Garon, who during the Thameshaven fires, had fought back burning oil from a leaking holder, thus saving five other tanks nearby.[47] Specific dates are not recorded in the citations for these decorations; they refer in retrospect only to "when serious fires were caused on oil depots", otherwise simply to incidents "last autumn". Heptinstall's brave record, when commemorated the year following in Thurrock Council's minutes, would note a date of October 5th, a month after the first conflagration. Even his award would be wrongly identified by the minutes-secretary.[48]

Seventeen tanks had been ignited by now, the sundown of 6th September and already across the channel, General Grauert, commander of No. 1 Air Corps, had issued his historic Operations Order for further high intensity attacks upon Southern England. Tomorrow, Thameshaven, Shellhaven, were to be mere incidentals to the main objective. "In the evening of 7.9" (the order read) "*Luftwaffe* 2 will conduct a major strike against target *Loge*" – Hitler's code word

46 G.T.G. 14th September, 5th October, 1940 and 1st March ,1941.

47 G.T.G. 7th December, 1940 and 1st March, 1941.

48 T.U.D.C. Special Council minutes 22nd February, 1941. Correctly given as M.B.E. in G.T.G. 4th April, 1942. The Rev. E. A. Gardner's contribution to the local war effort would earn him a Deputy Lieutenancy of the County, gazetted during November, 1940.

for London, named from the god who had forged the mythical sword of Seigfried. Upon the 7th, *Reichsmarschall* Goering would strut the clifftop of *Cap Blanc Nez*, watching his air armada – nearly 1000 'planes – pass overhead for the ultimate thrust into the heart of Britain.

Wave by wave, *Luftwaffe* formations droned away upon their northwesterly course toward Sevenoaks, a vast, impeccably ordered mass that was stepped in layers 1½ miles deep and covered an area close upon 800 square miles of sky. Despite concerns for the dangerous task ahead, yesterday's victory could hardly go forgotten. "Right from the French coast on the way in", recalled bomber *Gruppe* leader Paul Weitkies (whose target today was to be the India Docks) "we could see the columns of smoke from Thameshaven's burning tanks." To American correspondent Vincent Sheean, crouched alongside C.B.S. newscaster Ed Murrow later this day upon the Kent hills, these towers of smoke, surmounting "Great blobs of flame" stained the horizon like "monstrous signals of destruction."[49]

Since well before noon, there had been a full 6 hours of quiet readiness upon R.A.F. Fighter Command stations. Worn gramophone records turntabled round, favourite tunes dinned scratchily: Hoagy Carmichael's *Heart and Soul; Tuxedo Junction.* Sleek cowlings of *"Spits"* and *"Hurris"* stood poised against hazy airfield horizons. At 15.54 hrs., Bentley Priory placed initial radar information of enemy movement onto its plotting table and by 16.20 hrs. Observer Corps posts were telephoning sightings of "many hundreds" of aircraft crossing coastlines between Deal in Kent and the North Foreland. Squadrons and flights on guard over Guildford, Croydon, Biggin Hill and North Weald were urgently redeployed onto Fobbing's oil installations and Tilbury Docks. Scrambling at 16.55 to join 11 Group's battle for the first time, came Douglas Bader's "Big Wing" of *Hurricanes* and *Spitfires* out of 12 Group at Duxford, climbing straight to Angels One-Five[50] and making for North Weald. Already smears of Ack-Ack over the eastward estuary could be seen breaking along the path of the oncoming bandits. They were high, moving at 20,000 feet and Bader climbed his fighters at boost, attacking as soon as in range with 19, 242 and 310 squadrons, though his hoped-for impact of all 36 aircraft had been lost in the unequal struggle for height.

Albeit, within minutes one *Dornier* 215 could be seen falling in vertical crashdive and Bader himself was sending a maimed *Me* Bf.109 nosing into the patchwork of farms west of Wickford. F/Lt. Powell-Sheddon of (Bader's) 242 Sqdn., leading Blue Section *Hurricanes*, would remember "Volumes of jet smoke ... cascading up" from the refineries as he pursued and gunned another 109, caught in the identical killing mode behind a stricken *"Hurri"*. Pieces were flying off the

---

[49] *Between the Thunder and the Sun,* V. Sheean, 1941.

[50] Angels: R.A.F. radio transmission term for altitude in thousands of feet: 15,000.

cannon-torn *Hurricane*, and Blue Leader was able to confirm both aircraft plunging to destruction amidst a "dense blackness" beneath. At around 5,000 feet, Sub Lt. Gardner of the Fleet Air Arm selected a *Dornier*, putting in 3 short bursts at 250-50 yards, and blasting it earthward ahead of its baled-out crew into clearer countryside "about three miles north-west of Shellhaven".

For Bader's Duxford wing, today's sortie had been something of a combined baptism of fire. To Sergeant F. Koukal of 310 (Czech) Sqdn. it proved literally and individually so. Blown from his *Hurricane* when a wing tank exploded in the attack of 109s, he had delayed opening his parachute, dreading that his blazing uniform should set fire to its webbing shrouds. He landed in terrible condition on the Swale marshes, alive but grievously burned.[51] In days far ahead Koukal's aircraft would be exhumed from the Sheppey clay, one component of its Merlin engine being eventually brought to Fobbing as a memento of this September's sacrifices above the village.[52]

Both the oil installations at Purfleet (Anglo-American) and Thameshaven had been subsidiary targets on this Saturday, one fireman dying at each location. The district's *"Gazette"* could do no more than outline what most readers might have described first-hand anyway: another "terrific battle" and how, at a single moment, "no fewer than fifteen men could be seen descending by parachute" – stirring enough material, sufficiently nebulous to evade the censor's crayon. In truth, the combined strikes on city and suburbs today had cost the R.A.F. 25 'planes and 19 pilots; among them the inimitable South African Ceasar Hull of 43 Sqdn. Tangmere, and Dick Reynell, one of the few civilians in aerial combat during the Battle of Britain, shot down over Thames during the late afternoon. Despite *Luftwaffe* losses of 37 aircraft, the much debated adage of pre-war days – "The bomber will always get through" – seemed to have been proven amply enough.

Perhaps today it looks unpatriotic to suggest that the Royal Air Force did not exactly win the Battle of Britain; that the main thrust of Germany's offensive was simply withdrawn before the duel could be lost. September 7th was to be the ebbing point of a fierce tide, which Fighter Command could never have resisted, even a few weeks. Those experienced pilots who had escaped death since early summer, were fatigued beyond reasonable endurance, the young arrivals from O.T.U.s[53] insufficient in skill to combat so seasoned an enemy. Germany's fatal error had been in Hitler's change of policy – his turning from the eradication of the young defenders, their bases, radar equipment and fuel supplies, to the

[51] Koukal is the unnamed Czech. sergeant in hospital with Richard Hillary, *The Last Enemy*, 1942.

[52] In the possession of Susan Flanders of Fobbing.

[53] O.T.U. Operational Training Unit.

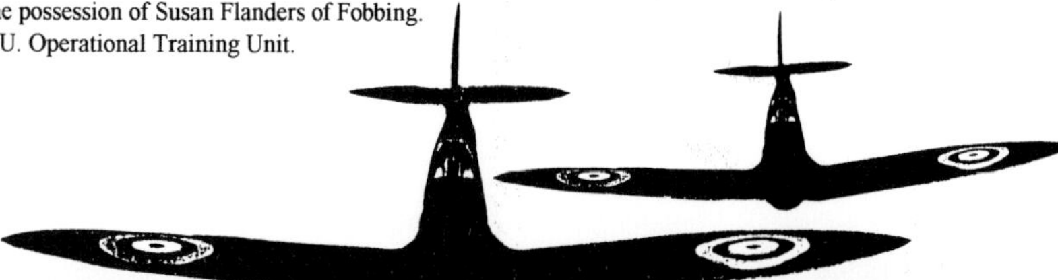

destruction of civilian targets. If Churchill's war cabinet did not cheer publicly as the bombs thundered into East End tenements and terraced streets over the next fifty nights or more, it must have felt privily heartened for what had been gained in terms of eventual survival: immediate respite and rebuilding for the R.A.F.'s fighter arm, a surer sight of America's full commitment in Europe.[54] Strategic architect of Fighter Command's wondrous performance through the battle, Air Chief Marshall Hugh Dowding's reaction had been one of "intense relief ... I could hardly believe that Germany would have made such a mistake".[55] *That* was the honest view.

To the last, Hitler's closest commanders felt that the *blitz* of London had been a decision taken with regret, that their *Fuhrer's* Reichstatt speech of July 19th had represented a genuine final call for peace. Britain's new Prime Minister, they concluded, had snubbed that offer with an intentful silence, while forcing Germany's hand politically by raining hasty death upon the innocent citizens of Berlin. Tonight, and for many other darknesses ahead, Thameshaven's fiery plain would stand as an eastward beacon, guiding his sky warriors to the amphitheatre of a great revenge.[56]

Hours after sunset, patterns of lurid light coloured the Vineyard grasses, rippled the grey masonry high upon St. Michael's tower, where roosting birds sought an uneasy, chackful rest. Along winding creek edges, the

---

[54] Joe Kennedy, U.S. Ambassador, had openly declared to the neutral press his belief that Germany would be master of London by mid August, 1940. *Fighter,* L. Deighton, 1977.

[55] Later, the sensitive Lord Dowding was to remark of his Prime Minister, *'he didn't seem to believe in working for peace'*, that Churchill really considered *'an atmosphere of struggle'* (war) necessary to avoid decadence in nations: *Dowding and the Battle of Britain,* R. Wright, 1969.

[55] *The Battle of the East Coast 1939-1945*, J. Foynes, 1994.

Postscript: Essex Chronicle 20 April, 1928, Rev. E. Gardner and *A Detective in Essex,* D. Maxwell, 1933.

tide-slapped mud shone beautiful, metal-foiled in the far flame's play. Squares of Georgian glass in recesses of old black cottages answered the burning distance. Even at midnight in Fobbing's lumpy burial yard, family names upon ancient headstones stood sharply discernible. From the Tudor porchway a little droop-hatted man carved in oak continued his centuries-old dance with a stub winged dragon.

Somehow, the ordinary pieces of the past had a trick of making themselves visible at pertinent moments – in times of private concern, of simple village occasion, at hours of group crisis. You could either dismiss the fabric of time or respect it; draw strength from its peculiar redolence. One thing was sure; *backwards* was the sole direction in which folk would ever be given the means to see. For every village individual born, tomorrow was always going to be a blindfold land. So who, in 1940, would have conceived that a community which so wished escape from the wreck of bombs, could mutilate, knock holes in itself in the quieter years to come?

D. Maxwell

FOBBING HARBOUR

POSTSCRIPT

"There on a bluff, sloping steeply down to the marsh", mused the romantic Reverend (Gardner) back in April 1928, *"stands a grand old Church embowered in lofty trees. Nestling below it lie the old cottages gathered round the little harbour ... There is not a thing to be seen out of harmony with ancient peace and beauty ... "*. The few photographs that remain, two or three blithe pen sketches by the wandering Donald Maxwell, taken at about the same period, suggest that a scenic perfection still really *did* exist. It wasn't a fantasy. And it wasn't to endure.

Elm decline in the '60s made a vast difference everywhere; but so did a dozen other kinds of wilful defacement to Fobbing's villagescape – some the result of achieving an undeniably less toilsome life for its inhabitants, but bringing monotony and ugliness in its wake – ribbon development, unsympathetic street furniture, a mess of road markings and carpark lots, and nasty curtilage fences displacing once decorous tea-tree hedging and mellow brick walls.

At the same time – in half a life's span – some of the best, most curious and pleasant of its buildings were to vanish; the eccentric *Glass Bottle* house; most of Vineyard farm: the neat Georgian *Brickhouse* by Wheeler's Lane; *Black Cottages* on Wharf Road and the workaday wharfside cluster itself, besides other proletarian features such as the weatherboarded carpenter's workshops upslope of the *"Lion"*, Fobbing's schoolhouse and *Sheepstealers* tar-painted barn. The toll of the 1950s and onward snatched as much as *one half* of the structural heritage of this settlement away, and though its replacement housing was not to be visually disastrous, it could by no means compensate for an absolute seemliness that had been.

And yet something remains. For all Anphilogoff's prophecy, Fobbing has come through the 20th century more fortunately than most other villages within its borough district. It's still a *place*, recognisable and not yet quite like anywhere else. If these essays have had a main purpose, it has been to give an idea of how one present piece of territory came to be, in its own particular way. Knowing something of *that* is no mere retrospective dalliance: it offers the argument by which a community may sometimes hold out (and sometimes win) against further erosion of what seems (to itself) most worthy about a landscape it calls *"home"*.

Finis

R.B.

Black cottages

ACKNOWLEDGEMENTS

Primary thanks go to Joyce Shaw, M.A., of Corringham, not only for seeing word-processing through from messy manuscript to legible copy, but for medieval discussion besides. John Webb, Chairman of the Thurrock Local History Society, Stuart Brand and Alan Leyin have each read-through the draft and been helpful with their comments as well as in practical ways. Curators Terry Carney and Jon Catton remained tolerant and productive of assistance to their old associate and I am indebted to Thurrock Borough Council's museums service for its financial encouragement of the project.

I would like to express my appreciation for sponsorship from the committee and members of Fobbing Friends, a body actively involved with the concerns of village environment and one which, I trust, will find my volume a pertinent reference document in future decisions and skirmishes. Essex and Suffolk Water, a member of the Lyonnaise des Eux Group, has celebrated a near-century-long association with pumping from Fobbing's substrata, with a welcome grant, enabling me to add an important photographic section to the work.

The Rev. George Davies was so amenable as to trust me with his handsome original registers and other parish documents in his keeping, though to minimise the handling of these, microfilm supplied by the Essex Record Office through Essex County Libraries, Grays branch, was routinely consulted. I am grateful to both organisations for many other resources along the way, as I am also to the city of Norwich Libraries, the Hunts. Record Office, Sylvia Hopkins, Keeper of Uniforms at the National Army Museum, Chelsea and Arthur Wright of Southend-on-Sea Borough Museum.

Within the neighbourhood patch, a kindly response flourished: Andrew Young, farmer, gave leave for general landscape investigation; Roy Eaton sportingly agreed I might steal a passage from his already published material upon children's education in Fobbing and turned up essential photographs, while headmaster M. Colvert of Herd Lane Primary School permitted reference to logbooks for the 1939-45 war. Ted Bandick and Len Chappell are but a couple of our parish denizens who contributed moments of conversation which rendered confused things clearer. Among others who gave time to discuss their perspectives of the past were Mr. and Mrs. George Robinson of High Road, Rowland Partridge of Dry Street and Cllr. Maurice Meen and his wife Marie, of Corringham. Most particularly I mention the generous understanding given me by Mrs. Julia Coffey of Mill Cottages and her sons, with regard to parts of the book.

In only one or two instances have I been denied my doorstep request to gather interior details of surviving agricultural or domestic buildings. A single important and ancient cottage is therefore absent from this record, since I could not make any purposeful statement. To everyone who let me get on with it – Len Cook of Whitehall, John Sell at Dry Street farm and Frances and Jean Paul Lafage of Ship Cotts., Trevor and Jeanette Jolly at Prosbus and many others – I declare my indebtedness: but most of all to Mike Valente, who was at pains to keep me posted upon all remedial works at his medieval home (*'Copeland'*) also allowing excavation of its earth-floor.

Roger Pickett of Aveley has an enthusiasm for wartime aircraft-recovery and he outlined the way it seemed Pilot Officer Hemingway's 'plane came down aside Fobbing Creek in 1940. To Allan Bennett, whose contribution to the district's archaeology through responsible field prospecting has been significant, I say 'much obliged' for frequent updates upon his pottery findings as they were deposited with Thurrock Museum.

An outright enhancement of my text through the talents of its illustrators is acknowledged with pleasure: firstly a delightful few pre-war vignettes which Donald Maxwell draughted in the Fobbing vicinity for his own books, *Unknown Essex*, 1925 and *A Detective in Essex*, 1933, reproduced by permission of the Donald Maxwell Estate, Dodding Green, Mealbank, Kendal. Fred Roe's virile pencilsketch of St. Michael's wooden porch is also here; it appeared originally in *'Essex Survivals'* published by Messrs. Methuen in 1929, from which company copyright permission has been diligently sought through Reed Books, Rushden, Northants. I am beholden, too, to Alan Leyin for his painstaking computer-generated improvement of my very inferior sketchmaps, to Dave Ross of KiM Colour Print of Grays, for laser copying, offered entirely *gratis* as a gesture toward the book's advancement and to Clive and Lynn Whipps of Provident Print, Chadwell, for photographic reduction aspects.

For some years I had admired John Garbutt's perceptive way of expressing in penline the essence of local buildings: I was both surprised and gladdened when, to a tentative plea for collaboration, he assumed the burden of preparing those thirty or so key drawings which now bear his signature. They were sometimes based upon mere shades of old photographic evidence and we have considered in most cases, the look and veracity of each individual line. During this project, I found John's patience and goodwill entirely remarkable and am proud to have my word-sketches so moodfully mirrored by his art.

The following persons have also eased the journey by their thoughtfulness or guidance and to them all I add, too briefly, my thanks:

Arts-leisure Manager for Thurrock Borough Council, Mark Allinson; Barry and Sheila Barnes; A. (Tony) Benton of Upminster; Jack Brown; Geoff Burton, churchwarden; Bob Cardy; Simon Carter; Mary Cartledge née Smith; Meryl Catty; Brian and Richard Coffey; Audrey Dann; John Dowson; Dr. Ian and Moira Frood of Old Hall; churchwarden Derek Gilman; Gordon Hales; Michael Ffitch of Mealbank, Kendal; Dinah Mullins; Secretary of the Fobbing Friends Marilyn Munt; Hazel Nevard; Fred Partner of Fishers farm cotts.; Dawn and Geoff Roots; Lily Sadler née Wells; Gladys Smith; Win and Stan Tinworth and their daughter Winifred Scott; Andrew Young snr. of Fobbing Hall and Mrs. Susan Young.

Randal Bingley

ABBREVIATIONS

A.F.	Essex Assize Files
C.C.	*Chelmsford Chronicle* newspaper series
C.B.A.	Council for British Archaeology Reports
C.R.O.	Cambridgeshire Record Office
D.N.B.	*Dictionary of National Biography*
E.A.S.	Essex Archaeological Society transactions
E.C.	*Essex Countryside* magazine
E.C.C.	Essex County Council
E.C.L.	Essex County Libraries
E.R.	*Essex Review*
E.R.O.	Essex Record Office, Chelmsford
G.L.	Guildhall Library, London
G.T.G.	*Grays & Tilbury Gazette* newspaper series
I.G.I.	International Genealogical Index
N.A.M.	National Army Museum, Chelsea
N.R.O.	Norfolk Record Office, Norwich
O.G.R.D.	*Orsett & Grays Rural Deanery Magazine*
O.S.	Dept. of Ordnance Survey
PAN.	*Panorama* series, journal of Thurrock Local History Society
P.C.C.	Fobbing Parochial Church Council
P.L.A.	*Port of London Authority Monthly* Magazine
P.R.O.	Public Record Office
R.E.	Royal Engineers records, Brompton
R.C.H.M.	Royal Commission on Historical Monuments
S.A.S.	Surrey Archaeological Society transactions
S.C.	*Stanford le Hope Courier* newspaper series
T.E.	*Thurrock Express* newspaper series
T.M.	*Thameside Mail* newspaper series
T.MUS.	Thurrock Museums Service
T.U.D.C.	Thurrock Urban District Council
V.C.H.	*Victoria County History of Essex*

SITE INDEX

Buildings, farmsteads and main structures

n = footnote p = picture ph = photo section (numbered)

(see also maps, pp. 22, 54, 63)

ALEHOUSES (various) 66, 104-5, 142, 197
ALEXANDER'S BARN, 72
AVENUE COTTS, 74, 74n, 190, 200, 230, ph 8, 29
BAKEHOUSE, 186-7, 194-5, 194p, 201, 213, 217, 217n
BAKER'S (rebel) Fm, 10-11, 14-5, 88
BARGE aleho, Vange, 190
BARLEYS Fm, 85
BARN, Sheepstealers, 163p, 164, 256p
BAY COTTS, 74, 74n, 190, 203, ph 29
BEACON, sites, 89-90
BECKSLAND Fm, W. Tilbury, 170
BELL, aleho, Horndon, 30
BELMONT CASTLE, Grays, 166, 168, 168n
BELVEDERE Ho, 234
BLACK COTTS, 94-5, 94n, 95p, 251p, 252, 253p, ph 7, 17
BLACKMANS Fm, L. Hills, 12
BLACKSMITH'S Premises, 38, 179, 252 (at Bells Hill) 195, 201
BLUEHOUSE Fm, W. Tilbury, 170 (Pitsea) 214n
BOORMANS MILL, Stanford le H, 187-8
BORLEY Fm, 5, 8, 41-3, 74, 87, 171, 180, 204-5
BRAZIERS HALL (see Great Ho)
BRICKFIELDS (Rushbrook's) 38-9, 202, 202n (Defoe's) 38, 38n (Ingram's) 164
BRICKHOUSE, 16, 160-1, 160n, 160p, 197, 234, 252, ph 22
BRIDGE RD. SNR. SCHOOL, Grays, 231
BROOKHOUSE Fm, 13, 58, 58n, 172, 172n, 178
BUNTINGS Fm, W. Thurrock, 171
BUSH HOUSE Fm, Corringham, 171
BYRONS Fm, 58, 58n, 160, 169-72, 210, ph 8
CATTLE-LANDING DOCKS, 45, 47-8, 199-200
CHALLACES Fm (see Prosbus Hall)
CHAPPELL'S AUTO GARAGE, 227
CHURCH (see St. Michael's)
CLAY HALL (see Hill Cotts)
COASTGUARD STNS, 40-1, 40n
COCK aleho, Orsett, 176n
COCK AND MAGPIE aleho, Stanford le H, 44, 161
COLEMAN'S Ho, 73
COOTE'S Ho, 71
CO-OPERATIVE HALL, Stanford le H, 238
COPELAND COTTS, 57-8, 57p, 58n, 92-5, 92n, 159, 200
CORONATION VILLAS, 8, 8n
CORRINGHAM HALL Fm, 171
CORRINGHAM LIGHT RLY (line, area) 46n, 216, 216n, ph 7
CORYTON (wks, area) 215, 215n, 228, 244, 246-7
COTTAGES (Bells Hl) 192p, 227 (Dry St) 193-4 (nr Five Bells) 94 (Lion Hl) 1, ph5 (Shellhaven) 20, 42, 44, 244 (Shell Cotts) 215 (Thameshaven 'new' cotts) 47 (Wharf Lane, unnamed) Title page, ph 16
COUNCIL HOUSES, 224-5
CRANES Fm, 85
CROOKED BILLET aleho, Stanford le H, 157, 162
CURTIS' Fm, 1p, 13-4, 58, 58n, 76p, 130, 164-5, 165n, 170, 212p, 231p, ph 8
DENEHOLE MINES, Grays, 26-7
DOCK HOUSE aleho, 177, 177n, 199-200, 222, 226
DRY STREET Fm, 14, 35, 83p, 130, 188-9, 188n, ph 20
EASEBORNE PRIORY, Sx, 115-6
EAST TILBURY, Gun Site (Bowaters) 243
EWEN'S SHOP (see Halston's)
FAIRGROUND (see market site)
FIRE BOX, 210
FISHERS Fm, 58, 93, 93n, 93p, 95, 103, 130-1, 159 ph 11, 12
FIVE BELLS aleho, Vange, 58, 61, 176, 218, 229

FOBBING Fm (see also Leesons) 8, 14, 35, 165, 169, 169n, 189, 210 (cotts) 194
FOBBING HALL Fm, 35, 53, 64-66, 64n, 83, 86, 88p, 93-5, 151, 159, 169, 193, 202n, 204, 213p, 232, 236
FOBBING INST, 74, 204
FOBBING WHARF, vip, viiip, 5, 30, 38-9, 38n, 39p, 53, 65-6, 96-7, 145, 151, 176, 184, 196-8, 251p, 252, ph 7, 23, 24
FOWLERS premises, 32n, 35
FRANKLIN'S SHOP, 227
FULLERS Fm, 85
GATEHOUSE, (rly) 198
GLASS BOTTLE Ho, viiip, 39p, 162, 162n, 202-3, 215, 252, ph 7, 17, 18
GLASCOCK'S SHOP, 179
GLEBE Fm, 112-3, 165, 173, 180-1, 186 (cottage) 112, 230
GOLDSMITHS Fm, L. Hills, 101, 212
GOWERS TENEMENT, 148
GREAT HOUSE Fm, 10, 52, 52n, 150, 152, 172, 226 (Chase) 9
GREAT ILFORD (Elford) 5, 5n, 27, 27n, 32n, 35, 35n, 55, 172-3, 172n, 206
GROVE, (The) 66, 76p, 158, 172, 172n, 189-90
GRUB'S BARN, 72
HALSTON'S SHOP, 76p, 195-6, 209-10, 213, 216, 226, ph 21
HARRIS' (see Hill Cotts)
HASSENBROOK HALL, Stanford le H, 86, 160
HAVEN HOTEL aleho, 226
HAWKESBURY Fm (also Manor ho) 2, 14-7, 35, 60, 60n, 62n, 69, 84, 84p, 85, 96, 99-100, 115-6, 115n, 126, 130-1, 135, 137, 143, 146, 201 ph 19 (gun site) 115, 219-20, 219n
HERD Fm (Colony) Corr, 215
HIGH Ho, W. Thurrock, 150
HILL COTTS, 94, 94n, 159, 162, 231p, ph 5, 8
HILLCREST COTTS (Peasants Croft) 94, 94n, 197
HOVELS Fm, 17, 35, 58, 58n, 95, 95n, 100-01, 165, 165p, 172, 172n, 200, 223
ISLAND MILL (see Oil Mill)
IVY WALLS, Stanford le H, 126n
JUBILEE CHAPEL (see Wesleyan Chpl)
JUDD'S TEAROOMS, 227
KINGS HEAD aleho (see The Ship) (Stanford le H) 7
KING'S TERRACE, 8, 8n, 218
KYNOCHS' FACTORY (wks area) 8n, 74, 204-6, 204n, 205p, 209-10, 215-6, 217-22, 217n
KYNOCHTOWN SCH, 204, 204n, 204p, 215, 219-20, 220n, 228
LANDISH'S Ho, 51
LEESONS (see also Fobbing Fm) 95, 95n, 101, 121
LITTLE ILFORD Fm (Lady's Island, Iron Latch) vp, 55
LOCKHART'S SHOP, 227
LONDON AND THAMES HAVEN OIL WHARVES, 222, 226, 228, 234, 244, 246-7
LYON aleho (see White Lion)
MARKET SITE, 56, 67
METHODIST Chpl, E. Tilbury, 189
MILL COTTS, 74-5, 74n, 74p, 212, 226, 234, 238
MILL Ho, 187-8
MISSION HUT, 190 (Bells Hill) 8
MOATED SITE, 52, 52n
MOUND SITE (raised house) 31, 32n, 51, 51n
MUCKING HALL, 166-8
MYRTLE Ldg, 238
NAZEWICK Fm, 35, 51, 138, 171, 216
NORDEN'S BARN, 72
OIL DEPOTS (see Coryton, Shellhaven etc)
OIL MILL Fm, 33p, 36, 36n, 41, 45-6, 61, 66, 72, 135-6, 193, ph 30
OLD HALL Fm, Corr, 96, 206
OLD MILL Ho, 5, 20, 24, 159, 159n, 226, 226n
OOZEDAM Fm, 23, 31-2, 35, 133, 206, 206p
ORSETT (hall) 169 (hospital) 230, 245 (meeting ho) 188 (police stn) 200 (work ho) 183-4
PAYNE'S Chpl (see Wesleyan)
PAYNE'S COTTS (see also Post office, Rural sub) 76p, 171, ph 8
PEASANTS CROFT (see Hillcrest Cotts)
PECULIAR PEOPLE'S Chpl, ph 5
PELL Ho (see Rectory ho)
PEVEREL MANOR, Grays, 168
PIG AND WHISTLE aleho (old, new) 47, 198-9

PITSEA HALL, 101, 101n, 121
POST OFFICE, rural sub, at Payne's, 190, 190p, 212-3, 230
PROSBUS HALL (Sprivens) 13, 30, 74, 76p, 95, 103, 130, 159, 161-3, 177, 200, 210, 228, 231p, ph 8, 15
PURFLEET GUN SITES, 217-8 (Anglo-American Oil wks) 249
RAILWAY COTTS (various) 45, 198
RAILWAY Tvn, aleho, Stanford le H, 1
REAMES Fm, 149
RECTORY Ho, vii, 112-3, 119, 129, 137, 152, 180, 180p, 182, 182n, 195, 197, 202, 225-6, 235, ph 4
REEDHAM Fm (Buttons) Corr, 21
REGAL Moviehouse, Stanford le H, 233 (various) 75
ROCHFORD RAF Stn, 241
ROOKERY Fm, Mucking, 235
SALT COTE, 37, 37n
SCHOOLHOUSES (various) 181, 202-4, 203p, 208, 212-4, 214n, 224, 236, 236n, 240-1, 240n, 242, 252, ph 28
SHEEPSTEALERS BARN, 163p, 164, 252, 256p
SHELLHAVEN Fm, 5, 20, 20n, 35-6, 42-5, 42n, 49, 49p, 133, 136, 199, 209, (poss) ph 26
SHELLHAVEN (wks, area) 4, 20-21, 28, 30, 35, 41, 56, 215, 222-3, 225, 229, 229p, 232p, 234-5, 237, 244, 246-7, ph 32
SHEPHERD AND DOG aleho, Crays Hill, 2
SHIP aleho and cotts, viiip, 5, 39, 39p, 88p, 104, 144-5, 144n, 162, 171, 173, 175-7, 176n, 177n, 179, 251p, 253p, ph 17, 23, 24
SHIP aleho, L. Thurrock, 209
SLATEY HOUSE Fm, (see Great Ilford)
SNAILS Fm, Gt. Burstead, 219, 219n
SPARKES' SHOEMAKER'S SHOP, 186
STAPLERS Fm, Stanford le H, 167
STIFFORD CLAYS Fm, (Crawfords) 243n, 244-5
STIFFORD Ldg, 167
ST. JOHN'S PRIORY, 231
ST. MARY'S Ch, Corr, 152, 182
ST. MICHAEL'S Ch (incidentalia such as marriages, headstones, not inc) Jacket, vip, viip, 8p, 14p, 26p, 59, 76, 89-90, 98, 106n, 108n, 108p, 110p, 111-14, 113p, 116-20, 117p, 120p, 123-4, 124n, 129p, 133-5, 146p, 147-54, 147p, 149p, 152n, 154p, 156-8, 158p, 166, 174, 174n, 180-83, 181n, 182n, 182p, 183n, 190p, 192, 211-2, 214-5, 227-8, 228n, 231p, 233-5, 237, 239p, 242, 250-2, 251p, ph 3, 5, 15, 27
ST. NICHOLAS Ch, Laindon, 172
SUTTONS Fm, Hornchurch (RFC; RAF stn) 219, 239, 241, 243-4
TANHOUSE, Corr, 62, 103
THAMESHAVEN (jetty and wks) vii, 45-9, 207, 216, 222 (rly terminus) 198
TILBURY FORT, 12, 219 (blockhouses E. W. Tilbury) 102, 143
VANGE PARK (development) Fobbing, 210-11, 210n
VANGE WELLS, Fobbing, 223-4, 223n, 224n, 224p
VINE Ho, 160
VINEYARD Fm, and cottage, 18, 18n, 19p, 65-6, 130, 135, 137, 163, 171-2, 178, 230-1, 234, ph 15
WALTON HALL, Mucking, 168, 243n
WATERWORKS COTT, 226
WATTS (see Ship aleho)
WELLS, WATERMAINS, PUMPS, 35, 74-5, 74n, 210, 223-4, 224p, 226
WESLEYAN METHODIST Chpl, 74, 190, 203-9, 208p, 225-6, 238, 243, ph 8, 29
WEST TILBURY HALL, 170
WHEELERS Ho, 58, 94-5, 95n, 103, ph 6, 13
WHEELWRIGHT'S, CARPENTER'S Shops (see The Grove)
WHITEHALL Fm, 11, 13, 35, 153, 159, 163
WHITE HART aleho, Brentwood, 30
WHITE HORSE (enigma) 162
WHITE LION aleho, 1, 3, 16, 18, 39, 58, 93, 93n, 95, 104-5, 105n, 130, 154-7, 162, 169, 173-7, 174n, 175n, 184, 197-8, 198n, 200, 202, 209, 212, 221, 229, 252, ph 5, 14
WINDMILL(S) and house, 8p, 14p, 81, 98-100, 98n, 137, 137n, 184, 186-8
WOMEN'S COLONY, Corr, 215
WORLD'S END aleho, Chadwell, 4, 209
WORKHOUSES (various) 183-4, 184n

LANDSCAPE INDEX

Fieldnames, highways and broader topographical features
n = footnote p = picture ph = photo section (numbered)
(see also maps, pp. 22, 54, 63)

ABBOTS (upper, lower) 11, 16
ABREY Fld, 16
ALLOTMENT gdns, next Avenue, 230, 237, ph 8
BAKERS CROFT, 10-11, 14-15, 88, 88n
BARN Fld, 82
BARLEYS, 80
BARR Ln, 10, 18
BELL Fld, 17-18
BELLS HILL, 8, 12-13, 12n, 64, 195, 210, 216, 227
BIG BARN Fld, 17
BILLERICAY HIGHWAY, 2, 12
BLACK LANDS, 85
BLACK SHIPP MARSH, 149
BLIND Ln, 10
BORLEY Fm, 21, 30, 32
BRAZIERS HALL (see Great Ho)
BROAD GATES (great, little) 149
BROOKHOUSE, grounds, 7
BULLOCK LODGE Fld, 17
BURGEYSCROFT, 14
BUSH Fld, 85, 115
BYRONS, 16, 169 (acre piece) 16
CALVES CROFT (Calves Crotes) 14
CASTELL (LE) 21, 24, 82
CASTLEWICK, 24
CHASE Ln, 10
CHERRYDOWN, 64
CHURCH HILLS, 7, 12
CHURCHYARD, St. Michael's, 113p, 129p, 146p, 147p, 158p, 162p, 190p, 203p, 255, ph 3
COLEMANS Fld, 61-2
CRANES, 80
CREEK nr. Marsh Lane foot, 53-5
CROOKED BROOK, 12n, 17, 28, 59, 64, 64n
CROUCHMANS CROFT, 14
CURRY MARSH, Corr, 28
CURTIS Fm, 170, 241
DEDEFELD (Diddles) 18
DOUBLE SHOTS, 13
DRY STREET, 8, 9, 12, 59, 62, 83-4, 83p, 91, 99, 139, 193, 216
EASTHAVEN (see Holehaven)
EAST HILL (see Whitehall Hill)
FAYERS, 160
FENNY Fld, 85
FLEET ST (Kynochtown) 221, 247
FOBBING Fm (see Leesons)
FOBBING (parish) 24, 50-1, 60, 60n (creek) vip, viiip, 23, 37, 39p, 55, 171, 223, 229, 242, 251, 251p, ph 23 (general ridge) 8p, 51-4, 59, ph 8
FOBBING HALL Fm, 17, 17n, 21, 64, 80, 83, 169, 192, 232
FOBBING HORSE, 4
FRITH, (The) 151
GLEBE LANDS (see also Rectory) 7, 30, 123, 154, 158, 165n, ph 15
GREAT HOUSE Fm, 10, 241 (chase) 9
GIBSONS DITCH, 61, 215, ph 1
GREAT ILFORD, 21, 23-5, 32
GUN MEADOW, 219n
HADLEIGH TURNPIKE, 7, 7n, 189
HALL CROFT, 14
HANGING HILLS, 85
HASSENBROOK STREAM, Stanford le H, 62
HAWKESBURY, 9, 12-13, 15, 50, 59, 60p, 82-5, 85n, 91, 99, 114-5, 139, 192 (Bush) 115 (Hook) 84, 126n
HEGGEMANS, 82
HIGH Rd, 2, 10, 12n, 13, 20, 52, 67, 74p, 76p, 93p, 95, 113p, 142, 210, 216, 225, 231p, ph 6, 8, 11, 13, 21
HOCKLEYS Ln, 227, 227n
HOLEHAVEN, 3-4, 21, 32, 42-3, 132, 135, 171, 186, 217-8, 228, 237
HOPES, (The) 24, ph 15
HORSES (see Fobbing)
HOVELS, 7, 17, 95, 95n, 141
HOVELS CHASE Rd, 211
INGLEFIELD Rd, 211
IRON LATCH (see Little Ilford)

IVY Rd, 211
KNIGHT Fld, 146
LADY DAVALL'S MARSHES (see Little Ilford)
LADY'S ISLAND (see Little Ilford)
LAINDON LINK, 64
LAMBERT MARSH, 84
LANDSEND, 84
LEESONS, 17, 17n, 82 (see also Fobbing Fm)
LION HILL, 1, 1p, 6-7, 57, 158, 200, 223, 225-7, ph 5
LITTLE ILFORD, 21, 23-4, 28-9, 29n, 32, 55, 168, 177-8
LONDON HIGHWAY, 141, 210-12, 227
MANORWAY FLEET, 20, 56, 206p
MANORWAYS, DROVEWAYS, marsh, v, 25, 30-1
MARSH Ln, 8p, 9-10, 14, 18, 25, 53-4
MARTINHOLE (Meaden hole) 7, 12p, 16p, 17, 85, 223n
MILL Fld, Hill, 17, 65, 83, 98, 188
MILL HOPE, 66,
MILL Ln, 10, 52, 211, ph 2
MOAT Fld (great, little) 52-3
MOTTS CROFT, 14
MOUNT DRIVE, 211
NAZEWICK MARSHES, 21, 23, 23n, 33, 51, 132p, 138
NORTH HOPE, 24, 27, 87
NORTHLANDS WOOD, Corr, 49
NORWICH HOSP LANDS (see Borley)
OIL MILL MARSHES, 21, 24, 29, 87n (fleet) 21, 24, 30
OLD BAR Fld, 18
OOZEDAM, 21, 21n, 30, 35, 206p
PALM Rd, 211
PARISH BOUNDARY LINES (also manor) 1, 12n, 12p, 16p, 17-18, 28, 40, 59-64, 60p, 64n, 215, ph 1, 5
PARTING GUT CREEK, 28, 28n
PEAR TREE Fld, 18
POCKATS (PICKETTS) CROFT, 14
PONDS (various) 18, 88p, 96, ph 6
PROSBUS HALL (see Sprivens)
REAMES premises, 149
RECREATION Grnd, 225, 230, 233, 233n, ph 6, 13, 29
REDMERS, 151
RICHERNESS, Canvey I, 33
ROGERS Fm, Stanford le H, 162
ROGERS CROFT, 14
RUGWARD MARSHES, Mucking det, 28
SANDALS, 16
SEA REACH, 4
SHEEPSTEALERS Fld, 16-17, 149
SHELLHAVEN CREEK, 36, 45, 55-6, 180, 186, 198, ph 32
SLATED (SLATEY) HOUSE (see Great Ilford)
SMALL MEALS, 85
SPOORHAMS, 164
SPRIVENS HALL, 84
STRAIGHT SHOT, 13
STRAW STACK Fld, 18
THAMESHAVEN, vii, 45, 45n, 47-8, 47n, 237, 240, 244, 246, 246n, 247-50
THISTLEY Fld, 10
UPPER MAYNE, 64
VANGE PARK ROAD (estate) 210-11
VINEYARD Fm, Flds, ip, 16, 18, 18n, 19, 19n, 30, 231, 233-5, 250, 251p (poss) ph 10
WADMERS, WADWICK, 23-4, 82, 87
WAITES, 18, 61
WALDEGRAVE, 64
WANT Fld, 10, 18-19
WATERWORKS Ln, 10n, ph 2
WELL Fld, 18
WEST St, 9, 9n, 10n (hill, see Whitehall Hill)
WHARF Ln (Rd) ip, 55, 57, 94, 95p, 174, 197, 210, 215, 217, 225, 229, 252-3, ph 7, 16, 17, 18
WHEELERS Ln, 8p, 10, 160, 252 (meadow) 225, ph 13, 29
WHITBREADS Fm, (see Leesons, Fobbing Fm)
WHITEHALL Fm, 9, 21, 86, 86n, 241 (hill) 162, ph 25 (ln) 9, 11 ('sixacres') 14

WHEN ADAM DELVED
AND EVE SPAN
WHO WAS THEN THE
GENTLEMAN
R.B.